Toward the Millennium

Also by Larry J. Sabato

Feeding Frenzy
American Government (with Karen O'Connor)
Campaigns and Elections
PAC Power
The Party's Just Begun
The Rise of Political Consultants
Goodbye to Good-Time Charlie
Dirty Little Secrets (with Glenn R. Simpson)

Toward the Millennium

The Elections of 1996

Edited by

LARRY J. SABATO

University of Virginia

ALLYN AND BACON

Boston • *London* • *Toronto* • *Sydney* • *Tokyo* • *Singapore*

Copyright © 1997 by Allyn & Bacon
A Viacom Company
160 Gould Street
Needham Heights, MA 02194

ISBN 0-205-19907-0

Printed in the United States of America
00 99 98 97   10 9 8 7 6 5 4 3 2 1

To the memory of Professor Weldon Cooper

Contents

Introduction   ix
Acknowledgments   xi

Chapter 1   1
The Road to Here

Tom Rosenstiel
Project for Excellence in Journalism

Chapter 2   19
Where Did All the Candidates Go?

Linda Fowler
Dartmouth College

Chapter 3   37
Presidential Nominations: The Front-loaded Frenzy of '96

Larry J. Sabato
University of Virginia

Chapter 4   93
**The Conventions—One Festival of Hope,
One Celebration of Impending Victory**

Larry J. Sabato
University of Virginia

Chapter 5   121
**The 1996 Presidential Election: A Tale of a Campaign
That Didn't Seem to Matter**

Paul S. Herrnson and Clyde Wilcox
University of Maryland and Georgetown University

Chapter 6   143
The November Vote—A Status Quo Election

Larry J. Sabato
University of Virginia

Chapter 7   163
Campaigning for Congress: The Echo of '94

Richard E. Cohen
Congressional Correspondent, National Journal

Chapter 8   189
The State Elections of '96

Thad Beyle
University of North Carolina–Chapel Hill

Chapter 9   205
The Press' Performance

Diana Owen
Georgetown University

Chapter 10   225
Financing the 1996 Campaign: The Law of the Jungle

Brooks Jackson
Political Correspondent, CNN

Chapter 11   261
Final Thoughts

Ken Bode
DePauw University
Moderator, PBS "Washington Week in Review"

Introduction

Larry J. Sabato

University of Virginia

The 1996 election captured the rootless and unpredictable nature of American politics at the end of the twentieth century. Prior to the onset of the election year, few pundits believed that President Clinton could survive a Republican onslaught clearly foretold (they believed) by the earthshaking GOP takeover of Congress in 1994. But the soothsayers were breathtakingly wrong. Whereas the voters had wrestled the presidency away from the Republicans in 1992 and the Congress from the Democrats in 1994, they chose to maintain a divided government in 1996—apparently trusting neither party fully and preferring to build in yet another major check and balance into the American system.

It was not quite *that* rational, of course. The year 1996 was an exciting and surprise-filled ride on the roller coaster of ambition, less so than historic 1992, certainly, but still worth the voyage. The most recent presidential contest was unique in the century, however, because it was held on the cusp of a new millennium.

End-of-century elections are inevitably tied to both the past and the future. In 1896 statesmen spoke of American exceptionalism and the dawn of a new age of global free trade, and they hoped finally to bury the bitter divisiveness of the Civil War and Reconstruction. In 1996, the candidates for the White House were struggling to define the post–Cold War era, and they cast their rhetoric in terms of both the glorious past (Bob Dole) and the promising future (Bill Clinton).

Future trumped past in 1996, and President Clinton's "bridge to the 21st century" theme was not unlike the stirring call at the 1896 convention for "a new republic, [to] greet the new century whose dawn is already purpling in the east."[1] The GOP nominee in 1896, William McKinley, in whose honor those words were spoken, was (like Clinton) the November victor.

In policy terms, McKinley and Clinton have little in common other than their distinction as the people's choice to lead America into a new century. Yet politically, the two presidents are twins. McKinley and his chieftains ran a brilliant campaign to take the White House, just as Clinton and company managed a shrewd effort to keep his Pennsylvania Avenue address. This volume—a collaborative effort among six scholars of presidential politics and four prominent journalists—is an attempt to explain how Clinton did it, along with an analysis of all the other critical elements of the election of 1996. Tom Rosenstiel, formerly of *Newsweek* and now Director of the Pew Charitable Trust's Project for Excellence in Journalism, sets the stage in Chapter One, skillfully taking us from the presidential battle in 1992 to the one in 1996. Next in Chapter Two, Professor Linda Fowler of Dartmouth College examines the candidates' decisions to run (or not run) for the White House. My discussion of the GOP nomination fight follows in Chapter Three, and in Chapter Four I examine the Democratic, Republican, and Reform Party conventions that nominated the three musketeers of '96 politics (Clinton, Dole, and Perot). Professors Paul Herrnson of the University of Maryland and Clyde Wilcox of Georgetown University take up the general election campaign in Chapter Five, reviewing the debates, polls, and gaffes—and yes, the substance—of the trail. I discuss the voters' final judgment, rendered on November 5, in Chapter Six.

A good argument can be made that the more significant elections in 1996 occurred for Congress and at the state level. In Chapter Seven Richard E. Cohen, congressional correspondent of the *National Journal*, perceptively analyzes the fascinating House and Senate races, and Professor Thad L. Beyle of the University of North Carolina–Chapel Hill does the same for the gubernatorial and state legislative races in Chapter Eight.

With each passing election, greater attention is properly devoted to two vital parts of the campaign process, the press and political money. We do the same here, thanks to the superior efforts of Professor Diana Owen of Georgetown University in Chapter Nine on the press and CNN's Brooks Jackson in Chapter Ten on campaign financing. Jackson's eye-opening essay on the collapse of campaign rules in 1996 is particularly significant as the search for political reform intensifies. Bringing it all together in a forward-looking essay that combines the lessons of 1996 and the prospects for 2000 is Ken Bode, moderator of PBS's "Washington Week in Review" and a DePauw University professor.

---

[1] From the speech of U.S. Senator Charles Fairbanks of Ohio, quoted in Lawrence Prescott, *The Great Campaign of 1896* (Washington, D.C.: Loyal Publishers, 1896), p. 57. The author wishes to thank former University of Virginia student Scott Bates for unearthing this rhetorical gem.

We hope that these eleven chapters will shed some light on a many-faceted election. Whatever history's final rendering on its importance, the 1996 contest produced a president who is the last one of the 20th century and the first one of the 21st. The real bridge thus built is a continuation of an electoral pathway reaching back to 1789 and stretching into, one hopes, a far distant future of further progress and reform in American politics.

ACKNOWLEDGMENTS

I wish to thank all contributors for their truly first-rate work under tight deadlines; my editors and staff at Allyn and Bacon, especially Joseph Terry–senior editor, Sean Wakely–vice president and editor-in-chief of social sciences, Bill Barke–president, Quinn Perkson–marketing manager, and Susan Hutchinson–editorial assistant, for their partnership and spectacular cooperation on this book; a team of superb University of Virginia students headed by project manager Justin Sizemore and deputy manager Jeff Manns, and including researchers Stan Humphries, Rick Mayes, Michelle Baker, Michael Smith, and Steven Betz; my administrative assistant Nancy Rae; Joshua Rales, U.Va. Class of 1979, for his essential support; and the many dozens of campaign staffers and party officials who agreed to be interviewed. This volume is dedicated to my longtime mentor and friend, Professor Weldon Cooper, who passed away in May 1996. I hope that Mr. Cooper, a man of exacting standards, would be satisfied with our work. I shall depend on his wonderful wife Mildred to tell me.

L.J.S.

CHAPTER 1

The Road to Here

Tom Rosenstiel

Project for Excellence in Journalism

Robert Dole looked at the crowd of fruit packing workers and mustered a grim, mid-afternoon smile. The day had already been long, another parade of holding rooms, rope lines, and respectful but passionless strangers, and it was still hours from over. After this, there was an airport rally and a flight from Oregon to Arizona. Dole shifted his feet slightly and tugged on his shattered right arm, hidden under his smoothly tailored blue suit. The longest-serving Republican Senate leader in history breathed the ways of governing, of making laws and making deals, but he bore campaigning like a wound. Selling oneself was unseemly, even unmanly. He managed it only with pain. But Dole's dignity was always defined by sacrifice, by gutting things out.

At least the speech he was about to deliver here was familiar territory. He was at the Naumes fruit company in Medford, Oregon to talk about agriculture. Dole had spent 36 years, longer than most Americans had lived, talking farming with voters, and protecting farm programs in government. The event in Medford had also been skillfully arranged, which often made Dole perform better. His team of advance people had set him up to stand in front of a 30-foot wall of Oregon produce, apples, pears and peaches stacked in wooden crates 30 feet high. It was an interesting and appealing picture. A distracted TV audience—chasing kids, making dinner, readying children for bed—might remember it. Even if one saw the event only in passing, with the sound off, the message came through in tableau: Bob Dole was the candidate for agriculture. Dole also could fairly claim to be champion of agricultural exports in this race. His primary rival, Patrick Buchanan, advocated trade tariffs to protect American workers. By all appearances, this Medford event had been skillfully conceived.

Except for one thing. It was actually a fake. Until that morning, the fruit packing plant Dole was standing in had been vacant, the machinery idle. The boxes of pears and apples behind him had to be trucked in for the cameras

1

from another plant. The workers didn't work here. They'd arrived by bus to play audience. If one looked closely, their vaguely irritated expressions betrayed something odd.

Suddenly, somewhere toward the middle of his speech, Dole himself seemed affected by the contrivance. "I'm not certain what everybody is looking for in a candidate for president," he began.[1] "Maybe as soon as not have any at all. Just leave it vacant." Only a smattering of laughs answered him back, uncertain laughter at that. Was he joking? "But there's going to be one," Dole ventured on. "Every country ought to have one. So, we're out here campaigning."

Dole wasn't connecting, and he knew it. Maybe it was because he was tired. Or maybe it was because he was worried. Dole's candidacy was on life support. He had narrowly won Iowa, narrowly avoided third in New Hampshire, and was now trailing in the next big primary, Arizona. Maybe it was because Dole was simply confounded by the election itself, worried that the old values he cared about most—service, loyalty, a record—seemed to matter less than they used to. ("I get to thinking, maybe experience doesn't mean anything," he would tell me wistfully a few days later on his campaign plane.[2] "Maybe people just want somebody standing there saying, 'I got an idea, everybody gets a tax cut.' I think you've gotta be real. You gotta tell the truth." The remarks would later seem sadly ironic when he decided to bank his faltering campaign on a tax cut plan.)

Whatever the reason, in Medford this day Dole's sarcasm seemed to veer suddenly toward nihilism. This whole exercise, campaigning, primaries, meeting voters, was a vacant sham, and we both know it, he seemed to suggest. "You never really know much about these candidates. They blow into town, they blow off, then they blow out again."

When you come right down to it, you might as well ignore his words altogether.

"Even if you don't like me you ought to vote for me."

The audience stared back at Dole in mystification.

The Medford event might be written off as one of those strange days on the trail. But some of the jokes were part of Dole's regular repartee on the stump—just this day a little darker, a little weirder. Dole's cynicism was his way of reaching out on the campaign trail in 1996, of trying to connect with voters sour about the process. In one sense, Medford even captured something about the spirit of the 20th century's final campaign in general. An American electorate that rose up in anger in the last two elections of 1992 and 1994 seemed to have lost its ire. Voter turnout, after surging four years earlier, sagged to its lowest level in 70 years. The third party candidacy of Ross Perot petered out. In an age of skepticism, Clinton became the first Democrat in 50 years to win a second term not so much for what he was as what he wasn't—

not a liberal or a conservative, not an environmentalist or a free marketer, not a clear tax cutter or a tax increaser.

The voters had much about which to be skeptical. At a level unseen before, both candidates' campaigns were born at times out of research rather than conviction. Bob Dole, who'd devoted most of his career to whittling away at the federal deficit, based his fall campaign on tax cuts that even many of his own advisers fretted he didn't believe in. Bill Clinton, whose first two years as president were marked by liberal adventures such as a dramatic overhaul of health care, ran as a virtual Republican, signing bills like welfare reform he had earlier vetoed, and asking his own party activists to then attack him for doing so. By the end of the campaign, the combatants seemed like soldiers engaged in war games, aiming high-tech weapons with skillful precision but firing only blanks, no stomach for the live ammo of big ideas.

It would become quickly fashionable to declare all this a sign of some bankruptcy. The race seemed a disappointing case of stagecraft over substance. The abler TV performer won, the poorer campaigner lost. With both candidates running away from their parties, the race did little to answer whether the nation was moving left or right. Some would even suggest the campaign of 1996 was a signal of something wrong, of some frightening turn against politics and public life on the part of the American voter, perhaps even of a disintegration in the great American experiment in democracy.

If the candidates seemed unnerved, so was the press. Increasingly, the country's journalistic establishment was no longer confident about what was appropriate to cover and what was not. "The profession is sick," professed *Newsweek* Washington bureau chief Evan Thomas.[3] The public, which once tended to believe events they saw on television more than those from their daily lives, had become cynical about what came over the screen—and politicians knew it. "Staging photo-ops like Ronald Reagan won't work anymore," said chief White House speech writer Michael Waldman. "The question for us at the White House is how does the President communicate in a post-television age."[4] Surveys suggested viewership of network news was shriveling, down in May by 30 percent from 1993.[5] The networks in turn stopped covering the campaign. The number of campaign stories on the news fell 40 percent from four years earlier.[6] The Republicans staged the most carefully crafted convention ever, and only 30 percent of those watching TV cared to tune in.[7] The networks threatened not to come back again. Mused Dole's media strategist at the time, Mike Murphy: "This is the last TV convention. We will have to think of a new way of doing this from now on. We've taken this as far as we can."[8] The basic notion that had governed politics over the last half century—that pictures never lie, that seeing is believing—seemed in question. The cynicism went beyond politics, or the means of communication. It was cultural. We were a nation of doubters.

Perhaps. But the democracy had endured civil war, scandal, assassination, presidential resignation, and more. It could probably survive voter disgust. The evidence just as easily points to a turning point in our politics at the end of the century. Americans, schooled by a skeptical press and impatient after years of political gridlock, were rightly turning cool to the increasingly polarized and professionalized politics as it had come to be played out over the last quarter century. And that would surely be the only thing that would force any real change. The political class—the politicians, consultants, the surrogates— had refined their technique to new levels of expertise. The bus trips, train tours, the one liners with the press, the seemingly intimate moments of spontaneity between candidates and their wives that just happened to be captured on camera, all were conceived and rehearsed with greater skill than ever before. (Democrats had refined the art of "rapid response" to such an art that in the spring they were faxing reporters their rebuttals to Dole's attacks before Dole had delivered them.) Yet hardly anyone seemed impressed. The public was tuning out the manipulations, and responding to the campaign based on a more basic, and perhaps sensible, level.[9] It supported Clinton because it feared the influence of Newt Gingrich and the Republican Congress.

Yet it also wanted the general direction Gingrich was moving, toward finally balancing the budget bloated out of control in the years led by Ronald Reagan, and reexamining the social programs extended under Lyndon Johnson and Richard Nixon.[10] There were even signs, subtle but not to be dismissed, that one of two great parties might be in fatal decline and that a new party might rise to replace it. It had happened before, when Whigs gave way to Republicans 150 years earlier. Then, as now, the party had lost any clear meaning in people's lives and began casting about for new, often contradictory, positions in each election, just as Clinton seemed to move toward running as a bleeding heart Republican, and Dole, in some moments, as a tough minded Democrat. What's more, as his own popularity waned, the fledgling Reform Party Ross Perot financed and built showed signs of outgrowing him. Many of the politicians touted as presidential material, from Bill Bradley among Democrats to Warren Rudman among Republicans, were uncertain they had homes in either party anymore. To what new beginning was uncertain. But the end of the century saw the climax of the era of the photo-op and the age of television, and the decline of politics as it had come to be known. People no longer bought it.

How had it come to this? Actually, the concept of presidential candidates campaigning at all was largely a twentieth century experiment. The idea that voters would pick their party nominees is even newer. Until Richard Nixon's second term, party professionals picked the nominees, largely in private. The first modern presidential primary was not held until 1952, and it didn't mean much. These early primaries were political dress rehearsals for aspiring candidates to show party bosses they had electoral charm. But they caught on. By 1960, an appealing young Democrat named Jack Kennedy used the growing number of primaries to convince party elders that he, rather than more experienced candidates, had the charisma needed to take on the GOP nominee, Vice President Richard Nixon. Eight years later, Senator Eugene McCarthy was able to embarrass President Lyndon Johnson into retiring merely by coming in second in the now much watched New Hampshire primary. Party bosses still made the decisions. They picked Vice President Hubert Humphrey as the Democrats' nominee at their national convention, though he had not won a single primary. The public outrage was so great, reformers forced wholesale changes in the system. Party professionals conferring in private would never again pick their party nominees after 1968. The smoke filled room was locked. Under new rules, instituted by an aspiring presidential candidate named George McGovern, voters voicing preferences in primaries would decide nominees. Whoever won the most votes in the primaries would have the most delegates at the convention.

The echo was profound. Since they no longer picked the party nominees, political conventions became fully scripted commercials, important as political communication but devoid of surprise. Since party pols who knew the candidates personally were no longer calling the shots, the press began covering the personal side of politicians more, so voters could judge these matters for themselves. Less obvious, the reforms were a first step toward polarizing American politics. Primary voters tended to be true believers, while the party professionals they replaced tended to be pragmatists. When the true believers got to pick their party nominee, they picked more for passion—and they picked people more from the political extremes.

The first non-incumbent presidential candidate to be picked through primaries, George McGovern in 1972, was probably the most liberal candidate ever picked by a major party. And his nomination helped ensure Nixon's landslide re-election. Four years later, Republican activists were so moved by the sunny passion of Ronald Reagan that the party's right wing nearly took the nomination from a sitting president, Gerald Ford. These internal party feuds between pragmatists and idealists had always simmered. But in the days when the party pros sat down behind closed doors, hashed out the pros and cons, and often settled on compromise candidates, the fissures were bridged, or at least kept from public view.

In the years since, parties have struggled with how to mitigate the passion the primaries created and the scar tissue they left behind. They've enjoyed only limited success. Today, many of the worst attacks in presidential politics come initially from fellow party members. Al Gore unearthed the charge that Michael Dukakis was somehow to blame for a black convicted murderer named Willie Horton committing rape while on a weekend furlough from a Massachusetts prison. The efforts to quell the bitterness have had their own problems. In 1996, Republicans tried to minimize the ravages of the primaries by compressing the process so that the nominee would be picked within a month. The effort required such expense that by March 2, only two weeks after the first-in-the-nation New Hampshire primary, Bob Dole had already spent nearly all of the $36 million allowed him under federal matching fund rules. Dead broke, the Dole campaign was unable to answer blistering Democratic attack ads for the next six months. The parties had only slightly more success trying to project images of unity at their televised conventions. The bitterness of the primaries ruined George Bush's last realistic chance of a comeback in 1992. When the parties glossed over or controlled their differences in 1996, the press denounced the conventions as fraudulent, not because they were scripted, but because they did so little to reflect the real face of the two parties.

In the early days of his own re-election campaign, Bill Clinton succeeded largely by eliminating the primaries. No president had won re-election if challenged during the primary season by his own party. Clinton's success in avoiding that drag as 1996 began was one of the first signs of his campaign's sudden, unexpected strength.

Only a few months earlier, such muscle had seemed improbable. After two years in office, Clinton had emerged as a undisciplined, unpopular leader, full of good intention but seemingly lacking either a philosophical core or a keen instinct for the public mood that might have helped make up for it.

The first cause of Clinton's failure was personal. When he arrived in the Capitol at age 47, William Jefferson Clinton was still a man in search of himself. He was, arguably, the most unfinished personality ever elected to the office. "Character," he had told the *Wall Street Journal* during the 1992 campaign, "is a quest."[11] Perhaps for Clinton, but hardly for most of the presidents who had preceded him. Ronald Reagan and George Bush had a firm grasp of who they were, and while that might have meant a certain closed mindedness to their presidencies, they also did not evince the meandering Clinton would. Clinton's capacity for growth was also a capacity to err. The Arkansas governor had run in 1992 as a "New Democrat," one more centrist and friendly to the marketplace, espousing targeted capital gains tax relief and welfare reform. In office, Clinton's first policy priorities were traditional and liberal. He alienated much of the culturally conservative southern vote he had picked up in the election by making his first action as president an attempt to provide legal and civil rights to homosexuals in the military. Then, when he ventured into the major policy initiative of his first term, his ill-fated attempt at reforming America's health care system, Clinton and his wife Hillary, who quarter-backed the effort, quickly wandered away from their stated purpose of controlling costs. Instead, their plan put emphasis on expanding health care to 100 percent of the American public, which made it enormously expensive. They also distrusted the marketplace and insisted on creating a government bureaucracy to impose price controls. Their system was close enough to nationalized health care that Republicans were able to depict Clinton as trying to socialize American medicine and crush the effort. Even many Democrats, particularly in the South, could not support it. And when Republicans sensed support fading, they ordered party members who would have voted for modified versions to oppose any health care reform in order to weaken Clinton. The President had overreached. He naively had tried to accomplish something as extraordinary as revolutionizing health care without making any attempt to be bipartisan. To his enemies, Clinton was a closet leftist. To his friends, he was politically inept. To a doubting public, he was a man without conviction—a politician who talked one way and governed another.

The second failing of the administration was hubris. Though he had won in the three way contest of 1992 with only a minority of support of 43 percent of the electorate, Clinton did not make winning over the independent vote that had eluded him a priority, in the way Richard Nixon had after his own three-way victory in 1968. The independent Perot voter of 1992 was interested in deficit reduction and political reform. On taking office, Clinton introduced a liberal budget that included a jobs-stimulus package to help satisfy traditional Democratic constituencies. Influential moderate Democrats, like David Boren of Oklahoma, bolted and began to denounce Clinton for being a too liberal. Republicans defeated the plan, and turned Clinton's budget into a deficit reduction package instead, one Clinton did little initially to champion.

Aside from his policy mistakes, Clinton also lacked technical skill over the presidency. Where the Reagan White House planned the priorities of the administration months ahead—and plotted a carefully controlled communications strategy to carry out those priorities—Clinton operated week to week. "At first, we didn't realize how big a megaphone we had," admitted political adviser Paul Begala.[12] Even the basics, such as the care and feeding of the press corps, were mishandled. Clinton's first communications director, George Stephanopoulos, held the press corps he was supposed to work with in a certain contempt. At his twice a day press briefings, for instance, Stephanopoulos thought his goal should be not to make news or give the press anything new to write. "Your job on the podium is to do nothing," Stephanopoulos said. "You should not be trumping the president."[13] Reporters knew they were being stonewalled, and sometimes misled, especially when Stephanopoulos claimed ignorance of matters reporters knew had taken place and that he knew about. "These guys definitely believed in the efficacy of spin," said ABC White House correspondent Brit Hume. The White House did not begin to right itself on these technical matters until two years in, when Leon Panetta took over as chief of staff and Mike McCurry came over from the State Department as press secretary. By then, Clinton's health care plan was dead, and congressional Democrats were finding that Clinton was about to cost many of them their jobs.

The fourth obstacle troubling the administration was not of Clinton's making. The President was victim of a changing political culture, one which might have daunted any president. Where Ronald Reagan could communicate to the country by sending his press secretary out to talk to the three TV networks, two wire services, and a handful of national newspapers, Clinton took office at a time when the media spectrum had become huge and uncontrollable. In the age of 24-hour news, there was no news cycle to control. The news was continuous. Everything had accelerated. Within two weeks, the press had declared Clinton's honeymoon over, and his presidency faltering. Journalism had become relentlessly interpretative, and the judgments rendered by the new subjective press were often rendered inoperative, in the famous phrase of the Nixon White House, for statements that proved to be untrue. Over the span of only a few months, for instance, *Time* magazine's covers heralded the scope of the Clinton ambition with "You Say You Want a Revolution," to calling him "The Incredible Shrinking President," to extolling the enormity of his agenda again: "Overturning the Reagan Era."[14] The new media of talk radio, meanwhile, purveyed rumor and innuendo alongside news. When a rumor surfaced in a conservative fax newsletter that White House Counsel Vince Foster had died in a Washington safehouse and that persons unknown had moved his body to the park where it was found, talk radio hosts reported it as fact, until it moved the stock market, and turned up in a financial story the next day in the *Washington Post*.

Two years in, the public wanted change again. Americans were not so much fickle as fed up. Polls showed for some time they thought the country was on the wrong track, and government seemed gridlocked about doing anything about it. For a decade, politicians had talked about shrinking the deficit, and it had only swollen. For a decade, politicians had talked about declining education, and people saw no results. For years, lawmakers had talked about shrinking government, and it had only grown. Voters were running out of patience. They'd flirted with a non-politician populist in Ross Perot two years earlier. They summarily fired George Bush, who had enjoyed close to 90 percent approval ratings only a year earlier. When they elected Clinton, they did so with misgivings. It was less an embrace of the young Arkansan than a rejection of Bush. And they were allowing the new president a short leash.

By the summer of 1993, Clinton was so unpopular, fellow Democrats running for re-election had to repudiate Clinton to have a chance of winning.

Republicans ran mainly by identifying any Democrat with the President—particularly, in the style of the day, by using new video technology to "morph" the face of whatever Democrat was running with a particularly unflattering image of Clinton. Just as the 1992 election had been a referendum on Bush, which left Clinton as the winner, 1994 was a referendum on Clinton, even though he wasn't on any ballots. When Clinton invited losing Democrats to the White House for a farewell after the election, one congresswoman stood uncomfortably in the receiving line and said in a stage whisper, "what do you say to the man who cost you your job."[15]

Earlier that summer, the House Minority Whip, Newt Gingrich of Georgia, had begun to sense Republicans could win the House and Senate for the first time in 40 years. He was mostly alone. But Gingrich believed that what Republicans needed to move over the top was an agenda that would appeal to the Perot swing-voters Clinton had never won over. Written agendas had become the fashion. In the 1992 presidential race, Paul Tsongas had defined himself as a new kind of more credible politician by personally writing a frank 87-page manifesto, which voters were calling away for and actually reading. Clinton's "me-too" manifesto had become a national best seller. Gingrich's idea of a manifesto went one better. He would not only draft an agenda; he would get all his fellow House Republican candidates to sign it. The effect shouldn't be overstated. "It was a photo-op," scoffed one prominent Republican consultant, who helped elect a number of Republican candidates.[16] But it gave Republican challengers who might have seemed otherwise unprepared a specific legislative strategy to campaign with. The existence of the Contract with America, regardless of what it said, gave them credibility.

Gingrich didn't read it that way. He saw the Contract as a literal promise of what the new Republican Congress would do. Two days after the elections, Gingrich held his first press conference in Washington with reporters and announced that the new Congress would do nothing for three months except work on passing the Contract. Gingrich believed voters had embraced it. He was mistaken, and it was a first sign of how hubris would blind him, just as it had Clinton before him.

Gingrich also saw the Contract as a way to aggregate power in his own hands. It had become conventional wisdom that the era of the strong-armed political bosses, like Sam Rayburn or Lyndon Johnson, were over. The age of television had made politicians free agents, who could gain power of their own through staging televised hearings or raising money through political action committees (PACs). Gingrich defied that. He wanted to be a new kind of political boss for a new era, who used the tools of television and PACs not to build the party but to build himself as the personification of the party. While most politicians had personal PACs to help funnel money to fellow Republicans, Gingrich had a different idea. He used his PAC not to raise money but to recruit budding politicians, train them, and then finance them. He called these recruits his "Farm Team," and they traveled their districts listening to his audio tapes on politics and campaigning. Once Republicans had won the House, Gingrich tried further to exert control. The Contract was the final element in the Gingrich plan to transform himself into a new kind of political boss. When Gingrich announced Congress would work only on the Contract for nearly four months, it meant that Gingrich would have essentially total control over committee agendas—and not just for 100 days. When the Contract period was over, Congress would have to turn to writing the budget. Since the Contract mandated that the budget be balanced, it really took Congress through Christmas, at least. Gingrich would effectively control every aspect of Congress for a year. In the guise of needing people who could ram the Contract through according to schedule, Gingrich next chucked the seniority system for picking committee chairs. Personal loyalty to the Speaker became the criteria. As leverage over the senior members, Gingrich gave power to freshmen, the most conservative group in his conference. Gingrich imagined they would be loyal to him. He had recruited and trained many of them. Again, he was mistaken.

The American system of government was designed to resist any one source of power from dominating the political process, even the president, let alone a speaker of the House. For all his attempts to exert total control, in fact, Gingrich's efforts to railroad his agenda through Congress meant that he needed to keep his right-wing happy—since he would be winning few votes from Democrats. Early on, he allowed some of the more extreme members of the Republican conference enormous range. To keep his coalition together on the balanced budget, he allowed supply-siders to build huge tax breaks for business and the wealthy into the economic plan. During appropriations, he allowed some of the most anti-environmental members to attach a series of politically disastrous riders onto the bill, including one that would have cut the budget of the Environmental Protection Agency to enforce popular clean water and air laws by 30 percent. (Gingrich and his aides knew the environmental efforts were politically damaging, but he was confident they could be fixed later.[17]) He allowed his House Whip Tom DeLay to also use a form of extortion with lobbyists, which reinforced the idea of a government that could be bought. DeLay made it clear to lobbyists that if they wanted to have influence with Republicans, they had to cut off funding to Democrats. Then DeLay and others allowed some of these lobbyists to write whole bills.

Gingrich's catering to his right wing, with whom he felt he had more ideological sympathy, undermined the notion he had tried so assiduously to create that this was a "new" Republican Party—just as Clinton's early actions undermined his own aspirations of being a "New Democrat."

These appeared to be old Republicans, only more blatant and uncompromising.

Then add to that Newt Gingrich's own personal chemistry with the public. The face of this Republican revolution was not warm. The more exposure he had, the worse it got. By summer, Gingrich was conducting secret studies to find out why he was so wildly unpopular.[18] The results showed the problem was visceral. The very things that some people liked about Gingrich, that he was shaking things up, struck others as a sign of a man who was dangerous. One internal adviser to Gingrich fretted that there was nothing the Speaker could do. He cited research in which voters in the United States were shown pictures of politicians from Canada. Knowing nothing other than the photos, their impressions eerily matched what the Canadians who knew these leaders thought of them. Some impressions were visual, subliminal, ineffable, in much the same way that some actors in Hollywood play leading men, others play characters, some heroes, some villains. Gingrich, said one aide privately, was destined to play the didactic professor, lecturing and hectoring people. It was just who he was and who he appeared to be. It may not be fair, but it was the way it is.

It also may have been fair. One component of Gingrich's success—and failure—was hubris. A powerful arrogance allowed him to think he could balance the budget when others had lacked the nerve. That arrogance had allowed him to think he could reform entitlements when other politicians had lacked the nerve. That arrogance had also allowed Gingrich to imagine Americans had embraced his Contract, against most empirical evidence, and to imagine that his freshmen would be supremely loyal. Gingrich had harnessed his arrogance at times in the past. "Newt had been very careful before the election about holding his tongue, about being strategic about what he said. After the election, he operated more on instinct. His arrogance got the best of him," said one of his closest advisers who was involved in these discussions with Gingrich.[19]

Nowhere was Gingrich's arrogance played out more than in his budget strategy, which he conceived and sold fellow House Republicans on. The plan was simple. The Republicans would pass a balanced budget and then shut the government down to force Clinton to sign it.[20] Gingrich made two tactical errors. He misjudged Clinton, particularly his ability to blast Gingrich's laudable plan to take on Medicare entitlements. And he had no plan of what to do if Clinton didn't blink. When the strategy didn't work, Gingrich shut the government down a second time. His already damaged popularity sagged even further.

Gingrich's failure was the prelude to the '96 race. It catapulted Dole, whose poll ratings climbed as Gingrich's dropped, as the responsible Republican. Dole relished the role as the reluctant revolutionary. His instinct for compromise seemed a sign of maturity when he stood in press conferences next to Gingrich and his freshmen. And Dole's skill at sending subtle signals, using body language, winces and nods, actually worked well on television. As primary voters watched Gingrich and Dole standing next to each other at podiums during the budget battle, Dole repeatedly made subtle references to acting like adults, turned away when Gingrich was speaking, and looked uncomfortable with the whole situation. The very uneasiness and mixed signals that would later mar his campaign served his purposes perfectly in the pre-primary season. Dole became the prohibitive favorite to win the GOP nomination. It was his to lose, and he avoided doing so, however barely.

Clinton's task was nearly as simple. Having avoided a primary challenge, Clinton prepared for the election with twin strategies. Humiliated in the midterm elections, he turned to an old friend, an ideologically ambidextrous political consultant named Dick Morris, who lately had taken to working with Republicans, in particular staunch conservative Mississippi Senator Trent Lott. Morris was a cynical but creative strategist whose instincts were always to move his candidates to the center on issues, where they could co-opt popular turf occupied by their opponents. Morris persuaded Clinton to adopt a strategy he called "triangulation," in which the President would position himself in a separate spot from congressional Democrats and Republicans. In the spring of 1995, Clinton at Morris' urging distanced himself from his party by presenting his own balanced budget plan, one that involved fewer tax cuts and fewer cuts in the growth of entitlement programs like Medicare. While it lacked specifics, it gave Clinton credibility in criticizing the Republican plan, which was still being debated in Congress. It also angered Democrats, some of whom had wanted to have their own balanced budget plan but had simply opposed the Republicans in Congress at the White House's behest. They felt betrayed, and their pique served Clinton's and Morris' purpose. The concept of triangulation, and the sometimes agile ideological hopscotch it involved, saw its zenith after the budget fight, when Clinton in his 1996 State of the Union Address declared "the era of big government is over." The man who had tried to add government into American health care had become a small government advocate.

Second, Clinton began to behave like a president. After the disastrous 1994 elections, political consultant Frank Greer made Clinton review video tapes of how Ronald Reagan comported himself as president, especially on camera. Watch his bearing, Greer advised. Before long, Clinton was no longer seen with a cup of takeout coffee, a sheaf of papers, and surrounded by young aides, as he had been in the early days. Now, Clinton walked to and from helicopters or meetings alone, striding with a purpose, a straight back, often with his eyes set faraway. Greer also showed Clinton video tape of a CBS Evening News program with no fewer than six White House stories. Clinton had been told he had to be more disciplined about his message before, but the CBS video was a reminder that was too painful to forget. There should be only one story a day. Clinton also became more aloof about engaging in the back and forth of issues. Over the course of the summer of 1995, while Congress was hashing it out over GOP budget cuts, he gave a series of speeches that struck a higher and more thematic tone. Known as "the common ground" speeches, they dealt with subjects like self-reliance, civility, optimism, and reason. They won little praise at the time, but Clinton was finding his voice as one above the fray. He was no longer the leader who took the lead on most issues, as he had done on health care. Now, he set a moral tone, and let the Congress get muddy over the details. What bills would Clinton veto, and which not? Washington began to wait expectantly for him. And if Clinton found himself only in reaction to Gingrich, using the easier-to-manipulate levers of government to stop things rather than to accomplish them, he did so with far greater skill than he had demonstrated before. When the budget battle became more focused that fall, Clinton let his chief of staff, Leon Panetta, do most of the negotiating. Not till later did Gingrich and Dole meet with Clinton, and then only on the President's turf, at the White House.

Finally, Clinton began to sense that people now doubted his ideological promises. So as the 1996 election commenced he began to campaign not with grand promises but small bore initiatives, many of which did not involve the federal government but were entirely hortatory. He advocated uniforms in public schools, the V-chip to allow parents to censor what their kids saw on TV, local teen curfews, a constitutional amendment protecting the rights of crime victims. The initiatives served many purposes. One was, as Clinton explained to an aide, that the President understood he could no longer talk in broad generalities about "reinventing government," or "ending welfare as we know it."[21] People didn't believe his broad political promises. So he spoke with small, illustrative actions. He was trying to establish his own character by policy espousal; and it was all about social discipline, the very qualities Clinton had lacked earlier in his term. These small policy initiatives also showed that Clinton now had command of the symbolic powers of his office, or the bully pulpit. That made him seem more presidential. Finally, many of these issues were once Republican initiatives, and they were aimed at key swing voter groups, particularly suburban parents. Clinton was no longer going to be John Kennedy. Now he was running for re-election as the national crossing guard.

This wasn't merely a move to the center. It was more subtle than that. Over the course of 1995, Clinton also became more of an environmentalist. It began when Vice President Al Gore asked environmental groups to assemble all the data they could that the environment was a strong issue. The data showed something Clinton and the Republicans had missed. Voters, even those who felt there was too much government red tape, liked environmental laws that protected clean air and water. (They were less tolerant about laws that told landowners what they could with their property.) People had misunderstood the Republicans' intentions. They thought the GOP plan to cut back on regulations would help the EPA enforce the laws, not that the GOP wanted to roll back the laws themselves. Soon, Democratic pollster Celinda Lake found in her focus groups something else she hadn't expected to come up when voters talked about the environment. Bob Dole's record on the environment reminded them of his age. Voters tended to think only younger Americans—kids or parents who had kids in school—cared about the environment. It was their kids, coming home from school pestering them about recycling and global warming, who had taught them to care, parents said. Seeing Clinton, whose daughter was in high school, talking about the environment, the voters said, reminded them that Bob Dole was old. The environment was not only good politics, it was a way of subtly reinforcing the age issue, Democrats found. Clinton was not exactly leading. He campaigned on self-selling environmental issues, like cleaning up toxic waste sites, or strengthening the Clean Air and Water Act. He made a point of swapping federal land with a drilling company that had rights to mine in Yellowstone National Park. He was not out campaigning on issues environmentalists thought most important, like global warming. But a comeback was not built simply on moving to the center. It was built on depicting the President as a popular opponent to the Republican charge in Congress.

In the end, what moved voters in the 1996 election? For all the changes in technology, it was not about staging photo-ops. Nor has it ever been. Just as they did in the age of the torch light parade, the penny press, the mass rallies, or the fireside chats on radio, voters at the end of the century still cared about peace and prosperity first. Indeed, a candidate's ability to perform on television has never been decisive. Patrick Buchanan was the best performer on television in the 1996 race, but his ideas were too extreme to make him electable. Only twice in the TV age, with John Kennedy and Ronald Reagan, did an extraordinary TV performer win. Most presidents are merely adequate on television. What TV did was bring politicians we once saw only from a distance of hundreds of feet, or heard through the radio, into our living rooms at a distance of about six feet away—a distance earlier we only saw people we knew personally. That did make Americans want to know more about the personal lives of their leaders, to know about them things they would want to know about friends. What kind of people were they? What was their marriage like? Looking this fellow over, what do I make of him? But those personal factors only became part of a larger mix, a mix that still relied much more heavily on ideas. By any measure, Bob Dole was an admirable man, a hero. By the conventional definition of character, Dole, a war hero, a stoic, a politician whose word really was his bond, was an extraordinary man. He never cursed, never spoke ill of colleagues, never lied, and seemed somehow to suffer his indiscretions more than most. He was, in many ways, the better man, just as in 1992 voters knew that George Bush was a war hero and a loving husband, while Clinton was a draft evader who had a difficult marriage. But voters in both elections were more concerned with ideas and the character of the public rather than the private man. They wanted someone who they thought would empathize with average people. In 1996, the race boiled down to something quite simple. Voters, particularly the growing number of independent voters, wanted someone who would be a check on Newt Gingrich and the House Republicans. And they thought that was Clinton, who had stood up to Gingrich over the budget, while Dole had to play a more subtle game of consent. Indeed, Dole's complicity with Gingrich undermined his hope of eventually moving to the ideological center as a moderate conservative. In time, Dole tried to move toward the Republican Party's other moderate wing, that of Jack Kemp's "compassionate conservatism" and supply-side tax cutting. He made a 15 percent across the board tax cut the cornerstone of his campaign, and named Kemp his running mate. But even many of his own aides doubted it would ever work. "The country wasn't in recession, Clinton wasn't advocating tax increases, and Dole didn't really believe in it," said one of Dole's top aides.[22]

In an odd way, much of the campaign that Dole and Clinton waged was beside the point. Dole ran in the end as a supply-side tax cutter. Clinton campaigned as a budget balancer who would trim the books and cut taxes but in a less draconian way. Voters doubted many of their claims. Most Americans didn't watch the conventions, or the debates. Fewer and fewer watched the network news or read newspapers. Most of what the press focused on, the horse race and the internal machinations of scandals involving Dick Morris, or the staff shakeups in the Dole campaign, were irrelevant. Voters understood a more basic dynamic. The handlers had perfected their craft. The parties had put up controlled messages, communicated with skill and discipline. Voters didn't believe most of it and didn't care. They wanted government to work, and they didn't want either party's extreme to have undue influence. As with all elections, the last one of the century told us much about the nation and its people. It did not, however, tell us much of where the two parties were headed. Nor did it tell us whether the country was becoming more conservative, or which party voters favored. In an age of skepticism, Clinton won because he was the none-of-the-above candidate, a pragmatist who moved to the places where the public wanted him.

Clinton's legacy would be more than the man who vetoed the budget. Whether by skill or lack of principle, he would succeed as no politician had since Richard Nixon in 1972, by governing in the middle, borrowing ideas from both sides, and eschewing polarization—though not attack. He made interdisciplinary politics a winner again, after years in which the two parties were moving further away from it. And he put an end to an era, epitomized by the phrase made popular by aides to Reagan, that the only thing to be found in the middle of the road were yellow lines and dead armadillos. But it seemed unlikely, or at least some time away, that this would change the direction of either party, or convince other politicians they could run on ideas rather than attacks. The only thing that was clear was that voters were turned off by politics, and their non-involvement could no longer be dismissed as mere apathy.

NOTES

1. Author was at this event covering it for *Newsweek* magazine.
2. Interview with the author, February 29, 1996.
3. Interview with the author, summer, 1996.
4. Interview with the author, summer, 1996.
5. Pew Research Center for the People and the Press Survey, May 13, 1996.
6. A Markle Foundation study conducted by Robert Lichter of the Center for Media and Public Affairs in August, 1996.
7. Howard Kurtz, "As Vote Nears, Americans Are Tuning Out Campaign '96," *Washington Post*, October 10, 1996.
8. Interview with the author, August 15, 1996.
9. Four in ten Americans made up their minds about whom they would vote for before 1996, according to a major post-election poll published November 15, 1996, by the Pew Research Center for the People and the Press examining how people got their information about the election. Another 13 percent had decided before the primaries ended, they told Pew, meaning the majority of Americans had settled on their choice before the general election even began. Given the natural pressure not to appear closed-minded in a poll, I believe the actual number is probably even higher. Furthermore, a growing number of Americans seemed to be tuning out the campaign as presented through the traditional mainstream press and gravitating to new, longer form media such as the Internet and Talk Radio. The number of Americans who reported receiving most of their information about the campaign from network television was down 40 percent from four years earlier to just four in ten, according to the same post-election Pew survey. The number who relied on local TV news was down 20 percent to two in ten. The number who relied on radio was up 30 percent, to two in ten. Ten percent reported relying on the Internet. And 60 percent, about the same as four years earlier, relied on newspapers.
10. Polling data suggested that nearly 70 percent of Americans were happy that the election resulted in divided government. Indeed, nearly 40 percent of Clinton voters, and even 40 percent of voters who supported Democrats in congressional races, reported they were "happy" Republicans had retained control of Congress. Poll by the Pew Research Center for the People and the Press, November 15, 1996.

11. Interview between Clinton and David Shribman, published in the *Wall Street Journal*, July 1992.

12. Interview with the author, March 1993.

13. Tom Rosenstiel, The Beat Goes On, Clinton's First Year with the Media, Twentieth Century Fund monograph, summer 1994.

14. Ibid.

15. This episode was recounted to the author by three different members of Congress at the White House event.

16. Interview with the author, January 5, 1996.

17. Interviews with Gingrich and several of his top aides throughout the first three months of 1996.

18. The details of this study were revealed to the author by several people on Gingrich's staff and other outside advisers involved in preparing the study and who were familiar with its results.

19. Interview with a senior Gingrich aide by the author.

20. Gingrich not only conceived of the strategy; he openly bragged about it in interviews with reporters, including the author.

21. A senior Clinton aide, in an interview with the author, related how Clinton had absorbed this skepticism about him, May 1996.

22. Interview with the author, August 1996.

CHAPTER 2

Where Did All the Candidates Go?

*Linda L. Fowler**

Dartmouth College

Before voters ever cast their ballots in November 1996, political commentators had already begun arguing about the reasons for Bill Clinton's seemingly inevitable victory. Some contended that Clinton could not lose given the robust economy and his winter rebound in the polls. For these analysts, the campaign was largely irrelevant because the factors that drive presidential politics had aligned in the Democrat's favor many months before. Other observers, however, thought the Republicans could have won if Bob Dole had run a different campaign or the party had selected a different nominee. In their view, Dole failed to define himself as an attractive alternative to a deeply flawed incumbent and missed numerous strategic opportunities to capitalize on the President's weaknesses.[1] These explanations not only reflect contradictory views of American electoral politics, but they also are short-sighted in overlooking the important events—and non-events—that set the stage for the 1996 election. President Clinton's popularity recovered in the polls because he escaped a bruising renomination fight within his own party. Senator Dole stumbled through a lackluster campaign because the GOP lacked an alternative candidate who could unify its myriad of factions. In short, the defining moments for this race were the decisions of numerous Democrats and Republicans *not to seek the presidency.*

Forecasts of presidential election results are often quite accurate; indeed, a variety of political scientists predicted Clinton's November victory back in August using his Gallup approval ratings, growth in Gross Domestic Product (GDP) and, in some cases, controls for the number of terms the administration's

*The author gratefully acknowledges the research assistance of Caroline D. Langsdorf and Meredith L. Martin and the editorial assistance of Anita K. Brown.

party had controlled the presidency.[2] Yet sometimes these models miss the mark. In 1992, for example, failure to account for the strength of Ross Perot's candidacy and historical trends in party control of the presidency led to the erroneous prediction of Bush's re-election. And in 1994, the relatively healthy growth of 4.1 percent in GDP nevertheless led to a resounding rejection of Clinton and his party.[3] An additional weakness of the forecasting approach, however, lies in its inability to explain movement in presidential popularity. We know that the approval ratings of modern presidents are increasingly volatile and that they are closely tied to political events, such as war or recession. But the president's standing in the polls is also dependent upon his own actions and upon the strategic behavior of rivals, as George Bush learned to his sorrow in 1992. Clinton emerged from the doldrums by the late fall of 1995 and held steady at 50 percent to 58 percent throughout the spring and summer[4] in large part because he did not have to defend his record against a primary challenger.[5]

In Dole's case, his liabilities as the GOP standard-bearer were obvious right from the start. After a long public career, his deficiencies as a public speaker, his preoccupation with legislative jargon, and his inability to delegate to subordinates were well known. But it does not necessarily follow that the Republicans had a better alternative. Dole was the front-runner by the fall of 1995 because thousands of party officials and GOP contributors had backed his candidacy with endorsements and money. Savvy handicappers, who well understood the opportunities Clinton's first-term performance presented, seem to have made hard-headed calculations about the rest of the Republican field rather than indulged in the sentimental claim that it was Dole's turn.

Where did all the candidates go? Among potential Democratic aspirants, the strategic environment discouraged presidential ambitions. The combination of a sitting president and a demoralized party was a powerful inducement to remain on the sidelines. Among Republicans, the factionalism inside the party made it difficult to mobilize the necessary resources for an effective candidacy. Under the best of circumstances, raising the money, enduring the media scrutiny, and running the gauntlet of an increasingly front-loaded primary schedule is a daunting task.[6] Despite the fact that Bill Clinton made an inviting target for Republican hopefuls, relatively few of the prospective contenders had the stomach for the fight in the party's highly charged atmosphere.

THE COMEBACK KID

At the close of New Hampshire's presidential primary in 1992, Bill Clinton labeled himself the "comeback kid." Bruised by disclosures of an extramarital affair, Clinton plummeted in the polls, but fought back to a second-place finish, just nine points behind Democratic rival Paul Tsongas.[7] He went on to clinch his self-styled title by becoming the first candidate to win the presidency after a loss in the New Hampshire primary. By the fall of 1995, Clinton once again proved himself the master of comeback politics, as his potential opponents for the Democratic nomination took themselves out of the running one by one.

Clinton's success in staving off rivals was one of the most significant happenings in the 1996 election. No single event marked the triumph within his own party, and yet the quiet withdrawal of several prospective challengers had enormous strategic significance for the fall campaign. First, it enabled Clinton to rise above the political fray and gain maximum advantage from the office of the presidency. Second, it permitted him to reposition himself as a moderate for the fall campaign. As a result, Clinton headed to the Democratic Convention in August with a 12-point to 20-point lead in the polls,[8] an astonishingly strong position for a president who had been all but eclipsed by the Republican congressional leadership just a year previously. Looking back to 1995, however, Clinton's renomination seemed far from inevitable.

The president's low level of approval and high negatives among voters were matched by disaffection among Democratic activists and public officials, who blamed him for the party's calamitous showing in the 1994 midterm elections. Moreover, Clinton alienated the most liberal factions in the party at the start of the 104th Congress by his tepid defense of cherished Democratic programs against the new Republican majority, which claimed a mandate to roll them back. Privately, many Democrats feared that if Clinton ran again, the long-predicted realignment giving Republicans lasting control of the federal government would finally occur in 1996.[9] Publicly, veiled hints circulated that the Democratic Party might be better served if its standard-bearer stepped aside.

During the winter of 1995, the press carried what were known as ABC stories—Anybody But Clinton. Talk show hosts joked about pictures from a New Year's hunting expedition that showed the President holding a dead duck. Interviews with members of Congress after Clinton's interminable 87-minute State of the Union Address suggested forthcoming challenges. As Senator Bill Bradley noted on a talk-radio show: "I think people are going to look at the President in the next six to nine months . . . anybody could step up to the plate if the circumstances are right."[10] A CBS News poll revealed that 53 percent of the public thought Clinton should not be renominated, and 47 percent agreed with the statement that he should not seek re-election.[11] Even the Democratic National Committee sent out a fundraising letter that startled campaign professionals with the headline: "Should President Clinton be Re-Elected?"[12]

Why did Clinton's opponents fail to mobilize against him, and how did the absence of a challenger benefit his re-election bid? Clinton earned his un-contested nomination partially through adroit maneuvering within his own party, and against the Republican Congress over the budget in the fall of 1995. Yet, he also benefited from the political calculations of his likely rivals, as well as some fortuitous circumstances that were well beyond his control. In many ways, the disarray within the Democratic Party after its drubbing in 1994 helped to shield the President from the consequences of his own political weakness.

Comparing Clinton's circumstances with those of previous incumbent presidents makes his good fortune seem even more striking. In the post–World War II era, incumbent presidents who faced tough primary challenges have in-variably lost their bids for re-election. None of the few presidents who gained a second term—Truman, Eisenhower, Nixon and Reagan—had to compete in primary contests, and all of those who lost—Ford, Carter and Bush—carried the burden of their primary challengers' charges of weak leadership into the fall campaign. Arguably, had party rules encouraged primary challengers in the 1940s to the extent that they do now, Harry Truman might not have sur-vived the Democratic Convention to eke out a victory in 1948.[13]

Although primary contests appear to be lethal to the re-election hopes of incumbent presidents, it is unclear whether they are merely a *symptom* of a failed presidency, or a *cause* of defeat. On the one hand, challengers within the president's party typically emerge from a disaffected faction that objects to some aspect of the incumbent administration's policy agenda. Ford and Bush had to contend with discontent within the conservative wing of the GOP, and Carter came under attack from angry liberal Democrats. Such factional disputes are common to both parties, but they generally do not flare into open rebellion unless the president's viability in the general election is opened to question. All three losing incumbents presided over a weak economy and inspired doubts about their leadership abilities, issues that first surfaced in the primaries but then carried over into the general election.

On the other hand, presidents caught in a primary contest consume po-litical capital that otherwise would be useful in the general election. Ameri-cans prefer the presidency to be above politics and are uncomfortable when presidents turn into candidates.[14] By extending the period in which presidents must play an overtly political role, primaries undermine their capacity to in-voke the powerful symbolism of their office. Moreover, a secure president can reserve his energy and resources for his opponent and avoid the factional strife that alienates party activists, whose efforts are critical to the fall campaign. By denying an incumbent president these strategic advantages, a primary lev-els the playing field somewhat for the opposing party.

Primaries also tend to restrict a president's ability to seek the political center. Voters in primaries tend to be more extreme than voters in general elections, and therefore pull candidates toward the left or right of the ideological spectrum.[15] By adopting issue stances to placate the vocal minorities who participate in primaries, incumbent presidents incur the same liabilities as their challengers in positioning themselves to appeal to November's centrist voters. In sum, sitting presidents who are already vulnerable because of their performance in office pick up tactical liabilities during the primary season that weaken them even further.

Despite the fact that primary challenges spell electoral trouble for sitting presidents, incumbents are seldom denied their parties' nomination. With the exception of Lyndon Johnson, who decided in 1968 not to seek a second term after a poorer-than-expected showing in the New Hampshire primary, presidents bent on renomination prevail inside their party.

Given these odds, why would any politician contest a primary against a sitting president? Two very different motivations appear to be at work: 1) extraordinary circumstances marring the president's first term appear to raise the likelihood of success for a challenger; 2) intense activists opposing the president's policies field an opponent to pressure him to change course. In the former case, the incumbent party's control of the presidency is sacrificed to the personal ambitions of a rival, who calculates that the president is going to lose anyway. In the latter case, it falls victim to the political passions of a faction which would rather see its party lose the presidency than perpetuate wrongheaded policies.

Although Clinton was unpopular with the general public and suspect among liberal activists, his administration's shortcomings and scandals were not as serious as those that plagued his defeated predecessors. The economy was relatively robust and the international scene was fairly quiet. Pitfalls lurked in both domains, but there were no crises on either front to galvanize an opponent. Indeed, the majority of indicators that analysts think predict the return of the president's party to the White House favored Clinton.[16]

The President capitalized on these advantages with some adroit maneuvering. As one White House aide noted in October 1996: "The election was last year."[17] Replaced on the evening news by House Speaker Newt Gingrich, Clinton nevertheless was highly visible on the fundraising circuit, and he had raised over $25 million by October 1995.[18] Having upped the ante for any would-be challenger, he also attempted to pre-empt prospective opponents with displays of presidential clout. Clinton's myriad of visits to California, so useful in securing the state's 54 electoral college votes for the general election, sent a message to his rivals that he was prepared for a fight. Clinton's lieutenants delivered similar messages privately to those who were thinking of running or supporting an alternative candidate. Complementing this behind-the-scenes effort, the President began to stiffen his opposition to the Republican budget, setting the stage for the ultimately successful showdown over two government shut-downs.

If Clinton's renomination were to come under attack, the challenge would most likely come in the form of a Pat Buchanan–style assault from the left by factions within the party bent on preventing accommodation with congressional Republicans. Potential antagonists existed among several groups in the party's left wing: African-American politicians worried about preserving civil rights' policies, old-guard liberals anxious about the future of the welfare state, environmentalists disappointed at the administration's half-hearted regulatory enforcement, and labor unions angry about Clinton's support for NAFTA.

Clinton's fundamental strategic problem in winning re-election, however, was to reclaim his identity as a "new Democrat" by moving toward the electoral center, precisely the behavior most calculated to infuriate liberals. Clinton had been pulled to the left early in his presidency—through a series of controversial appointments, his efforts to alter policy on gays in the military, his support of tax increases on gasoline and high income voters, and his ambitious health care reform plan. The President badly needed the time and the leeway to reassure voters that he was not the tax-and-spend liberal Republicans portrayed him to be. He also needed to counter the appeal of third-party advocates, such as businessman Ross Perot and former Connecticut Senator and Governor Lowell Weicker, who argued that the two-party system was increasingly irrelevant to the concerns of the majority of American voters. Yet, it would be impossible for Clinton to reposition himself as a social and fiscal moderate with a primary challenger attacking his left flank. Fortunately for Clinton, his potential opponents made this task much easier by bowing out of the race.

In retrospect, the threat to Clinton from within the Democratic Party was probably not as serious as the press reports suggested, for the list of credible candidates was never very long. Some of the politicians on it had too much baggage of their own to take on the President; others seem to have decided to wait for a better opportunity and avoided playing the role of spoiler. Ironically, the very weakness within the party arising from the Republicans' triumph in the 1994 congressional elections helped to insulate the President from possible rivals.

Two perennial names on the roster of presidential aspirants who could have mustered old-guard liberals and labor to their banners, New York Governor Mario Cuomo and Missouri Representative Richard Gephardt, lost much of their luster in November of 1994. As governor of the third largest state, Cuomo had a solid base to launch a presidential bid and had been the hope of many liberals in the party ever since his electrifying defense of the welfare state at the 1988 Democratic Convention. When he lost his re-election bid for a fourth term, he not only forfeited his platform as a national party spokesman but raised doubts about his future electoral viability. Gephardt first sought the presidency in the 1988 primaries, but his candidacy did not last very long and he never succeeded in gaining more than 6 percent of the national primary vote.[19] He was popular with organized labor because of his strong support for protecting American jobs, but as majority leader in the House, he was tainted with the Democrats' humiliating defeat in the 1994 elections.

Another frequently mentioned prospective candidate, the Reverend Jesse Jackson, also was poorly situated to challenge Clinton. The President's active courtship of prominent African-American leaders had partially diffused some of the appeal of the civil rights activist and former presidential candidate, but Jackson himself was not in a strong position to contest the nomination. Having gained national attention when he garnered 18.2 percent of the national vote in the 1984 primary against former Vice President Walter Mondale,[20] Jackson did not hide his continuing interest in becoming president. But several things had changed since then. First, the novelty of the Jackson candidacy that brought him so much favorable press coverage in 1984[21] had worn off by 1995. Twelve years later, Jackson was not only old news, but had also been supplanted as a darling of the media by General Colin Powell.

Powell had not declared his affiliation with any political party, and although he had served under President Bush as Chair of the Joint Chiefs and briefly under President Clinton, he still invited speculation that he might rehabilitate the Democrats. Powell's flirtation with a presidential bid ended in November 1995, but by that time it was too late for Jackson to mount a serious primary challenge to President Clinton.

But Jackson had other liabilities. He had lost some credibility by talking about running for the presidency in 1992 and instead remaining on the sidelines. Furthermore, he had not succeeded in establishing a base beyond the black community, despite his efforts to attract low-income whites and women to his "Rainbow Coalition." This failure was particularly critical for Jackson's hopes because the early contests in Iowa and New Hampshire, where challengers typically pick up momentum, had minuscule populations of black voters. Most important, his issues of social justice for the disadvantaged were increasingly overshadowed by middle-class angst over job security, rising public sentiment against affirmative action, and low participation within his core constituency. In the end, Jackson confined his challenge to threats of a third-party candidacy, which sounded increasingly hollow as the 1996 campaign season began in earnest.

Another group of potential Clinton rivals lurked in the U.S. Senate. These included Nebraska Senator Bob Kerrey, who had contested the 1992 primary, and Senators Bill Bradley of New Jersey and Sam Nunn of Georgia, whose reputations for policy leadership inside the Senate earned them frequent mention in the press as presidential aspirants. Each senator was attractive to middle-of-the-road voters; none had the burden of personal scandal that haunted Clinton; and both Kerrey and Nunn had strong credentials in one of the President's weak areas—national defense.[22] All three men were ideological centrists and had a history of bipartisanship in dealing with major legislative issues—Kerrey on social security, Bradley on taxation, and Nunn on defense. Kerrey had often been at odds with Clinton, but neither he nor his colleagues was a likely figure to rally aggrieved liberals in a crusade against the President.

Without a cadre of intense activists to fuel a primary challenge, each senator had to make some hard-headed calculations about the likelihood of winning and the costs of losing. In the summer of 1995, when they were making such decisions, the odds looked far from promising. Democrats across the country were still in shock over their losses from the previous year, and Republicans appeared to be well on their way to securing a veto-proof Congress. The public reaction to the hubris of Speaker Gingrich and the intransigence of the GOP freshmen over the 1995 federal budget would come later. With national tides seeming to flow with the Republicans and with modest increments in economic growth favoring the President, the chances for a successful primary challenge looked exceedingly low. Nunn and Bradley had press conferences to renounce the role of spoiler, although Bradley kept the door open to a third-party challenge for several months afterward. Kerrey remained discreetly silent. All three men were young enough to try again in the year 2000, when conditions might be more favorable to centrist Democrats.

With the party's biggest guns trained on the next election, Clinton's remaining rivals posed no more than a minor inconvenience to his renomination. Pennsylvania Governor Robert Casey caused some speculation in the press that he might run on an anti-abortion platform. Denied an opportunity to express his views on abortion at the 1992 Democratic Convention, Casey was a symbol of the cross-pressures within the party's core constituency of working class, Catholic voters, who were torn between their traditional support of Democratic economic policies and their dismay over its social agenda. Yet, for all the emotional power of the abortion issue to galvanize people, the arithmetic was against a Casey insurgency. The primary electorate inside the Democratic Party was not only heavily pro-choice, it was prepared to bury Casey in a show of force to discourage future politicians with similar ideas from seeking the party's nomination.

Through a gradual process of elimination, Clinton's sole remaining rival was former Colorado Senator Gary Hart who emerged from obscurity for a brief survey of the electoral terrain before once again disappearing from view. Hart had mounted a serious challenge to former Vice President Walter Mondale in 1984 and enjoyed a brief flurry as front-runner in 1988 before floundering amidst press stories of extra-marital affairs. Having spent so many years out of national politics, he excited little notice for his presidential ambitions.

In the end, the Democrats' non-primary in 1996 was notable for the absence of fresh faces to mobilize the party's disaffected activists and primary voters. Having lost control of the Senate, Democrats forfeited the chairmanships that enabled them to command a national audience and were all but eclipsed by the GOP leadership team of Dole and Gingrich. Most important, however, the Democrats held relatively few governorships after the 1994 election, and had relinquished all of the major states, except Florida, to Republicans. Lacking politicians with either the clout or the political bases to attract media attention and financial contributors, the party was stuck with its seemingly crippled president and closed ranks to avoid further erosion of his re-election prospects.

THE REPUBLICAN FREE-FOR-ALL

If the Democrats suffered from a dearth of viable alternatives to Bill Clinton, the Republicans appeared to be awash in presidential aspirants. Eleven candidates eventually filed with the Federal Election Commission (FEC), and numerous others explored the possibility of running before eventually dropping out. Prospective nominees included senators, governors and former governors, House members, former Cabinet officials, and media personalities. For all the apparent interest in the GOP nomination, however, the field of possible contenders was weak. Those politicians who might have wrested the nomination from Senator Bob Dole opted out of the race, and the ones who remained lacked the resources and electoral appeal to do anything more than damage the front-runner. Among the declared candidates, Dole probably was the GOP's *best* bet, a fact which underscores the party's ongoing crisis of succession in the aftermath of the Reagan years.

For nearly three decades, the Republican Party was the party of the presidency. Jimmy Carter's election in 1976 by a bare margin and Bill Clinton's win in 1992 were but brief interruptions in a long chain of Republican victories and occasional landslides. Fueled by the momentum of the 1994 GOP sweep, presidential ambitions among Republicans flourished, as potential contestants considered the possibility of becoming the first Republican president to lead a GOP-controlled, and possibly veto-proof, Congress. Yet, the party was in transition, torn between nostalgia for its past glories under Ronald Reagan and uncertainty about its future direction. The magnitude of the prize simply exacerbated all the inherent tensions and contradictions within the GOP coalition.

Against this backdrop of uncertainty, it is not surprising that Republicans reached back to the past for Senator Bob Dole. Many of Dole's critics contended that his drive for the nomination was a selfish assertion of his prerogative as the party's senior statesman, and instead of claiming "his turn" at the helm he should have stepped aside for a younger and more politically nimble Republican. Yet, this line of reasoning ignores several important facts. First, Dole became the front-runner because large numbers of party leaders and contributors, who provided his formidable arsenal of endorsements and funds for the primaries, did not see a viable alternative. Second, Dole's limitations—his age, demeanor, and penchant for legislative dealmaking—did not seem insurmountable when weighed against the weaknesses of Bill Clinton. Third, early in the game many of the party's most promising presidential contenders took themselves out of the race. At the time, Dole's candidacy seemed to provide a way of postponing the showdown among the party's rival factions until 2000 without seriously compromising its chances for victory.

THE DECLARED CANDIDATES

By October 1995, the "invisible primary" leading up to the presidential election was nearly over.[23] Eleven men had formally proclaimed their candidacies, and one, California Governor Pete Wilson, had already taken himself out of the pack after a month of campaigning when he was unable to raise enough money to stay in the race. Any latecomers would have to declare themselves during the first two weeks of December, when the deadline for entering the New Hampshire primary came due.

The dynamics of the race were already clear. Bob Dole was the undisputed front-runner, but his electoral support was shaky. Dole's challengers, however, were in even worse shape—either the voters had never heard of them or they had strong dislikes about the ones they did recognize.

Table 1 gives the standings of the 10 declared candidates plus retired General Colin Powell (who remained a source of speculation until mid-November) among likely Republican primary voters in New Hampshire. Although Dole commanded 35 percent of the likely vote, he had very high negatives for a supposed front-runner, with a third of the respondents reporting an unfavorable opinion of him.

Well behind Dole was a second tier of candidates that included political commentator Pat Buchanan, Texas Senator Phil Gramm, former Education Secretary and Tennessee Governor Lamar Alexander, and *Forbes* magazine publisher Malcolm "Steve" Forbes. Among this group, both Buchanan and Gramm had negative ratings that exceeded their favorability ratings—in

Table 1   **Candidate Preferences among Likely Republican Voters in New Hampshire**

Candidate	% Vote	Favorable	Unfavorable	Undecided	No opinion
Dole	34.9	42.0	33.0	22.2	2.8
Alexander	6.6	21.3	21.4	22.7	34.7
Buchanan	8.8	25.9	48.3	17.1	8.7
Forbes	6.7	14.1	14.1	15.1	56.7
Gramm	6.2	25.0	32.8	21.8	20.4
Dornan	0.3	3.7	16.0	6.6	73.8
Keyes	0.3	8.9	11.9	8.6	70.6
Lugar	1.2	8.1	20.7	15.1	56.1
Specter	1.9	10.3	36.9	14.0	38.1
Taylor	1.0	6.1	14.1	7.9	71.9
Powell[a]	31.0	46.3	16.5	26.0	11.1
Clinton	N/A	21.4	60.6	17.2	0.8

N = 483

[a] The vote for Powell was measured with a separate question.

Source: Linda L. Fowler and Tami Buhr, Dartmouth/WMUR-TV New Hampshire Primary Poll, October 1–4, 1995.

Buchanan's case by nearly two-to-one. Alexander and Forbes were evenly split in terms of the positive or negative feelings they engendered, but suffered from low name recognition among voters. At the back of the pack clustered the long-shot candidates: Pennsylvania Senator Arlen Specter, Indiana Senator Richard Lugar, California Representative Bob Dornan, Maryland talk show host and former GOP Senate candidate Alan Keyes, and businessman Morry Taylor. None of this latter group was a serious contender.

Dole had already run three presidential campaigns, in 1976, 1980, and 1988. Known for his acerbic wit and his stoic efforts to overcome wounds from World War II, Dole was a master craftsman of the legislative process, first as chair of the Senate Finance Committee and then as Republican leader. Although every piece of important legislation in the past 15 years bore his stamp, his political priorities were remarkably unclear. Such flexibility might help him during the general election, but it caused mistrust among the hard-line conservatives who vote in primaries. As he honed his increasingly right-wing message to woo them away from Gramm, however, he risked leaving his flank open to moderates like Alexander and Forbes. He was eventually caught between the two rival factions within the party.

The weakness of the candidate field emerged from this early snapshot of the key New Hampshire electorate in several ways. Multimillionaire Steve

Forbes, a political novice and virtual unknown, moved immediately into the second tier of candidates upon his September announcement, even before the massive advertising barrage that became the hallmark of his campaign. Attracting voters with his outsider's stance and proposals for radical changes in the tax code, Forbes identified with the socially moderate wing of his party, but his principal constituency was adherents to supply-side economics. His comparatively warm reception so early in the race heralded the divisions over economic and social policy that plagued the GOP throughout the campaign. But in the end, Forbes's ability to spend lavishly on television ads did not dispel the fact that he was a single-issue candidate.

Adding to the confusion within the GOP was General Colin Powell's strong showing in the early polls. As Chair of the Joint Chiefs during the Gulf War, Powell developed an avid following in the press and among the public. His prior service as Reagan's National Security Advisor and his criticism of President Clinton's stance on gays in the military gave him Republican credentials even though he had kept his party affiliation a secret, but his African-American heritage made many observers suspect he was a closet Democrat. Powell had a reputation as a man of probity, talent, and moderation, but his chief appeal was that he appeared to be above politics, much as General Dwight Eisenhower had been in an earlier era.[24] As the data make clear, Powell had the only strong ratio of favorable to unfavorable ratings among any likely GOP contender. Most important, Powell was the only Republican who bested Bill Clinton in a head-to-head contest among the general electorate in New Hampshire, a result that held in early national polls as well.

Yet Powell probably could not have won the GOP primaries in a crowded field because of his pro-choice stance on abortion, his support for affirmative action, and his reservations about scrapping the welfare state. With the party's more moderate wing divided among Forbes, Alexander, and Dole, Powell would be vulnerable to the wrath of the Christian Coalition and various anti-abortion groups. Comprising an estimated third of the Republican base vote, this threat from the Christian Right was serious, indeed.

Moreover, Powell's lengthy and well-publicized deliberations about running had cost him time and money. Needing an estimated $30 million to $40 million to stay the course in the intense primary season,[25] Powell was poorly positioned by the fall to assemble the war chest he would need to compete against Bob Dole. Since 1980, success in early fundraising has been a powerful predictor of a candidate's capacity to capture the nomination, and in every case but one—Democrat Michael Dukakis in 1988—the financial front-runner has emerged the winner.[26] Although Powell personified the type of centrism and inclusive politics that many voters found lacking in the two major parties, the rules of the game operated against such a candidate surviving the primary season. And as he admitted during his press conference to announce his decision, he lacked "a passion and commitment that, despite my every effort, I do not have for political life."[27] The weight of a hostile minority, the deficit in fundraising, and the personal costs to his family were too heavy a burden.

If General Powell found American-style electioneering distasteful, columnist Pat Buchanan appeared to thrive on it. An effective orator whose skill at the rough and tumble of political argument had been honed on the Beltway television news circuit, Buchanan plunged into crowds with enthusiastic abandon. Under-funded and decried in GOP circles as a hothead and extremist, the former Nixon speechwriter who had never won public office was prepared to demonstrate the lesson he had taught the party in 1992—that a small, intense following of activists can give a candidate a disproportionate advantage in nomination politics.[28] Like evangelist Pat Robertson in 1988, Buchanan attracted anti-abortion activists and fundamentalist Christians; yet unlike Robertson, he also appealed to some working class voters with a combustible mix of protectionist and nationalist rhetoric. In the end, Buchanan's views were too far to the right even for the GOP primary electorate, and his lack of resources caught up with him once the primary season intensified. But his presence in the campaign was a constant reminder of deep splits in the Republican Party.

Lamar Alexander's candidacy was predicated on the unusual premise that a politician who was everyone's second choice could win the nomination. Cultivating a nice-guy image with his trademark red flannel shirt, Alexander was dubbed the "Republican lite" candidate by journalists. Claiming conservative credentials, Alexander softened the edges of the anti-government, moralistic invective that eventually dominated the GOP primaries by proposing to turn matters over to the states. In that way, he could run against Washington, but still leave the door open to compromise positions on tough issues, such as abortion. Alexander calculated that in a crowded field in which everyone was attempting to demonstrate his credentials as a "true" conservative, things would get nasty and personal. He hoped that when the bloodletting was over, he would be the only candidate left who would be acceptable to a majority in the party. In another era his low-key strategy might have worked, but he was not the only moderate in the race and his blurred image never attracted the activists who would have enabled him to stay the course in the front-loaded primary system.

THE MIGHT-HAVE BEENS

Was there another candidate who might have unified the Republicans during the primaries and emerged as a viable competitor for President Clinton?

Could former Vice President Dan Quayle, former Secretary of State James Baker, Wisconsin Governor Tommy Thompson, ex-HUD Secretary Jack Kemp, or any of the other names circulated by the "great mentioners" have led the GOP to victory in 1996?

The Republicans had an abundance of potential candidates because of their past control of the White House and their increasing dominance of governorships around the country. But from the lengthy list of well-credentialed politicians who might have considered running, no one stepped forward. However much Senator Dole's critics might have longed for a younger and more nimble party champion, they lacked a willing substitute.

What was striking about the decision to "just say no" was the similarity of the reasons different individuals gave for remaining on the sidelines. Many of those who declined to run cited the huge personal burdens of a presidential campaign, the sacrifices of family time, privacy, and in some cases financial well-being that a presidential campaign demanded. The truncated primary season described in Chapter Three appears to have made the onerous job of fundraising even more daunting because of the large sums of early money it required. Among those rejecting candidacy because of its costs were Baker and Kemp, as well as former Education Secretary and drug czar William Bennett, former Defense Secretary and White House Chief of Staff Dick Cheney, and former South Carolina Governor Caroll Campbell. Vice President Dan Quayle remained the darling of many religious conservatives and had built support inside the party. But he stepped aside because he found the logistics of fundraising overwhelming, although many attributed his unexpected announcement to health problems that had hindered him in preparing for a campaign.[29]

For other prospective candidates, the opportunity simply came at the wrong time in their political lives. For the Republican governors who were beginning to attract national attention—Wisconsin's Tommy Thompson, Michigan's John Engler, and Massachusetts' William Weld—the 1996 race was a bit premature. Tough managers who had cut expenditures, streamlined programs, toughened criminal penalties, and in some cases cut taxes, these men epitomized the Republican ideal of smaller, more efficient government. All were in their second terms, but none had developed the networks of support outside their home states they would need to sustain a primary bid. Weld left the door open to run if California Governor Pete Wilson declined to enter the race, and was let off the hook by Wilson's eventual declaration.

Surveying the Republican field, it is important to remember that under the best of circumstances a party that does not believe in government faces obstacles in recruiting men and women to public service. Professing a commitment to free markets and private charity, Republicans have been less inclined than Democrats to view governmental office as a worthwhile career.[30]

Thus, the party has typically drawn its leaders from a small group of business people, professionals, and those with inherited wealth (although in recent years it has relied more frequently on media figures and celebrities).[31] Certainly, many prominent Republicans feel a sense of civic obligation or a desire for political power, but their feelings of duty or ambition compete with the comforts of an affluent lifestyle and the opportunities to exercise considerable influence without the inconvenience of public scrutiny in a campaign.

Adding to the general skepticism about public office is the widespread perception in both parties that contemporary electoral politics is a particularly nasty business. Negative ads, pack journalism, and the length and complexity of the nomination process seem to grind down even the most experienced and qualified participants to a lowest common denominator. As one observer noted:

> The long intra-party squabble that lies at the heart of the new system . . . requires candidates to toot their own horns endlessly and to undermine their partisan colleagues at every turn . . . Much of this activity is inherently demeaning . . . and virtually guarantees that the stature of the players will be diminished.[32]

In such an environment, the politicians who stay out of the race always end up looking better than those who enter the fray.

For Republicans with a political bent it is often not necessary to seek office to exercise political power. The myriad of think tanks, media outlets, policy institutes, and lobbying organizations that have grown up in recent years have created an enormous demand for political commentary and connections. Although the opportunities to appear on "Washington Week in Review" or the lecture circuit do not compare to the American presidency, they are lucrative, stimulating and have the aura, if not the reality, of power—and they are available at a much lower price.

In sum, Senator Bob Dole had few rivals who could match his experience, resources, and ambition for higher office. He did *deserve* the Republican nomination, not because it was his turn, but because he had skillfully positioned himself to exploit the rules of the game and because he was willing to make the personal sacrifices for the chance to be president.

CONCLUSION

The 1996 election hit a new low in voter turnout and public dissatisfaction. Bill Clinton won re-election even though a majority of those who voted for him thought he was untrustworthy. The loser, former Senate Majority Leader Bob Dole, lost the confidence of even his fellow partisans in Congress. With results like these, many political observers and citizens wondered why more appealing candidates had disappeared. Yet, as we have seen, powerful strategic incentives kept prominent Democratic aspirants sitting on the sidelines. And factional strife within the GOP, plus the already formidable costs imposed by the front-loaded primary system, produced a relatively weak field.

Dissatisfaction with the choices on the ballot have fueled public support for the formation of a third party. A bipartisan group that included Senator Bill Bradley, former Connecticut Governor and Republican Senator Lowell Weicker, former Colorado Governor Dick Lamm, and former Massachusetts Senator Paul Tsongas, began meeting in 1995 to consider such an option, although they never pursued it. Billionaire businessman Ross Perot led a successful effort to establish his Reform Party on a national footing. Consumer advocate Ralph Nader also became the standard-bearer for the Green Party in California in an effort to revive the political left in the American system.

Third parties cannot resolve whatever problems of candidate recruitment exist in American politics today, however. Their limitations are not simply a function of the first-past-the-post electoral system, which largely negates third party votes. Rather, they too suffer from the shortcoming that plagues the two major parties—the costs of seeking public office fall disproportionately on individuals rather than on organizations. As long as we require heroic efforts from our would-be leaders before they even get elected to office, we will find relatively few individuals willing to put themselves forward.

The difficulty of recruiting and training talented individuals for governance is an old refrain in American politics, noticed by Alexis de Tocqueville in the 1830s and echoed in successive generations ever since. As long as Americans insist on an open and decentralized party system that admits amateurs and tolerates defection, they will continue to repeat Lord Bryce's haunting question: why are there so few great [men] in American public life? There is a certain rough utility to a process that reserves its greatest prize for those who have the strategic instincts, the unflagging energy, and the single-minded ambition to capture a presidential nomination. Yet, we should not be surprised that the men and, some day the women, who have these attributes make us slightly suspicious and more than a little uncomfortable.

NOTES

1. Adam Nagourney and Elizabeth Kolbert, "Missteps Doomed Dole from the Start," *New York Times* (November 8, 1996), pp. 1, 28.

2. See the special edition of *American Politics Quarterly,* edited by James C. Garand (October 1996, v. 24, n. 4), which includes seven articles employing variations on the basic econometric model above. All predicted a Clinton victory.

3. Figures for 1994 are from Harold Stanley and Richard Niemi, *Vital Statistics on American Politics*, 5th ed. (Washington, DC: Congressional Quarterly Press, 1995), p. 384. GDP figures for 1996 are 4.7 percent for the second quarter and 2.2 percent for the third quarter [World Wide Web: WWW.Whitehouse.gov./Fsbr (bea.doc.gov) (stat-usa.gov)].

4. Richard Berke, "Poll Indicates Stable Ratings," *New York Times* (June 5, 1996), p. 1; Richard Berke, "Public Favors Democrat New Poll Finds," *New York Times* (August 8, 1996), p. 1.

5. Note that his ratings fell short of other incumbent presidents who had won re-election, with the exception of Ronald Reagan. Summer presidential approval ratings for re-elected incumbents: Truman: 39–69; Eisenhower: 67–72; Nixon: 53–62; Reagan: 52–57. Taken from *Vital Statistics on the Presidency from Washington to Clinton*, Lyn Ragsdale (Washington, DC: Congressional Quarterly Press, 1996), pp. 189–193.

6. Emmett H. Buell, Jr. and James W. Davis, "Win Early and Often: Candidates and the Strategic Environment of 1988," in E. H. Buell, Jr. and Lee Sigelman, eds., Nominating the President (Knoxville, TN: University of Tennessee Press, 1991), pp. 1–41; William G. Mayer, "Forecasting Presidential Elections," in W. G. Mayer, ed., *In Pursuit of the White House* (Chatham, NJ: Chatham House Publishers, Inc.), pp. 44–71.

7. John L. Moore, ed., *Congressional Quarterly's Guide to U.S. Elections*, 3d ed. (Washington, DC: Congressional Quarterly Inc., 1994), p. 552.

8. Agence France Presse, "Good Poll News for Clinton," (August 26, 1996).

9. Michael Kramer, "Campaign '96 Briefing: The Race for the White House," *Time* (March 13, 1995, V. 145, N. E10) pp. 66–73.

10. Melinda Henneberger, "Clinton May Face a Rival From Party, Bradley Says," *New York Times* (January 31, 1995), p. A12.

11. Walter Shapiro, "Our Man in the White House," *Esquire* (March 1995), p. 60.

12. Richard L. Berke, "His Party Asks, Elect Clinton in '96?," *New York Times* (March 29, 1995), p. A16.

13. The Southern Democrats who walked out of the party convention to form the Dixiecrat Party were limited in their ability to hurt Truman because the nation's first past-the-post electoral system handicaps third parties.

14. Ralph L. Ketcham, *Presidents Above Party: The First American Presidency 1789–1829* (Chapel Hill, NC: University of North Carolina Press, 1984); see also Fred I. Greenstein, *The Hidden Hand Presidency: Eisenhower as Leader* (New York, NY: Basic Books, 1982).

15. A study of the 1988 delegates to the Iowa caucuses suggests that participants were not as extreme as earlier studies by political scientists have indicated. See Alan I. Abramowitz, Ronald B. Rapoport and Walter J. Stone, "Up Close and Personal: The 1988 Iowa Caucuses and Presidential Politics," in Emmett H. Buell and Lee Sigelman, eds., *Nominating the President* (Knoxville, TN: University of Tennessee Press, 1991), pp. 42–71. However, a more recent and comprehensive study confirms the strong partisanship and ideological extremism of party activists. See James A. McCann, "Presidential Nomination Activists and Political Representation: A View from the Active Minority Studies," in William G. Mayer, ed., *In Pursuit of the White House* (Chatham, NJ: Chatham House Publishing, Inc., 1996), p. 90.

16. Allan J. Lichtman, *Keys to the White House 1996: A Surefire Guide to Predicting the Next President* (Lanham, MD: Madison Books), 1996. C. F. Steven J. Rosenstone, *Forecasting Elections* (New Haven, CT: Yale University Press, 1983).

17. Alison Mitchell, "Clinton Campaign Finds Harmony After a Swift Exit by Morris," *New York Times* (October 15, 1996), p. A25.

18. J. Gruenwald, "Campaign: Who's In, Who's Out?," *Congressional Quarterly*, V. 53 (October 7, 1995), p. 3084.

19. *Congressional Quarterly's Guide to U.S. Elections*, p. 551.

20. *Congressional Quarterly's Guide to U.S. Elections*, p. 543.

21. Adolph Reed, *The Jesse Jackson Phenomenon*, (New Haven, CT: Yale University Press, 1986).

22. Kerrey had lost a leg in the Vietnam conflict and had been awarded the Medal of Honor; Nunn was widely respected for his expertise on military expenditures.

23. Emmett H. Buell, Jr., *The Invisible Primary* (Englewood Cliffs, NJ: Prentice Hall, 1976); Emmett H. Buell, Jr., "The Invisible Primary," in William G. Mayer, ed. *In Pursuit of the White House* (Chatham, NJ: Chatham House Publishers, Inc., 1996), pp. 1–43.

24. Fred I. Greenstein, "Colin Powell's *American Journey* and the Eisenhower Precedent: A Review Essay," *Political Science Quarterly* (10, 4), pp. 625–629.

25. Berke, p. 31.

26. Mayer, "Forecasting Presidential Elections," pp. 49–51.

27. Francis X. Clines, "Powell Rules Out '96 Race; Cites Concerns for Family and His Lack of Calling," *New York Times* (November 9, 1995), p. 1.

28. Duane M. Oldfield, "The Christian Right in the Presidential Nominating Process," in W. G. Mayer, ed., *In Pursuit of the White House* (Chatham, NJ: Chatham house Publishers, Inc., 1996), pp. 254–282.

29. Richard L. Berke, "Facing Financial Squeeze, Quayle Pulls Out of '96 Race," *New York Times* (February 10, 1995), p. 16.

30. Alan Ehrenhalt, *The United States of Ambition: Politicians, Power and the Pursuit of Office* (New York: Random House, Inc., 1991).

31. James A. Schlesinger, *Ambition and Politics: Political Careers in the United States* (Chicago, IL: Rand McNally and Co., 1966).

32. W. Wayne Shannon, "Evaluating the Nominating System: Thoughts after 1988 from a Governance Perspective," in E. H. Buell, Jr. and L. Sigelman, eds., *Nominating the President* (Knoxville, TN: University of Tennessee Press, 1991), p. 270.

CHAPTER 3

Presidential Nominations

The Front-loaded Frenzy of '96

*Larry J. Sabato**

University of Virginia

The 1996 presidential nominating process was quasi-Hobbesian—nasty, brutish, but short. The former qualities were due to the combustible mix of candidates and their willingness to pummel one another senseless on the stump, across the airwaves, and by means of mail and telephone. The latter, rare quality of brevity was the result of "front-loading"—the scheduling of a record number of primaries early in the election year calendar. Front-loading was the most electorally critical innovation in 1996, and its effects were noteworthy in both major parties. On March 19, 1996, Bob Dole easily swept the four Midwestern states on "Big Ten" Tuesday and went over the top in the delegate count, the quickest that any candidate has ever clinched a contested party nomination. While running essentially uncontested, President Clinton wrapped up the Democratic nomination by March 12, which was extraordinarily early even for an unchallenged incumbent. By comparison, it took President Ronald Reagan, more popular than Clinton at the same time in 1984, until May 16 to finally amass the necessary number of delegates to claim his party's mantle.

Despite front-loading, the 1996 nomination process was not entirely devoid of drama, and it was fascinating in substance as well as procedure. The Republican contest was made more portentous by the partisan battles being waged between President Clinton and the Republican-controlled Congress.

*The author gratefully acknowledges the invaluable help of University of Virginia graduate students Stan Humphries and Rick Mayes and undergraduate student Justin Sizemore in the research, drafting, and presentation of this chapter. Also making contributions were Michelle Baker, Steven Betz, Jeff Manns, and Michael Smith.

37

While a return to a Republican presidency in 1996 had seemed very likely in the aftermath of the 1994 Republican congressional coup, the GOP's momentum began to wane by early 1996, especially because of the battle over the federal budget. The influence of this event became all the greater because of the Republican Party's ultimately fruitless search for a presidential candidate who could match Clinton's telegenic presence and for issues that would overpower Clinton.

In this chapter we will review the initial nominating battles of 1996, explore the implications of the compressed primary schedule, and travel the road that led to the August party conventions. Our focus will be on the issues and strategies that produced the major party nominees, as well as the minor parties' bids (especially that of the Reform Party).

DOLE AGAINST THE REST OF THE FIELD

How the Front-runner Got There

By 1996 Bob Dole was a familiar face to GOP primary and caucus-goers. This was his third race as a presidential aspirant, and fourth race for national office (including his unsuccessful vice-presidential bid in 1976). In his first outing as a presidential hopeful in 1980, Dole entered the Republican presidential nomination battle against a strongly favored Ronald Reagan. While Dole had already received substantial exposure during the 1976 elections as President Gerald Ford's running mate, this coverage was not entirely positive. The 1976 campaign had left many voters with an impression of Dole as a mean-spirited partisan, mostly remembered for his suggestion in a debate that Democrats were responsible for the American wars of the twentieth century.

By contrast, Ronald Reagan was well poised for the 1980 Republican nomination battle. In 1976, the former California governor had come within sixty delegate votes of beating the incumbent Ford at the Republican National Convention and by 1980 the dominant conservatives within the party were nearly unanimous in their support for Reagan. Dole never broke out of the pack of challengers to Reagan, and his first attempt at the party nomination ended in dismal failure.

His next, better chance to become the nominee came in 1988 as he challenged Vice President George Bush. Dole scored an early, stunning upset over Bush in the 1988 Iowa caucuses. In New Hampshire, however, Dole was outmaneuvered by Bush and his sponsor, Governor John Sununu. After losing the Granite State, Dole was never able to regain momentum, and Bush's subsequent victory in South Carolina gave the Vice President unstoppable momentum going into the "Super Tuesday" contests in the South. Again, Dole's presidential aspirations were crushed, and this time they looked permanently extinguished.

But George Bush's 1992 defeat for re-election changed the calculus. The GOP was reeling and rudderless following its loss of the presidency, and there was no obvious leader or path out of the wilderness. After waiting for more than a decade and a half for his turn at the party nomination, Dole gradually became the clear party favorite and early front-runner in the 1996 campaign, by virtue of both luck and shrewdness. First, Dole saw an opening in Bill Clinton's 43 percent showing in 1992, and he seized the mantle of the loyal opposition immediately. Only hours after Clinton's election as president, Dole acknowledged that Clinton would get the traditional "honeymoon" but only with Dole serving as "chaperone." Moreover, Dole's claim to the party mantle was advanced early in the pre-campaign season by announcements of non-candidacy by several potential rivals such as former Vice President Dan Quayle, ex-Congressman Jack Kemp, and former Defense Secretary Dick Cheney. Former Chairman of the Joint Chiefs of Staff, General Colin Powell spent a period of time flirting with a candidacy, but ultimately he also decided against entering the nomination contest. Powell's behind-the-scenes explorations of a candidacy and the intense media speculation about his prospects actually aided Dole because it kept Dole's challengers out of the news for the most part, in effect locking in Dole's early lead. Dole's ascension to Senate Majority Leader in January of 1995 also enabled him to dominate the news and keep the edge on competitors. Finally, a potentially serious rival, California Governor Pete Wilson, was forced to withdraw from the race even before the primary season opened due to financial and political difficulties. (Voters in Wilson's state were furious that he had broken a pledge made in his tough 1994 re-election race to serve out his term if he won.) Dole had finally and fully paid his dues and become the presumptive front-runner in the Republican Party. Among the rank-and-file of the hierarchically thinking GOP, the Senate Majority Leader had become the crown prince—he was next in line for the throne and it was *his turn.*

Doubts about Dole

While Dole became the early favorite, troubles soon developed in the campaign that the 73-year-old Dole referred to as his "last mission." An early bump in the road was a highly publicized Republican straw poll at a convention of party activists in Iowa in August of 1995. Dole, who had been expected to win, ended up in a tie with Gramm for first place. Gramm's surprising strength shocked the Dole organization, which immediately made minor adjustments in campaign personnel.

While Dole overcame this minor setback, the front-runner's campaign suffered another more serious blow when Dole inartfully delivered the GOP response to President Clinton's January 23, 1996, State of the Union Address. Dole's stumbling, cadaver-like performance was ridiculed by both pundits and his Republican rivals, and it exacerbated concerns about Dole's ability to compete with Clinton on television. His staff offered some reasonable excuses. Apparently, Dole was never sure that he wanted to deliver the response, and thus never fully prepared for it. Moreover, Dole was fighting a cold and had taken medication, leaving him dry-mouthed and looking tired and haggard. Nonetheless, it left many Republicans with a foreboding sense of unease.

These pre-primary missteps would pale, though, by comparison to the troubles Dole would experience in the initial primaries and caucuses. Dole would soon be shaken in Iowa, defeated in New Hampshire (for the third time), and not see another victory until twin wins in the Dakotas on February 27.

THE CAMPAIGN SEASON

Opening Rounds

For more than a year, political analysts had predicted that the inevitable Republican nominee would be Bob Dole. For a brief period of time it looked as though the analysts would have egg-covered faces.

The first hint that the pre-ordained script would be rewritten came in the late-January Alaska caucus. Pat Buchanan won the low-turnout event with 32.6 percent of the vote, with Malcolm S. "Steve" Forbes, Jr., in a close second place at 30.7 percent (Bob Dole was third at 17.1 percent, Alan Keyes fourth at 9.8 percent, and Phil Gramm fifth at 8.6 percent).

Buchanan reveled in his victory despite the fact that none of Alaska's 19 national convention delegates were at stake and that fewer than 10,000 voters even bothered to participate. The Buchanan triumph was not unusual given that Alaska was one of the few states that religious broadcaster Pat Robertson won in first-round caucus voting in early 1988.

Nevertheless, proclaiming himself "King of the Klondike," Buchanan quickly moved on to the Louisiana caucus slated for February 6. Phil Gramm had literally created and arranged the rules of the Bayou caucus to benefit his campaign, since he assumed he could easily carry a neighboring state on his own terms. In January, Gramm boasted that he would win all 21 delegates. Again, however, with the strong support of the most conservative elements of the GOP, especially evangelical Christians, Buchanan came away with a shocking victory, garnering 13 of the event's 21 delegates. Buchanan proclaimed the results "a victory for a 'new conservatism of the heart,' which features concern for the lives of the unborn, the livelihood of struggling middle-class workers, and an America that controls its own destiny."[1] Gramm was left politically hemorrhaging in second place with an embarrassing 8 delegates. Gramm's campaign premise was that he, not Bob Dole, was the "real" conservative in the race. But Louisiana seemed to send the signal that Buchanan, not Gramm, deserved the sought-after label of Mr. Conservative. As for the campaign, it saw Gramm's pitch failing in the other direction as well. "Basically, the Gramm campaign disintegrated because they were trying to say that Bob Dole wasn't a real conservative," asserted a Dole aide. "It was as if we had embarked on a campaign to beat Phil Gramm by proving that Gramm wasn't really a Texan, because he was [born in] Georgia. Well, he is from Georgia, but he is [also] a Texan. People intuitively know this."[2]

Gramm's collapse and Buchanan's rise came as an enormous surprise to the Dole campaign. Dole's then-manager, William Lacy, remembered,

> We felt that Phil Gramm was our principal opponent from day one, both because of his money and because he was the best "athlete" in the race. And so the campaign was geared mainly towards dealing with him. As long as we hugged Gramm and kept him close to us philosophically, we felt we couldn't lose the nomination.
>
> At the same time we—and everybody else—grossly underestimated Pat Buchanan. We felt that some of the things he had said and written in the past disqualified him fairly automatically and that he would be remembered as the guy who took George Bush down, and that he wouldn't have any money and he wouldn't be able to build much of a campaign. All those assumptions were generally correct, with one exception: Everybody underestimated the power of ideas and the power of Pat to communicate those ideas.[3]

All the other competing candidates, minus Alan Keyes, skipped Louisiana in deference to Iowa's long-standing claim to being the first legitimate battleground for presidential aspirants. Previously thought to be nothing more than a contest for second place behind the Dole juggernaut, Iowa rapidly developed into a surreal circus of warring caricatures. Gramm limped into the fray after his humiliating loss in Louisiana. Buchanan, invigorated by his early victories, portrayed himself to the voters as the most electable of the Republican candidates. Dole found himself in a position with much to lose in momentum and excitement, but little to gain.

A new challenger had also emerged on the political horizon—Steve Forbes, the free-spending, multimillionaire magazine publisher. Forbes' wealth granted the first-time candidate two significant advantages. First, he was able to refuse federal funds and the accompanying spending limits, and thus he was free to spend as much as he wanted wherever he wanted. (Forbes opted primarily for negative advertising and lots of it.) Second, Forbes did not have to waste any effort on fund-raising—an activity that consumed a third or more of his opponents' energies and time. The results were apparent to all television consumers. Ordinarily accustomed to traditional grass-roots campaigning and door-to-door vote-seeking, Iowans could literally not watch more than 15 minutes of television without seeing a Forbes ad hawking his flat tax proposal or attacking one of the other candidates, usually Dole. Forbes's television assault came to be labeled "an electronic drive-by shooting."[4] In addition to his relentless television advertising, the Forbes campaign made 4,000 calls nightly to Iowa residents, and Republicans received upwards of seven pieces of direct mail from Forbes. "Without the Forbes advertising," a Dole staffer grumbled, "Dole would have won Iowa with 35 percent of the vote, and would have won New Hampshire with 33 percent of the vote. I can prove it; it's a statistical fact."[5]

By the time the phones had stopped ringing, the televisions had been turned off, and the polls had closed, Dole had eked out a bare "survival" victory in Iowa with 26.3 of the vote to Buchanan's second-place finish at 23.3 percent (Lamar Alexander was third at 17.6 percent, Forbes was fourth at 10.2 percent, and Gramm was fifth at 9.3 percent). Gramm's feeble fifth-place showing effectively deposited his candidacy at the local morgue. He officially bowed out two days later on February 14. After Iowa, the race quickly headed on to chilly New Hampshire and its primary eight days later with four horses still in the field—Dole, Buchanan, Alexander, and Forbes. Dole's Iowa win did not count for much, historically, as Table 1 shows. Five of the last nine winners of the Iowa caucuses have lost their party's nomination. And so have four of the last nine New Hampshire primary victors, including 1996's winner, Pat Buchanan.

Table 1   **Where's the "Iowa Bounce"?**

Year	Party	Iowa winner[*]	New Hampshire winner	Nominee
1972	Democrat	Edmund Muskie	Edmund Muskie	George McGovern
1976	Democrat	Jimmy Carter	Jimmy Carter	Jimmy Carter[†]
1980	Democrat	Jimmy Carter	Jimmy Carter	Jimmy Carter
1980	Republican	George Bush	Ronald Reagan	Ronald Reagan[†]
1984	Democrat	Walter Mondale	Gary Hart	Walter Mondale
1988	Democrat	Richard Gephardt	Michael Dukakis	Michael Dukakis
1988	Republican	Bob Dole	George Bush	George Bush[†]
1992	Democrat	Tom Harkin	Paul Tsongas	Bill Clinton[†]
1996	Republican	Bob Dole	Pat Buchanan	Bob Dole

[*]Only contested Iowa caucuses are listed here.

[†]elected President

New Hampshire

Arguably the most shocking and unpredictable moment of the Republican nomination process occurred in New Hampshire on February 20, when TV commentator Patrick Buchanan pulled off the unthinkable. Buchanan upset Senate Majority Leader Bob Dole, still the presumed front-runner, by receiving 27.4 percent of the vote to Dole's 26.3 percent (Alexander finished third at 22.8 percent, Forbes plummeted to fourth with 12.3 percent, and the other minor challengers divided the remaining 11 percent). The pool of real candidates seemed to be just three—Dole, Buchanan, and Alexander—but a fourth (Forbes) was still well financed and could not be written off, as he soon proved.

Although Buchanan *appeared* to be the most threatening candidate following his victories in Alaska and Louisiana and impressive second place showing in Iowa, the Dole camp was primarily worried about Alexander. "We knew that Alexander could ultimately deny us the nomination and so we were very concerned about him," said Dole's former deputy campaign manager William Lacy. "We wanted to raise doubts about Alexander and we already had an ad that we had tested with three focus groups; it just tested off the charts. We knew we had the goods on him."[6] The Dole campaign plotted its attack coordinates on Alexander and patiently waited.

The opportunity came four days before New Hampshire voted, as the Dole campaign concocted a back-handed television attack-trap designed to sink Alexander. The Dole staff leaked to the press that they were preparing a negative TV ad barrage aimed at Buchanan for the weekend prior to Tuesday's voting. But when the time came, the barrage struck Alexander instead. "It was a deliberate strategy, a sort of head feint," said a Dole media adviser. "You didn't want to start attacking Alexander a day after Iowa, because that would give Alexander a boost. He would then be seen as Dole's primary challenger. We wanted to pick a fight with Buchanan."[7] It was a tricky balancing act, aimed less at boosting Dole than picking off his real principal challenger (Alexander) as he rose in the polls.

Lamar Alexander and his staff were not unaware of the Dole campaign's chessboard moves, but, in Alexander's words, "We were coming up two or three points a night, and that's one of the rarest things in politics, to be coming up like that. You never quite know what the ingredients of that are, and you've got to be careful about changing anything you're doing." With no cash reserves, Alexander would have had to take off the air his positive TV ads and quickly substitute negative ones to counteract the Dole ads and phone calls. The Alexander organization chose to do nothing, a decision that retrospectively may have been one of the most fateful of 1996.

As late as the very day of the New Hampshire primary, however, it was the Dole campaign, not Alexander's, that was panicking, unsure of whether or not their strategy would prove successful. "On Tuesday afternoon or early Tuesday evening we got the most devastating news of the entire primary election which was that in one set of exit poll data we were actually *behind* Alexander," said William Lacy. "There was some concern that we could finish third at that point. Dole was very concerned about that. He felt that he would be forced to withdraw if he finished third."[8] Stuart Stevens, a Dole media adviser, confirmed this when asked what the ramifications might have been had Alexander come in second. "It could very well have ended Dole's candidacy," said Stevens.[9]

The negative TV spots, however, coupled with extensive telephone push-polling (to be discussed later), effectively stalled Alexander's steady rise in the polls between Iowa and New Hampshire, and kept Alexander in third place. "I'm convinced it was the combination of advertising and phones that slowed the rate of Alexander's rise, and kept him from slipping past Dole," claimed Alexander pollster Whit Ayres.[10] Steve Forbes' spending also had an effect, noted veteran New Hampshire politician Tom Rath, a senior adviser to the Dole campaign: "Forbes' tremendous expenditures kept him at 14 percent in New Hampshire, when otherwise after his poor showing in Iowa, he would have collapsed. If he had gone down, Alexander would have picked up most of the Forbes voters, who were turned off to Dole and more centrist than Buchanan. That would have been Alexander's margin of victory."[11]

Had Alexander finished first or second in New Hampshire, the former Tennessee governor might well have emerged as the GOP nominee. He certainly would have defeated Buchanan in a one-on-one contest (and Dole has admitted he would have dropped out if he had run third in New Hampshire). An Alexander versus Dole race would have been close, but a growing number of Republicans was beginning to look for an alternative to the Kansas senator's disappointing bid for president. After New Hampshire, Lamar Alexander's position was less clear. Although he finished only third in both Iowa and New Hampshire, this was higher than expected, and consequently, his candidacy was given an "extension" by political pundits. This quickly translated into a tantalizing (but brief) surge in financial contributions that enabled Alexander to entertain notions of glory.

But after New Hampshire, the cold reality of a possible Buchanan nomination changed the dynamics of the race totally. Dole became the only game in town to stop Buchanan, a candidate most Republicans saw as a ticket to a Goldwater-style electoral debacle. Dole's flaws, which had earlier loomed large, were put into perspective by the Buchanan threat, and a panicked rush of GOP officeholders and voters began to move toward Dole.

Looking back, Lamar Alexander recognizes that Dole's strategy worked beautifully:

Dole's prompt, post-Iowa effort to slow me down was effective. Of course, those negative ads also hurt Dole's image, and Pat [Buchanan] popped through in New Hampshire. And in the next ten days the media created the "Buchanan scare." Pat never had a chance at being our nominee, but it was portrayed as "Somebody's got to stop Buchanan." Because Dole was the better-known figure who nosed ahead of me in New Hampshire, he became that person. So there was very little steam left in my campaign.

The transition to Dole's inevitability was not a smooth, straight-lined process, though. In the chaos following the New Hampshire primary, it was every candidate for himself. Often, New Hampshire has provided the initial requisite momentum for one candidate to emerge from the pack. This time, however, the state's primary turned conventional wisdom on its head and actually generated a confusing, uncertain muddle. Grumbling over Dole's ineffectual campaign style and doubts about his comparison to the youthful and charismatic Clinton increased substantially. Buchanan was attracting most of the press attention, and thus was setting the terms of the debate. Political success has its price, however, and temporary front-runner Buchanan quickly became the focus of increased press scrutiny and controversy. For example, shortly after his New Hampshire triumph, Buchanan accepted a leave of absence from Larry Pratt, co-chair of his campaign, after it was disclosed that Pratt had spoken at rallies held by white supremacist and militia movements. Additionally, Sandy Lamb, the chairman of the Buchanan campaign in a Florida county, was forced to resign after it became known that she was an official of the National Association for the Advancement of White People, an organization founded by former Ku Klux Klan leader and Louisiana politician David Duke. (Phil Gramm also accused Buchanan of relying on Duke supporters to win the Louisiana caucuses.)

Given all this, the post-New Hampshire mad scramble boiled down to a few immutable facts. Steve Forbes had vast amounts of money but little momentum. Pat Buchanan had the momentum and the charismatic presence, but a skeletal national organization and little money. Lamar Alexander had some organization, some money, and a little momentum, but not enough of any of the three to ignite his candidacy. That left Bob Dole with the strongest organization, the lion's share of endorsements of governors and other elected officials, and sufficiently deep pockets to wage a national campaign, even bereft of momentum.

Four small-state primaries were next, followed by March's maelstrom of twenty-nine contests in every region of the country. These primaries and caucuses would have the collective task of clearing the muddle.

Delaware, Arizona, North & South Dakota

The final four primaries in February before "March Madness" ensued were held in Delaware (12 delegates, February 24), Arizona (39 delegates, February 27), North Dakota (18 delegates, February 27) and South Dakota (18 delegates, February 27). Because the contests were so widely dispersed geographically, most candidates decided not to mount a full-scale effort in each.

Steve Forbes was the only finalist to campaign vigorously in Delaware, airing extensive television advertising there. Still, public and private polls showed Dole ahead, so it was a mild surprise when Forbes won his first state with 32.8 percent of the vote to Dole's second place finish of 27.2 percent (Buchanan was third at 18.6 percent and Alexander finished fourth at 13.4 percent). Due to its winner-take-all nature, all 12 of Delaware's delegates went to Forbes.[12]

Arizona was the next major event and, in numbers, the largest contest yet in the nomination process with 39 delegates at stake in another winner-take-all scenario. It was the first Sun Belt arena for the Republican candidates, but it was also the state's first-ever presidential primary. Arizona's inclusion so early in the schedule was the work of Gramm supporters including Gov. Fife Symington and Sen. John McCain, in the belief that the Texan would have regional strength. Gramm was not around to take advantage of the primary, though, and McCain backed Dole. Yet Forbes was, again, spending an unprecedented amount of money (about $4 million) and Buchanan was fresh off his New Hampshire victory. Stung by a string of second place finishes, Dole tried to avoid raising the stakes in Arizona and perhaps unwisely skipped a television debate held just days before voting, leaving Buchanan to dominate the event. Chastened by criticism of his negative advertising, Forbes switched to predominantly positive spots touting his "flat tax" initiative. Only Alexander, who preferred to spend his time and financial resources on the South Carolina primary in his native region, essentially skipped Arizona.

Ultimately, Forbes parlayed his Delaware "little mo(mentum)" into an Arizona victory with 32.8 percent of the vote. Dole finished second for the third time in a row with 30.1 percent, and Buchanan was close behind with 27.3 percent. (Alexander finished fourth with a paltry 7.1 percent.) Forbes' twin victories in Arizona and Delaware had rescrambled the contest again. As with Buchanan, the Dole campaign had miscalculated Steve Forbes' potential, former Dole manager Bill Lacy admitted:

> By January we found we were getting a new principal challenger in Forbes because we suddenly saw him leading us in Arizona and pulling within a few points of us in South Dakota. Wherever he was doing his heavy negative advertising, he was really taking a toll on Dole. Forbes forced us away from our game plan, away from focusing on Dole's positives, and it was very damag-

ing to the Dole candidacy in the long run. We had to turn on a dime and reinvent our whole campaign.

We went from a very traditional, positive-oriented campaign strategy for a front-runner, designed to cruise to success, to a largely tactical campaign designed to kill Steve Forbes, because we felt we had no choice. In our focus groups, people were literally using the terms "American hero," "the exact kind of man we need in Washington," to describe Forbes. They were saying things about Dole like "yeah, every time he talks about getting shot, it's because he's trying to get votes." One lady said, "You know Elizabeth Dole? She's president of the Red Cross. Well she got that because of the political influence of Bob Dole." We could not believe this. These people had sat there for two months and watched millions in advertising from Forbes with no response from us at all, and they believed all the charges. They absolutely believed all of it.

So you've got to give Forbes and his campaign people credit, even though we could debate until the cows come home the accuracy of his advertising and how misleading and inaccurate it was. It was an audacious and bold strategy and it worked to the extent that we let it work.[13]

Incidentally, some of the television networks publicly apologized for mistakenly projecting Buchanan finishing second and Dole third in Arizona. As ABC's Ted Koppel put it, "A lot of us in the news business woke up this morning with egg on our collective faces." CBS's Dan Rather added, "Despite our internal system of checks and balances, we made a wrong call based on our polling data. . . . I consider it a humiliation, not just a reminder, that those of us who live by the crystal ball sometimes wind up eating broken glass."[14]

The Republican Party also saw mainly broken glass in the chaos that followed New Hampshire, Delaware, and Arizona. With no obvious front-runner then, it was not immediately clear what would happen. For a brief time, Republican National Committee Chairman Haley Barbour said he "thought there was a real possibility, though not a probability, that the nominee would actually be chosen at the convention."[15] Barbour is quick to insist that the RNC never showed any favoritism to Dole, despite the general fear of Buchanan and the fact that Barbour's executive director, Scott Reed, became Dole's campaign manager:

We not only didn't help any of the campaigns, but as best as possible, we stayed away from them. I hardly ever talked to anybody at any campaign or any of the candidates throughout the nomination process. We did nothing organizationally, or materially, or programmatically for anybody. We met periodically with representatives of the various campaigns so that they would know what we were doing, know what our plans were, know what we had going on that would be of importance for whoever won the nomination. The Gramm campaign was constantly quoted to me as saying that we were for

Dole, but Phil on more than one occasion told me that he personally didn't believe that, and for a very right reason. It would be against my own interests to do that.

Let me just say, I never thought Buchanan had any chance to win the nomination. I like Pat, we worked together at the White House, and if the voters had chosen him to be the nominee, that would have been all right with me. But I never thought he had a chance of winning; I never thought Steve Forbes had a chance of winning. The only people I thought had a chance of winning were Dole, Gramm, and Alexander, and after Gramm got out, it looked to me like you had four people running: Dole, Alexander, Buchanan, and Forbes, and only [the first] two of them actually could be nominated.[16]

February 27 was not a complete shutout for Senator Dole; he finally won some primaries in his native Midwest, in the Dakotas. In North Dakota, he had the support of Gov. Edward T. Schafer and much of the Republican establishment. Dole made quick work of his opponents, racking up a commanding 42.1 percent of the vote (Forbes was second at 19.6 percent, Buchanan was third with 18.3 percent, and Gramm, who had already pulled out of the race, beat Alexander 9.4 percent to 6.3 percent, respectively). South Dakota was much the same. Dole had the endorsements of both Gov. Bill Janklow and Sen. Larry Pressler, and won with 44.7 percent of the vote (Buchanan finished second with 28.6 percent, Forbes third with 12.8 percent, and Alexander fourth at 8.7 percent).

South Carolina: Dole's Salvation

The critical turning point of the 1996 Republican presidential selection occurred in the Palmetto State. Billed as the political gateway to the South, South Carolina held the region's lead-off Republican presidential primary in both 1980 and 1988. The victories recorded there by Ronald Reagan in 1980 and George Bush in 1988 propelled them to sweeps of other Southern primaries. Bush was helped by the vigorous support of then-Gov. Carroll A. Campbell. This time, former Gov. Campbell, along with Gov. David Beasley and Sen. Strom Thurmond, were all in the Dole camp.[17] South Carolina was one of Bill Clinton's weakest states in the 1992 general election, and a win here would award any candidate solid conservative credentials. This was precisely what Bob Dole needed as he sought to eliminate the Buchanan threat and emerge—finally and firmly—as the front-runner.

In a South Carolina straw poll held one year earlier, Phil Gramm had finished first with 35 percent of the nearly 1,200 ballots cast, followed by Alexander with 26 percent, and Dole with 21 percent.[18] As is frequently the case with straw polls, the actual primary outcome in 1996 bore no resemblance to the straw poll results. With support among Christian conservatives equal to that of Buchanan's and the vote-producing machines of former Gov. Campbell and current Gov. Beasley in full swing, Dole won going away with 45 percent of the vote, and pluralities in 43 of South Carolina's 46 counties. Buchanan came in a distant second place with 30 percent (Forbes was third with 13 percent and southerner Alexander brought up the rear with 11 percent).[19]

Governor Beasley, a born-again Christian, was especially effective in diluting Buchanan's strength among rank-and-file Christian conservatives, who made up more than a third of the primary electorate. While exit polls showed Buchanan beating Dole handily in New Hampshire (five to one) and Arizona (two to one) among those who identified themselves with the religious right, Dole pulled even with Buchanan in South Carolina.[20] Equally important to Dole's smashing triumph was former Gov. Carroll Campbell, who made no secret that he wanted to be considered for the vice-presidential spot on the Dole ticket.[21] As governor from 1987 to 1995, he assiduously assembled a formidable organization through his personal popularity and powers of patronage. The result was a broad-based network of experienced campaigners who could staff telephone banks, put up signs, turn up at rallies and—not least—get out the vote.[22]

With South Carolina's big win as desperately needed fuel, the re-started Dole juggernaut set its sights on March's contests which, if won, would mark the effective end of the nomination phase of the 1996 presidential election.

Junior Tuesday and the Yankee Primary

March Madness began with the so-called Junior Tuesday, consisting of primaries and caucuses in ten states held on Tuesday, March 5. It included Colorado, Connecticut, Georgia, Maine, Maryland, Massachusetts, Minnesota, Rhode Island, Vermont, and Washington, with a total of 208 delegates, most of which were at stake in winner-take-all allocation systems—that is, the top vote-getter in a district or state wins all the delegates assigned to that district or state.

In nearly sweeping all contests, Dole won 185 of the 208 delegates; Buchanan, his nearest competitor, picked up just 14 delegates, and Forbes took only 9. None of Dole's Junior Tuesday week victories were close. He won every primary by better than 15 percentage points with one exception (Georgia). And even in Georgia, which held arguably the most important of the contests on March 5, Dole's victory margin topped 12 percentage points.[23]

If South Carolina was Dole's "springboard," Junior Tuesday virtually clinched his nomination. Disappointed with weak showings in southern regions such as South Carolina and Georgia, Alexander announced his withdrawal from the race on March 6, the same day the little-noticed Senator Richard Lugar made his "exit" announcement. Dole's superior national organization was able to keep him afloat in the face of surprisingly strong Buchanan and Forbes challenges and in the long run it proved simply invincible. Even potentially strong challengers such as Lamar Alexander did not have the time or money to introduce themselves to voters in several states at once, as did Dole.[24]

In retrospect, the Dole staffers were particularly critical of Alexander's effort, given his real potential for success. "Alexander ran an extraordinarily flawed campaign," said one Dole aide. "He ran as the Republican Bill Clinton. . . .A guy from Maryville [Tennessee] against a guy from Hope [Arkansas]." They maintained that Alexander failed to do his homework and learn from history. "Whenever the White House changes parties, it goes to someone who is a mirror opposite of the person holding it: Kennedy-Eisenhower; Nixon-Johnson; Reagan-Carter; Clinton-Bush," the Dole staffer added. "Worst of all, [Alexander] ran against politics using the worst of politics, which is political gimmickry." This was a reference to Alexander's summer walk across New Hampshire, wearing the same plaid shirt he chose as the campaign symbol in his successful 1978 run for the Tennessee governorship. "In our early surveys, what struck me was that people were turned off by the shirt. They wanted to know who this guy was walking across the state wearing this shirt in July," said Steve Forbes's campaign manager.[25] "The reason it worked when he walked across Tennessee was because he had to prove he wasn't an uptight Nashville-Washington lawyer," said a Dole campaign aide. In the end, "I think Alexander, a terrifically appealing person, sold himself short."[26]

The day after Alexander withdrew, the New York primary was held. Because of Byzantine ballot-access rules designed to enhance the power of state GOP leaders (who backed Dole), only Dole gained immediate access to the ballot in all thirty-one New York congressional districts. After a successful court challenge, however, Steve Forbes managed to get on the ballot everywhere, and he was Dole's main challenger in the Empire State.[27] Interestingly, just before the election, Forbes was personally endorsed by his supply-side tax-cutting colleague, former New York congressman and Buffalo Bills quarterback, Jack Kemp. But Dole beat Forbes by twenty percentage points on March 7 (52 percent to 32 percent). Afterwards, according to Dole campaign staffers, the senator angrily proclaimed he would never deal with "the quarterback" [Kemp] again. Of course, all that would change by August.

One other footnote to this phase of the nominating season was Pat Buchanan's somewhat surprising capture of the Missouri caucuses on March 9. With a strong turnout among antiabortion forces producing 36.5 percent of the vote for him, Buchanan edged Bob Dole, who had only 28.1 percent despite the support of the state's major GOP officeholders. However, Buchanan's Show Me State victory was to be his last hurrah in the 1996 election season.

Super Tuesday

In 1992 Democrat Bill Clinton lost the New Hampshire primary, recovered in the South, and headed into the primaries of the industrial Midwest with unstoppable momentum and a large delegate lead that proved more than any rival could match. In 1996, Dole simply grabbed Clinton's playbook and flawlessly repeated the same scenario.

Minus Oregon, Super Tuesday is, for all intents and purposes, a Southern primary, featuring Florida, Louisiana, Mississippi, Oklahoma, Tennessee, and Texas. Of the 362 delegates up for grabs, Dole amassed all but thirteen of them, leaving ten for Buchanan and three for Forbes. Forbes quietly bowed out two days later at a Washington, D.C., hotel saying he would "support Sen. Dole wholeheartedly," while working to keep his message of "hope, growth and opportunity" on the party's agenda. Dole's overwhelming success catapulted him to a grand total of 710 delegates, almost three-quarters of the way to the finish line with all his competitors vanquished, though Pat Buchanan stubbornly continued his campaign. Yet Dole clobbered Buchanan in a primary held in Louisiana, the site of Buchanan's caucus victory just five weeks earlier. (Some of Louisiana's delegates were awarded in the caucuses, the rest in the later primary.) As this result suggests, Buchanan usually did better in low-turnout caucuses, worse in high-turnout primaries. New Hampshire was an exception, but even here Buchanan won only because about three-quarters of the vote was split among several other candidates.

Big Ten Tuesday: The Rust Belt Primary

One week after Dole's mega-victory on Super Tuesday, the Midwest was called upon to register its opinion on the shrunken field of Republican nominees, and no surprises were in store. Dole was actually gaining strength and momentum as evidenced by his winning an increasing share of the vote percentage as the nominating season progressed (see Table 2). A total of 219 Republican delegates were at stake on March 19 in Illinois, Michigan, Ohio and Wisconsin, and Dole captured 196 of them. Dole surged to overwhelming victory in Illinois and Ohio, collecting 64.3 percent and 66.4 percent of the vote, respectively. In Michigan and Wisconsin, Dole won less impressively, carrying bare majorities with Buchanan winning about a third of the vote.

Golden California

On March 26, Dole capped off his lengthy winning streak in California, going 25 wins for 25 contests in March, by gobbling up all of the Golden State's 165 delegates. His 65.9 percent of the vote was more than three times that of his

Table 2   **"Freight Train" Dole: Unstoppable Momentum**
           Percentage of Primary/Caucus Vote

	February contests	Junior Tuesday	Super Tuesday	Big Ten Tuesday	California Tuesday	Remaining Stragglers	TOTAL
Dole	31%	52%	55%	60%	65%	72%	59.0%
Buchanan	26	22	21	27	18	15	21.3
Forbes	24	13	14	5*	8*	4*	10.1
Alexander	12	9	3*	2*	2*	3*	3.6
Others	6	5	5	6	7	6	6.0
Votes Cast	706,855	2,102,273	3,091,811	2,847,624	2,492,952	2,637,007	13,878,522

Compiled from: *Congressional Quarterly Weekly*, and assorted newspaper and wire services.
*indicates candidate had already withdrawn

single remaining opponent, Pat Buchanan, who received 18.5 percent of the vote.

California had traditionally concluded the primary season in early June, but for 1996 it moved its primary to late March, ostensibly to play a larger part in the nominating process. But even the new date was woefully late. The large cache of delegates that Dole received in California's winner-take-all primary provided only an exclamation point on a nomination story that had lost all of its drama two weeks earlier. Dole won convincingly throughout California, carrying every county with ease. Even in that quintessential bastion of Sun Belt conservatism, suburban Orange County, Dole pummeled Buchanan, 64 percent to 18 percent.

In retrospect, then, Dole and his campaign proved extremely effective in building an organizational advantage throughout the country that could not be overcome despite the manifest weaknesses of Bob Dole. The process was quick and brutally effective, as candidates Alexander, Buchanan, and Forbes could attest. After stumbling momentarily in February, Dole regained his footing by March 2 in time for South Carolina's primary and proceeded to win the next 43 contests in a row. The entire process was over in less than a month, but even within that time-frame, the outcome was only in doubt for upwards of one week. Buchanan did not officially drop out of the race and endorse Dole until the GOP convention in August, but it hardly mattered. Even with a very conservative activist electorate, Buchanan could never manage to attract much more than a third of the vote in any GOP primary. This unofficial ceiling for Buchanan's support guaranteed Dole's eventual nomination, once the front-runner helped to create a one-on-one contest with the maverick populist firebrand. Buchanan never had enough strength to capture the nomination,

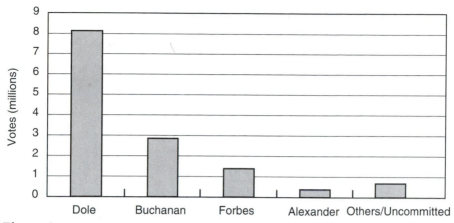

Figure 1   Primary Vote Total—National

but his insurgent candidacy had just enough fire to incinerate the bids of the two men (Phil Gramm and Lamar Alexander) who might actually have been able to give Bob Dole a real race.

Looking back, one thing seemed apparent to everyone: 1996's radically front-loaded schedule probably delivered Dole from defeat. "Structure saved Dole," Forbes said. "He lost Alaska. He couldn't even compete in Louisiana. Did very badly in Iowa. Lost New Hampshire. Lost Delaware and lost Arizona. Normally, that would have been the end of a front-runner . . ."[28]

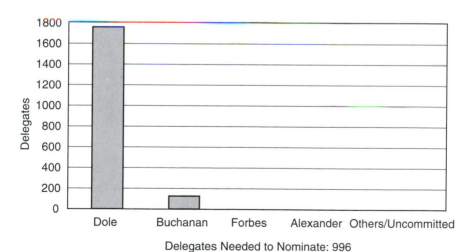

Delegates Needed to Nominate: 996

Figure 2   Delegate Total—National

Table 3   **State-by-State Primary and Caucus Results**

(by vote percentage)

	Date	# of Delegates	Alexander	Buchanan	Dole	Forbes	Others
Alaska [c]	(1/29)	19	—	32.6%	17.1%	30.7%	19.6%
Louisiana [c]	(2/6)	21	—	13 (delegates)	—	—	8 (delegates)
Iowa [c]	(2/12)	25	17.6	23.3	26.3	10.2	22.6
N. H.	(2/20)	16	22.8	27.4	26.3	12.4	11.1
Delaware	(2/24)	12	13.4	18.6	27.2	32.8	8.0
Arizona	(2/27)	39	7.1	27.3	30.1	32.8	2.7
N. Dakota	(2/27)	18	6.3	18.3	42.1	19.6	13.7
S. Dakota	(2/27)	18	8.7	28.6	44.7	12.8	5.2
S. Carolina	(3/2)	37	10.5	29.3	44.8	12.7	2.7
Wyoming [c]	(3/2)	20	7.2	19.8	40.4	17.6	15.0
Puerto Rico	(3/3)	14	0.5	0.4	97.9	0.5	0.8
Colorado	(3/5)	27	9.7	21.5	43.6	20.8	4.3
Minn. [c]	(3/5)	33	4.6	33.1	41.2	10.3	10.8
Connecticut	(3/5)	27	5.4	15.2	54.5	19.9	5.0
Georgia	(3/5)	42	13.5	28.8	40.9	12.7	4.1
Maine	(3/5)	15	6.7	24.6	46.3	14.9	7.5
Maryland	(3/5)	32	5.4	21.1	53.5	12.7	7.3
Mass.	(3/5)	37	7.6	25.0	47.9	14.1	5.3
Rhode Island	(3/5)	16	19.9	—	66.8	—	13.2
Vermont	(3/5)	12	10.8	17.2	41.0	16.3	14.7
New York*	(3/7)	102	—	15.0	52.0	32.0	1.0
Missouri [c]	(3/9)	36	—	36.5	28.1	0.9	34.5
Florida	(3/12)	98	2.0	18.1	56.9	20.2	4.8
Louisiana	(3/12)	9	3.0	32.7	47.3	13.2	6.9
Mississippi	(3/12)	33	2.0	26.0	61.0	7.9	3.1

THE 1996 NOMINATION SCHEDULE

Increased Front-loading in 1996

Since the advent of the modern nomination process, the states that held their contests early in the process have received increasing media attention, thus affording these early states a disproportionate influence on the selection of party nominees. Other states, desiring to capture some of the attention and influence of the early contests, have scheduled their primaries and caucuses earlier and earlier in the nomination process in a trend called "front-loading."

In an attempt to combat front-loading, Democrats in 1980 tried imposing a "window" during which all nomination contests could be held. This time period established by the Democrats initially began on the second Tuesday in

Table 3 **(continued)**

	Date	# of Delegates	Alexander	Buchanan	Dole	Forbes	Others
Oklahoma	(3/12)	38	1.0	21.5	59.3	14.1	4.1
Oregon	(3/12)	23	7.0	21.8	51.5	13.4	6.3
Tennessee	(3/12)	38	12.0	25.1	51.1	7.7	4.0
Texas	(3/12)	123	0.0	21.4	55.7	12.8	10.1
Illinois	(3/19)	69	3.0	22.5	64.3	4.8	5.4
Michigan	(3/19)	57	1.0	33.8	50.8	5.0	9.3
Ohio	(3/19)	67	2.0	21.6	66.4	6.0	4.0
Wisconsin	(3/19)	36	2.0	34.0	53.0	6.0	5.0
California	(3/26)	165	2.0	18.5	66.0	7.5	6.0
Nevada	(3/26)	14	2.0	15.2	51.9	19.2	11.7
Washington	(3/26)	18	2.0	20.8	63.2	8.7	6.3
Penn.	(4/23)	73	—	18.0	63.0	8.0	11.0
D.C.	(5/7)	14	—	10.0	77.1	—	12.9
Indiana	(5/7)	52	—	18.8	70.0	11.2	—
N. Carolina	(5/7)	58	3.0	13.0	72.0	4.0	8.0
Nebraska	(5/14)	24	3.0	10.0	76.0	6.0	5.0
W. Virginia	(5/14)	18	3.0	16.0	69.0	5.0	7.0
Arkansas	(5/21)	20	—	23.0	77.0	—	—
Idaho	(5/28)	23	—	22.0	63.0	—	15.0
Kentucky	(5/28)	26	3.0	8.0	74.0	3.0	12.0
Alabama	(6/4)	40	—	16.0	76.0	—	8.0
Montana	(6/4)	14	—	24.0	61.0	7.0	7.0
New Jersey	(6/4)	48	—	11.0	82.0	—	7.0
New Mexico	(6/4)	18	4.0	8.0	75.0	6.0	7.0
Total	(6/15/96)	1,884[†]	3.6	21.3	59.0	10.1	6.0

Compiled from: *Congressional Quarterly Weekly*, *The Hotline*, assorted newspapers and wire services.

[c] caucus

*approximation

[†]includes other contests such as Guam and Puerto Rico

March and ended on the second Tuesday in June, but in 1992 the opening date was moved forward to the first Tuesday in March. The Democratic Party has granted Iowa and New Hampshire an exception to this window since the laws of both states require that they be the first nomination contests. At least through 1996, the Republicans have not mandated any guidelines about primary scheduling. Since states incorporate their nomination procedures into law, however, the Republican and Democratic contests usually take place on the same date within each state, and thus the general window of nomination contests looks relatively similar for both parties.[29]

Table 4   **Final Candidate Scorecard—National Cumulative Totals**

	Bob Dole	Pat Buchanan	Steve Forbes	Lamar Alexander	Others— Uncommitted
Primary vote	8,147,882	2,944,117	1,396,766	498,626	819,577
% of the vote	59	21.3	10.1	3.6	6
Delegates won	1,739	146	0*	0*	9

Compiled from: *CQ*, June 15, 1996, p. 1704 and CBS Campaign '96, July 2, 1996

* withdrawal forfeits any delegates won

Obviously, the creation of a nomination window has not prevented front-loading within the window itself. States have increasingly scheduled their nomination contests earlier within the established time-frame (see Figure 3). As Republican National Committee Chairman Haley Barbour said about the front-loaded 1996 schedule, "This is about compression; it is not about who goes first."[30] In 1972, the Democrats had no primaries in February, only three in March, and fifteen in May and June. By 1976, the number of primaries scheduled by the Democrats before April doubled to six of the twenty-seven presidential primaries held that year. In 1988, with the help of Super Tuesday in which fourteen Southern and border states held their primaries on the second Tuesday of March, the number of Democratic primaries held in February

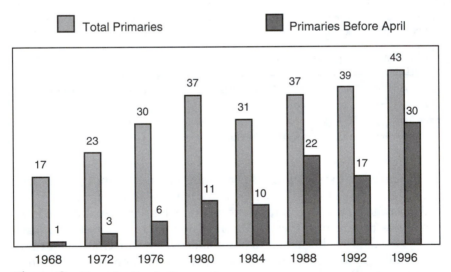

Figure 3   Front-loading in Perspective
Source: *Congressional Quarterly's Guide to U.S. Elections,* 3d ed. (Washington, D.C.: CQ Press, 1994).

or March jumped to twenty-two of the total thirty-seven primaries. Seventeen of thirty-nine Democratic primaries took place before April in 1992.

As just noted, since most of the primary rules are established by state law, the Republican nominating schedule has undergone front-loading similar to the Democrats.[31] In 1996, thirty of forty-three Republican primaries and ten of the eleven Republican precinct-level caucuses were held before the end of March. *In total, seventy-four percent of all Republican convention delegates were chosen before April.*

The Effects of Front-loading in 1996

Front-loading has exaggerated the importance of what Arthur Hadley called the "invisible primary," or the period between the last presidential election and the next round of presidential nomination contests.[32] It is during the invisible primary that candidates begin campaigning unofficially, raising money and establishing the semblance of a campaign organization. All this activity often occurs long before they have actually officially announced their candidacies. While this early jockeying of presidential aspirants is nothing new, the increasingly front-loaded nominating process places overwhelming significance on the early events, which for all practical purposes determine the identity of the nominee and make most late contests pointless and anticlimactic.

Front-loading has several important consequences for candidates, voters and the overall system. With respect to the fates of the 1996 candidates, front-loading amplified the advantages of the front-runner, leaving little time for his opponents to regroup after inevitable setbacks. Bob Dole's assets of money and organization could be matched in the first few contests but proved overwhelming once the battle quickly moved into a large number of states scattered across the nation. Not surprisingly, the ultra-front-loading of 1996 was accomplished with the approval and assistance of Dole allies working with many of the state legislatures.

Other candidates besides Dole, especially Pete Wilson and Phil Gramm, hoped that front-loading would work to their advantage.[33] Wilson orchestrated the California legislature's shift of the state's primary from early June back to March 26 in order to give an early boost to his nomination effort. As it turned out, of course, Wilson not only dropped out of the race before the start of the official season, but Dole clinched the nomination even before California voters cast their ballots. Similarly, Gramm persuaded friendly Louisiana GOP officials to move their primary back to February 6 in the hope that an early win in a neighboring state would give him momentum for Iowa and New Hampshire. Instead, Gramm lost to Pat Buchanan in Louisiana, crippling the Texan's campaign.

While many commentators viewed the Republican primary schedule as a tremendous advantage to the Dole campaign, they also saw that the process could become quickly unpredictable and chaotic if Dole stumbled in the first few contests. In fact, this situation almost did unfold as Dole's performance was far weaker than expected in Iowa, New Hampshire, and Delaware. As we discussed earlier, many saw New Hampshire as a bullet that narrowly missed Dole, with the senator edging Lamar Alexander for second-place by roughly 7,500 votes. Stuart Stevens of the Dole campaign admits that "had Alexander come in second [in New Hampshire], it could have very well ended Dole's candidacy."[34] Dan McLagan, Alexander's press secretary assets that "Lamar would have been the nominee" had he taken second place in New Hampshire,[35] and Dole himself apparently realized on primary night that a third-place showing would have finished him off.[36]

The week following New Hampshire produced mixed results for Dole with wins in the Dakotas and a close loss in Arizona to Steve Forbes. (Buchanan placed third in Arizona.) Dole's salvation was South Carolina, the "firewall" primary which Lee Atwater had created in 1988 as an insurance policy for George Bush's nomination campaign. In the 1988 campaign, Atwater arranged for South Carolina to hold its primary on the Saturday before Super Tuesday when fourteen southern and border states held their primaries. The Bush campaign realized that a victory in South Carolina would give Bush momentum over Bob Dole going into Super Tuesday, and the strategy worked beautifully. While Bush placed third in Iowa, he came back to win New Hampshire, then swept South Carolina and went on to capture all but one of the Super Tuesday states. Following Bush's example with no little irony, Dole invested heavily in the 1996 South Carolina primary and lined up the state party machinery in his corner. The effort paid off with an easy victory in the Palmetto state, which provided Dole with unstoppable momentum going into the Yankee Primary and Junior Tuesday contests. Bob Dole had learned a bitter lesson from George Bush, but the lesson served him well in the end.

While Dole, the early party favorite, did win the 1996 front-loaded schedule, front-loading aided Dole less than his other advantages such as money, organization, and the winner-take-all rules used for most Republican contests. But front-loading clearly backfired for Gramm and hurt Forbes, whose lavish spending on advertisements began to offset Dole's early advantage in voter familiarity. Whether Forbes could have continued to gain on Dole had it not been for the nomination schedule is, of course, unknowable.

But with front-loading, Dole (or someone like him) was nearly a leadpipe cinch to win. With almost three-quarters of the convention delegates selected before the end of March, candidates with strong name recognition and financial backing were heavily favored. Since the nomination process was over less than six weeks after it started, those without familiarity or money had precious little time to gain. The reality that candidates must have substantial financial resources long before the official process begins creates enormous advantages for both nationally known candidates and the independently wealthy.

The effects of front-loading on how and where candidates allocate their resources are obvious. Candidates devote huge resources to the early contests in hopes that momentum can be gained which will then carry them into the later contests. Almost all of the candidates, if they spent at all, spent heavily in the two key early contests, Iowa and New Hampshire. Dan McLagan, Alexander's press secretary, has noted that "[I]ronically, the race by all the states to move their primaries up earlier in the process had the reverse effect of what was intended. The idea was for [the other states] to lessen the importance of Iowa and New Hampshire. What they really did was make them more important."[37]

Some candidates managed to add unusual wrinkles to the Iowa-New Hampshire axis. As already noted, Phil Gramm invested heavily in Louisiana. Steve Forbes, following his "4-3-2-1 strategy" of placing higher in each successive contest, invested heavily in Delaware and Arizona in addition to Iowa and New Hampshire. His victory in Delaware paid off with momentum going into Arizona. Lamar Alexander focused on the Florida Presidency III straw poll, which received considerable media attention. Alexander also spent heavily in South Carolina, which has become almost as much a key early contest as Iowa and New Hampshire. Buchanan pursued a low-budget campaign in Alaska and Louisiana, relying on free media and fiery rhetoric to make up for his lack of funds.

Many critics of front-loading argue that it significantly alters the manner in which candidates campaign and, thus, the way in which voters familiarize themselves with candidates and issues. William Dal Col, Forbes's campaign manager, sees front-loading as yet another way that incumbents and career politicians benefit from the process because "it doesn't give the electorate a sufficient opportunity to contemplate, observe, and absorb the ideas that are presented by all the candidates, but especially new candidates."[38] A GOP task force which examined the impact of the compressed 1996 nomination schedule acknowledged that the process forced candidates to spend more time raising money and less time campaigning before the voters.[39] The emphasis on fundraising has an influence on the type of forum in which candidates will campaign in person. Alexander's press secretary McLagan noted that Alexander "had to spend a third or more of his time on the fundraising circuit, talking to . . . small groups of very nice people, who in addition to being nice, also had the ability to write $1,000 checks. Every minute he spent doing that was a minute that he wasn't able to spend talking to larger groups of people or getting his message out. Every time you're meeting with a hundred people, it's time that you're not meeting with five hundred people."[40]

Besides altering the type of candidates and campaigns offered to primary voters, the front-loaded schedule also reduces the number of voters who actually have a voice in the process. Only a handful of states really had any influence on the 1996 Republican nomination process. As a report from a committee of the National Association of Secretaries of State claimed, the current process produces a "feeling of irrelevancy" on the part of many voters and states.[41] This "irrelevancy" is not just because some candidates have already dropped out of the race by the time many states vote. It is also because most states see only superficial campaigning and many voters have not had time to hear the candidates' issues and deliberate before they must cast a ballot.

One recommendation to improve the ability of candidates to campaign in person and for voters to get to know candidates better is to spread the contests more evenly over March, April, May, and June. Lamar Alexander, among the critics of the 1996 nominating process, has said that such a revised system "would give winners a chance to capitalize on successes, voters a chance to digest new faces, and candidates a chance to actually meet voters."[42] The Republican Party has indicated that it may try to encourage just such a system for the year 2000.

Not everyone agrees that front-loading is deleterious. The Republican Party has traditionally placed emphasis on a hierarchical deference to the "next in line" candidate, which favors a front-runner every bit as much as front-loading. From the party's perspective, front-loading may also seem attractive since it reduces the period of intra-party divisiveness and allows the party to more quickly turn its sights to the other party.

The Struggle Over Who Goes First

Although much of the debate in 1996 about the schedule of the GOP nominating process concerned the front-loading of the contests, there was some controversy about which state would go first. In particular, Louisiana and Delaware challenged Iowa and New Hampshire's "first in the nation" status, creating some early sparks in the nomination process.

As we have already mentioned, Phil Gramm worked behind the scenes to arrange the Louisiana caucus; he anticipated a win in the Bayou State that would generate momentum going into Iowa. Obliging Louisiana GOP officials scheduled their caucuses on February 6, six days before the Iowa caucuses. However, Iowa officials were outraged over the attempt by Louisiana to usurp Iowa's status as the opening round of the nomination process, and Iowa Republicans requested all GOP candidates to pledge not to compete in Louisiana. While most candidates did forgo entering the Bayou caucus so as not to offend the Iowans, Gramm, Buchanan, and Keyes decided to compete in Louisiana.

As it turned out, there was sparse participation in the Louisiana caucuses due to widespread voter apathy and a lack of information about the times and locations of the caucuses. Another problem was the accessibility of the polling locations. There were only 42 caucus sites around the state despite the fact that Louisiana has close to 4,000 voting precincts.[43]

The other controversy between New Hampshire and Delaware erupted when state officials in Delaware announced plans to hold their primary February 24, only four days following the New Hampshire election. New Hampshire has traditionally insisted on a full week between its primary, the first in the country, and that of any other state. Delaware officials hoped that by having their primary closely follow New Hampshire, the state would reap a bonanza of national publicity and expanded influence on the nomination of the Republican candidate. State officials also touted the fact that Delaware has supported the winner of every presidential election since 1952, and it is much more demographically representative of the nation than New Hampshire.[44]

Just as Iowa officials did with Louisiana, New Hampshire officials including Gov. Steve Merrill (R) applied pressure to the other GOP candidates to stay out of Delaware. New Hampshire Secretary of State William Gardner characterized Delaware's primary as "a desperate attempt to gain some political recognition" and "some depraved version of a kangaroo straw poll." While Gramm readily endorsed Delaware's early date since it was crucial to his strategy of creating early contests to offset anticipated losses in Iowa and New Hampshire, most of the other Republican candidates deferred to New Hampshire and did not register in Delaware.[45]

Delaware Republicans were predictably upset by the widespread boycott of their primary, but in the end, only Forbes, Gramm, and Keyes officially filed in Delaware. Not to be defeated, however, the Delaware legislature passed a special law that required the names of *all* candidates who qualified for federal matching funds to appear on the primary ballot. As it happened, though, only Forbes and Keyes seriously campaigned in Delaware; Gramm withdrew from the race the week before the primary, and Dole had pledged in New Hampshire not to do so. This decision clearly cost Dole. Originally predicted to win the state easily, Dole was caught flat-footed there, with Forbes winning the state after he aired extensive media advertising.

ANALYSIS OF ELECTION RESULTS[46]

Voter Turnout

Nearly 14 million voters participated in the 1996 Republican primaries, an unimpressive percent of the potentially eligible electorate (all voters age 18 and over). Nonetheless, this total vote was a record number for the GOP, and far exceeded the nine million voters who cast votes in the essentially unopposed 1996 Democratic contests.[47] The 1996 primaries were the first time since 1952 that more people participated in the Republican than Democratic primaries, although the Democrats' lack of presidential competition in 1996 makes this statistic of dubious worth. Republican turnout in 1996 was roughly comparable to that of GOP presidential primaries since 1980, but about 20 to 25 percent lower than GOP turnout in the 1960s and early 1970s.[48] As expected, turnout was greatest in some of the early contests when the nomination was still up for grabs.

Voting by Gender

The Republican Party has become the party of choice for a disproportionate number of men, and this becomes evident when examining the participants in GOP primaries. Overall, considerably more men than women turned out to vote in the 1996 Republican primaries. The gender differential varied by state. One of the largest gaps occurred in New Hampshire, where 14 percent more men than women voted for Republican candidates. The gender gap was 10 percent in the March 5 New England primaries and a relatively small 4 percent overall in the southern states voting on Super Tuesday.

The gender ratio of each candidate's supporters varied dramatically as well (see Figure 4). Buchanan consistently drew substantially more men than women to his banner; his gender gap ranged from a low of 8 percent in the Super Tuesday contests to 24 percent in New Hampshire. Similarly, the Forbes and Gramm candidacies were more attractive to men. Forbes' gender gap ranged from 8 percent on Super Tuesday to 18 percent in Iowa. Gramm drew 18 percent more men than women in the Louisiana caucus and 22 percent more men than women in Iowa.

Dole and Alexander consistently had a much more balanced ratio than the other major candidates. Dole's gender gap was generally just 2 to 4 percent, except for Iowa and New Hampshire (16 and 12 percent more men, respectively). Alexander generally drew, at most, 2 percent more men than women except Iowa, where he drew 12 percent more men than women. In the Junior Tuesday contests overall, Alexander actually captured 2 percent more *women than men*, rare among the Republican field. Alexander achieved a similar result in South Carolina.

Voting by Income

Since economic issues figured prominently in the campaign themes of Buchanan and Forbes, it is not surprising to find that the candidates appealed

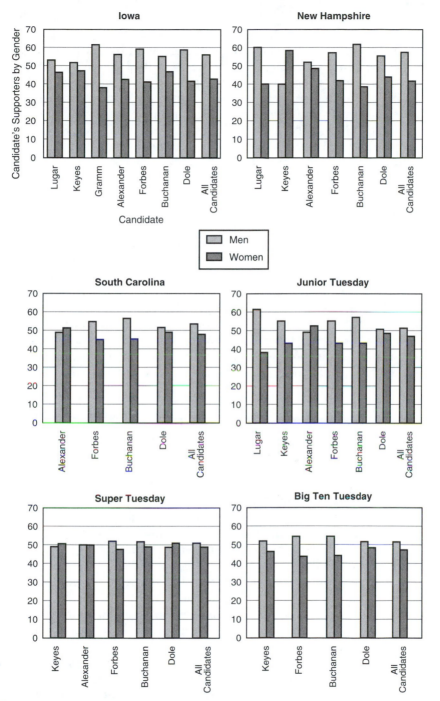

Figure 4 Support for Candidates by Gender

63

to widely divergent income groups. Consistent with his message aimed at working and lower-middle class families concerned about economic dislocation, Buchanan's biggest constituency was the "Under $30,000" and "$30–50,000" income brackets, where he consistently garnered a disproportionate share of the vote, roughly twice his support in the "Over $75,000" income bracket. His victory in New Hampshire was aided by an 8 percentage point boost in the "$15–30,000" and "$30–50,000" income brackets over his overall percentages. In South Carolina, he drew 11 percentage points more in this bracket than he did overall.

While early polls showed widespread support for Forbes' flat tax proposal, media scrutiny of the flat tax's possible adverse implications for middle income workers reduced Forbes' backing in middle and lower income brackets. Forbes' voters, then, were concentrated in the income groups with the most to gain—those in higher tax brackets. So Forbes' support picked up in the "Over $75,000" income group, primarily because of a strongly disproportionate share of voters earning above $100,000. Except for New Hampshire and the Big Ten Tuesday primaries, Forbes generally captured 4 to 7 percentage points more in the "Over $100,000" group than his overall percentage vote.

By comparison to Forbes and Buchanan, Dole generally performed about equally across the income brackets, except for a slightly better showing among the highest income voters.

Voting by Age

In one important way, Bob Dole's age showed in the GOP primaries: his fellow seniors staunchly supported him while younger voters did not. Dole under-performed by 5 to 8 percentage points in the 18 to 29 age group versus his overall vote percentage in South Carolina and the Junior Tuesday and Super Tuesday contests. Dole also under-performed by 5 to 9 percentage points in the 30 to 44 age group. He generally took his proportional share of the 45 to 59 age group, and drew 9 to 14 points more of the over-60 age group. In Iowa, Dole drew an astounding 35 percentage points more of the oldest age group than his overall percentage vote.

Alexander did particularly well among the youngest voters in the early contests. In Iowa, New Hampshire, and South Carolina, Alexander drew 6 to 8 percentage points more of the 18 to 29 age group than he drew overall. His performance among the other age groups was generally proportional to his overall percentages.

While Dole performed best among the oldest age group, Buchanan and Keyes generally performed the worst. Buchanan drew roughly 5 percentage points less in the over-60 group than his overall percentage vote in Junior Tuesday, Super Tuesday, and Big Ten Tuesday.

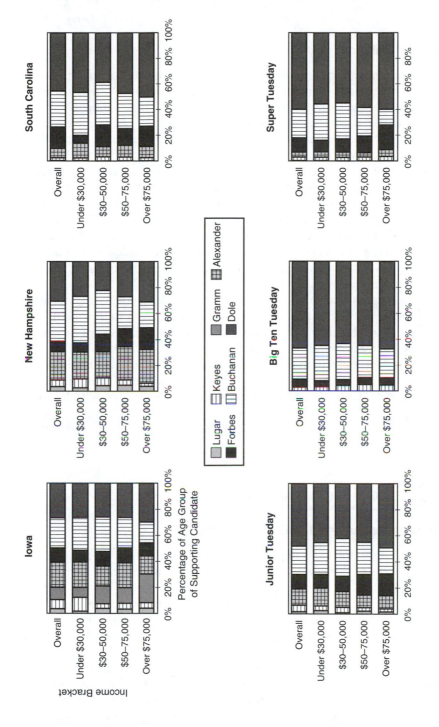

Figure 5 Support for Candidates within Income Brackets

65

Voting by Religion

One distinctive pattern among religious groups was Pat Buchanan's success among self-identified members of the "Religious Right," which comprised about a third of the GOP primary electorate. Buchanan consistently drew 15 to 20 percentage points more of the Religious Right than he did overall. Alan Keyes also appealed heavily to this group, generally capturing twice the percentage of conservative Christians as he captured overall. New Hampshire was atypical of most states in that the portion of the electorate identifying itself as Religious Right was roughly half that of other states (17 percent in New Hampshire). While fewer in number, though, the Religious Right of the Granite State displayed an even more pronounced preference for Buchanan and Keyes. In New Hampshire, Buchanan drew a full 27 percentage points more of this group than he drew with all voters combined, while Keyes' portion of the Religious Right voters was three times more than his portion of the overall voters in the state.

The success of Buchanan and Keyes with the Religious Right was largely at the expense of the front-runner. Dole generally drew 5 to 9 percent less of this group than he did overall, except for New Hampshire were he drew 15 points less than his overall vote percentage.

Interestingly, even with the presence of Buchanan, a devout Catholic, on the ballot, there was generally little differentiation between Catholic and non-Catholic voters. The only real exception was New Hampshire which featured a higher proportion of Catholic voters than many other contests (36 percent Catholic). In the Granite State, Buchanan drew 7 percent more among Catholic voters than overall.

ANALYSIS OF THE CAMPAIGNS

Campaign Issues and the GOP Factions

The candidates in the 1996 Republican nomination contest represented a variety of schools of thought within the party. The two primary themes common to all the candidates were social and economic issues, although candidates had varying approaches. In many respects, the different ways in which the candidates struck these themes revealed the intra-party cleavages associated with the new issues and interests that began to be reflected in the party two decades ago.

During the late 1970s, the so-called New Right began to emerge representing culturally conservative voters who were energized by issues such as school prayer, abortion, gun control, affirmative action, and welfare dependency. While the social conservatism of the New Right did not necessarily

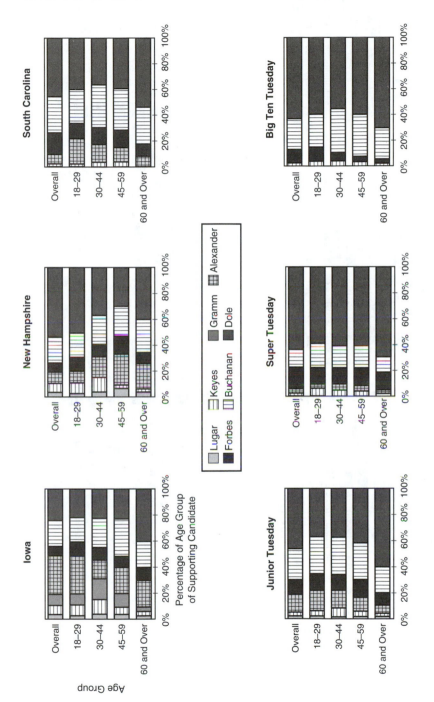

Figure 6   Support for Candidates Within Each Age Group

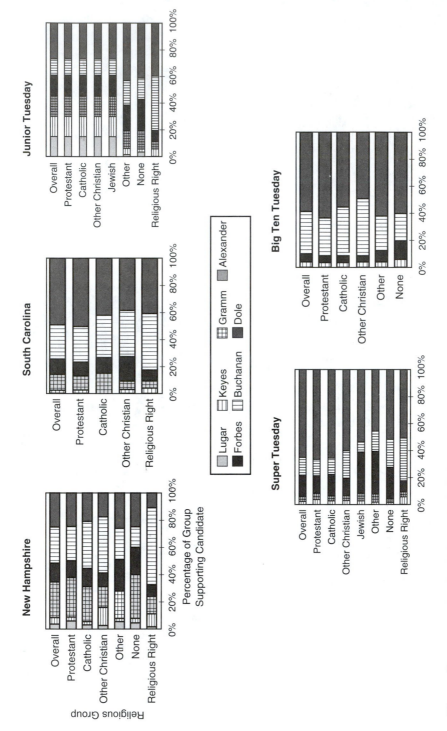

Figure 7 Support for Candidates within Religious Groups

mesh with the economic conservatism of the Old Right (oriented towards traditional Republican themes of fiscal responsibility, limited government, laissez-faire economic regulation, and free trade), they were tactically joined in the candidacy of Ronald Reagan in 1976, 1980, and 1984. The elements of this coalition have not always coexisted easily, since economic conservatives are not necessarily socially conservative (and vice versa). Republican leaders have long feared splits between their social and economic wings, because in order to win, the GOP, of course, must unite both groups.

These old tensions between economic and social conservatives re-emerged with a vengeance in the 1996 nomination battle thanks mainly to Pat Buchanan. Buchanan attempted to capture the social conservative elements of the party while rejecting the views of the economic conservative wing of the party. On the social agenda, Buchanan was hard right, and fervently embraced the anti-abortion position. Like Phil Gramm, Buchanan sought to appeal to the Reagan-mobilized New Right, and both furiously competed to control this crucial segment of the GOP.

Buchanan, however, did not subscribe to traditional Republican free-trade conservatism. Instead of budgetary or tax policy, Buchanan's economic message was keyed to nationalism and free trade protectionism. Much like Ross Perot, Buchanan argued that foreign economic competitors were taking unfair advantage of overly generous international trade agreements such as the North American Free Trade Agreement (NAFTA) and the General Agreement on Trade and Tariffs (GATT), both passed during the Clinton administration. In articulating protectionism, Buchanan sought to tap into lower- and middle-class anxiety about economic dislocations and widespread private-sector downsizing. His blue-collar platform of social conservatism and economic populism had clear antecedents in the 1972 campaign of George Wallace. In fact, in 1976 Buchanan had published *Conservative Votes, Liberal Victories: Why the Right Has Failed*, in which he argued that the Republican Party should fully absorb the Wallace constituency in order to achieve majority-party status.[49] In the 1996 Republican presidential fight, Buchanan worked to bring about the party realignment he had discussed in 1976. Buchanan relished portraying candidates Forbes, Alexander, and Dole as liberal both on social issues such as abortion (despite the fact that all of them professed to be pro-life to varying degrees) and on economic issues because of their support for free trade and opposition to tariffs on foreign goods.

Another Reagan-era division within the Republican Party was exposed anew during 1996—the split between traditional balanced budget advocates and proponents of supply-side economic philosophy. Unlike the traditional, fiscally prudent Republicans who consistently sought a balanced budget, "supply-siders," who came to power under Reagan, viewed tax cuts as a beneficial economic stimulus even if they resulted in larger budget deficits temporarily.

In 1996 two major candidates—Bob Dole and Lamar Alexander—were fiscally conservative but socially moderate, and they thus faithfully represented the traditional core of the Republican Party during the primaries. Consistent with the traditional principles of his party, Dole had been a long-standing champion of balanced budgets (at least until he embraced supply-side economics in the general election campaign of 1996). Indeed, it was because of Dole's overriding commitment to the principle of balanced budgets that he refused to join George Bush in his "no new taxes" pledge during the 1988 New Hampshire Republican primary campaign. (Bush was able to take tactical advantage of Dole's stand on this issue to win in anti-tax New Hampshire.) Dole's dedication to the balanced budget was further confirmed in 1990 when he supported Bush's tax increase in order to ease the budget deficit, even though Newt Gingrich publicly rebuked Dole at the time by calling him the "tax collector for the welfare state."

The views of Dole (and Alexander) on balanced budgets separated both men from the newer supply-side believers in the party, represented in 1996 by Steve Forbes. The traditional dichotomy within the Republican Party on economic philosophy is clearly seen in the differing views of Dole and Forbes on tax policy. Dole grudgingly accepted tax cuts included in the 1996 budget resolution (a capital gains tax cut and a child tax credit) since it was part of an overall balanced budget proposal. Forbes, on the other hand, proposed a 17 percent across-the-board flat tax but he did not explicitly incorporate the tax cut into an overall budget proposal, much less identify any spending cuts needed to offset the tax cuts. With a flat tax, Forbes argued, families "would have a chance to get off the treadmill," and he prophesied "economic boom and spiritual renewal."[50] Forbes' supply-sider credentials were further enhanced by a key endorsement from Jack Kemp, one of the original supply-side advocates in the Reagan era. Ironically, as noted earlier, Dole converted to the supply-side in the general election with a large tax cut proposal, and he cemented his born-again status by asking Kemp to be his running mate.

Economically, Gramm seemed somewhere between Dole and Forbes, advocating a flat tax plan similar to Forbes but continuing to talk about a balanced budget. Conservative socially as well, Gramm sought to integrate evangelical Christians into his support base through strident opposition to affirmative action, gun control, and abortion. As a social conservative, Gramm's rivals were Buchanan and Keyes, who were even further to the right.

Given the Christian Coalition's large GOP constituency, there was considerable attention paid to all the candidates' views on abortion. One example was the candidates' debate just prior to the South Carolina primary, held on February 29 in the city of Columbia. When asked what they would do in a hypothetical situation where a woman was raped and became pregnant, Dole gave an answer that seemed to rule out an abortion, contradicting his

Abortion Question in South Carolina Debate

QUESTION (Sandra Myree—audience participant): If I am brutally raped by a vicious criminal and become pregnant, would you oppose a first-trimester abortion, knowing that a continued pregnancy would cause me mental and emotional anguish?

DOLE: Yes, I would. I'm opposed to abortion, as I've indicated before. I have a strong pro-life record, a consistent record, in the Congress of the United States, and I would keep it that way.

BUCHANAN: Let me say this. If that happened to you, that would be a horrendous atrocity and it's happened to too many women across this country, and what I believe should happen to the rapist in a case like that, if it's particularly vicious and you had a serial rapist, I would vote for his execution. . . . As for you, I would try to counsel you to go to my friend . . . and put [the child] up for adoption. I would try to counsel you to do that because I believe your unborn child is innocent, and the only guilty party here is the rapist.

ALEXANDER: . . . I would say in that instance I would create an exception to the law against abortion and the decision, in that case, of rape would be yours.

FORBES: I believe in the cases of rape, incest, or the life of the mother is genuinely at stake, then there is a right to an abortion.

DOLE: I only thought we had 10 seconds on the last statement. Now, let me suggest that I support the exceptions to rape, incest, life of the mother, and I would do pretty much as Bill—or as Pat Buchanan indicates in this case. I want to make that clear. I thought we had just a short answer. But I want to underscore my strong pro-life record for people who have that view, and again, I think we can have different views and still be good Republicans.

Source: Federal Document Clearing House, Inc.

previous statements on rape. Dole was clearly uncomfortable with the abortion issue, and during the primaries, the Kansan repeatedly stumbled over his statements, costing his campaign valuable time and effort.

The Christian Coalition notwithstanding, national surveys and exit polls frequently indicated that economic concerns tended to outweigh social and

moral issues among primary voters. The three issues that figured most prominently during the 1996 nomination season were: (1) economy/jobs; (2) taxes;
and (3) the budget deficit (see Table 5). In virtually every poll, abortion placed
a distant fourth. And when asked about the most important presidential qualities, voters regularly opted for "standing up for his beliefs," ahead of "conservative values," "vision for the future," or the fact that the candidate was
"not a politician" (see Table 6).

Whether issues really mattered much in this race is debatable. Once
again, front-loading is the reason. The horserace took center stage throughout
the month that mattered (early February to early March), and very quickly
candidates were not being asked anymore about their policy positions but
rather their electoral status. "As soon as the Delaware primary (Feb. 24), several reporters were asking me, 'When are you going to get out?' " remembered
Alexander. "By South Carolina (March 2), that was almost the most frequent
question I got."[51]

TV Advertising

All the major GOP candidates used TV advertising, of course, but 1996 will
be remembered more for Steve Forbes's ads than anyone else's. In 1995 alone
Forbes spent $12.5 million on television and radio, and by the end of his cam-
paign Forbes shelled out over $23 million for advertising. Just in Iowa and Ari-
zona, the Forbes advertising blitz cost $8 million.[52] While the spots were a
mix of positives and negatives, the most memorable were Forbes's pointed
attacks on Bob Dole.

Table 5   **Most Important Campaign Issue**

Issue which mattered most	New Hampshire (2/20/96)	Arizona (2/27/96)	South Carolina (3/2/96)	Junior Tuesday (3/5/96)	New York (3/7/96)	Super Tuesday (3/12/96)
				all states		*all states*
Environment	3	—	1	2	—	—
Foreign trade	6	4	7	6	2	4
Taxes	21	27	22	21	29	21
Education	6	3	5	5	4	7
Economy/jobs	27	15	22	23	25	20
Budget deficit	15	17	20	19	15	22
Abortion	9	10	13	11	8	12

Compiled from: CNN/TIME Voter News Service Exit Polls; the following are the numbers of those
polled after having participated in their respective primary: 2,556 (New Hampshire), 2,102 (Arizona),
1,894 (South Carolina), 6,394 (Junior Tuesday), 1,553 (New York), and 9,911 (Super Tuesday).

Table 6   **Most Important Presidential Quality**

Quality which mattered most	New Hampshire (2/20/96)	Arizona (2/27/96)	South Carolina (3/2/96)	Junior Tuesday (3/5/96)	New York (3/7/96)	Super Tuesday (3/12/96)
				all states		*all states*
Vision for future	14	13	9	11	14	10
Stands up for beliefs	25	21	25	22	17	24
Can beat Clinton	13	12	17	14	13	14
Conservative values	13	19	18	17	12	21
Not a politician	9	13	7	7	11	3
Experience in D.C.	10	10	13	14	19	16
Not too extreme	9	7	7	9	6	6

Compiled from: CNN/TIME Voter News Service Exit Polls; the following are the numbers of those polled after having participated in their respective primary: 2,556 (New Hampshire), 2,102 (Arizona), 1,894 (South Carolina), 6,394 (Junior Tuesday), 1,553 (New York), and 9,911 (Super Tuesday).

The Forbes television campaign certainly had an impact, especially on Dole, Alexander, and Gramm. "The primary was about one thing, and that was Steve Forbes's negative advertising," said a Dole adviser. "They set out on a policy to destroy Bob Dole. It's that simple. . . . The Forbes advertising was a nuclear bomb that was dropped on this race. The entire race was played out in the fallout of this bomb."[53] Mark Merritt, Lamar Alexander's communications director, seemed to agree, "There is such a thing as overkill when it comes to negative campaigning and that line was crossed and, in fact, I think Steve Forbes admitted it."[54] Charles Black, Phil Gramm's senior political adviser, expressed his exasperation with Forbes's television blitzkrieg: "The only people who really could have been nominated and gone the distance were Dole, Gramm, and Alexander. Forbes could never have been nominated, but by seizing the stage and spending all his money and dominating the airwaves, he kept the other two guys from having a real shot at Dole. [Moreover], he gave Dole some horrible negatives which hurt Dole's image by the time he clinched the nomination; it greatly weakened him."[55]

Naturally, the Forbes campaign takes a different view, contending that their television advertising actually left Dole in a better position for the general election. "If anything, what it did was make him stronger; had Steve Forbes not been in the race, Bob Dole wouldn't have been forced to focus on the issues that he's going to need to win in the general [election]."[56] "Well, that's like someone in Seattle denying that it rains," a Dole media adviser retorted. "The Forbes candidacy was a vanity candidacy that was driven by someone who had never really done much in his life, trying to do something. [It was] a rich man's fantasy, and the opportunity for a bunch of consultants who had been left out of the presidential political process to make a lot of money."[57]

As for Forbes' competitors, television advertising was not the highest priority. Even for cash-laden front-runner Bob Dole, less than 20 percent of his budget went to broadcast advertising, and of that $6 million, only $1 million went to produce commercials.[58] For those without large warchests, like Buchanan, free media exposure became an alternative to paid advertising. With a professional expertise in media, Buchanan developed strategies whereby television crews filmed him making calls to local talk radio shows—media on top of media. While surrendering complete control over what went out over the airwaves, Buchanan's tactics were a tonic for an underfunded insurgency.

The reality of Campaign '96 was that it was over almost as soon as it began, and this reality obviously dictated the timing of television advertising. On the last two days before the New Hampshire primary, Dole, Forbes, and Buchanan aired more than 500 television commercials in Boston and Manchester, N.H. On the last weekend before the Texas primary, held just a few weeks later but once the outcome was clear, Buchanan and Forbes ran no television ads in Dallas, one of the two biggest media markets in Texas, and Dole aired fewer than 60 spots.[59]

Push-Polling

As a vicious negative tactic, push-polling (also called negative persuasion phoning) is ethically questionable but also sadly efficient and effective. A push-poll is a candidate's survey that attempts to change the opinion of contacted voters, usually by introducing highly negative information about the opposing candidate(s).[60] Television advertisements have to be broadly acceptable and in-bounds even when negative, because the candidate's name is attached. By contrast, push-polling does not require a statement or tag identifying the campaign that paid for it and, consequently, it has become a stealth way to smear an opponent, with tens of thousands of voters targeted.

Steve Forbes first raised the specter of push-polling in 1996 when he accused the Dole campaign of using push-polling to portray him and his positions in an unflattering way to religious conservatives in Iowa.[61] While Dole denied the charge at the time, others inside the Dole campaign acknowledged that they had conducted at least a small sample (up to 600 interviews) and mentioned critical information about Steve Forbes."[62] Months afterward, when we asked a high-level Dole campaign aide about it, he brushed aside the subject as a non-issue: "The whole thing about push-polling is a total joke. It never had an impact on the campaign," he argued. "This is whining by other candidates. . . . Instead of saying, 'I lost because I had a flawed strategy,' they say, 'I lost because of push-polling.' "[63]

The Forbes campaign saw it differently, and insisted the polling was more extensive than acknowledged by the Dole team. Forbes himself pointed to push-polling as "a critical factor" in his Iowa loss, and added that it lowered voter turnout. In Iowa Forbes noted that, "You had [pre-caucus] estimates [of voter turnout] ranging from 135,000 to 175,000 voters, but [on election night] it barely broke 100,000."[64] Forbes campaign manager Bill Dal Col saw other sinister motives in the Dole push-polling. "Push polling [was] used as a vehicle to gather information," Dal Col said. "What the Dole campaign did would be more correctly termed 'negative canvassing'. . . . It wasn't, 'If you knew Steve Forbes did this, would you be more or less likely to vote for him?' It would be, 'Hi, I'm Joe Smith. Did you know that Steve Forbes supports X?' Click, hang up the phone."[65] Another trick, as Forbes pointed out, was late-night phoning in the Granite State: "In New Hampshire several people said they got calls at three o'clock in the *morning* saying, 'This is the Forbes Committee—vote for Forbes.' "[66] This was no minor effort by the Dole campaign either, with reported telemarketing expenditures of $3 million or more in January and February 1996.[67]

Lamar Alexander appeared to be another victim of Dole push-polling. Reflecting on the Dole calls in Iowa and especially New Hampshire, where Alexander was poised to pass Dole in the polls and conceivably come in first, Alexander noted, "They would say, 'Who are you for?' And if [the answer was] 'Alexander,' they'd say, 'Did you know thus and so?' . . . [S]ometimes it was about abortion . . . or that I had sponsored an income tax [in Tennessee], which I had in fact rejected."[68] Added Alexander's New Hampshire campaign director, Steve Watson: "Dole employed [Steve] Goldberg, the premier Republican telemarketer stationed out of New York City with his company Campaign Tel, to do their push polling. I was told by pretty good sources in the Dole campaign . . . that they made approximately 250,000 push calls, and in a state the size of New Hampshire, that number of calls is going to have an impact." Watson concluded, "Honestly, and I say this unfortunately for us, it was, I believe, the most effective tactic used in the Dole campaign and if you talk with [the Dole staff], I think they would admit it was probably what saved them in the campaign."[69]

Indeed, one of Dole's most senior staffers admitted on a not-for-attribution basis that the campaign's push-polling in Iowa and New Hampshire was "very, very heavy . . . a real barrage," and one of the reasons why Lamar Alexander and Steve Forbes were unable to gain more traction. With most of the other candidates' fire trained on front-runner Dole, "there was nothing we could do to drive our numbers up," said the Dole staffer. "So with our limited market share, we were asking, how do we keep everybody else's market share [of votes] down?" Push-polling was clearly their technique of choice.

Dole's campaign was not alone in conducting push-polling (although its effort was unquestionably the largest). The Gramm and Buchanan campaigns also used negative telephoning, especially in Iowa where the phone lines were clogged with these calls. Mary Boote, Lamar Alexander's Iowa campaign manager, reported that her husband took five push-poll calls in a single weekend night: "We were getting reports of three to seven phone calls per household, all very negative and many centering on abortion."[70]

Staff Wars

The three "handlers" for the major presidential campaigns presented a striking contrast in personality and style. Scott Reed, who managed the Dole campaign, adopted a corporate supervisory role. Bill Dal Col, Forbes' manager, constantly shadowed his candidate and made decisions with him on an hourly basis. Meanwhile, strapped for money, Buchanan kept his staff skeletal and his manager "in the family" by tapping his sister, Angela (Bay) Buchanan, as "chairwoman" of his campaign.

One of the first "staff wars" was comparatively minor. Marlene D. Elwell, who had previously worked on religious broadcaster Pat Robertson's 1988 campaign, joined Buchanan's staff. Elwell had been Robertson's national field director and played a large role in his stunning second-place finish in Iowa; she signed on to develop Buchanan's grassroots organization in the same state. But in December of 1995 she left Buchanan's organization to join Gramm's operation. In doing so, she faulted Buchanan's top advisers for their tendency to "micro-manage."[71]

It was Dole's campaign that featured most of the infighting. After his disappointing second place finish in Delaware, Dole sacked two of his senior strategists—campaign deputy chairman William B. Lacy and chief pollster William D. McInturff—in hopes of revitalizing his faltering bid for the nomination.[72] Dole considered McInturff's polling data to have been too rosy and Lacy's decision to go negative after Iowa, notably labeling Buchanan an "extremist," as a strategic mistake. Prior to his departure, Lacy had been essentially a co-equal with Reed in Dole's campaign. Yet Lacy was somewhat more cautious in management style, while Reed favored making quick decisions.

The Delaware primary was the flash point, when McInturff presented final pre-election numbers showing that Dole would win comfortably (instead of finishing second behind Forbes). McInturff also allegedly failed to predict Buchanan's victory in New Hampshire. But basically, McInturff was Lacy's lieutenant, and when Reed and Dole lost confidence in Lacy, Lacy and McInturff's fates were both sealed. Replacing Lacy as Dole's chief message strategist was GOP media consultant Don Sipple, who was recruited by campaign manager Reed after Sipple's first boss, California Governor Pete Wilson, dropped out of the presidential race. Tony Fabrizio, who had already been in charge of some polling duties, took over McInturff's responsibilities. Ironically, Sipple was the victim of the next Dole campaign shake-up in September, when Scott Reed became dissatisfied with Sipple's TV ads.[73]

One of the principals in the first 1996 Dole campaign upheaval, William Lacy, described the situation from his perspective as the fired manager. While others on the Dole staff may dispute some of his assertions, Lacy's account well reflects the Machiavellian maneuverings present in just about every big-league campaign:

> After the Delaware loss, Scott Reed went on a plane with Dole. Apparently he engineered, uh, he convinced Dole that changes needed to be made in the campaign. Dole has a tendency to feel the heat and make staff changes to buy more time; that's been his style in the past. Scott called me in my car the day after Delaware. He said, "Dole's totally lost confidence in you." I said, "Oh, really?" And he said, "Yeah, and we're going to have to do something about it." I said, "O.K." So I went in to see Scott. He at one time said he had a direct order from Dole to remove me, and this I found later to be totally untrue. He said I could still be involved in the campaign, but that I wouldn't be responsible for strategy or advertising or polling.
>
> So I said, "Fine, under those conditions you guys can just have it. I'll resign." And then we agreed, and this is the final part of it that makes me sick, then we agreed to have the massacre on the day of the next primary so that you're not responding to a primary loss. It doesn't look like panic, and at the same time it doesn't become a big national news story before the primary. So, let's wait until Tuesday's Arizona primary and do it. The other condition was that I insisted on talking with Dole.
>
> Scott said, "No problem. Dole will be back on Tuesday and you can see him then and then we will announce this on Tuesday afternoon." I said, "Great." And that was the end of our discussion, and then about 10 o'clock that night [Sunday] was when I started getting phone calls from people saying, "Have you heard on CNN that you've been thrown out of the campaign?"
>
> I thought we'd had a very unified team. I was shocked that it happened . . . In retrospect, I don't think there needed to be a shake-up of the team. We just needed to suck it up and wait for things to unfold; just hang on to South Carolina, because once you got out of Arizona and the Dakotas, which were the final states where Forbes had poisoned the well, it was a cakewalk. They didn't change a damn thing after I left.[74]

Staff wars, of course, are not exclusively internal, as the various staff and campaign consultants for presidential rivals frequently develop a healthy dislike of each other over the months of battle. Generally, the acrimony between the Dole and Forbes campaigns was the most intense. Looking back on Forbes' candidacy with disgust, one senior Dole aide declared, "The reason I think Forbes is not President of the United States is because the majority of people don't want to elect someone president who's never had a job his parents didn't give him. . . . Someone who on the front page of the *Wall Street Journal* cites day-camp as one of his primary character-building experiences is not a man [Americans] want as president."

Press Coverage

Despite promises to delve deeper into issues than in previous years, the media covered Campaign '96 superficially and very critically. Perhaps because of the compressed schedule of primaries and caucuses, the press turned heavily to "horserace" coverage of who was ahead in the polls, who was climbing, and who was fading. Forbes campaign manager Bill Dal Col argued, "[T]he most interesting thing is to watch the political media, how they cover the process rather than the issues. They're always process driven."[75]

Researchers at the Center for Media and Public Affairs found that the network evening news covered the horserace twice as much as the issues leading up to the Iowa caucuses, while averaging twelve complaints per night about the negative campaign in Iowa.[76] Dal Col asserted that there was a strong bias against Forbes in the media (a complaint borne out by the Center's data): "There was a slant against Forbes and the reason for that was, one, we were total outsiders. Two, none of the 'boys in the beltway media' had had lunch with [Forbes]. They tend to be friendly with people they've had lunch with. . . . And, three, [Forbes] came from the media."[77]

By the conclusion of the New Hampshire primary in the latter part of February, candidate soundbites were averaging only seven seconds, compared to eight seconds in 1992 and nine seconds in 1988. The nine GOP candidates received a combined 79 minutes of airtime, compared to 453 minutes for the journalists who covered them. Only 17 out of 78 stories (22 percent) discussed any of the candidates' policies, proposals, or qualifications. The leading news topics were: campaign trail conduct (37 stories), horserace standings (32), and campaign strategy and tactics (27). The top stories were the campaign's negative tone (11 stories), allegations of Buchanan's bigotry and extremism (10), and Alexander's past personal finances (4).[78]

A peculiar dynamic of the race was Buchanan's treatment by his fellow journalists and commentators. Many felt that, at times, he received gentle treatment that occasionally verged, as *National Journal's* Richard E. Cohen put it, "on sycophancy as pundits from the political Left and Right . . . appeared to bask in his reflected glory, rather than focus on Buchanan the candidate."[79] Others, such as Lamar Alexander, saw it differently: "The news media . . . were terrified of a Pat Buchanan [presidency]. I think the media knew so little about the Republican primary process that they thought he might actually have a chance to win," said Alexander. "The contest was portrayed as a 'somebody versus Buchanan' race and . . . Dole . . . looked like he was the somebody to beat Buchanan."[80]

Another interesting aspect of the relationship between the media and the unfolding drama of the nomination process was the apparent impotency of "talk radio" to influence the overall outcome and Dole's refusal to utilize the medium for campaign purposes. Dole did appear on the *Oliver North Show* on March 12 and a handful of local-market shows around the time of the Junior Tuesday primaries, but that was about the extent of it. He also turned his back on talk TV, appearing only once as guest on CNN's *Larry King Live* (on March 1).[81]

For a more detailed discussion of the press's role in the nomination process, please see Diana Owen's examination in Chapter Nine.

Time Allocation

One of the most important resources in any campaign is the candidate's personal time. Where he campaigns tells a great deal about his strategy. In 1996, the personal visits to each state also reflected the front-loaded schedule, of course. Iowa and New Hampshire received the lion's share of candidate time, and other early-voting states were favored with visits, too.

Lamar Alexander was the Iowa-New Hampshire champion, with 35 visits to his credit. His walk across New Hampshire enabled him to log more days in the state than any other candidate.

Despite being Senate majority leader, Dole was close behind Alexander, having logged 28 visits to Iowa and New Hampshire. Buchanan, at 25 visits to Iowa and New Hampshire, could also boast the most diverse travel schedule, with special attention paid to Louisiana, California, and Arizona. By contrast, Forbes was probably seen on his television ads more than in person in most places, though he did manage 10 trips each to Iowa and New Hampshire. His days in Delaware and Arizona were well rewarded, though his New York effort less so.

Endorsements

With notable exceptions—Jack Kemp endorsing Steve Forbes in New York and William Bennett endorsing Lamar Alexander in New Hampshire—Dole was the endorsement king of the race. Not only did he have the largest number of endorsements, but he also had the most important ones—GOP governors, and the vast majority of them, such as William F. Weld of Massachusetts,

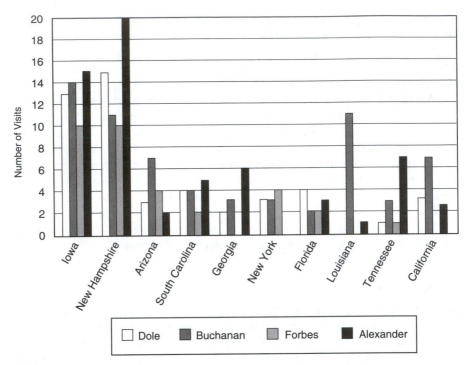

Figure 8   Candidate Visits to Selected States

George Allen of Virginia, Tommy Thompson of Wisconsin, Christine Todd Whitman of New Jersey, Stephen Merrill of New Hampshire, David Beasley of South Carolina, and George Bush of Texas, just to name a few. By the time the most critical week of the nominating process, the first week in March, rolled around, Dole had secured the endorsements of 37 of the 53 Republican senators and 25 of the 31 Republican governors.[82]

A notable exception to Dole's impressive list of endorsements was Louisiana Governor Mike Foster who endorsed Pat Buchanan, to the detriment of Phil Gramm. In fact, some have suggested that Dole played a role in Foster's endorsement of Buchanan. They allege that after Dole decided against contesting the Louisiana caucus, he orchestrated a scenario whereby a less competitive opponent, Buchanan, would defeat a more competitive one, Gramm.

Whatever the truth of this, the governors, said Lamar Alexander, clearly played a critical role for Dole. The early endorsements in Iowa and New Hampshire may not have mattered as much to Dole since all the candidates could spend time in those states and the voters had a chance to get to know them. "But then you start going lickety-split from one place to the next," Alexander

Table 7   **Candidate Visits to Each State***

(primary/caucus dates in parentheses)

	Jan.12–March 26	Alexander	Buchanan	Dole	Forbes	Total
Iowa [c]	(2/12)	15	14	13	10	52
N. H.	(2/20)	20	11	15	10	56
Delaware	(2/24)				3	3
Arizona	(2/27)	2	7	3	4	16
N. Dakota	(2/27)		1	1		2
S. Dakota	(2/27)		1	3		4
S. Carolina	(3/2)	5	4	4	2	15
Wyoming [c]	(3/2)					0
Puerto Rico	(3/3)					0
Colorado	(3/5)	1		2		3
Minnesota [c]	(3/5)					0
Connecticut	(3/5)			1	1	2
Georgia	(3/5)	6	3	2		11
Maine	(3/5)			3	1	4
Maryland	(3/5)					0
Mass.	(3/5)	2			1	3
Rhode Island	(3/5)	1		1		2
Vermont	(3/5)	1		1		2
New York	(3/7)		3	3	4	10
Missouri [c]	(3/9)	1		1		2
Florida	(3/12)	3	2	4	2	11
Louisiana	(3/12)	1	11			12
Mississippi	(3/12)			1		1
Oklahoma	(3/12)		3	2		5
Oregon	(3/12)			2		2
Tennessee	(3/12)	5	3	1	1	10
Texas	(3/12)	1	4	3	1	9
Illinois	(3/19)		2	4	1	7
Michigan	(3/19)		4	3	1	8
Ohio	(3/19)		1	2		3
Wisconsin	(3/19)		2	2		4
California	(3/26)	2	7	3		12

Compiled from: *The Hotline*

*approximation

[c] caucus

noted. "That's when it is essential to tap into existing political networks. The voters are looking for a clue about what to do. In this roller coaster of a presidential race coming after New Hampshire, the governors are a big help."[83]

THE DEMOCRATIC NON-CONTEST

As Linda Fowler has already explained in Chapter Two, no well known Democrats challenged President Clinton for renomination, making him the first Democratic incumbent since Franklin Delano Roosevelt to be so blessed. Thus there was no drama or excitement whatsoever in the contest for the Democratic nomination, except perhaps for one revealing episode. As Table 8 illustrates, Clinton cruised to an easy victory, winning every single state contest and all but 21 of the 4,135 delegates up for grabs. Nevertheless, Clinton's poorest showing in the country was in none other than his home state, Arkansas, where he had been governor for a dozen years. Of the 320,609 Arkansans who voted in their presidential primary, 87,909 (27 percent) refused to vote for their former governor, now President of the United States.[84]

Advantages for Clinton

Of the previous six presidents, only one, Ronald Reagan, had escaped a challenge for renomination. In 1992 television commentator Pat Buchanan took on President Bush; in 1980, Senator Ted Kennedy challenged President Jimmy Carter; in 1976, Reagan opposed President Gerald Ford; in 1972, Representatives Pete McCloskey of California and John Ashbrook of Ohio challenged, albeit feebly, President Richard Nixon; and in 1968, Senators Eugene McCarthy and Robert Kennedy attempted to wrest the nomination away from President Lyndon Johnson. After Senator Estes Kefauver defeated Harry S. Truman in the 1952 New Hampshire primary, Truman opted not to run for another term. Finally, even at the zenith of his popularity, President Johnson still faced a challenge from Alabama Governor George C. Wallace in 1964.

Given his predecessors' woes, how did Clinton manage to avoid a bruising, debilitating, and possibly fatal battle after leading his party to its worst midterm defeat in almost five decades? Potential Democratic presidential aspirants Senators Bob Kerrey of Nebraska and Bill Bradley of New Jersey, House Minority Leader Richard Gephardt of Missouri, and political activist Jesse

Table 8   **Final Democratic Tally**

	Primary Vote	Percentage of the Vote	Delegates Won
Bill Clinton	7,482,656	87.3%	4,114
Others/Uncommitted	1,090,813	12.7	21
Total	8,573,469	100	4,135
Needed to Nominate			2,146

Compiled from: *Congressional Quarterly Weekly Report* vol. 54 (June 15, 1996): p. 1704.

Jackson all declined to run against Clinton, and the most important explanation was the 1994 Republican landslide that resulted in the Democrats' loss of both houses of Congress for the first time since 1952.

Democrats feared that the GOP might be on the verge of achieving total enactment of their conservative agenda. Only the White House remained out of the Republican orbit; with it, Speaker Newt Gingrich and his fellow House revolutionaries would probably be able to work their will and control the national agenda. Hatred and fear of Gingrich and his compatriots generated a 'rally-round-the-president' effect that spared Clinton the usual fate of unsuccessful presidents.

In addition, Clinton helped to scare off potential rivals for the party nomination by his prodigious fundraising. Early in 1995, several Clinton advisers developed a preemptive plan called "Peace through Strength." The purpose was to deter any challenger by raising an enormous amount of money. By the end of 1995, Clinton had raised a record amount of cash in record time, $27 million.

Democratic officials insist that no overt efforts were made to clear the field for Clinton. Democratic National Committee chair Donald L. Fowler noted that only former Governor Robert Casey of Pennsylvania, a pro-life Democrat, indicated any real interest in challenging Clinton, and Casey decided against a candidacy in the end. With Casey and all the other potential challengers, says Fowler:

> As strange as it seems, there were no special inducements, sessions of persuasion, or any other efforts that were unusual or out of the ordinary that were pointed toward keeping the slate clean. It is clear that these people were treated kindly and with deference and their calls were returned, but that was all.
>
> Everybody who might have been interested had a different reason [for not running]. Bill Bradley lives life by hunches, and I think it was his hunch that it was not his time, or the right time. I think Dick Gephardt probably felt that the '94 congressional defeats were in part his responsibility, and as a consequence he didn't feel very confident about placing himself at the public's will. As for Jesse Jackson, it was clear in my mind from a number of conversations with him that he knew that he couldn't win and he knew that if he ran and lost again he would be a complete outsider. I also detected some lack of fire in him that clearly had been there in '88 and '84.

INDEPENDENTS AND THIRD PARTIES

Third parties and independent candidates have periodically been vital throughout American history, but the television age is creating a new breed

Table 9   **Presidential Popularity**

Spring Ratings, Fall Outcome

President	April approval rating	November election result
Lyndon B. Johnson, D (1964)	75	Won by 23 points
Dwight D. Eisenhower, R (1956)	69	Won by 15 points
Richard M. Nixon, R (1972)	54	Won by 23 points
Ronald Reagan, R (1984)	54	Won by 18 points
Bill Clinton, D (1996)	*54*	Won by 8 points
Gerald R. Ford, R (1976)	48	Lost by 2 points
George Bush, R (1992)	42	Lost by 5 points
Jimmy Carter, D (1980)	39	Lost by 10 points
Harry S Truman, D (1948)	36	Won by 4 points

Compiled from: *Congressional Quarterly Weekly Report* vol. 54 (April 27, 1996): p. 1100.

of media-savvy contenders such as George Wallace in 1968, John Anderson in 1980, and Ross Perot in 1992 and 1996. Perot received 19 percent of the 1992 presidential vote, roughly 20 million Americans. Having spent $60 million of his own money on his independent candidacy, by 1995 the Texas billionaire had formed the Reform Party as the successor to his 1992 United We Stand organization. The Reform Party qualified for the ballots of all fifty states in 1996.

Former Colorado Governor Richard D. Lamm challenged Ross Perot for the nomination of the Reform Party in the summer of 1996. The three-term former governor, whose ideas have included partially privatizing Social Security and rationing health care, had always been a Democrat, but became disenchanted with the national party. Perot and Lamm made their nominating speeches at their August 11 convention in Long Beach, California. Members then voted by ballot and electronically during the following week. Perot was declared the easy victor on August 18, at the convention's second session in Valley Forge, Pennsylvania. (The Reform Party's activities will be discussed in greater detail in the Conventions chapter to follow.)

The Reform Party race might have been more interesting had Ross Perot been more successful in his recruiting of other candidates to run for the party's presidential nomination. Some Reform Party officials have privately hinted that Perot would have stepped aside had he been able to attract a strong, nationally recognized figure willing to carry the party's banner in the autumn. Other observers outside the Reform Party believe that Perot was simply looking to "set up" a high-caliber candidate whom Perot could defeat for the party nomination, as a way of legitimizing Perot's presidential bid. The beaten candidate might also have been a logical vice presidential running mate for Perot.

Table 10   **How Recent Third-Party and Independent Candidates Have Fared**

Election year	Candidate	Highest point in the polls	Percentage of popular vote
1948	Strom Thurmond	2.4%	2.4%
1948	Henry Wallace	7	2.4
1968	George Wallace	23	13.5
1980	John Anderson	22	6.6
1992	Ross Perot	39	19

Source: Steven J. Rosenstone, Roy L. Behr, and Edward H. Lazarus, *Third Parties in America: Citizen Response to Major Party Failure.* Second edition. (Princeton, N.J.: Princeton University Press, 1996), p. 106, 112, 118, 119, 238, 231.

Whom did Perot contact for these purposes? The list included retiring U.S. Senator Sam Nunn (D-Georgia), former U.S. Senator David Boren (D-Oklahoma), and—remarkably—Jack Kemp. In an interview with us a week before Bob Dole tapped Kemp for the GOP ticket (and before Kemp even knew he was under consideration), the future Republican vice presidential nominee disclosed the Reform Party's spring wooing process, and the factors behind his eventual rejection of the offer:

> I had talked to the Reform Party mostly at the urging of my old friend [economist] Jude Wanniski who was enamored with the Reform Party and wanted me to at least put myself in the position of a possible candidacy for president or vice president. But that really was Wanniski. I met with [Reform Party political director] Russ Verney, who's a really nice guy, and I've thought Perot was a great entrepreneur and had some good ideas. I had some fundamental disagreements with his protectionist attitude towards NAFTA, but I liked his idea of reforming the tax code. And I did take a call from Perot about [the Reform Party ticket]. They wanted me to put my name on a list that would go

Table 11   **Key Facts and Statistics for Independent and Third-Party Candidates**

Total signatures required nationwide: Approximately 700,000
First state deadline: Utah, March 1
Last state deadline: Vermont, September 19
Most signatures required: California, 147,238
Number of states with no signatures required: 13

Compiled from: *U.S. News & World Report,* "Election 96" and *Ballot Access News* vol. 12 (May 28, 1996): p. 18.

Table 12   **Ballot Access for Third-Party and
             Independent Candidates**[85]

	Requirements		Deadlines	
State	**Full Party**	**Candidate**	**Full Party**	**Candidate**
Alabama	36,060	5,000	July 1	August 30
Alaska	2,586	2,586	in doubt	in doubt
Arizona	15,062	7,813	May 18	June 27
Arkansas	21,506	0	in doubt	September 15
California	89,007	147,238	October 24 ('95)	August 9
Colorado	no procedure	0	—	July 16
Connecticut	no procedure	7,500	—	August 7
Delaware	191	3,828	August 17	July 15
D.C.	no procedure	3,500	—	August 20
Florida	196,788	65,596	July 16	July 15
Georgia	30,036	30,036	July 9	July 9
Hawaii	4,889	3,829	April 24	September 6
Idaho	9,644	4,822	August 31	August 26
Illinois	no procedure	25,000	—	August 5
Indiana	no procedure	29,822	—	July 15
Iowa	no procedure	1,500	—	August 16
Kansas	16,418	5,000	June 1	August 5
Kentucky	no procedure	5,000	—	August 29
Louisiana	0	0	June 30	August 29
Maine	25,565	4,000	December 14 ('95)	May 24
Maryland	10,000	72,785	August 5	August 5
Michigan	30,891	30,891	July 18	July 18
Minnesota	89,731	2,000	May 1	September 10
Mississippi	1,000	1,000	September 6	September 6
Missouri	10,000	10,000	July 29	July 29

out to the Perot people as a potential presidential candidate. Perot basically suggested that if things did not turn out very well in the Republican Party, I might want to consider getting into the nominating process of the Reform Party. Now Jude thought I could get the nomination, but that was his fantasy, and he's always been that type of person. But I didn't get from Russ Verney and Ross Perot anything more than just, "would I get into the process?" and help legitimize their nominating process.

And I saw that as a danger for them and for me, because with Lamm on the left and Perot occupying the vast majority of the hearts and minds of the Reform Party, and then me on the right, it would look like a set-up [for Perot]. I don't mean they did it intentionally, but it looked like it would be a very serious problem for me. I did discuss it with [Senate Majority Leader Trent] Lott and [House Speaker Newt] Gingrich, and of course they disagreed with it. I

Table 12   **(continued)**

| State | Requirements | | Deadlines | |
	Full Party	Candidate	Full Party	Candidate
Montana	10,471	10,471	March 14	July 31
Nebraska	5,773	2,500	August 1	August 27
Nevada	3,761	3,761	July 11	July 11
New Hampshire	9,584	3,000	August 9	August 7
New Jersey	no procedure	800	—	July 29
New Mexico	2,339	14,029	April 2	September 10
New York	no procedure	15,000	—	August 20
North Carolina	51,904	80,684	May 16	June 28
North Dakota	7,000	4,000	December 29 ('95)	September 6
Ohio	33,463	5,000	August 22	August 22
Oklahoma	49,751	41,711	May 31	July 15
Oregon	18,316	14,601	August 27	August 27
Pennsylvania	no procedure	24,425	—	August 1
Rhode Island	18,069	1,000	August 1	September 6
South Carolina	10,000	10,000	May 5	August 1
South Dakota	7,792	3,117	April 2	August 6
Tennessee	37,179	25	April 3	August 20
Texas	43,963	61,541	May 27	May 13
Utah	500	300	March 1	September 1
Vermont	unclear	1,000	September 19	September 19
Virginia	no procedure	15,168	—	August 23
Washington	no procedure	200	—	July 6
West Virginia	no procedure	6,837	—	August 1
Wisconsin	10,000	2,000	June 1	September 3
Wyoming	8,000	9,810	May 1	August 25

didn't want to do anything that would hurt the Republican leadership in Congress, all of whom are dear friends. So I just told Perot and Verney that I could not put my name on their ballot.[86]

As it turned out, Jack Kemp was a popular choice for vice president in 1996, because not just Bob Dole but also Ross Perot tried to enlist Kemp for his party ticket. Perot raised the subject, Kemp reported, "and he told me I didn't have to make up my mind until after the Republican convention," where a funny thing happened.

It is clear that Kemp was not unalterably opposed to a Reform Party candidacy under all conditions. In the interview a week before Dole chose him, Kemp had this to say about his eventual running mate:

Now, if Bob Dole came out and said he was going to raise taxes, I would run. I mean, I really would, but I know for a fact Dole is going to advocate a very strong growth package. Not everything that I would want, but it's certainly going to be consistent with where I think we should go the next two years. It's closer to Kemp than what I've heard from Perot. I've not heard a growth message from Perot.

And since Perot ended up attacking Dole's 15 percent tax cut plan throughout the 1996 general election campaign, the tax-cut-loving Kemp undeniably picked the right horse.

ON TO THE CONVENTIONS

The nominating process can be messy, especially for a party with a large field of candidates and no obviously superior contender. Such was the Republicans' fate in 1996. Bob Dole's embarrassingly obvious inadequacies as a candidate helped to fuel several challengers, and produced early chaos in the nominating season. In the end, though, Dole was saved by his years of careful preparation for the race that yielded an unbeatable combination of money, organization, and "next-in-line" status after two previous unsuccessful runs for the presidency. This ended the contest quickly, but a battered, financially exhausted nominee remained on the field to survive for months on little sustenance. All the while, the unopposed Democratic president stayed fresh, hoarded tens of millions of dollars in unspent primary campaign treasure, and launched a massive television advertising campaign promoting himself and attacking Dole and the "Dole-Gingrich Congress."

Gradually but steadily, Bob Dole drifted downward in the polls as Bill Clinton steadily rose. Dole's resignation from the U.S. Senate in June got good press reviews but had little lasting impact on public opinion. The Republican candidate lurched from gaffe to gaffe, declaring tobacco not necessarily addictive and refusing an invitation to address the NAACP. Meanwhile, Ross Perot made it clear that he would run again for president as the candidate of the Reform Party, a move likely to split the anti-Clinton vote and make it exceedingly difficult for Dole to win under any circumstances.

As the two August party conventions approached, the political situation looked nearly hopeless for Dole, and demoralized Republicans saw defeat over the horizon not only for the presidency but for control of Congress. Dole knew that any regeneration of his candidacy would have to begin at the Republican National Convention with his choice of a running mate and the image projected from the podium.

NOTES

1. Rhodes Cook, "Gramm's Candidacy Teeters After Loss in Louisianan," *Congressional Quarterly Weekly Report* vol. 54 (February 10, 1996): p. 363.

2. Stevens interview.

3. Interview with William Lacy, August 5, 1996.

4. Jack Germond and Jules Witcover, "Forbes Makes Race Costlier for All," *National Journal* vol. 28 (February 3, 1996): p. 274.

5. Stevens interview.

6. Lacy interview.

7. Stevens interview.

8. Lacy interview.

9. Stevens interview.

10. Interview with Whit Ayres, August 6, 1996.

11. Interview with Tom Rath, August 5, 1996.

12. Michael Kranish, "Forbes Wins in Delaware," *The Boston Globe* (February 25, 1996): p. 23; Tom Keyser, "Forbes' Lone Campaigning Pays Off," *The Baltimore Sun* (February 25, 1996): p. 6A.

13. Lacy interview.

14. Eric Mink and Richard Huff, "All but Peacock Eat Crow in Arizona," *The New York Daily News* (February 29, 1996): p. 7.

15. Interview with Haley Barbour, September 24, 1996.

16. Ibid.

17. Roger K. Lowe, "Georgia a Key to Survival for Some GOP Candidates," *The Columbus Dispatch* (South Carolina), March 5, 1996, p. 1A. Thurmond had backed Dole in 1988 as well.

18. "Gramm Wins Straw Poll in South Carolina," *Congressional Quarterly Weekly Report* vol. 53 (March 11, 1995): p. 764.

19. Richard Berke, "Politics: Changing Direction," *The New York Times,* March 3, 1996, p. 1.

20. Howard Troxler, "Dole Gets First Big Win," *St. Petersburg Times* (Florida), March 3, 1996, p. 1A.

21. John King, "Dole Wins South Carolina," *The Sunday Gazette Mail* (Charleston, South Carolina), March 3, 1996, p. 1.

22. "Campaign Organization: Welcome to the Machine," *The Economist* vol. 338 (March 9, 1996): p. 26.

23. Finlay Lewis, "Dole Surges With Sweep in New York," *The San Diego Union-Tribune,* March 8, 1996, p. A1.

24. Alan Greenblatt, "Lugar, Alexander Withdraw," *Congressional Quarterly Weekly Report* vol. 54 (March 9, 1996): p. 641.

25. Interview with William Dal Col, July 18, 1996.

26. Stevens interview.

27. Buchanan was on the ballot in only twenty-three districts, and eventually received 15 percent of the statewide primary vote.

28. Interview with Steve Forbes, July 29, 1996.

29. Stephen J. Wayne, *The Road to the White House: 1996* (New York: St. Martin's Press, 1996), pp. 96–101.

30. Dan Balz, "GOP Panel Begins Study Of Nominating Process," *The Washington Post,* May 31, 1996, A14.

31. Emmett H. Buell, Jr., "The Invisible Primary," in William G. Mayer, ed., *In Pursuit of the White House* (Chatham, NJ: Chatham House Publishers, Inc., 1996), p. 7.

32. Arthur T. Hadley, *The Invisible Primary* (Englewood Cliffs, NJ: Prentice Hall, 1976).

33. Claude R. Marx, "He Who Writes The Rules Wins," *Investor's Business Daily* (March 22, 1996): A1.

34. Stevens interview.

35. Interview with Dan McLagan, July 17, 1996.

36. Bob Woodward, *The Choice* (New York: Simon & Schuster, 1996), p. 385.

37. McLagan interview.

38. Dal Col interview.

39. Republican National Committee, "Presidential Primary Task Force," Washington, D.C., May 30, 1996.

40. McLagan interview.

41. Report from the National Association of Secretaries of State, in a memo format dated May 22, 1996 from New Hampshire Secretary of State William Gardner to the president of the National Association of Secretaries of State.

42. Lamar Alexander, "What I Learned About How We Pick A President," *The Weekly Standard* 1:27 (March 25, 1996): p. 26.

43. William Booth, "Buchanan Stuns Gramm in Louisiana," *Washington Post,* February 7, 1996, A1.

44. Bill McAllister, "Candidates Show Up Short and Late for Delaware's First Presidential Primary," *Washington Post,* February 24, 1996, A10.

45. David S. Broder and Howard Kurtz, "Delaware Goes On The Attack For Early Primary Date," *Washington Post,* January 14, 1996, A22.

46. All data about voting patterns are extracted from exit polling conducted by Voter News Service for the commercial television networks and other news outlets.

47. Rhodes Cook, "Primary Season Concludes Without Much Drama," *Congressional Quarterly Weekly Report* vol. 54 (June 15, 1996): p. 1701.

48. Excerpt from a discussion with voting expert Curtis Gans, "Over So Soon," *The Brookings Review* vol. 14 (Summer 1996): p. 42.

49. Patrick J. Buchanan, *Conservative Votes, Liberal Victories: Why the Right Has Failed* (New York: Quadrangle, 1975).

50. Burt Solomon, "In Frigid Iowa, A Political Circus," *National Journal* vol. 28 (February 10, 1996): p. 324.

51. Interview with Lamar Alexander, August 1, 1996.

52. James A. Barnes, "In Iowa, The Buzz Versus the Buzzsaw," *National Journal,* vol. 28 (February 3, 1996): p. 272; and Rhodes Cook, "GOP 'March Madness' May Be Turning Point in Campaign," *Congressional Quarterly Weekly,* vol. 54 (March 2, 1996): p. 571.

53. Stevens interview.

54. Interview with Mark Merritt, July 20, 1996.

55. Interview with Charles Black, July 17, 1996.

56. Dal Col interview.

57. Stevens interview.

58. Ruth Marcus, Walter Pincus, and Ira Chinoy, "Dole's Aggressive Maneuver: Spend Early and Freely," *Washington Post* (April 18, 1996): p. A1.

59. Blaine Harden and Dan Balz, "Compressed Primary Schedule Leaves Some Looking for Better Way," *Washington Post* (March 14, 1996): p. A6.

60. See Larry J. Sabato and Glenn R. Simpson, *Dirty Little Secrets: The Persistence of Corruption in American Politics* (New York: Times Books, 1996), Chapter Nine.

61. *Wall Street Journal* (February 12, 1996): p. A16; Thomas Edsall, "Dole Camp Acknowledges 'Push Poll'," *Washington Post* (February 12, 1996): p. A8.

62. *The Hotline* (February 12, 1996).

63. Stevens interview.

64. Forbes interview.

65. Dal Col interview.

66. Forbes interview.

67. Dan Balz, "Dropping in Polls, Forbes Lashes Out," *Washington Post* (February 10, 1996): p. A1.

68. Alexander interview.

69. Interview with Steve Watson, August 2, 1996.

70. Interview with Mary Boote, August 5, 1996.

71. "Not My Echo, My Shadow and Me," *National Journal* vol. 28 (January 1, 1996): p. 11.

72. James A. Barnes, "Shake-up of Dole's High Command," *National Journal* vol. 28 (March 2, 1996): p. 494.

73. Media consultant Mike Murphy was also dropped from the campaign with Sipple in September.

74. Lacy interview.

75. Ibid.

76. "Election Watch," Center for Media and Public Affairs (February 16, 1996).

77. Dal Col interview.

78. "Election Watch," Center for Media and Public Affairs (February 21, 1996).

79. Richard Cohen, "Not Their Finest Hour," *National Journal* vol. 28 (March 3, 1996): p. 565.

80. Alexander interview.

81. Paul Starobin, "Bob Who?", *National Journal* vol. 28 (April 27, 1996): p. 926.

82. The Economist, March 9, 1996, p. 26.

83. Jill Zuckman, "Dole Calls in the Chits for Many Past Favors," *The Boston Globe*, March 11, 1996, p. 1.

84. "Arkansas Primary," *The Commercial Appeal* (Memphis), May 23, 1996, p. 15A.

85. Richard Winger, *Ballot Access News* vol. 12 (May 28, 1996): p. 18.

86. Interview with Jack Kemp, August 2, 1996.

CHAPTER 4

The Conventions

One Festival of Hope, One Celebration of Impending Victory

*Larry J. Sabato**

University of Virginia

The national conventions of great parties are Rorschach tests of political moods and electoral fortunes. At least since 1964, it has been easy to spot the likely November winner based simply on the tone of the proceedings. Upbeat, confident conventions mean victory: Democrats in 1964, 1976, and 1992, and Republicans in 1968, 1972, 1980, and 1984. Fractious, quarrelsome conventions signal defeat: Democrats in 1968, 1972, 1980, and 1984, and Republicans in 1964, 1976, and 1992.

Occasionally, there are exceptions, of course. In 1960 and 1988 *both* major parties had successful, optimistic conclaves without deep divisions. In the former year, Republican Richard Nixon and Democrat John Kennedy were evenly matched, giving both parties cautious cheer, and in the latter year, Democrat Michael Dukakis led in the polls, thrilling Democrats, but Republicans correctly had confidence that the winning Reagan formula would elect George Bush in the end.

Like 1960 and 1988, the 1996 conventions were a closer call for soothsayers. Both parties ran relentlessly bright and meticulously scripted affairs

*The author gratefully acknowledges the invaluable help of University of Virginia graduate students Stan Humphries and Rick Mayes and undergraduate student Justin Sizemore in the research, drafting, and presentation of this chapter. Also making contributions were Michelle Baker, Steven Betz, Jeff Manns, and Michael Smith. The author attended both national party conventions in 1996, and wishes to thank the Democratic and Republican parties for their help in securing credentials.

93

that projected a winning image. Both conventions were almost entirely designed for television, with the delegates serving as enthusiastic props for
pre-chosen nominees. And both conclaves shrewdly achieved their main
objective—to produce a "bump" in the public opinion polls for the presidential nominee.

Yet just beneath the surface there was a very clear difference between the
two major-party conventions. Far behind in the polls, *the Republicans ran a
festival of hope*—hope fueled by Dole's selection of the popular Jack Kemp as
his vice presidential running mate and Dole's 15 percent across-the-board income tax cut proposal. These last two developments were the first pieces of
good news that Republicans had received in months, and euphoria was
thereby generated in delegates who feared they were slated to attend a funeral
in San Diego. By contrast, *the Democrats held a celebration of impending victory* in Chicago. Party brass and delegates were thoroughly confident about
the November outcome, and they were willing to submerge literally every difference, major and minor, to reinforce President Clinton's substantial lead.

How each party attended to its task, and juggled the many demands of interest groups and elected officials, is the focus of this chapter.

CONVENTIONAL WISDOM

The planning for the national party conventions begins in earnest *at least*
eighteen months in advance, long before the nominees are known for certain.
The Republican and Democratic National Committees choose their site and
organize the program and financing. While $12.4 million in taxpayer funds is
provided to each party for the convention, the Democrats and GOP (along
with their host cities) each privately raise *in addition* more than twice that
amount, by means of a "host committee," a tax exempt organization located
in the convention localities.[1] The host committees were bipartisan and secured money from civic boosters of both parties in San Diego and Chicago.
Debra DeLee, Chief Executive Officer of the 1996 Democratic Convention,
estimated that the Chicago host committee, co-chaired by Illinois Gov. Jim
Edgar (R) and Chicago Mayor Richard M. Daley (D), raised 70 percent of its
funds from Republicans.[2]

Local parties at the convention sites can be a minefield for the organizers.
When DeLee, a native Chicagoan, first met with the mayor's brother Bill, he
made two requests on behalf of the Daleys: "He said all I am going to ask from
you is A) no surprises, and B) do nothing that interferes with our local politics." DeLee tried to follow those guidelines while attending to the party's
needs, such as working closely with the Chicago African-American community that was not always enthralled with Daley. Inevitably, some conflict

arose. At one public meeting held to announce Democratic convention investments in local banks, Congressman Bobby Rush (D), a potential African-American challenger to Mayor Daley, unexpectedly told the press he saluted DeLee for "standing up against the hooliganism of the Daleys." DeLee was distressed, but silently took her medicine (a critical press column about her engineered by the Daleys) and went on.

Still, conventions are about national, not local, politics, and both parties in 1996 fully grasped the job that needed doing. Republican convention manager Bill Greener truly spoke for the GOP *and* the Democrats when he boiled down the modern party convention to its essence:

> We just formally pick a president and vice president, the nominees give their speeches, and that's all people really remember. This is a TV show, and if you stay disciplined, you can leave a good basic impression of your party and nominees.[3]

THE 1996 REPUBLICAN NATIONAL CONVENTION (AUGUST 12–15)

The Republican National Convention was held in San Diego soon after the closing ceremonies of the 1996 Atlanta Summer Olympic Games. The convention officially nominated Bob Dole as the party's presidential nominee, but because Dole had already amassed the lion's share of delegates via primaries and caucuses, the event was primarily a showcase and advertisement rather than a deliberative gathering. Not surprisingly, by the time it was over, many were labeling the whole exercise an "infomercial" for both Dole and the Republican Party. The hard-right platform, drafted the previous week by conservative activists who dominated the Platform Committee, was virtually ignored; Dole, Newt Gingrich, and RNC Chairman Haley Barbour indicated that they hadn't even read it. Any politician who threatened a discordant message on such issues as abortion (such as Gov. William Weld of Massachusetts) or immigration (including Gov. Pete Wilson of California) was struck from the speakers' roster. Minorities and women were widely featured on the rostrum to emphasize moderation and diversity in a party often perceived as exclusive and too conservative. As Barbour put it, "We needed to let the public understand that we are not a party of just seventy-year-old white men."[4] Finally, the presumption that unsuccessful rivals for the nomination, especially Pat Buchanan, were entitled to some convention time was unceremoniously exploded. Few previous conventions of either party had ever demonstrated such tight control over image and message.[5]

THE RUN-UP TO THE REPUBLICAN CONVENTION

A party naturally tries to make news, heighten the suspense, and downplay distracting controversies in the days prior to its national convention. This is not easy when the presidential nominee is known well in advance, but three opportunities presented themselves to the GOP: Dole's announcement of a tax cut package, his choice of a vice presidential running mate, and the formulation of the Republican platform. All of the three went reasonably well for Dole, although the tax cut idea was heavily criticized and the platform debate on abortion made the Republicans look intolerant at a critical juncture.

The Tax Cut Package

On August 5 in Chicago (site of the Democratic Convention to be held three weeks later), just one week prior to the convention's kick-off in San Diego, Dole announced the centerpiece of his campaign—a 15 percent across-the-board income tax decrease. Also included was a 50 percent cut in the capital gains tax and a $500-per-child tax credit to low- and middle-income families. Added together, the cost of Dole's tax cuts was estimated to be at least $551 billion. At the same time, Dole pledged to keep the budget balanced without touching such huge and popular entitlement programs as Medicare, Social Security, and veterans' benefits.

The goal of the tax package was to raise economic growth 1 percent to an annual rate of 3.5 percent. It was an unusual initiative for Dole, who had routinely derided "supply-siders" for proposing tax cuts without providing offsetting spending cuts. Nevertheless, portraying his plan as benefiting working families, Dole argued that the increase in economic growth resulting from the tax cuts would be the answer to the middle class's economic anxieties. "Growth will put those women and men back on the jobs, paychecks in their pockets," Dole said. ". . . But let me be very clear, the purpose of tax cuts is to leave more money where it belongs—in the hands of the working men and the working women."

The criticism the Dole tax cut plan generated—and there was a great deal of it in the press and from both Democrats and Republicans—was that there were no specified spending cuts and no plan to have the tax cut pay for itself. Dole avoided specifying spending cuts, because it would have generated organized resistance from the groups that had a vested interest in keeping various programs. Instead, Dole pointed somewhat vaguely and unconvincingly to increased revenues resulting from economic growth stimulated by the tax cut, and also the elimination of the Energy and Commerce Departments as well as the auctioning off of portions of the broadcast spectrum by the Federal Communications Commission.

The Battle over the Platform

The Republican platform deliberations were held one week before the Convention between August 5–7. The high profile participants included conservative activists Phyllis Schlafly (president of the Eagle Forum), Gary Bauer (president of the Family Research Council), Paul Weyrich (head of the Free Congress Research and Education Foundation), Ralph Reed (executive director of the Christian Coalition), and Angela "Bay" Buchanan (chairwoman of her brother Pat Buchanan's campaign).

As anticipated, the most heated debates raged over the issue of abortion and the platform's call for a constitutional amendment to ban abortion. Specifically, the disputants wrangled over Dole's attempt to include a "tolerance language" addendum that said, in essence, that one could be pro-choice and still a good Republican.

Back in June, Dole had brokered a deal for some tolerance language with the platform committee chairman, Rep. Henry J. Hyde (Ill.). But Bay Buchanan led a successful public fight to render the Dole-Hyde deal "dead-on-arrival," although Dole was able to squeeze out a minor, face-saving victory by having the failed tolerance language included in an appendix to the platform. The platform went on to quiet passage and it was approved without debate on the first day of the convention, garnering little additional attention.

In retrospect, while the abortion debate was not helpful to Dole, it could have been far worse but for a stratagem conceived by Haley Barbour, the wily RNC chairman. Barbour explained it this way:

> I announced in '95 that we wouldn't begin the platform process until April. And the rationale was that by April we were likely to know who our nominee would be, and the nominee ought to have a voice. Now that's true, but every bit as true was that we needed an excuse to put it off, and we wanted to make the platform process as short as possible. So we canceled the field hearings, which saved another two weeks. We took these steps because once the platform process started, all the press would want to talk about was abortion. And if we started it all in January, they *would* have talked about abortion.

The Vice-Presidential Selection

Surprising almost everyone, including the eventual choice himself, Dole finally settled upon a long-time rival and opponent in choosing Jack Kemp as his running mate. Dozens of names had been bandied about in the days and weeks leading up to the convention, including Wisconsin Governor Tommy Thompson, Pennsylvania Governor Tom Ridge, Michigan Governor John Engler, Ohio Governor George Voinovich, Arizona Senator John McCain, former South Carolina Governor Carroll Campbell, and Florida U.S. Senator Connie Mack.

In an interview with the author one week prior to his being tapped, Kemp confided that he was convinced that " . . . the odds-on favorite for Vice President [was] Connie Mack of Florida,"[6] and indeed, Mack was the runner-up for the post. But in the end Bob Dole's deteriorating position in the polls forced him to view his vice-presidential choice (and the convention) as critical to getting him back into the game. Consequently, he came to focus on Kemp, someone with previous presidential campaign experience, exuberant charisma, and the credibility to sell the supply-side tax cut. Kemp's years as a professional football quarterback (winning two American Football League championships with the Buffalo Bills in the 1960s) and his close connection to Reagan's tax cut legacy made him an ideal ticketmate for Dole.

The match-up was an uneasy one, however. Dole and Kemp had a long history of political and personal disagreements, from immigration and affirmative action to tax cuts and deficit reduction. (Dole once quipped that "Kemp never met a deficit he didn't like," while Kemp replied that "Dole never met a tax he didn't hike.") Dole's choice of Kemp was all the more surprising since Kemp endorsed Dole's opponent, Steve Forbes, even after Dole had courted Kemp with considerable ardor. Once chosen, however, both Kemp and Dole dutifully downplayed their antagonisms, and sought to portray their union as "Exhibit A" for the so-called Republican "big tent."

The formal marriage was prearranged. Dole called Kemp at 10:06 p.m. on Friday, August 9, from his boyhood home in Russell, Kansas, to ask him officially to be his running mate. Kemp took the call in a waiting room at the Dallas airport, accepted, and headed for Kansas to meet up with Dole. Then it was on to San Diego.

The San Diego Pep Rally

Rarely have delegates to a national party nominating convention gathered together more dispirited and with a collective sense of such dark foreboding as did the Republicans in 1996. Bob Dole had fired up few, had made frequent summer stumbles (such as his suggestion that nicotine might not be addictive), and had shown little ability to connect with swing voters.

Yet the triumph of the GOP conclave was its transformation of defeatism into genuine excitement and hope. While Dole proved incapable of sustaining his party's upbeat mood following the convention, the temporary restoration of energy was a minor miracle in itself.

After quickly adopting the party's platform without controversy at a sparsely attended opening session on Monday morning, August 12, the stage was set for an evening of nostalgia and a tone of moderation and inclusiveness. Speeches by former presidents Ford and Bush reminded the party and home viewers of the GOP's presidential past (a mixed blessing, perhaps). The evening took a decisive turn when Nancy Reagan made an emotional address that included a videotape tribute to her husband, former president Ronald Reagan, now suffering from Alzheimer's disease. Then retired General Colin Powell electrified the convention with an enormously effective address. Powell stressed the need for the Republican Party to be the party of inclusion. "It is our party, the Party of Lincoln," Powell said, "that must always stand for equal rights and fair opportunity for all." Powell—whose image had been basically nonpartisan—made his most valuable contribution to the party and its nominee by explicitly endorsing and promoting Bob Dole. "In an era of too much salesmanship and too much smooth talking, Bob Dole is a plain-spoken man," said Powell. "He is a man of strength, maturity and integrity. He is a man who can bring trust back to government and bring Americans together again."

Tuesday night's agenda focused on two objectives: (1) to continue to project a moderate, inclusive party image by showcasing prominent women such as Rep. Susan Molinari (N.Y.), who gave the keynote address; and (2) to stress the GOP's winning issues, including taxes and welfare, and the contrast with President Clinton's views. This was clearly the night for sharp partisan attacks on President Clinton. "Americans know that Bill Clinton's promises have the life span of a Big Mac on Air Force One," asserted Molinari, referring to the President's penchant for fast food and position flip-flops.

Bob Dole's wife, Elizabeth Dole, stole the Tuesday show. Breaking with tradition by leaving the podium, Mrs. Dole took to the convention floor much like an Oprah Winfrey or Phil Donahue. Without use of the omnipresent teleprompter, she strolled among the delegates introducing ordinary individuals who had played pivotal roles in the life of Bob Dole, such as the family of the doctor who operated on Dole's devastating war wounds, a Capitol Hill aide who noted that Dole consistently won the "most friendly" senator designation among staff employees, and a handicapped individual who gave Dole the idea of starting a foundation to help disabled Americans.

The night ended with Sen. John McCain (Ariz.) placing Dole's name in nomination for president, followed by a carefully scripted roll call vote of the states that ended with Kansas putting its "native son" over the top. Immediately afterwards, Kemp was nominated by Gov. George Pataki (N.Y.) and confirmed in the vice presidential slot by voice vote. Also notable on Wednesday evening was what did *not* happen: the nominations of the other GOP presidential candidates, especially Pat Buchanan, who kept his challenge technically alive until the convention. Given Buchanan's harsh "culture war" speech at the 1992 Houston Republican National Convention, the Dole staff was not anxious to give Buchanan another forum, especially given the Dole message of moderation and inclusiveness. Argued GOP convention planner Bill Greener: "There's no requirement in law or politics that forces you to let the losing candidate dictate the terms of the convention. Michael Dukakis didn't get much out of Jesse Jackson's speech in '88 and George Bush sure didn't get anything from Pat Buchanan's in '92."[7]

The following evening, Jack Kemp provided Dole with a "warm-up" act in his acceptance speech for the vice presidential nomination. Refraining from partisan or personal jabs at Clinton or the Democratic Party, Kemp declared that the Dole-Kemp ticket would aggressively pursue the vote of every segment of the American electorate, an attempt to build upon the "inclusion" theme of the convention. "We will carry the word to every man, woman and child of every color and background that today, on the eve of the new American century, it is time to renew the American promise to recapture the American dream," declared Kemp.

Dole followed Kemp by first walking around the convention floor shaking hands and working the crowd before ascending to the podium for his acceptance speech. What followed was a nearly one-hour dissertation that attempted to touch on virtually every aspect of his campaign: personal recollections of his recovery from debilitating war wounds; potshots at Clinton for passing a large tax increase and Mrs. Clinton for her book *It Takes A Village;* a clarion call for strengthening family values; and a focus on rebuilding the economy by means of the campaign's central plank, a 15 percent across-the-board income tax cut. Clearly, different speechwriters had written various portions of the speech, and consequently Dole had some difficulty adjusting his tone and delivery to accommodate the changing subject matter. Never-

---

JACK KEMP

Born: July 13, 1935, Los Angeles, California

Age: 61

Education: Occidental College, B.A., 1957

Military Service: Army Reserve, 1958–'62

Occupation: Professional football player

Family: Wife, Joanne Main; four children

Religion: Presbyterian

Political Career: U.S. House, 1971–'89; candidate for president, 1988; secretary of Housing and Urban Development, 1989–'93

LIST OF SPEAKERS: MONDAY, AUGUST 12

Nostalgia and Inclusion Night

Haley Barbour, Republican National Committee (RNC) chairman
Evelyn McPhail, RNC co-chairman
Jack Ford, host committee director
U.S. Sen. Alfonse M. D'Amato (N.Y.)
U.S. Rep. Bill Paxon (N.Y.)
Gov. John Engler (Mich.)
Mary Fisher, AIDS activist
Gov. George V. Voinovich (Ohio)
U.S. Rep. Rob Portman (Ohio)
Susan Golding, San Diego mayor
U.S. Sen. John McCain (Ariz.)
Gov. George W. Bush (Tex.)
Former president Gerald R. Ford
Former president George Bush
Former first lady Nancy Reagan
Retired Gen. Colin L. Powell

LIST OF SPEAKERS: TUESDAY, AUGUST 13

Issues and Clinton Contrast Night

Gov. George Bush (Tex.)
U.S. Sen. Bill Frist (Tenn.)—health care
Gov. Tommy Thompson (Wis.), Gov. Marc Racicot (Mont.)—welfare
Gov. Tom Ridge (Penn.)—crime
Gov. John Engler (Mich.), Lamar Alexander, Gov. Arne Carlson (Minn.)—education
U.S. Sen. Kay Bailey Hutchison (Tex.)—the Clinton record
U.S. Rep. J.C. Watts (Okla.)—minority issues
Gov. John Rowland (Conn.), Malcolm S. "Steve" Forbes, Jr.—taxes
U.S. Rep. John Kasich (Ohio), Sen. Phil Gramm (Tex.)—balancing the budget
U.S. Rep. Susan Molinari (N.Y.)—keynote address

LIST OF SPEAKERS: WEDNESDAY, AUGUST 14

Nomination Night

Gov. George Bush (Tex.)—the "common sense" Republican Congress

U.S. Rep. George Radanovich (Calif.), Rep. Sue Myrick (N.C.)—GOP
  congressional scorecard

U.S. Sen. Ben Nighthorse Campbell (Colo.)—party switchers

Chris DePino (Conn. GOP chairman)—union members

Matt Fong (Calif. treasurer)—government waste

Morry Taylor—Dole economic agenda

Carol Keaton Rylander (Texas railroad commissioner)—immigration

Kim Alexis (model), Alan Keyes, Ralph Reed, William J. Bennett,
  Rep. Steve Largent (Okla), Dan Quayle (former vice-president)—
  strong families/values

U.S. Sen. Richard Lugar (Ind.), Rep. Robert K. Dornan (Calif.), Rep. Lincoln Diaz-Balart (Fla.), Sen. Arlen Specter (Pa.), Jeanne Kirkpatrick
  (former U.N. ambassador), James Baker (former Secretary of
  State)—foreign affairs

U.S. Sen. Nancy Kassebaum (Kan.), Sen. Fred Thompson (Tenn.), Robin
  Dole (Dole's daughter), Elizabeth Dole (Dole's wife and American
  Red Cross president)—Bob Dole the man

Gov. George Pataki (N.Y.)—nomination of Jack Kemp

U.S. Sen. John McCain (Ariz.)—nomination of Dole

LIST OF SPEAKERS: THURSDAY, AUGUST 15

The Acceptance Address

Gov. Christine Todd Whitman (N.J.)—listening to America

U.S. Rep. Nancy L. Johnson (Conn.), Sen. Connie Mack (Fla.)—women
  and health care

Mayor Steve Goldsmith (Indianapolis), Gov. Mike Leavitt (Utah)—
  states' rights

Gov. Steve Merrill (N.H.), House Majority Leader Richard K. Armey
  (Tex.)—Dole economic agenda

Senate Majority Leader Trent Lott (Miss.)

Gov. Whitman—introduction of Jack Kemp

Kemp's acceptance speech

Film about Robert J. Dole

Dole's acceptance speech

theless, for an individual not known for his stirring rhetoric or charismatic oratory, Dole managed to project the image of someone at peace with himself who had an overarching vision for where he intended to lead the country. In a touching passage that attempted to capitalize on his age and experience, Dole argued that he could "be the bridge to an America that only the unknowing call myth. Let me be the bridge to a time of tranquillity, faith and confidence in action. And to those who say it was never so, that America's not been better, I say you're wrong. And I know because I was there. And I have seen it. And I remember."

THE 1996 DEMOCRATIC NATIONAL CONVENTION (AUGUST 26–29)

Held in Chicago two weeks after the Republican gathering, the Democratic Convention was designed to emphasize the party's achievements over the past four years. After all, the Democrats came into Chicago with their incumbent nominee, President Clinton, comfortably ahead in all the major polls and more popular than at almost any other point in his presidency. The mission, then, was simple—remain upbeat and avoid mistakes. With the exception of a last-minute embarrassment (the Dick Morris affair), the Democrats did just that. Their platform deliberations were a love-fest, the run-up to their convention was attention-grabbing, and the convention itself was a Hollywood production that put the Academy Awards to shame. Front and center, on-stage and off-stage, was Bill Clinton, who as the incumbent president was the focus of the entire election year. "This was not so much a party convention as a Clinton White House convention," DNC chairman Donald Fowler noted, adding that the president had been "intimately involved" in planning the entire affair.[8]

The Platform Pax

In contrast to the Republicans' battle over the language of their platform, Democrats agreed not to disagree. They began and calmly wrapped up their deliberations on the platform in Pittsburgh on August 5, with the 186-member Platform Committee completing its business in just three-and-a-half hours. There were a few protests over Clinton's signing of Republican-written welfare reform legislation, but the controversy was quickly glossed over. Contrary to the Republicans' internecine warfare over abortion, the Democrats simply added a "conscience clause" to their traditional abortion-rights plank, welcoming people of all views to their party. The language of the platform invariably reflected the moderate course that Clinton had set for his second presidential campaign, a supposed "middle way" between the Democrats' old liberalism and the hard-right policies of the GOP Congress. "That," said the platform, "is what today's Democratic Party offers: the end of the era of big government and a final rejection of the misguided call to leave our citizens to fend for themselves . . . ."

Train Ride to the Convention

In order to build suspense in an otherwise suspense-less convention, the Democrats (at the suggestion of the Clintons' Hollywood pal Harry Thomason) decided to have President Clinton ride a train to Chicago through key swing states in the first days of the convention. Don Foley, the Democrats' national convention manager, noted two initial and conflicting worries, concern about a potential news void in a happy-talk convention, and the leftover 1968 legacy—memories of the last, disastrous Democratic conclave in Chicago: "We didn't know what would happen, the fear being that Chicago would again become a place for a lot of dissidents to converge and protest."[9] The train trip worked on both counts, providing attractive television pictures each evening that could fill a news hole or counteract noisy demonstrators (who never showed up).

So as the convention prepared to open, Clinton boarded the customized "21st Century Express" on Sunday, August 25 in Huntington, West Virginia, for a four-day journey that became a media extravaganza. From Huntington the President went to Ashland, Kentucky; Chillicothe, Columbus, Arlington, Bowling Green and Toledo, Ohio; and Wyandotte, Royal Oak, Pontiac, East Lansing, Battle Creek, and Kalamazoo, Michigan. The train stopped frequently so that Clinton could deliver brief partisan remarks attacking unpopular Republicans such as Newt Gingrich. It was a throwback to an older style of politicking made famous by presidents Franklin Delano Roosevelt and Harry Truman. Finally, on the evening of Wednesday, August 28, Clinton arrived in Chicago to much fanfare, and just 24 hours before his acceptance address in the convention hall.

A United Party in the United Center

The first night of the Democratic Convention was purposely a politician-free zone during the prime-time hours covered by the networks (10–11 PM EDT). The Democrats' preferred focus was on sacrifice and suffering, beginning with a video tribute to former Secretary of Commerce Ron Brown, who died along with thirty-four others in a plane crash over Croatia in April 1996. Brown's wife, Alma, followed the video with an emotional appearance to the convention. The evening then turned to another story of pain and loss. Sarah Brady, wife of former White House press secretary James Brady, delivered a powerful message supporting gun control. She attacked the gun lobby for its opposition to the pro-gun control Brady Bill and praised Clinton for signing the bill into law. Her husband, still suffering the effects of his near-fatal wounds suffered during the Reagan assassination attempt in March 1981, also walked a few steps and spoke a few halting words. The Bradys, of course, are Republicans, making their endorsement of Clinton all the more effective. Referring to the Republican Convention two weeks earlier, Sarah Brady joked, "Jim, we must have made a wrong turn. This isn't San Diego."

As moving as the Bradys' presentation was, the night belonged to Christopher Reeve. Paralyzed from the neck down in an equestrian accident in May 1995, Reeve was forced to abandon his acting career and the roles that made him internationally famous, such as Superman. With halting speech made possible by an artificial breathing device, Reeve addressed the need for more research into neurological injury. Just as the Republicans had their American hero (Colin Powell) on opening night, the Democrats chose to feature a man whose almost apolitical message of caring was reinforced by the messenger's brave struggle against the odds.

Politics returned in force on Tuesday night, the evening for "family values" rhetoric. Keynote speaker Gov. Evan Bayh (Ind.) and First Lady Hillary Rodham Clinton—whose speech was the media highlight of the day—targeted their messages on issues that Democrats argue are family-centered—education, health care, crime-control, tax cuts, gun control, and welfare reform. Hillary Clinton's address to the convention was designed to convey a different persona than the one she acquired as her husband's chair of health care reform two years earlier. Gone was the picture of a co-president and political manager; instead, she spoke almost solely on issues concerning families and children. The goal was obviously to soften her image in the public's eye and de-emphasize the controversial aspects of her tenure as First Lady. Former Governor Mario Cuomo and Jesse Jackson were also featured (though not in prime time), and they expressed a bit of disagreement with Clinton over his signing of the Republican-sponsored welfare reform bill just prior to the convention. But their mild dissents were portrayed as a strength of the Democratic Party—the ability to tolerate diversity in opinion while maintaining unity.

Finally on Wednesday, the convention proceeded to its real business, the renomination of its presidential candidate. As with the Republicans, the official roll call of the states, in earlier times a dramatic and tense spectacle, was an anticlimactic chore sure to yield the predetermined result.

Clinton's renomination was such a foregone formality that the evening's focus became a change in convention tradition. In addition to having the vice-presidential candidate featured on the convention's last night, as had been customary, Vice President Al Gore—who had been President Clinton's virtual shadow during the entire first term and who was clearly being groomed to succeed Clinton in 2000—was also added to the Wednesday evening line-up. Gore gave an especially emotional address that ended with a soliloquy about his sister's death in 1984 from lung cancer. (Having picked up the smoking habit at age 13, she died in her mid-40s.) Citing his sister's fate, Gore pledged vigorously to fight the tobacco industry, supporting President Clinton's decision two weeks earlier to limit tobacco advertising aimed at children. "Until I draw my last breath, I will pour my heart and soul into the cause of protecting our children from the dangers of smoking," Gore pledged, his lip quivering. Usually known for his awkward stiffness at public events, Gore's animated address was a marked departure and, to many observers, a calculated attempt to change his stolid image.

However, the next day Gore was forced to explain how his remarks squared with his previous statements and actions on behalf of tobacco. In 1988, four years after his sister's death "in unbearable pain," Gore spoke to a campaign rally in North Carolina. "Throughout most of my life, I raised tobacco," he boasted. "I want you to know that with my own hands, all of my life, I put it in the plant beds and transferred it. I've hoed it. I've chopped it. I've shredded it, spiked it, put it in the barn and stripped it and sold it." He even continued to accept political contributions from tobacco companies as late as 1990. Gore gamely claimed that he had to cross an "emotional numbness" barrier after his sister's death before he could begin to change his position.[10]

Gore's tobacco hypocrisy was a minor controversy compared to the next day's feeding frenzy, though. Thursday was supposed to be centered completely around President Clinton's acceptance speech, but the speech had to share top billing with a scandal. The man most responsible for Clinton's political resurrection after the 1994 Democratic debacle, senior advisor Dick Morris, was forced to resign abruptly over convincing allegations that he had had a lengthy relationship with a high-priced prostitute, Sherry Rowlands. The *Star*, a supermarket tabloid, was preparing to run the story replete with photographs and scandalous details provided by Rowlands herself. Morris (and, more importantly, the White House) did not deny the essence of the story.

Rowlands claimed that she and Morris met for sex almost weekly at the Jefferson Hotel in Washington, D.C., while he was away from his home and wife, Eileen McGann, in Redding, Connecticut. According to Rowlands, Morris tried to impress her with advance news stories from the White House such as NASA's discovery of possible life on a Martian meteorite. Incredibly, Morris also allowed her to listen in on telephone conversations with the president himself and to read an advance copy of Hillary Rodham Clinton's convention speech. Moreover, Morris allegedly referred to President Clinton as the "Monster" because of his frequent temper tantrums, and to Hillary as the "Twister" for her propensity to stir up trouble. Ironically, the story broke the same week that Morris was featured on the cover of *Time* magazine as "the man who has Clinton's ear." Morris would grace *Time*'s cover again in four days, thereby becoming only the second person (after O. J. Simpson) to appear on the newsmagazine's cover two weeks in a row. All in all, the Morris affair was a costly and unwelcome distraction, said DNC chairman Don Fowler: "I believe that if we hadn't had the Morris thing we might have added five more points to the president's margin. It didn't last long, but it was clearly an interruption of the flow of our message."[11] As Fowler noted, though, the Democrats were almost lucky in the embarrassment's timing: "In other times the Morris story might have dominated the news for days. But the avalanche of convention news and the president's big speech helped to overwhelm it and cover it up."

Fowler's analysis is correct. Despite the titillating scandal and the press hubbub about it, President Clinton delivered a successful 66-minute oration that highlighted his generational differences with Dole. Seizing upon Dole's stated desire to be a "bridge to the past," Clinton countered, "With all due respect, we do not need to build a bridge to the past. We need to build a bridge to the future"— something that became a constant refrain for Clinton in the general election campaign. In contrast to Dole's 15 percent across-the-board tax cut, Clinton noted, "Every tax cut I call for tonight is targeted, it's responsible and it is paid for within my balanced-budget plan." Naturally, Clinton boasted with bravado and some exaggeration that his administration was responsible for the economic recovery and all manner of good things, including 10 million new jobs, 100,000 new police officers, 1.8 million fewer people on welfare, a 40 percent increase in child support collections, and the lowest combined rated of unemployment, inflation and home mortgage rates in 28 years. The president did not claim credit for Dick Morris, of course, and judging by polls, the unwelcome distraction mattered little. The Democratic Convention had masterfully launched Clinton toward a second four-year term.

Off the Script

Not everything can or does go well at even the best planned national party convention. After all, these gatherings of most of the nation's largest egos (politicians *and* press) naturally generate clashes of will and ambition. In addition to the Dick Morris incident, examples abound from both the 1996 major party conventions.

Table 1   **Breaking .500: Results After Democratic Conventions in Chicago**

Year	Candidate (D)	Election result
1864	George McClellan	Lost to Abraham Lincoln
1884	Grover Cleveland	Defeated James Blaine
1892	Grover Cleveland	Defeated Benjamin Harrison
1896	William J. Bryan	Lost to William McKinley
1932	Franklin Delano Roosevelt	Defeated Herbert Hoover
1940	Franklin Delano Roosevelt	Defeated Wendell Willkie
1944	Franklin Delano Roosevelt	Defeated Thomas E. Dewey
1952	Adlai E. Stevenson	Lost to Dwight D. Eisenhower
1956	Adlai E. Stevenson	Lost to Dwight D. Eisenhower
1968	Hubert H. Humphrey	Lost to Richard M. Nixon
1996	Bill Clinton	Defeated Bob Dole

While the Democrats featured 198 separate speakers during all their sessions combined, and the GOP about a hundred, only a handful could get prime-time, and most speakers were strictly limited on time at the podium. Some people took this news better than others. Secretary of Veterans' Affairs Jesse Brown "pitched a fit" when told he could not take a half hour at the Democratic Convention, recalled one official. (He received a five-minute slot despite his protests.) Other speakers, such as House Budget Committee Chair-

Table 2   **Delegate Demographics**

Democrats*		Republicans
4,320	total delegates	1,990
50%	male	66%
50%	female	34%
67%	white	90%
20%	black	3%
3%	Asian	1%
9%	Hispanic	3%
28%	union member	3%
18	youngest delegate	18
92	oldest delegate	93
46 years, 1 month	average age	46 years, 6 months
jobs/economy (40%)	most important issue	balanced budget (37%)

* Democratic rules require delegates to reflect the race and gender mix of the overall population. Republicans do not.

Source: Associated Press

Table 3 **Household Income of Delegates**

Annual income	Democratic delegates	Republican delegates
Under $12,000	1%	under 0.5%
$12,000–$20,000	1%	1%
$20,000–$30,000	6%	4%
$30,000–$50,000	18%	14%
$50,000–$75,000	25%	24%
$75,000–$1,000,000	38%	38%
over $1,000,000	8%	18%

man John Kasich (R-Ohio), simply ran over their allotted time even with the help of a teleprompter, as a GOP convention official recalled: "John sucked the energy right out of the audience by going seventy percent over-time. That's huge and he took a lot of grief for it."

The GOP presidential candidate's daughter, Robin, also refused to stick to the script. She wanted a prime-time appearance on Wednesday, even though she had been scheduled for pre-prime television. "At first, Robin was refusing to come on stage until the clock struck [10 p.m. EDT], and she had to be virtually dragged on early," noted an exasperated Republican convention official. Even sillier was the insistence of a singing group of four GOP U.S. Senators that they simply had to go on in a certain Wednesday time slot.[12] When told their appearance had to be delayed a day, one of the senators moaned, "Everybody was looking forward to this," while another cautioned, "Think about

---

LIST OF SPEAKERS: MONDAY, AUGUST 26

Sentiment Night

Debra DeLee (CEO, Democratic National Convention)
Don Fowler (National Chair, Democratic National Committee)
Senate Minority Leader Tom Daschle (S.D.)
House Minority Leader Richard A. Gephardt (Mo.)
Mayor Richard Daley (Chicago)
Tribute to the late Secretary of Commerce Ronald H. Brown
Mrs. Ronald H. Brown (Honorary Chair, Democratic National Convention)
Sarah Brady (Chairwoman, Handgun Control, Inc.) and ex-Reagan press secretary Jim Brady
Christopher Reeve (featured speaker)

LIST OF SPEAKERS: TUESDAY, AUGUST 27

Hillary's Night

Jesse Jackson (founder, The Rainbow Coalition)
Mario Cuomo (former governor of New York)
U.S. Sen. John D. Rockefeller (W. Va.)
Adoption of the 1996 Democratic Platform
Democratic congressional "Families First" agenda:
  U.S. House Minority Leader Richard A. Gephardt (Mo.)
  U.S. Rep. John Lewis (Ga.)
  U.S. Sen. Joseph R. Biden, Jr. (Del.)
  U.S. Rep. Lynn Nancy Rivers (Mich.)
  U.S. Sen. John F. Kerry (Mass.)
  Senate Minority Leader Thomas A. Daschle (S.D.)
Performance by Aretha Franklin
Gov. Evan Bayh (Ind.) (keynote address)
Carolyn McCarthy (candidate for the U.S. House from District 4, New York)
Victor Morales (candidate for the U.S. Senate from Texas)
Harvey Gantt (candidate for the U.S. Senate from North Carolina)
Tipper Gore (wife of Vice President Albert Gore)
Hillary Rodham Clinton (featured speaker)

how the crowd's going to react." An amused convention planner later remarked, "They actually thought people cared . . . Can you imagine?" This was not the Republicans' only problem with musical accompaniment. GOP national convention manager Paul Manafort admitted he did not pay much attention to the band being signed to play the convention hall but wished he had: "We needed an upbeat contemporary band but got one like Lawrence Welk. At least I finally got them to play 'Twist and Shout'."[13]

The most revealing backstage anecdote, though, occurred at the Democratic Convention and was a classic drawn from the playbook of "tit-for-tat" Chicago politics. The Democrats had long planned to drop a thousand pounds of mylar confetti at the conclusion of Wednesday evening's session. But suddenly on Wednesday afternoon the Chicago fire marshal objected, claiming the fireproof confetti might be a fire hazard. What had triggered this bizarre ruling? A Democratic Party official offered this informed theory: "Prior to Mayor [Richard] Daley's welcoming remarks on Monday, there were supposed to be two videos, one introducing the city of Chicago and the other the mayor. We had a technical glitch and couldn't air those videos. The mayor was pissed." Once Mayor Daley knew his message of displeasure had been received

LIST OF SPEAKERS: WEDNESDAY, AUGUST 28

Nomination Night

U.S. Sen. Frank Lautenburg (N.M.)—environment
Gov. Howard Dean (Vermont)—health care
Ellen Malcolm (Emily's List)—women's issues
John Sweeney (AFL-CIO)—labor
U.S. Sen. Kent Conrad (N.D.), Rep. Vic Fazio (Calif.)—budget and taxes
U.S. Rep. Maxine Waters (Calif.)—work
Gov. Robert J. Miller (Nev.)—crime
U.S. Sen. Joseph I. Lieberman (Conn.)—defense and security
Louis DeBerry—families
Gov. Roy Romer (Colo.)—education
Presentation by the Democratic women of the U.S. Senate
　Sen. Barbara Mikulski (Md.)
　Sen. Carol Mosely-Braun (Ill.)
　Sen. Diane Feinstein (Calif.)
　Sen. Patty Murray (Wash.)
　Sen. Barbara Boxer (Calif.)
Vice President Al Gore
U.S. Rep. Bill Richardson (N. M.)
Nomination of President Clinton
　U.S. Sen. Christopher J. Dodd (Conn.)
　Mayor Dennis Archer (Detroit)—seconding nomination
Roll call of the states

and a pound of flesh thus extracted, he (and the fire marshal) permitted the confetti to be dropped with the traditional balloons on Thursday evening after President Clinton's speech.

LIST OF SPEAKERS: THURSDAY, AUGUST 29

Clinton's Night

U.S. Sen. Edward M. Kennedy (Mass.)
Nomination of Vice President Al Gore
Vice President Al Gore
President Bill Clinton (featured speaker)

Despite these deviations from the script, both conventions were remarkably faithful to their planners' designs, and the proof is in the general praise the convention managers from opposite parties heap on their rivals. Some slight criticism was voiced, though. Republican Convention director Paul Manafort claims the GOP tracking polls showed "the Democrats' first two nights were a bust."[14] Allegedly, these sessions added nothing to Clinton's lead, in part because the convention was overshadowed by the "gimmick" of the president's train trip. Democrats dispute this assertion, of course, and insist that it was the GOP that failed to take into account a critical convention element—the delegates in the hall. Contends Democratic Convention manager Don Foley: "In contrast to the Republicans, we did some things, such as the use of the Macarena dance, to get the people in our hall excited. That is something that can be felt through the network camera lens. [The GOP] simply treated their delegates as if they were a studio audience that needed an applause sign to get excited."[15]

THE REFORM PARTY CONVENTION (AUGUST 11 AND 17)

In 1996 the Democrats and Republicans had company in the national convention spotlight. Ross Perot's Reform Party attracted a good deal of media attention, both because of his television-savvy persona and the 19 percent he secured in the 1992 presidential election.

After that failed 1992 bid, Ross Perot did not fade from public life. He continued a high public profile, appearing frequently on CNN's "Larry King Live!" and converting his grassroots political movement, United We Stand America, into the Reform Party, a full-fledged political party aiming for a place on the 1996 ballot in all fifty states. While most pundits believed that Perot's interest in the Reform Party was a vehicle for his enduring political aspirations, Perot insisted he was not interested in running for president again. Instead, Perot claimed to be seeking a credible nominee who would advance the Reform Party ticket, and he invited potential candidates to compete for the party nomination.

One person, at least, took Perot's invitation to compete for the Reform Party nomination seriously. On July 9, former Colorado Governor Richard D. Lamm, stating that "the torch must pass" from Perot to a new leader, announced that he would seek the party's nomination for president. Lamm, who served three terms as a Democratic governor in Colorado from 1975 to 1983, was the choice of many Reform Party activists in California and elsewhere who had become disillusioned with Perot's often self-absorbed leadership.[16] However, Perot remained a hero for most people in his movement; moreover, he still wanted to be president, despite occasional rhetoric to the contrary. So it came as no surprise that, less than 36 hours after Lamm's announcement of candidacy, Perot officially threw his hat into the 1996 ring.

A few weeks after his declaration that he would seek the Reform Party nomination, Lamm named former Republican congressman Edwin V. W. Zschau of California as his running mate. Perot had more difficulty than Lamm in nailing down his vice-presidential choice, since few if any establishment politicians wanted to be associated with the out-of-favor Texan. In July, he approached Democratic Congresswoman Marcy Kaptur of Ohio about being on the ticket with him. But Kaptur turned Perot down in early August in order to continue her tenure in Congress. Perot also approached retiring Democratic U.S. Senator Sam Nunn of Georgia and ex-senator David Boren of Oklahoma (currently president of the University of Oklahoma) about being his running mate, but Nunn and Boren also refused. Others who were mentioned as potential running mates included U.S. Senator Pete Domenici (R-N.M.), Lenora B. Fulani, who ran for president twice before under the banner of the leftist New Alliance Party, and Richard Toliver, an African-American former military officer who worked for Perot's Reform Committee.[17] Perot ultimately did not decide until early September, several weeks after receiving his party's nomination. Perot chose Pat Choate, a long-time economic advisor to Perot, noted for his protectionist trade positions and a best-selling book about the seedier side of U.S. trade with Japan. Choate had little name recognition and less political clout, though, and his candidacy was not considered particularly helpful to Perot's long-shot bid.

A Look at Reform Party Voters

Perot and Lamm campaigned together in two mass meetings on June 20, 1996, one held in Maine and the other in Virginia. We took the opportunity to conduct an informal straw poll of participants in the Charlottesville, Virginia meeting. The party's leadership urged participation in the study, and 148 of the approximately 200 attendees filled out a questionnaire. Not surprisingly, a large majority (96) preferred Perot as the Reform Party candidate, compared to 42 for Lamm with 10 people undecided. (These proportions were very close to the national vote totals for Perot and Lamm recorded in August.)

Just as in 1992, Reform Party supporters tended to be male (65 percent of the attendees), older (70 percent were over 45 years of age), and centrist in political philosophy (almost two-thirds described themselves as moderate, compared to a quarter as conservative and 12 percent liberal). While almost uniformly conservative on economic matters, the attendees were libertarian on social issues such as abortion (two-thirds were pro-choice).

Perot backers and Lamm supporters differed mainly by ideology and educational level. The higher the educational level, the more likely an attendee was to choose Lamm. By contrast, the more conservative the attendee, the greater the chance that Perot was his or her pick. These differences had an implication (or inference) for the Dole–Clinton match-up in the general election. As Figure 1 shows, a Lamm candidacy posed a bigger threat to Clinton, while a Perot candidacy most damaged Dole. Fully two-thirds of Lamm's supporters said that they would vote for Clinton if the Reform Party were not to have a candidate in the 1996 election. The numbers were exactly reversed for Perot supporters, with two-thirds saying that they would vote for Dole if the Reform Party did not field a candidate. Since the eventual nominee (Perot) drew disproportionately from pro-Dole conservatives, and it is likely that some Lamm supporters returned to their Democratic roots after he lost the Reform Party nomination, it seems reasonable that Perot hurt Dole more than he hurt Clinton on November 5. (The election-day exit poll cited in Chapter Six confirms this assumption.)

The Bi-Coastal Reform Party Convention

The Reform Party adopted an unusual split convention, opening in Long Beach, California and ending in Valley Forge, Pennsylvania a week later. The party members cast their ballots for the party nominee in a unique multi-mode voting process during the interim between the two meetings.

Long Beach

Both the location and the timing of the opening session in Long Beach were clearly intended to capitalize on the readily accessible media juggernaut in nearby San Diego for the Republican National Convention. Both Perot and

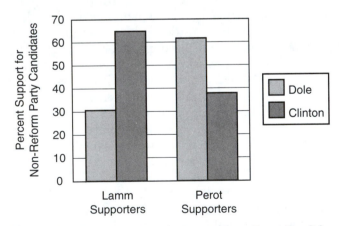

Figure 1   Percent Support for Non-Reform Party Candidates

Lamm spoke in Long Beach on August 11 (the day before the GOP conclave opened), but there was a sharp contrast between the candidates in terms of style and their reception by the audience. Lamm was much more specific in his policy recommendations, yet Perot clearly received more enthusiastic support from the crowd. As with most of his previous speeches to Reform Party audiences, Lamm argued that "the Reform Party is larger than just one individual."[18] The key themes in Lamm's speech were the need to control the growth of entitlement programs, especially Medicaid and Medicare, and pass a constitutional balanced budget amendment.[19]

Perot, the clear favorite of the attendees, spoke twice as long as Lamm. His speech was filled with the usual criticisms about the budget deficit, foreign trade, and the influence of special interests in Washington, and he declared, "I don't belong to anybody but you." Commenting on the alleged failings of the two major parties, Perot said that Americans must "demand an end to negative politics, mean-spirited name-calling, and demand that the candidates deal with the issues."

The Voting Process

Party supporters who had signed party petitions or officially registered with the party were mailed a Reform Party ballot in the mail. Attached to the ballot was a voter identification number for each member which, in theory, permitted only registered members to cast votes and ensured that each member cast only one vote. In keeping with its efforts to project a progressive, innovative approach to politics, the Reform Party allowed members to cast their votes either by mail, telephone, or e-mail. Separate companies were contracted to count the votes for each of these voting methods; MCI, the long-distance service provider, was responsible for telephone voting, American Caging Co. of Houston tabulated votes sent in by mail, and ConXion of San Jose counted votes cast via the Internet. Ernst and Young, a New York-based accounting firm, handled the overall coordination of the voting process, and thus was responsible for receiving the vote totals from each of these three firms and tabulating an overall vote total.

Unfortunately, the process did not go as smoothly as had been planned. Suspicion was aroused among Lamm supporters when the problems seemed to disadvantage Lamm more than they did Perot. For example, just days before the deadline for casting ballots, Lamm and his daughter still had not received ballots; they only secured them after the personal intervention of Perot. The Lamms were hardly alone in being left out. An official of New York's Independence Party (aligned with the Reform Party) said that as many as 30 percent of its 80,000 members did not receive their ballots. Overall, it is estimated that about 200,000 registered Reform Party members did not get a ballot which, according to party officials, was due to confusion over names and addresses. Yet, while many went without *any* ballot, some party members received *more than one* ballot and voter identification number, thus allowing them to vote more than once.

Complaints were not just confined to the voting process. There was also considerable controversy about the handling of the list of party members registered to vote in the nomination process. Initially, Reform Party officials refused to provide Lamm with access to the list. Perot noted that the member list was valued at $4 million, and giving it to Lamm might violate federal campaign spending rules. Thomas J. D'Amore, Jr., Lamm's senior adviser, also accused Perot of improperly utilizing both the list and official Reform Party literature. Specifically, D'Amore pointed to a postcard bearing Perot's picture that was mailed by the supposedly neutral Reform Committee to all 1.1 million party members. While the postcard merely encouraged members to vote in the nomination process, the presence of Perot's picture along with a greeting entitled, "A Message from Ross Perot," was clearly prejudicial. D'Amore asserted that both candidates had agreed not to send mail to party members, and that official correspondence from the party should not have had only Perot's picture on it. Perot's spokeswoman Sharon Holman claimed that there was no agreement between the candidates not to mail literature to the party members.[20]

Valley Forge

After a week of voting, Perot was pronounced the winner of the Reform Party's nomination at the opening of the second half of the convention in Valley Forge on Saturday, August 17. Perot beat Lamm by nearly a two-to-one margin, 32,145 votes (65.2 percent) to Lamm's 17,121 votes (34.8 percent); however, only five percent of the 1.1 million people who made the effort to sign a petition or register with the party actually cast ballots. It was unclear the extent to which the extremely low turnout was attributable to the problem-plagued voting process or to voter apathy about the party and the candidates. Lamm, speaking briefly before Perot delivered his acceptance speech, congratulated Perot on his victory, and stressed again the vital need for a third party in American politics. However, he pointedly did not endorse Perot.

Immediately following the Valley Forge session, Perot appeared on CNN's "Larry King Live!" and announced that he would accept federal campaign funds rather than bankroll his campaign himself. By taking the $29.2 million in federal funds to which he was entitled,[21] Perot was forced to limit his personal contributions to his general election campaign to a maximum of $50,000. In 1992 Perot spent about $60 million of his own money on his presidential effort.

The Reform Party did not leave its convention the picture of unity. Both Lamm and his running mate, Ed Zschau, had harsh words about the nomination process. "I'm not making any accusations," Lamm said, "but there were enough questions [about the results] that I don't want to endorse [Perot] at this time." As for Zschau, he admitted he could not say that Ross Perot was the candidate "best qualified to serve the nation as president of the United States."

PRESS COVERAGE OF THE CONVENTIONS

The American news media do not appreciate being used as a mere conduit for public relations, but at the same time they can perversely admire skillful manipulation. In a nutshell, this was the press's contradictory reaction to the 1996 Republican and Democratic Conventions. The networks and the major newspapers made certain their viewers and readers understood the parties were conducting made-for-Hollywood productions, even as they covered those productions and thereby helped the parties achieve their public relations goals. (ABC's "Nightline" was an exception. Citing a news-less convention, Ted Koppel and company announced mid-week in San Diego they were leaving town to return to Washington, and the show never moved to Chicago at all.)

The television coverage was severely limited in 1996, compared to the gavel-to-gavel coverage that was standard network practice from the 1950s to the 1980s. C-SPAN and CNN had nearly continuous coverage, but ABC, CBS, and NBC restricted their prime-time interruption of regular programming to one hour per night (usually 10–11 p.m. EDT). The featured speaker each evening was carried uninterrupted; of course, analysis and commentary preceded and followed every speaker.

The network evening news programs were harsh in their judgments about both conventions, as the Center for Media and Public Affairs has documented.[22] About six of every ten statements made concerning the nominees and their parties were negative, and fully 93 percent of the comments about how the conventions were run were negative. As usual, the horserace (Dole versus Clinton) received twice as much attention as the issues (140 horserace stories compared to 83 on policy), and the celebrity television anchors and journalists soaked up *twelve times* as much air-time as the convention newsmakers. Unsurprisingly, the convention managers in both parties were somewhat unhappy with the media, especially television. Republican Paul Manafort bluntly stated, "The networks did a very poor job."[23] Citing the withdrawal of "Nightline" as a prime example, Manafort continued, "They don't want to cover information and issues, just controversy." This view, prevalent within the GOP, is one reason why RNC Chairman Barbour arranged a $1.3 million private donation to cable's Pat Robertson-owned Family Channel to air the evening sessions, with the Republican Party's own commentators. This was the first time any party had televised its convention, and it will surely not be the last.

Given the news media's widely perceived tilt to the Democratic Party, Republican officials are particularly tough in describing the press's role at their convention. Haley Barbour is openly contemptuous because of what he sees as journalists' fixation on the abortion issue:

> The reporters in San Diego chased down any Republican who could spell the word abortion to try to see if they could stir up a fight, and when they couldn't, they got pissed off and went home. The press just wanted the convention to be about abortion. They chased the abortion thing hither, thither, and yon, and generally failed, but it wasn't for lack of trying.

What about the Reform Party? Ross Perot's convention was featured in only ten network evening stories, for a total of just 18 minutes. And 70 percent of the on-air comments were critical.

By the conclusion of all the party conventions, the three top commercial networks were already hinting that they would probably further cut back their convention coverage in the year 2000. Party leaders recognize as much; said one, "I understand that unless we have a mud wrestling fight, they will not be very interested in covering it." As a consequence, both Democrats and Republicans are willing to consider three-day conventions in 2000, possibly structured around a weekend. Naturally, much will depend upon the degree of competition remaining in the parties' presidential contests by convention time. If the primary season has left either nomination unsettled and therefore more newsworthy, the networks might be willing to cover a longer convention.

The possible cutback in network coverage in 2000 is regrettable but also dictated by declining audiences for the conventions. In 1996, both major-party conventions were watched by substantially fewer citizens than in 1992. On the three largest networks combined, about 23 million Americans tuned in each evening for the 1992 Democratic and Republican conventions; four years later, only about 17 million did so, on average.[24]

ON TO THE FALL CAMPAIGN

With the three conventions over, the official general election campaign began in earnest. There were the usual roller-coaster polls during the major-party conclaves, with Dole gaining during the GOP convention and Clinton during his. But as the convention bounces faded, it was abundantly clear that the incumbent was a strong favorite for re-election. Bob Dole and Ross Perot had to run a difficult race of catch-up, and as Paul Hernnson and Clyde Wilcox explain in the next chapter, Dole and Perot were unable even to run in place.

NOTES

1. For example, the Democratic host committee (called Chicago '96) was a 501(c)(3) group under contract with the DNC to raise $27 million, $21.6 million in cash and the rest in in-kind services.

2. Interview with Debra DeLee, October 3, 1996.

3. Interview with Bill Greener, October 3, 1996.

4. Interview with Haley Barbour, September 24, 1996.

5. The 1972 and 1984 Republican conventions, which renominated Presidents Nixon and Reagan respectively, were precedents for 1996, however.

6. Interview with Jack Kemp, August 2, 1996.

7. Greener interview.

8. Interview with Donald Fowler, September 24, 1996.

9. Interview with Donald Foley, September 23, 1996.

10. David S. Broder and Dan Balz, "Gore Had to Cross 'Numbness' Barrier to Change Stand," *The Washington Post*, August 30, 1996, A33.

11. Fowler interview.

12. The senators, whose favorite musical number is an off-key rendition of "Elvira," are Majority Leader Trent Lott of Mississippi, Larry Craig of Idaho, John Ashcroft of Missouri, and Jim Jeffords of Vermont. Of the four, Lott was the most cooperative and readily agreed to the rescheduling.

13. Interview with Paul Manafort, September 27, 1996.

14. Manafort interview.

15. Foley interview.

16. See Donald P. Baker and David S. Broder, "Perot Basks in Reform Party's Affirmation," *Washington Post*, August 12, 1996, A20.

17. See Donald P. Baker, "Reform Party's Unique Multi-Mode Vote Has Old Fashioned Result: Delay," *Washington Post*, August 18, 1996, A24.

18. AllPolitics. "Perot and Lamm Compete For Reform Party Support." August 11, 1996. <http://www.allpolitics.com> (September 13, 1996).

19. Donald P. Baker and David S. Broder, "Perot Basks in Reform Party's Affirmation," *Washington Post*, August 12, 1996, A20.

20. See Donald P. Baker, "This Time, 'Ross the Boss' Has Focused More on Party Than Candidacy," *Washington Post*, August 10, 1996, A10.

21. Based on his 19 percent share of the vote in November 1992, Perot received close to half the amount allotted to Bill Clinton and Bob Dole.

22. Center for Media and Public Affairs and the Markle Presidential Election Watch, "Networks Tune Out Both Parties" (Washington, D.C.: September 12, 1996), 2 pp.

23. Manafort interview.

24. See *Hotline* 9 (September 3, 1996): 14–15. More of the viewers may be turning to C-SPAN, CNN, and other cable channels, but it is doubtful that an additional six million abandoned the networks with the passage of only four years.

CHAPTER 5

The 1996 Presidential Election

A Tale of a Campaign
That Didn't Seem to Matter

Paul S. Herrnson

University of Maryland

Clyde Wilcox

*Georgetown University**

When Senate Majority Leader Robert Dole clinched the GOP presidential nomination in March, he trailed President Bill Clinton by roughly 15 percentage points. When the 1996 presidential campaign officially began on Labor Day, Dole continued to trail Clinton by about 15 points. During the campaign, the candidates engaged in two debates, their vice presidential running mates debated once, and all four contestants criss-crossed the country in a frenetic campaign schedule. The campaigns also aired hundreds of radio and television advertisements, convened dozens of focus groups, conducted nightly polls of prospective voters, and spent approximately $124 million in federal funds on their elections. In addition, the Democratic and Republican national committees spent hundreds of millions of dollars in connection with presidential, as well as some nonpresidential, elections. Yet, the day before the election the polls still showed Clinton holding the same 15-point lead he had held throughout most of the election. Although Clinton's final victory margin was somewhat smaller, the end results suggest that few votes were moved by the campaigns, and the campaigns were not decisive in determining the election outcome.

*We wish to thank Mary Bendyna, Mary Flanagan, and Wesley Joe for their research assistance on this chapter.

Journalists covered the internal mechanisms of the campaigns—the hiring and firing of various media teams by the Dole camp, the debates in the Clinton campaign over how to reach out beyond the traditional Democratic base without alienating minorities, workers, and other core constituencies—while prominent party members and pundits publicly advised Dole and Clinton on how to boost their standings. The Dole camp spent roughly $40 million on media buys, and as the campaign neared its end in late October, it could not point to a single state where the ads had helped narrow the lead.[1] Public sentiment remained remarkably stable throughout the campaign. On election day, Clinton won by 8 percent of the popular vote, becoming the first Democrat to get elected to a second term in the White House since Franklin Roosevelt.

The 1996 presidential campaign made little impact on voters, many of whom professed disinterest in the whole affair. The television audience share for the presidential and vice presidential debates was smaller than at any time in history. By the end of the Republican Convention most voters had made up their minds, and no amount of advertising, issue posturing, or debating points could change it. In 1996, the presidential campaign mostly didn't matter.

It is not uncommon for a presidential campaign to move few voters. In only two campaigns in the last 40 years has a candidate come from behind on Labor Day to win an election. In 1960 John Kennedy narrowly defeated Richard Nixon, after trailing at various times during the race, and in 1980 Ronald Reagan benefited from a last-minute surge that lifted him past Jimmy Carter and into the presidency. In a few other elections, notably 1968, 1976, and 1992, the losing candidate managed to narrow the margin during the campaign, but was unable to pull ahead.[2] Five times in the last ten elections—in 1956, 1964, 1972, 1984, and 1988—the winning candidate's percentage was similar to the support for that candidate in the first poll in early September when the campaign officially began.

This chapter examines the 1996 presidential campaign. We begin with a discussion of whether and when presidential campaigns matter, provide an analysis of the context of the 1996 election, and review the events that occurred before the campaign's official beginning on Labor Day that helped assure Clinton's victory. We then examine the strategic positions and the decisions of the two candidates, including the issues they chose to stress, their advertisements, and the geographical basis of their campaigns. We next turn to the two presidential and one vice presidential debates, the campaigns' closing messages, and then conclude with some thoughts about why the 1996 campaign did not matter.

DO CAMPAIGNS MATTER?

Campaign consultants, political actors, and journalists generally assume that presidential campaigns matter. When consultants attempt to explain who won or lost elections, they often point to strategic choices, good or bad performance in debates, and the quality of advertisements. This is not surprising, for candidates pay consultants large sums to help them win elections.[3]

Politicians also frequently point to campaigns as the source of election outcomes. Many prominent Democrats blamed Michael Dukakis for running a poor campaign in 1988 in a race they believed he could have won. During the 1996 campaign, Republicans argued at various times that Dole could win if he would attack Clinton, refrain from attacking Clinton, emphasize economic issues, emphasize social issues, or emphasize character issues, giving him little clear direction. Finally, journalists often argue that campaigns hinge on certain key events: Ford's denial of Soviet domination of Eastern Europe in the 1976 presidential debate, Reagan's light-hearted retort to the age question in his debate with Mondale in 1984, or Dukakis' wooden response to a question in 1988 about the death penalty for someone who (hypothetically) raped and murdered his wife.[4]

Yet many political scientists believe that long-term forces, especially the performance of the economy, usually determine election outcomes and that the vast energies and funds that are poured into campaigns seldom change many vote intentions. They note that most voters make up their minds by the end of the conventions, and that many of those who decide during the campaign are influenced by their partisanship or by ongoing economic news.[5] Although campaign events may move opinion for a short time, the effects of these events generally decay rapidly, returning to the equilibrium position. As Steven Rosenstone writes of the 1984 election, "the important determinants of the 1984 presidential election were in place long before most people heard of Geraldine Ferraro, long before the candidates squared off in front of the television cameras, and long before Americans met the bear in the woods (if there was a bear)."[6]

A number of political scientists have developed models that forecast presidential election outcomes based on long-term forces such as the economy, and some short-term forces such as approval of the incumbent president in early summer.[7] These models do not include any terms to measure the effects of presidential debates, advertisements, issues, or attacks. They do not specify which candidate is running (although most do include a variable to identify whether there is an incumbent seeking re-election). Instead, the models generally posit that economic factors are very important determinants of electoral outcomes, that incumbents have important advantages, and that public preferences in late summer are generally a good guide to electoral outcomes.

Many of these models are remarkably accurate. For example, several models during the summer of 1988 indicated that whichever candidate won the Republican nomination should beat the Democratic candidate by roughly 54 percent to 46 percent. These estimates were made when Dukakis held a double-digit lead, before Bush's strong convention speech boosted him to the front of the polls, before the Willie Horton advertisement helped narrow the gender gap, and before Dukakis' weak performance in the second presidential debate.[8] The prediction almost precisely matched the final margin, nonetheless.

In a comprehensive investigation of campaign effects, Thomas Holbrook comes to a somewhat more nuanced conclusion. He argues that "In years where national conditions overwhelmingly favor one candidate or another, it is unlikely, barring the total collapse of one side of the campaign, that campaigns can provide enough swing to alter the expected outcome. However, in years when the expected outcome is not so lopsided, campaigns may have enough influence to play a critical role in determining the outcome."[9] The 1996 campaign clearly falls into the former category, in which national conditions overwhelmingly favored the Democrats.

The Context

Clinton began his presidency without much of a mandate. Although he had received 370 Electoral College votes, Bush and Perot combined to win enough votes to deprive him of a popular majority, leaving him with just 43 percent of the popular vote. After the Republican landslide victories of 1994, many journalists and political pundits declared the end of the Clinton administration. The Republican Party had not held a majority in the House since 1952 or in the Senate since 1986, and Clinton's low approval ratings were widely blamed for the Democrats' defeat.

Journalists wrote that Clinton had wasted his precious first months battling over gays in the military, had mismanaged the health care issue by proposing a complex plan that involved too much government bureaucracy, and failed to deliver on his campaign promise of a middle class tax cut. The Whitewater, Paula Jones, and other alleged ethical transgressions—some real, some perceived—by the president, Cabinet appointees and officials, and members of the White House staff contributed to a growing disenchantment with Clinton and his administration. The president's low job approval ratings were credited with bringing about the first Republican majority in the House in a generation. Republicans talked publicly about what they would do when they defeated Clinton in 1996 and controlled both elected branches of government.

By July 1996, however, Clinton's job approval rating stood at 57 percent. One reason for the resurgence of Clinton's popularity was the state of the economy. Unemployment was at a seven-year low, inflation was at its lowest level in three decades, and interest rates remained low. The budget deficit had declined from roughly $290 billion in 1992 to roughly $109 billion in 1996. Moreover, the economy was creating jobs at a steady and rapid rate. Growth in the second quarter of 1996 was 4.8 percent, more than three times what it had been during the second quarter of 1992. Presidential job approval generally tracks quite closely with economic performance, and good economic news raises people's evaluation of the president.[10]

Although the public was generally upbeat about the economy, the electorate was not uniformly content. Indeed, a substantial number of voters told pollsters that things were off on the wrong track, and a majority in an August 1996 Gallup Poll indicated that they were dissatisfied with the way things were going in America.[11] Large majorities told pollsters that there was something wrong in America, and a majority attributed this problem to a moral decline.[12]

Moreover, the economic recovery provided significant income gains for those with high levels of education, but those whose formal education had ended at high school or before remained at the same stagnant income levels that they had experienced for the previous decade.[13] There remained a reservoir of anger in many sectors of the electorate. The Republicans had successfully tapped it in 1994, and Dole hoped to mobilize it again in 1996.

Overall, however, national conditions were quite favorable to Clinton. Most of the major political science forecasting models, using economic indicators and measures of public support during the summer, predicted an easy Clinton victory with between 53 percent and 57 percent of the two-party vote.[14] Although some Americans were unconvinced of the economic recovery, in August the Consumer Confidence Index was higher than even during the Reagan recovery in 1984, and by two-to-one Americans said they were better off in 1996 than in 1992.[15] More than half of the public polled by Gallup at the start of the campaign believed that the national economy was getting better.[16]

A second reason for Clinton's renaissance was his careful and concerted effort to position himself as a moderate who shared the basic values of Americans. Clinton reportedly read and was impressed with Ben Wattenberg's book *Values Matter Most.* Wattenberg argued that Democrats had in recent years found themselves on the wrong side of several issues involving core values of the American electorate—crime, school discipline, welfare, and affirmative action. Following the advice of Dick Morris and other White House advisers, Clinton adopted a "triangulation" strategy. By positioning himself in the center, between liberal Democrats and conservative Republicans in Congress, the president sought to portray himself as a moderate who would protect the American people from the excesses of each.

Between 1994 and 1996, Clinton focused on crime, touting the ban on assault weapons and the Brady Bill, pushing for funding for additional police officers on the beat, and supporting the expanded use of the death penalty in federal statutes. He made a public call for school uniforms, for the "V-chip" (which would curb children's viewing of violent television programs), and for greater school discipline. He advocated welfare reform, eventually signing during the campaign a bill that eliminated the social safety net of Aid to Families with Dependent Children and Medicaid, allowing states to determine eligibility and program benefits. He proposed a reassessment of affirmative action, although ultimately he made few changes in federal government programs in this area.

By moving aggressively to the center-right on symbolic and policy issues that related to these core values, Clinton left the Republicans little room to paint him as a cultural liberal and deprived his opponent of the opportunity to run as the champion of social conservatives. Before the campaign began he was well positioned in the center of the political spectrum. Indeed, one cartoon in the month before the GOP convention showed Clinton as the featured speaker at the Republican Convention, with an observer noting that Clinton articulated Republican values better than any Republican candidate. Clinton was endorsed later in the campaign by the largest police union in the country, and a *New York Times* poll in early September showed that the public thought Clinton was better able to deal with crime than Dole.

A third reason for Clinton's recovery was his skillful use of the advantages of incumbency. Chief executives can use their position to make decisions that attract tremendous amounts of media coverage.[17] Clinton traveled to California throughout the four years of his presidency, and took special care to announce programs and policies that would benefit the state. He had the Food and Drug Administration issue immensely popular, tough new regulations on tobacco sales to minors, directed that additional funds be spent researching women's health issues, created a national monument out of 1.7 million acres of federal lands in Utah, and sent federal relief to North Carolina, California, and other parts of the nation when they were wracked by disasters. Just as he had used the "bully pulpit" of the presidency to redefine his public image, Clinton used the powers of the presidency to build support among women, environmentalists, and other targeted constituencies. Both approaches demonstrate how a president can dominate and sometimes create news.

A fourth factor in Clinton's recovery was the performance of the Republican Congress. Although polls initially showed that the public was pleased with the flurry of activity that took place in the Republican-controlled House and that GOP House Speaker Newt Gingrich was popular, voters soured on the new GOP Congress within a few months and Gingrich became one of the most unpopular figures in America. As Republicans moved aggressively to reduce spending, cut taxes on businesses and wealthy citizens, limit environmental protection, and reduce the level of services distributed to Medicare recipients, Americans increasingly came to view the new Republican Party as threatening and radical. Gingrich himself was badly embarrassed after he complained petulantly that Clinton had ignored him during a flight on Air Force One, when the White House released a picture showing Gingrich chatting amiably with the president around a big table on the jet.

The new GOP majority allowed Clinton to position himself as in favor of policies like deficit reduction and welfare reform, but as the voice of reason on issues like spending on education, environmental protection, and Medicare. When an enduring budget dispute led to two shutdowns of the federal government, polls showed that voters blamed the Republican Congress far more than President Clinton. The federal shutdowns demonstrated the utility of Clinton's triangulation strategy, as the president's approval ratings began to improve.

The fifth factor that aided Clinton's standing in the polls was an uneasy accommodation he reached with congressional Republicans late in the 104th Congress. Throughout the early days of the first session, GOP legislators, especially in the House, sought to ram their bills through Congress and force the president to sign his name to policies he opposed or risk being blamed for Washington gridlock. Clinton showed a willingness to sign some Republican bills, but resisted on many others, including the GOP's budget and several appropriations bills. Toward the end of the 104th Congress, both Clinton and Republican legislators recognized that they would need to work together in order to avoid being blamed for political stalemate. The GOP-controlled Congress backed off on controversial spending reductions in Medicare, education, and other areas that Clinton had threatened to veto, and passed the president's minimum wage bill. Clinton acquiesced on several Republican proposals, including the signing of a historic welfare reform measure that eliminated the national social safety net for the poor. This "conspiracy of incumbents" deprived Democratic challengers of their ability to tag their opponents as members of "an extremist do-nothing Congress," and it deprived Dole of the chance to characterize Clinton as willing to let his liberal views stand in the way of progress.

In contrast to Clinton, who was able to capitalize on his incumbency, Dole found himself hamstrung in his position as Senate majority leader. Because he held this position, Dole was identified, perhaps somewhat unfairly, with the House-led government shutdowns and the far-reaching conservative legislation that emanated from the lower chamber. He was unable to oppose openly elements of the GOP's "Contract with America" without offending Republican conservatives, but could not fully embrace the Contract without risking alienating GOP moderates and independents. His inability to deliver Senate support for policies that were at the center of his platform made him appear ineffective to party hard-liners. Dole's treasured position as majority leader of the Senate hung like an albatross around his neck.

THE EARLY DAYS

Although presidential campaigns traditionally kick off on Labor Day, Clinton ran unopposed for the Democratic nomination and was able to campaign for the entirety of 1996. This gave him a tremendous advantage over Bob Dole, who like most nomination candidates, was bloodied while fighting off other contestants for the nomination. Dole wrapped up the GOP nomination by March and was the obvious front-runner even earlier. Yet because of campaign finance law, Clinton had a clear advantage after the mist had cleared and the two candidates had been determined.

The Federal Election Commission provides matching funds for all candidates for the major party nominations, including incumbents running unopposed for re-election. Candidates who accept these funds are limited in their total spending during the primary election campaign, which officially ends the day they are nominated. Dole spent all of his available funds seeking the GOP nomination, and was thus prevented from spending money on his general election campaign during the summer.

Taking advantage of some creative accounting rules, the nomination campaign managed to scare up some funds by selling—for cash in advance—office and computer equipment to the general election campaign. Dole was also able to travel across the country to Republican Party fundraising events, where he made speeches and attracted free media. Some of the money he raised at these events poured into the same soft money accounts that the Republican National Committee used to televise "issue advocacy" advertisements that publicized Dole's policy positions and personal attributes without directly advocating his election or Clinton's defeat.[18] Nevertheless, Dole's lack of campaign funds greatly limited his advertising.

In contrast, Bill Clinton was able to spend his entire primary election budget attacking not Democratic opponents but rather the Republicans, and eventually Bob Dole. Clinton ran a number of unanswered negative advertisements during the summer in key states, and was able to build a commanding lead over Dole during this period. In August Clinton spent nearly $4 million on television advertising before the Democratic Convention. He took every opportunity to link Dole with Newt Gingrich and the unpopular Republican Congress, leading Dole to eventually resign from the Senate in an effort to refocus the campaign. Yet Dole could not pay for the advertising he needed to answer Clinton's attacks, and his campaign got no real boost from his new status as full-time candidate. The 1996 election was only the second since the implementation of the matching fund system in which an incumbent president had faced no opposition for his party's nomination, and under these circumstances the incumbent has a substantial advantage.[19] Over the summer Clinton's job approval numbers crept up, and more importantly his negative evaluations dropped sharply, from 42 percent in mid June to 31 percent in September.[20]

Clinton's early spending defined the race, inoculated the incumbent against many attacks, and increased negative evaluations of Dole. This made it very difficult for Dole to find a sympathetic ear once the campaign had begun. One Dole official complained, "There's a point where your advertising becomes ineffective because the impression is so well set. They defined the race, they defined the issues that would decide the race, and they defined Bob Dole."[21]

Clinton's early ads sought to portray the Republicans as radicals who wanted to cut Social Security and Medicare, force children into poverty, cut Head Start and anti-drug programs, and allow toxic pollution. He repeatedly linked Dole, then majority leader of the Senate, with House Speaker Newt Gingrich, who remained unpopular. When Dole announced his tax cut package, Clinton attacked quickly with advertisements that labeled the plan "risky," charging that it would undermine the economic recovery.

Dole was forced to spend much of the summer healing an intra-party split between Christian conservatives and party moderates. The divisions between these two factions was quite intense in many states and threatened to split the party.[22] Prominent leaders of the Christian Right threatened to bolt the party if Dole chose a pro-choice nominee, while the GOP's social moderates indicated that they might withdraw support from the ticket if Dole chose a strong social conservative. The tension boiled over during a debate over language for the party platform on abortion; moderates were willing to accept the call for a constitutional amendment to ban abortion if the plank called for tolerance of those with opposing views, but Christian conservatives were unwilling to acquiesce to their request. Dole backed the moderates and said that the plank would include tolerance language, but Christian conservative control of the platform committee was sufficiently strong to block Dole's preference. Ultimately, the platform contained an appendix of defeated proposals, including the tolerance language.

Dole chose to side with the moderates at the convention, which featured a series of pro-choice speakers and was chaired by one pro-life and one pro-choice Republican. Although the word "tolerance" did not appear in the platform, it was spoken frequently from the podium, and indeed seemed to be the unofficial slogan of the convention. Dole announced that he had not read the platform, and in his acceptance speech invited those who could not be tolerant of legal immigrants (and by inference of those who took different views on other issues) to leave the convention. Christian conservatives were unhappy with the tone of the convention, but many acknowledged that the 1992 convention had frightened many social moderates. Clearly, the Dole campaign wanted no repeat of the "culture war" speech by Patrick Buchanan in 1992.

The choice of Jack Kemp as running mate helped to heal the rift in the party, at least temporarily. Kemp was popular among social conservatives and had been the strong second choice of Robertson's supporters in 1988.[23] Yet Kemp also appealed to moderates, for he had opposed efforts to limit benefits to immigrants, favored maintaining at least some affirmative action programs, and spoke constantly of the need to build an inclusive party. The Republicans left the convention united, at least for a time.

Ross Perot had considerable support in the early summer months, polling 17 percent in two polls in late June. Yet Perot's support faded throughout the summer for several reasons. First, in 1996 Perot lacked the novelty factor that he had in 1992, and his defeat in that previous election had convinced many of his past supporters that he could not win. In July 1992, nearly half of the public thought Perot was a viable candidate, but in July 1996, only 7 percent believed that he could win.

Second, Perot's actions in the summer alienated many Americans, including some of his past supporters. He accepted public funds for his presidential bid, something he had proudly denounced in 1992. The nature of the Reform Party's nomination—which was designed to be more of a coronation than a contested election—caused both the party and Perot to lose support among some voters.[24] The party mailed literature to voters who were eligible to participate in its nominating contest that included a picture of Perot but not his opponent, former Colorado Governor Richard Lamm. The party also refused to give Lamm a list of voters so that he could make his case using direct mail. Party leaders' refusal to insist that Perot debate Lamm prior to its convention also did little to boost either the party's or Perot's standing with the public, and made the nomination contest appear to be "fixed" in favor of Perot. Balloting irregularities resulted in many Reform Party members, including Lamm, failing to receive ballots. Public reaction was predictable. An ABC News/*Washington Post* poll taken in early September indicated that 79 percent of the public thought Perot lacked the personality and temperament to be president.[25] The nature of the Reform Party's nominating contest probably contributed to the public's assessment.

THE STRATEGIC CALCULUS

As the two camps looked forward to the start of the campaign, it was clear that Dole faced some daunting odds. A spate of positive economic news in August made his quest seem even more quixotic. Dole trailed by 15 to 20 points in most nationwide polls, and the Electoral College map did not look promising. At the start of the campaign, polls showed Dole comfortably ahead in only three states totaling 18 electoral votes, and slightly ahead in ten states that totaled only 95 electoral votes. Dole was not even solidly ahead in Kansas, his home state. Clinton had a commanding lead in states that totaled 298 electoral votes, and held a narrow lead in Florida, Arizona, Georgia, and Virginia, states that a competitive Republican campaign must be able to count on so that it can concentrate on "battleground" states. Dole trailed badly in many populous states that were key to any winning electoral strategy—California, Michigan, Ohio, New Jersey, Pennsylvania—and was behind in much of the South.[26]

This meant that Dole was forced to try first to solidify his base and spend time addressing groups of voters in states where he needed to be secure. In early September, Dole spent an afternoon speaking to a VFW Post in Nevada, clear evidence of his poor standing in the polls. Indeed, Dole's troubles were national, not geographic, and the only way to pull ahead in key states was to close the national gap in the polls.

But Dole was not well positioned to play catch-up, for several reasons. First, the easiest way to narrow a sizable gap in voter preferences is to run a negative campaign, attacking the personal or public performance of the opponent. Yet Dole was singularly limited in his ability to use this tactic because his previous campaigns had left him with a reputation as a mean-spirited campaigner. In his vice presidential debate with Walter Mondale in 1976, Dole had complained about the large numbers of Americans who had died in "Democrat wars" such as World War II. After he narrowly lost the New Hampshire primary to George Bush in 1988, he lashed out on television that he wanted to tell Bush to "stop lying about [my] record."[27] Focus groups showed that Dole would lose more support than he would gain by "going negative," a source of much frustration for the campaign because Clinton appeared vulnerable to a focused attack on his character.

Often, it falls on the shoulders of the vice presidential nominee to play the part of "pit bull" in a presidential campaign. Dole had played this role for Ford, attacking the Democratic nominee in the 1976 election. Jack Kemp, however, was unwilling to step into the pit bull role. As a congressman and one-time presidential candidate, Kemp had built a reputation as a genial, issue-oriented politician who reached out to diverse constituencies. His selection as the Republicans' vice presidential nominee had resuscitated what had appeared to be an expired political career. Now that he was back in the limelight, with his presidential aspirations rekindled, Kemp was wont to sully his largely positive image.

Dole's greatest liability was himself. Focus groups and surveys revealed that many voters, especially younger women, viewed him as too old, at age 73, to serve as president. Dole would have been the oldest president to be elected to a first term. Although Reagan had successfully defused the age issue with a joke in 1984, his inattentiveness to the details of policy during his second term and his advanced Alzheimer's disease in 1996 left many voters nervous about electing another individual who was old enough to be the grandfather of a substantial portion of the electorate.

Moreover, Dole was not a good candidate; indeed he was one of the weakest major-party candidates in the modern era. He was often inarticulate on the campaign trail and frequently used cryptic "inside-the-Beltway" language to refer to complex issues of which the public had little awareness. He also departed from his prepared speeches on numerous occasions and made off-the-cuff remarks that he was later forced to defend. Early in the campaign, Dole told an audience in tobacco country that tobacco was not addictive, and then spent a week answering reporters' questions about this claim. At one point, in response to a reporter's question, Dole maintained that the idea that tobacco was harmful was just a theory, and that "some people would say that milk is bad for you." He continued to mishandle the issue for several days, including on the "Today Show" when he attacked network correspondent Katie Couric. Clearly, the Dole camp did not plan to devote a week to defending tobacco, but their candidate's offhand remark cost them time and popular support.

Dole's task was greatly complicated by the fact that few voters were interested in the campaign, and most had made up their minds. A *New York Times* survey in early September revealed that only 8 percent of registered voters had not decided for whom they would vote, and that only 34 percent were paying a lot of attention to the campaign. In 1988, these same figures had been 14 percent and 50 percent, respectively.[28]

Dole decided to try to get the public's attention and unify his party with a proposal for a 15 percent across-the-board income tax cut, along with cuts in capital gains and other taxes. Although the proposal did serve to motivate many Republican activists, it struck most observers as a repudiation of Dole's long history as a deficit hawk. Indeed, the tax cut proposal and the selection of Kemp as running mate appeared to many to be a cynical election-year move from a man who had fought supply-side economics for the past 16 years.

Clinton's strategic considerations were considerably more rosy. With a comfortable lead in states with enough electoral votes to give him victory, he could run a low-risk campaign and coast to victory. Yet there were a number of reasons for Clinton to be nervous. First, a majority of Americans thought that he lacked many of the basic character traits that they wanted in a president. In one ABC News/*Washington Post* poll taken at the beginning of the campaign, voters rejected statements that Clinton was honest and trustworthy (52 percent to 43 percent) and that he had high personal moral and ethical standards (56 percent to 39 percent).[29] The great uncertainty about when the Whitewater prosecutor might move added to the nervousness of the Clinton camp. One of Clinton's former Whitewater investment partners, James McDougal, agreed to cooperate with Independent Counsel Kenneth Starr, but his former wife Susan McDougal refused to cooperate and went to jail for contempt, leading to speculation that she was waiting for a pardon from Clinton in his second term. Moreover, many speculated that Starr might indict Hillary Clinton on charges of obstruction of justice.

Other scandals simmered on the horizon. In June 1996, it was revealed that the Clinton White House had improperly received the FBI files of a number of Republicans who had served in the Reagan and Bush administrations. Although the Clinton administration maintained that its possession of the files was merely a bureaucratic snafu, the matter was turned over to Starr for further investigation. The sexual harassment charges filed by Paula Jones were also still in force, and Clinton had appealed to the Supreme Court to rule that he need not stand trial until after the end of his second term. Overall, it was clear that Clinton was vulnerable to attacks on character.

Yet Clinton continued to lead by a wide margin, leaving him with several options. He could run a safe campaign, appearing presidential and emphasizing only those issues on which his position was popular, and try to win by the largest possible popular or Electoral College margin, thereby earning a "popular mandate." Second, he could actively campaign for a "policy mandate" by staking out positions on key issues that he would pursue in his second term, making it easier for him to effectively push the legislation through Congress. Third, he could seek a "congressional mandate," devoting his resources to helping elect Democrats to the House and Senate in an effort to regain a majority in both chambers. Finally, he could seek an "extended mandate" by campaigning for Democrats everywhere, including governors and state legislators. All but the first choice would demand that Clinton sacrifice some of his double-digit lead to promote policies or candidates. After a number of high-level discussions, the Clinton camp decided late in the election to risk some of their candidate's lead in order to help Democrats recapture the House and Senate.

CAMPAIGN THEMES

The theme for the Dole campaign was "A Better Man for a Better America," suggesting that the campaign had initially decided to contrast Dole's and

Clinton's character. Yet Dole launched the campaign with a strong focus on his proposed tax cuts and publicly spent little time attacking Clinton. Kemp stated in the vice presidential debate that neither he nor Dole would run a negative campaign, but would instead wage a campaign of ideas. Although Dole ran negative television advertisements during the early weeks of September, his personal attacks on the president were muted.

Throughout September and the first weeks of October, the central message of the campaign was tax relief. So focused was Dole on the economic message that Pat Robertson sent a plea through Jack Kemp to remember the social issues that would move Christian conservatives. Dole ignored Robertson's request.

Clinton's campaign theme was "A Bridge to the 21st Century," a motto that subtly emphasized the difference in the age of the candidates and cast Clinton as a man of many ideas for the future. Clinton's early strategy was to highlight the positive things that government could do to affect people's lives, especially the Family and Medical Leave Act and the ban on assault weapons, both of which Dole had opposed. Clinton made a number of carefully targeted proposals to improve schools, extend family leave provisions, protect the environment, and build a new and expanded Internet. Although many of these proposals were barely sketched out, they struck a responsive chord among citizens who favored at least some government activity. He repeatedly drew attention to Dole's opposition to the creation of Medicare and his continued opposition to family leave and regulations on tobacco and firearms.

Clinton targeted much of his campaign to attracting women's votes and maintained a 20-point lead among likely women voters. At a rally in Virginia in late October, for example, he highlighted the efforts of his administration in breast cancer research, providing loans to small businesswomen, Head Start, school loans, and the Family and Medical Leave Act.[30]

The Clinton campaign was also notable for its tightly controlled communications. White House Press Secretary Mike McCurry and other White House and campaign spokespersons selected one thematic issue for each day and carefully coordinated their press releases and public statements to focus on that issue. This "message discipline" helped them put the spin they wanted on the president's activities. In addition, the campaign's rapid response team set a new record for responding to an opponent's campaign events. Within an hour of most major Dole speeches, the Clinton campaign would fax its reactions to reporters and news organizations. The speed and effectiveness with which Clinton's rapid response team reacted to the Dole campaign led some to speculate that there was a Clinton mole in the Republican camp.

In contrast, Dole, Kemp, and their campaign spokespersons frequently issued contradictory messages, causing reporters to point to inconsistencies in their issue stands. The Dole/Kemp campaign was also not as effective as its

Democratic counterpart in responding to speeches and policy pronounce-ments from the opposition. Dole's repeated firings of various media teams did not help his campaign deliver a focused message.

THE DEBATES

After some negotiation, the two major-party candidates agreed to two presi-dential and one vice presidential debates of 90 minutes each. The Dole camp insisted on the exclusion of Perot, whom they feared would undercut their support, although Perot's later attacks on Clinton's character suggested that this may have been a mistake on Dole's part. With few citizens paying much attention to the campaign, both camps believed that the debates would be Dole's last chance to influence the campaign.

In the first debate, however, Dole was quite circumspect in his attacks on Clinton and tried instead to persuade viewers that the economy was not as healthy as the president maintained and that Clinton's policies would lead to an intrusive big government. Dole stated, "I don't like to get into personal matters," and referred to ethical issues only obliquely when he asked Clinton to take a stand on pardons for Whitewater conspirators. Dole impressed many observers with his wit and his even temperament, but overall the viewers told pollsters that Clinton had won the debate, and Clinton got a short-lived bump in the polls.

In the vice presidential debate, Kemp also declined to attack Clinton per-sonally. Kemp even went so far as to state that it was "beneath Bob Dole" to make a personal attack on Clinton, a statement that ultimately demonstrated that Kemp is no prophet. In a wide-ranging discussion of economic, social, and political issues, Vice President Al Gore seemed better prepared and in better command of the facts, while Kemp had the advantage of enthusiasm. But Kemp appeared to contradict Dole's positions on several issues, including taxes.

Moreover, Kemp's handling of a question on affirmative action was widely believed to harm public perceptions of his party on racial issues. Gore had lauded Kemp's prior support for affirmative action, referring to him as "a lonely voice in the Republican Party over the years on this question" and then stating, "It is with some sadness that I refer to the fact that the day after he joined Senator Dole's ticket, he announced that he was changing his position and was . . . thereafter going to adopt Senator Dole's position to end all affir-mative action." Kemp in a lengthy response recited his history of support for affirmative action, but did not defend Dole's or his party's position on the issue. Kemp's failure to defend the party or to attack Clinton drew criticism from Republicans. As was the case with the presidential debates, the audience gave the edge to the Democratic ticket.

After the vice presidential debate, Dole still trailed badly in the polls, which consistently put his support at or below 40 percent. Many GOP activists pleaded with the campaign to attack Clinton. Even if such attacks might not help Dole they might energize the Republican base and help the GOP retain control of Congress. Attacks by surrogate campaigners had not received much public attention, as is usually the case. After weeks of refusing to attack the president directly, Dole finally began to attack Clinton's character with increasing force. His task was made easier by a late-breaking scandal involving campaign contributions funneled to the Democratic National Committee by Indonesians and a related story about a Democratic fund-raising event that Gore had attended in a tax-exempt Buddhist temple in California.

In the second presidential debate, Dole forcefully argued that Clinton was too mired in scandal to be a good role model and that the ethical lapses and scandals of his administration meant that he should not be re-elected. Clinton, confident with a 16-point lead, did not even answer the charges. Near the end of the debate the president proclaimed, "No attack ever created a job or educated a child or helped a family make ends meet. No insult ever cleaned up a toxic waste dump or helped an elderly person." Dole seemed to visibly tire after about 45 minutes and had difficulty answering a question about his age. Clinton retorted that Dole was not too old to be president, but that his ideas were too old. Once again, polls showed that the public believed that Clinton had won the debate.

THE CAMPAIGNS' CLOSING MESSAGES

Dole's advertising sought to stress character issues in the last month of the campaign, but his long history in the Senate made it easy for Clinton to counterattack. In one ad, Dole cited an increase in teenage use of marijuana, and then featured a clip from Clinton's appearance on MTV, where he had said that if he had it to do over, he would have inhaled. Yet Clinton's response ad was on the air in days, attacking Dole for voting repeatedly to cut spending on the war on drugs.

In the final weeks of the campaign, Dole attacked Clinton with increasing bitterness and seemed genuinely angry that his attacks were not moving the voters. He then attacked the press for burying his charges instead of trumpeting them on the front page. He scolded the voters for not being outraged by the Clinton administration's apparent ethical lapses. Yet as Dole's charges escalated, his own negative evaluations increased along with Clinton's lead.[31]

Why did the public not respond to Dole's attacks? Most of these charges were old news to the voters, who already believed that Clinton had smoked marijuana, had extramarital affairs, and dabbled in a slick real-estate deal. Moreover, public cynicism was so high that voters did not trust Dole either—by mid-October a majority of voters indicated that they trusted neither man. Indeed, even as Dole railed against the press for not following up on Clinton's questionable fundraising practices, Dole's former campaign finance co-chair was sentenced for laundering contributions, a fact that went largely unreported by the press.[32]

In late October, the Dole campaign decided to contest California, although they trailed badly there in the polls. In part, the decision was borne of necessity, for Dole was making little headway in battleground states in the East and Midwest. In part, the decision was one of opportunity; the race in California had narrowed a bit, and Dole's opposition to affirmative action and benefits for immigrants dovetailed with ballot initiatives in that state where the polls showed the public shared his views. And in part, Dole concentrated on California to help boost the chances of the GOP House candidates in that state. Dole spent many days in California and aired a number of commercials, but ultimately Clinton carried California with ease.

The desperation of the Dole camp was evident in late October when Dole sent campaign manager Scott Reed to plead with Perot to withdraw from the race. Perot responded that the request was "weird." When it became obvious that Dole would lose badly, the National Republican Congressional Committee (NRCC)—the campaign arm of House Republicans—announced that it would spend $3 to $4 million on television advertisements urging voters to return a Republican majority to Congress, so as avoid giving Clinton and "liberal special interests" a "blank check."[33] The ads, which were put on the airwaves in the 50 districts hosting the most competitive House races did little to help Dole.

In the final weeks of the campaign, Clinton began to focus on mobilizing turnout among the Democratic base and among voters more generally. He and Gore felt comfortable enough with their lead to begin to pursue a congressional mandate, campaigning in states with close Senate and House races and leaving it to the Democratic Party organizations and surrogate speakers to campaign for the ticket in Democratic strongholds. Clinton took part in several large Democratic National Committee (DNC) fundraising dinners to help channel money into close races and directed his top fundraisers to help congressional candidates.

In the last week of the campaign, Clinton's poll numbers slipped perceptibly under the barrage of criticism from Dole and Perot—whose unorthodox campaign made use of late infomercials to attack the president. Continued negative press attention to apparent DNC fundraising improprieties also hurt the president's standing. The *Washington Post* and other major media outlets continued to investigate a story about DNC fundraiser John Huang's efforts to collect large contributions from individuals and corporations with Asian roots, permanent residents of Asian ancestry, U.S. subsidiaries of Asian-based corporations, and possibly nonresident Asians and Asian businesses. An initial decision by the DNC (which was later reversed) not to file a routine report with the Federal Election Commission provided more fodder for Dole's attacks. Dole's efforts had the effect of siphoning away some of Clinton's support, but they made him look mean-spirited and desperate. As a result, the major polls showed that Dole's support remained static and that Perot was the major beneficiary of Clinton's declining support.

In the final days, both Clinton and Dole engaged in extended last-minute campaigning, including a 96-hour blitz by Dole, who crossed the country with little sleep in a marathon of speeches. This hectic schedule took a toll. Dole's voice gave out repeatedly, and at one stop he announced, "We are going to give you sex—satisfaction and your money back."[34] In this last spurt of campaigning, Dole largely abandoned his attacks on Clinton, instead giving short speeches on patriotism and small government and endorsing local Republican candidates.

AN EVALUATION

The 1996 campaign did not change the minds of voters, and although it is easy to criticize the Dole camp's failure to adopt a consistent strategy or to stay on message, it is difficult to imagine anything that Dole might have done to win the election. Moreover, it is unlikely that the other Republican hopefuls would have beaten Clinton in such a propitious Democratic year. Even Colin Powell, widely touted by the media as the best possible GOP candidate, would have divided his party and faced long odds to beat Clinton.[35]

In many ways, the 1996 election was a repeat of the 1984 election. In both years, America re-elected a popular incumbent in a time when the economy was rapidly improving. In both elections, the out-party complained that their attacks on the incumbent did not move the voters (Reagan was called the "Teflon President"), but in both cases the incumbent had been quite unpopular only two years before. In both 1984 and 1996 the challenger chose an unimaginative campaign theme. In 1984 Mondale promised to raise taxes, not to reform the tax code as many advisors had urged. In 1996 Dole campaigned on a promise to cut taxes, a pledge with much less resonance in light of the huge budget deficit that had ballooned after Reagan's 1980 tax cuts. The spotlight that the House Republicans' budget plan placed on the reductions in Medicare, education, and environmental protection that would be needed to pay for a tax cut also undercut support for large tax cuts.

In both elections, the incumbent also chose to focus the campaign on retrospective evaluations of the state of the economy, foregoing an opportunity to win a mandate for new policies in the second term. Indeed, the Clinton campaign carefully studied Reagan's re-election campaign and sought to copy its most successful elements.[36]

It is also worth noting that both Dole and Clinton turned their backs on issues about which they had great credibility and adopted positions that contradicted decades of previous work on their part. Clinton ultimately signed a welfare reform bill that did not provide poor Americans with either a federal safety net or the resources needed to find jobs or get out of poverty, promising only to "fix it" after the election. The president probably could have vetoed the bill and still won election. In doing so, he could have sparked a debate on the role of compassion and incentives in public policy. Dole's tax cut plan was a repudiation of a lifetime of careful attention to budget deficits. By adopting supply-side economics after years of wryly criticizing it, Dole lost one of his greatest advantages in early polls, the notion that he stuck by his beliefs. When it became evident he would lose, Dole also missed his chance to make a principled stand on some issues of real importance—how to deal with Medicare and Social Security, or the role of religious values in American politics—and to force Clinton to confront these issues head on.

The last few weeks of the Dole campaign were painful to watch, as Dole railed against the liberal media elite, made sharply negative attacks on Clinton, and tried desperately to get the public to listen. Dole, who had been an effective Senate majority leader and who was generally well-liked and respected by most Republicans and Democrats in Congress, watched Republican candidates run away from his presidential bid and ask him not to appear at their rallies. In the end, Dole was a man whose partisan message played poorly in a non-partisan year, who appeared too old to be president, and out of touch with his time.

Just as the campaign did not alter the outcome of the election, the election did not introduce any major changes into the balance of power that exists in Washington. Clinton's 379 to 159 Electoral College victory and 49 percent popular vote margin did not provide him with a large popular mandate. His party's failure to win control of the House or Senate, or take over any statehouses, left him with neither a congressional nor an extended mandate. Because the president's campaign was built around a core of loosely tied symbolic themes and rested on several modest policy proposals rather than one or two major ones, the election also did not give the president a policy mandate. As such, the president began his second term in a position remarkably similar to the one that existed prior to the election. His clout with the GOP-controlled Congress will be limited, necessitating that he lead through compromise and conciliation. Ongoing congressional investigations will probably strain relations between those who work at different ends of Pennsylvania Avenue.

The election outcome also extended some pre-existing trends that have important implications for the political parties. It showed that Democrats will probably continue to benefit from votes of women and draw disproportionate support from minorities, youthful and lower income voters, and liberals. The Republicans will probably continue to strengthen their hold over the South and draw support from economic conservatives and the Christian Right. Both parties will continue to battle for the great center—moderate and independent voters. Although the Reform Party continued to attract support from disaffected voters and won enough popular votes to qualify for federal campaign funds in 2000, it continued its downward spiral. The party's 8 percent share of the presidential vote highlighted its failure to come even close to achieving major-party status. It will have to battle even harder to be included in future presidential debates and to be perceived as a viable alternative to the Democrats and Republicans.

Overall, the results of the 1996 presidential election indicate that it was characterized more by continuity than change. Perhaps this is a fitting outcome for a campaign that didn't really seem to matter.

NOTES

1. Howard Kurtz, "Early Offensive by Democrats Blunted Effects of Dole Ad Blitz." *Washington Post*, Oct 25, 1996, A19.

2. In 1968, Hubert Humphrey had so much momentum in the final weeks that many observers speculated that he would have won had the election been held a week later.

3. Consultants for losing candidates, however, often blame long-term forces for their candidate's defeat.

4. Jack Germond and Jules Witcover, *Wake Us When It's Over: Presidential Politics in 1984*, New York: MacMillan (1985), p. 9; Jack Germond and Jules Witcover, *Whose Broad Stripes and Bright Stars? The Trivial Pursuit of the Presidency in 1984*, New York: Warner (1989).

5. Steven Finkel, 1993, "Reexamining the 'Minimal Effects' Model in Recent Presidential Elections," *Journal of Politics* 55: 1–21.

6. Steven Rosenstone, "Why Reagan Won," *Brookings Review* 3: 25–32. The "bear in the woods" refers to an advertisement by the Reagan campaign in which the bear was the Soviet Union.

7. For example, see Alan Abramowitz, 1988, "An Improved Model for Predicting Presidential Elections," *PS*. 21: 843–847; Michael Lewis-Beck and Tom Rice, 1992, *Forecasting Elections*. Washington, DC: CQ Press; James E. Campbell, 1992, "Forecasting the Presidential Vote in the States," *American Journal of Political Science* 36:

386–407; Ray C. Fair, 1978, "The Effect of Economic Events on Votes for President," *Review of Economics and Statistics* 60: 159–172; Steven Rosenstone, 1983, *Forecasting Presidential Elections*, New Haven: Yale University Press.

8. Dukakis was quite ill on the day of the second debate, and badly handled several key questions.

9. Thomas Holbrook, *Do Campaigns Matter?* (Thousand Oaks, CA: Sage, 1996), p. 158.

10. Richard Brody, *Assessing the President: The Media, Elite Opinion, and Public Support* (Stanford, CA: Stanford University Press); Henry Chappell, Jr. and William Keech, "A New View of Political Accountability and Economic Performance," *American Political Science Review* (1985) 79: 10–27; and Samuel Kernell, "Explaining Presidential Popularity," *American Political Science Review* (1978) 72: 506–522.

11. *Public Perspective*, October/November 1996.

12. Ibid.

13. For a detailed discussion, see Clay Chandler and Richard Morin, "Prosperity's Imbalance Divides U.S.," *Washington Post*, October 14, 1996, A1.

14. James E. Campbell and Thomas E. Mann, 1996, "Forecasting the Presidential Election: What Can We Learn from the Models?" *Brookings Review* Vol. 14 (Fall, 1996), 26–31. The exception was a purely economic model by Fair, which predicted that Clinton would receive 49.5 percent of the two-party vote. Fair's model did not include any measures of public opinion.

15. Richard Morin and John M. Berry, 1996, "A Nation that Poor-Mouths Its Good Times." *Washington Post*, October 13: A1, A38.

16. *The Public Perspective* October/November, 1996.

17. See for example, Doris Graber, *Mass Media and American Politics* (Washington, DC: CQ Press, 1997), p. 282.

18. "Issue advocacy" ads can be used to praise or attack a candidate's campaign positions or record as long as they do not expressly call for a candidate's election or defeat. "Soft money" refers to contributions made by individuals or organizations to political parties to help finance party building activity, voter mobilization drives, and party-focused generic campaign advertisements. Theoretically, these funds are not supposed to be linked to the election campaigns of specific candidates. However, because they help presidential candidates' campaigns, the candidates aggressively raise soft money.

19. The other case was Reagan in 1984, who had announced that he was opposed to matching funds, but accepted them despite the lack of intra-party opposition.

20. *The Public Perspective*, op. cit.

21. Cited in Howard Kurtz, "Early Offensive by Democrats Blunted Effect of Dole Ad Blitz." *Washington Post*, Oct 25, 1996, A1.

22. Mark J. Rozell and Clyde Wilcox, 1996, *Second Coming: The Christian Right in Virginia Politics*, Baltimore: Johns Hopkins University Press. Rozell and Wilcox, 1996, *God at the Grassroots: The Christian Right in the 1994 Elections*, Lanham, MD: Rowman & Littlefield.

23. Clifford Brown, Jr., Lynda Powell, and Clyde Wilcox, 1995, *Serious Money: Fundraising and Contributing in Presidential Nomination Campaigns*, New York: Cambridge University Press.

24. See, for example, Paul S. Herrnson, "Two-Party Dominance and Minor-Party Forays in American Politics," in Paul S. Herrnson and John C. Green, eds., *Multi-Party Politics in America* (Landover, MD: Rowman and Littlefield, 1997).

25. *The Public Perspective,* op cit.

26. Information obtained from www.politicsnow.com, which provided weekly electoral maps summarizing the latest polls in each state.

27. In fact, Bush had misrepresented Dole's record and position on taxes, but Dole's angry outburst in a time when civil congratulations are usually offered made a lasting impression on journalists, and on some voters.

28. Cited in "Maybe Not So Fickle." *New York Times,* September 22, 1996, A1.

29. *The Public Perspective,* op cit.

30. Alison Mitchell, "Clinton Campaign Puts an Emphasis on Female Voters," *The New York Times,* October 28, 1996.

31. Richard L. Berke, "Aggressive Turn by Dole Appears to be Backfiring." *New York Times,* Oct 22, 1996, A1.

32. Jonathan Alter, "A Man Not of This Time," *Newsweek,* November 4, 1996, p. 30.

33. Dan Balz, "GOP Stresses Division of Power in Ad," *Washington Post,* October 27, 1996.

34. Blaine Harden, "With Voice Giving Out, Dole Goes on His 96-Hour Tour," *Washington Post,* November 5, 1996, A1.

35. See James K. Glassman, "Could It Have Been Any Different?" *Washington Post,* Oct 29, 1996, A17.

36. Alison Mitchel, "Politics: The Democrat," *New York Times,* September 17, 1996, A1.

CHAPTER 6

The November Vote

A Status Quo Election

Larry J. Sabato*

University of Virginia

On the cusp of a new millennium—the ultimate change in the calendar—America's voters rejected change and chose to preserve the status quo by re-electing the Democratic president and the Republican Congress. Yet the election can still be viewed as appropriate to the *fin de siecle*. The electorate preferred the future-oriented, bridge-to-the-21st-century presidential candidate over a nominee who hearkened back to an earlier era of greatness. At the same time, citizens signaled their desire to continue the dramatic shift in legislative control and outlook begun just two years ago. Trusting no party or person completely, Americans moved in contradictory fits and starts toward the millennium. Bill Clinton became the first Democratic president since Franklin Roosevelt in 1936 to be re-elected, but also the only Democratic president this century to win office alongside a GOP legislature. The Republicans managed to re-elect a majority in both houses of Congress for the first time since 1928, but the voters administered a mild rebuke to Speaker Newt Gingrich by shrinking his House margin while increasing the GOP majority in the Senate.

ELECTION FACTS AND FIGURES

Looking strictly at the numbers, President Clinton won a comfortable, but not massive, re-election victory. Just as in 1992 when he garnered only 43 percent

*The author gratefully acknowledges the invaluable help of undergraduate student Justin Sizemore in the research and presentation of this chapter. Also making contributions were U.Va students Jeff Manns, Michelle Baker, Michael Smith, and Steven Betz.

of the popular vote, Clinton secured a second term with less than a majority of the vote, 49.2 percent to Bob Dole's 40.8 percent, Ross Perot's 8.5 percent, and 1.5 percent for other candidates. Clinton thus became the first two-term president since Woodrow Wilson never to win a popular vote majority. Also of note was the double-digit showing of the third parties, the first time since 1856–1860 that votes for all third-party candidates have topped 10 percent in two consecutive presidential elections. And since Ross Perot exceeded 5 percent, his Reform Party will be eligible for some public funding in the 2000 contest.

In the Electoral College, Clinton's 1996 total of 379 mirrored his 1992's 370. Once again Clinton swept the entire Northeast, carried most of the middle Atlantic states, won every industrial Midwestern state except Indiana, captured all the Pacific coast states save Alaska, and picked off a few Southern, Border, and Southwestern states to boot. Compared to 1992, the president carried one fewer state (31 in 1996, 32 in 1992) yet added two big normally Republican prizes, Arizona and Florida. In exchange, Clinton forfeited three states he won in 1992, Georgia, Colorado, and Montana. On the whole, the electoral map suggested considerable stability from four years ago, although the popular vote showed more variation. Nationally, Clinton ran 6 percentage points better than in 1992, Dole exceeded George Bush's vote proportion only

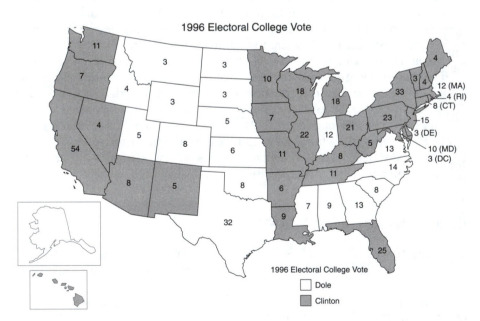

Figure 1   1996 Electoral College Vote

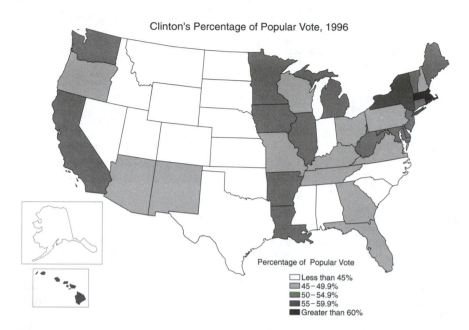

Clinton's Percentage of Popular Vote, 1996

Percentage of Popular Vote
- ☐ Less than 45%
- 45–49.9%
- 50–54.9%
- 55–59.9%
- ■ Greater than 60%

Figure 2 Clinton's Percentage of Popular Vote, 1996

by about 3 percentage points, and Ross Perot dropped over 10 percentage points (with his ex-voters quite possibly accounting for Dole's ability to carry the several states Bush lost). As Table 1 indicates, Clinton's vote proportion increased in all fifty states from 1992, ranging from +14 percent in Massachusetts to +1 percent in North Carolina. Yet because of a low voter turnout, Clinton garnered only about 887,000 more votes country-wide than in 1992.

The 1996 election was reminiscent in some ways of the one-sided 1972 and 1984 presidential contests. Like Presidents Richard Nixon in 1972 and Ronald Reagan in 1984, Bill Clinton benefited from a generally robust economy and basically peaceful conditions abroad. Nixon, Reagan, and Clinton were all re-elected easily, though Clinton's 1996 margin did not approach the 60 percent popular-vote, 49-state landslides of 1972 and 1984. Yet the congressional results were eerily similar in all three years (see Table 2, p. 147).

These numbers strongly suggest that electoral history is repetitive. Whenever the fundamental conditions of an election year are similar, human voting behavior is predictable, at least in outline form. Good times generate good feelings for most incumbents, and a positive economic stimulus can overcome many kinds of doubts and concerns about officeholders, as some exit poll results will show.

Table 1   The Presidential Vote - 1996

State	Clinton votes	Clinton percent	Dole votes	Dole percent	Perot votes	Perot percent	Clinton '92 votes	Clinton '92 percent	Clinton Gain percent
Alabama	664,503	42.9	782,029	50.5	92,010	5.9	690,080	40.9	+2.0
Alaska	66,508	33.5	101,234	51.0	21,536	10.8	78,294	30.3	+3.2
Arizona	612,412	46.9	576,126	44.1	104,712	8.0	543,050	36.5	+10.4
Arkansas	469,164	53.8	322,349	37.0	66,997	7.7	505,823	53.2	+0.6
California	4,639,935	51.2	3,412,563	37.7	667,702	7.4	5,121,325	46.0	+5.2
Colorado	670,854	44.4	691,291	45.8	99,509	6.6	629,681	40.1	+4.3
Connecticut	712,603	52.2	481,047	35.2	137,784	10.1	682,318	42.2	+10.0
Delaware	140,209	51.8	98,906	36.6	28,693	10.6	126,054	43.5	+8.3
District of Columbia	152,031	85.5	16,637	9.4	3,479	2.0	192,619	84.6	+0.9
Florida	2,533,502	48.1	2,226,117	42.3	482,237	9.2	2,072,698	39.0	+9.1
Georgia	1,047,214	45.7	1,078,972	47.1	146,031	6.4	1,008,966	43.5	+2.2
Hawaii	205,012	56.9	113,943	31.6	27,358	7.6	179,310	48.1	+8.8
Idaho	165,545	33.7	256,406	52.2	62,506	12.7	137,013	28.4	+5.3
Illinois	2,299,476	54.0	1,577,930	37.1	344,311	8.1	2,453,350	48.6	+5.4
Indiana	874,668	41.6	995,082	47.3	218,739	10.4	848,420	36.8	+4.8
Iowa	615,732	50.2	490,949	40.1	104,462	8.5	586,353	43.3	+6.9
Kansas	384,399	36.1	578,572	54.3	92,093	8.6	390,434	33.7	+2.4
Kentucky	635,804	45.9	622,339	44.9	118,768	8.6	665,104	44.6	+1.3
Louisiana	928,983	52.1	710,240	39.8	122,981	6.9	815,971	45.6	+6.5
Maine	311,092	51.7	185,133	30.8	85,290	14.2	263,420	38.8	+12.9
Maryland	924,284	54.2	651,682	38.2	113,684	6.7	988,571	49.8	+4.4
Massachusetts	1,567,223	61.7	717,622	28.3	225,594	8.9	1,318,662	47.5	+14.2
Michigan	1,941,126	51.8	1,440,977	38.5	326,751	8.7	1,871,182	43.8	+8.0
Minnesota	1,096,355	51.1	751,971	35.0	252,986	11.8	1,020,997	43.5	+7.6
Mississippi	385,005	43.8	434,547	49.4	51,500	5.9	400,258	40.8	+3.0
Missouri	1,024,817	47.5	889,689	41.3	217,103	10.1	1,053,873	44.1	+3.4
Montana	167,169	41.2	178,957	44.1	55,017	13.6	154,507	37.6	+3.6
Nebraska	231,906	34.6	355,655	53.1	76,103	11.4	216,864	29.4	+5.2
Nevada	203,388	43.9	198,775	42.9	43,855	9.5	189,148	37.4	+6.5
New Hampshire	245,260	49.5	196,740	39.7	48,140	9.7	209,040	38.9	+10.6
New Jersey	1,599,932	53.4	1,080,041	36.0	257,979	8.6	1,436,206	43.0	+10.4
New Mexico	252,215	49.4	210,791	41.3	30,978	6.1	261,617	45.9	+3.5
New York	3,513,191	58.8	1,861,198	31.1	485,547	8.1	3,444,450	49.7	+9.1
North Carolina	1,099,132	44.1	1,214,399	48.8	165,301	6.6	1,114,042	42.7	+1.4
North Dakota	106,405	40.1	124,597	46.9	32,594	12.3	99,168	32.2	+7.9
Ohio	2,100,690	47.4	1,823,859	41.1	470,680	10.6	1,984,942	40.2	+7.2
Oklahoma	488,102	40.4	582,310	48.3	130,788	10.8	473,066	34.0	+6.4
Oregon	326,099	47.0	256,105	37.0	73,265	10.6	621,314	42.5	+4.5
Pennsylvania	2,206,241	49.2	1,793,568	40.0	430,082	9.6	2,239,164	45.1	+4.1
Rhode Island	220,592	60.1	98,325	26.8	39,965	10.9	213,299	47.0	+13.1
South Carolina	495,878	43.8	564,856	49.9	63,324	5.6	479,514	39.9	+3.9
South Dakota	139,295	43.0	150,508	46.5	31,248	9.7	124,888	37.1	+5.9
Tennessee	905,599	48.0	860,809	45.6	105,577	5.6	933,521	47.1	+0.9
Texas	2,455,735	43.9	2,731,998	48.8	377,530	6.7	2,281,815	37.1	+6.8
Utah	220,197	33.3	359,394	54.4	66,100	10.0	183,429	24.7	+8.6
Vermont	138,400	53.6	80,043	31.0	30,912	12.0	133,592	46.1	+7.5
Virginia	1,070,990	45.1	1,119,974	47.1	158,707	6.7	1,038,650	40.6	+4.5
Washington	899,645	50.8	639,743	36.1	161,642	9.1	993,037	43.4	+7.4
West Virginia	324,394	51.5	231,908	36.8	70,853	11.2	331,001	48.4	+3.1
Wisconsin	1,071,859	48.9	845,172	38.5	227,426	10.4	1,041,066	41.1	+7.8
Wyoming	77,897	36.8	105,347	49.8	25,854	12.2	68,160	34.0	+2.8
Total/Average	**45,628,667**	**49.2**	**37,869,425**	**40.8**	**7,874,283**	**8.5**	**44,909,326**	**43.0**	**+6.0**

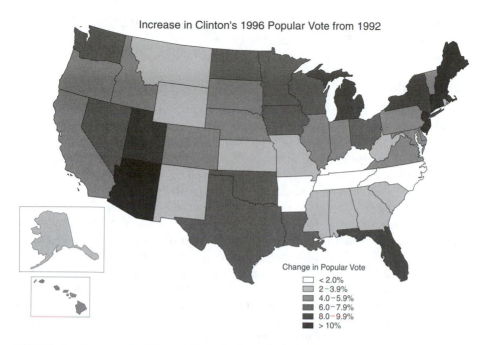

Figure 3 Increase in Clinton's Popular Vote from 1992

THE DEMOGRAPHICS OF THE BALLOT BOX

Unlike pre-election polling which can partially rely on guesswork in picturing the voting electorate, "exit-polling"—a random-sample survey of voters actually leaving the polling places—is highly reliable. The television networks (among others) contracted with Mitovsky International to conduct the 1996 exit polls, and it is a marvelous resource for analyzing the presidential contest. Over the next few pages, we draw directly from the networks' exit polls to explain Bill Clinton's victory. The numbers in the chart should be read horizontally. For example, under "Vote by Gender," men comprised 48 percent

Table 2

Year	Re-elected President	U.S. House Seats GAINED by President's party	U.S. Senate seats LOST by President's party
1972	Richard Nixon	13	2
1984	Ronald Reagan	15	2
1996	Bill Clinton	9	2

of the election-day voters, and they gave 43 percent of their votes to Clinton, 44 percent to Dole, and 10 percent to Perot.

Group Politics

The story of the 1996 presidential election begins with the gender gap, and especially the women's vote, since women literally overrode men and gave Bill Clinton a second term. Targeted early by the Clinton campaign as the president's best hope for re-election, women in the end made all the difference for the Democrats. Female voters, who comprised 52 percent of the electorate, backed Clinton 54 to 38 percent while men narrowly favored Dole, 44 to 43 percent. The gender gap was thus an enormous 17 percentage points, about 10 points larger than in 1992. More importantly, it was the first time since exit polling began that pluralities of men and women preferred different presidential candidates. Clinton's margins among some subgroups of women were even larger; for example, single working women, increasingly a Democratic mainstay, voted for Clinton over Dole by the enormous margin of 65 to 26 percent. Even married women, usually a Republican island in the female Democratic sea, voted for Clinton in 1996, albeit by only a few percentage points. Remarkably, nearly six of every ten votes cast for Bill Clinton were women's ballots. Interestingly, while Bob Dole's voters were 52 percent male, Ross Perot's supporters were even more male: 57 percent of the Reform Party candidate's ballots were cast by men.

Race has nearly consistently been a fundamental dividing line at the polling places, and 1996 was no exception. Whites backed Dole by 46 percent to 43 percent for Clinton and 9 percent for Perot, while African-Americans were solidly in Clinton's corner (84 percent to Dole's 12 percent and Perot's 4 percent.) Hispanics were almost as Democratic (Clinton secured 72 percent of their votes), but Asian-Americans as usual tilted to the GOP (Dole secured 48 percent, Clinton 43 percent). Compared to 1992, by the way, Clinton fared somewhat worse with whites, about the same with blacks and Asians, and fully 12 points better with Hispanics (who were a major factor in shifting Florida and Arizona out of the Republican column and in padding the Democratic margins in New Mexico and California). Most noteworthy was the shift among Cuban-Americans in Florida. Normally overwhelmingly Republican, they gave Bob Dole just a 4 percentage point plurality over Clinton in 1996.

With one exception, there was little differentiation in the vote by age group. Clinton won 48 percent among the 30 to 44s, 45–59s, and over 60s. It was with the young that he scored big: 53 percent of those aged 18–29 backed Clinton, compared to just 34 percent for Dole. However, only 17 percent of the voting electorate was 18–29, so the impact was limited.

Table 3   Presidential Election Exit Poll Results

Question	All Voters	Clinton	Dole	Perot	Question	All Voters	Clinton	Dole	Perot
	Horizontal %					**Horizontal %**			
Vote by Gender					Religion				
Men	48	43	44	10	Protestant	38	41	50	8
Women	52	54	38	7	Catholic	29	53	37	9
Vote by Race					Other Christian	16	45	41	12
Whites	83	43	46	9	Jewish	3	78	16	3
African-Americans	10	84	12	4	Other Religion	6	60	23	11
Hispanics	5	72	21	6	None	7	59	23	13
Asians	1	43	48	8	Religion - Whites Only				
Other	1	64	21	9	Protestant	56	36	53	10
Vote by Age					Catholic	29	48	41	10
18-29	17	53	34	10	Jewish	4	78	16	3
30-44	33	48	41	9	Other Religion	5	51	29	13
45-59	26	48	41	9	None	7	56	26	14
Over 60	24	48	44	7	White Religious?				
18-64	84	49	40	9	Yes	17	26	65	8
65 and Older	16	50	43	6	No	80	54	35	9
Vote by Income					Do You Own a Gun?				
Less than $15,000	11	59	28	11	Yes	37	38	51	10
$15-30,000	23	53	36	9	No	63	54	37	7
$30-50,000	27	48	40	10	Marital Status				
$50-75,000	21	47	45	7	Married	66	44	46	9
$75-100,000	9	44	48	7	Not Married	34	57	31	9
Over $100,000	9	38	54	6	Union Member in Household?				
Vote by Education					Yes	23	59	30	9
No High School	6	59	28	11	No	77	46	45	8
High School Graduate	24	51	35	13	First-Time Voter?				
Some College	27	48	40	10	Yes	9	54	34	11
College Graduate	26	44	46	8	No	91	48	42	8
Post-Graduate	17	52	40	5	Frequent Talk Radio Listener?				
Party Identification					Yes	36	45	46	8
Democrat	39	84	10	5	No	64	52	39	8
Republican	35	13	80	6	Are You Gay/Lesbian/Bisexual?				
Independent	26	43	35	17	Yes	5	66	23	7
1992 Vote					No	95	47	43	8
Clinton	43	85	9	4	Do You Smoke Cigarettes?				
Bush	35	13	82	4	Current Smoker	19	53	36	9
Perot	12	22	44	33	Former Smoker	30	49	41	8
Other	1	24	36	9	Never Smoked	49	46	45	7
Didn't Vote	9	53	33	11	Opinion of Federal Government				
Vote if Perot Were Not Running					Should Do More	41	72	20	6
Clinton	50	91	3	5	Should Do Less	52	30	60	9
Dole	43	4	90	5					
Would Not Vote	5	11	18	56					
Political Ideology									
Liberal	20	78	11	7					
Moderate	47	57	33	9					
Conservative	33	20	71	8					

(Continued)

149

Table 3 (continued)

Question	Horizontal %				Question	Horizontal %			
	All Voters	Clinton	Dole	Perot		All Voters	Clinton	Dole	Perot
New Federal Welfare Law					Feelings If				
Cuts Too Much	18	70	17	9	Clinton Wins				
Doesn't Cut Enough	39	33	58	8	Excited	13	91	7	2
About Right	37	55	37	7	Optimistic	34	83	9	6
More Likely to Cut					Concerned	30	28	56	13
Medicare					Scared	22	2	85	11
Only Democrats	17	45	48	6	Top Issue in Vote				
Only Republicans	42	68	24	6	Taxes	11	19	73	7
Both Parties	22	32	55	11	Medicare	15	67	26	6
Neither Party	16	27	63	8	Foreign Policy	4	35	56	8
Abortion Should Be					Federal Deficit	12	27	52	19
Legal In . . .					Economy/Jobs	21	61	27	10
All Cases	25	69	21	8	Education	12	78	16	4
Most Cases	35	55	33	11	Crime/Drugs	7	40	50	8
Few Cases	25	32	57	10	Top Factor in Vote				
Never	12	23	68	7	View of Government	20	41	46	10
Family Finances					Stand Up for Beliefs	13	42	40	16
Since 1992					Cares About People	9	72	17	9
Gotten Better	33	66	26	6	Honest/Trustworthy	20	8	84	7
Gotten Worse	20	27	57	13	In Touch	10	89	8	4
About the Same	45	46	45	8	Vision for Future	16	77	13	9
Condition of National					Dole's Age Affect				
Economy					His Ability?				
Excellent	4	78	17	4	Yes	34	79	12	8
Good	51	62	31	6	No	64	34	58	7
Not Good	36	34	52	12	When Decided				
Poor	7	23	51	21	Presidential Vote				
Direction of Country					In the Last 3 Days	11	35	38	22
Right Direction	53	69	24	5	Last Week	6	35	47	17
Wrong Track	43	23	61	13	Last Month	13	47	36	13
Clinton Honest and					Before That	69	53	41	5
Trustworthy?					Better First Lady?				
Yes	41	88	6	4	Hillary Clinton	43	86	7	5
No	54	18	67	12	Elizabeth Dole	50	16	75	8
Clinton and Whitewater					If Powell Were				
Told the Truth	33	89	6	4	GOP Candidate				
Did Not Tell the Truth	60	24	62	13	Clinton	36	93	5	1
Which is More					Powell	48	24	68	6
Important?					Perot	8	11	36	50
Issues	58	69	20	8	Would Not Vote	3	24	70	2
Character	38	18	71	10	Presidential Vote				
Concerned About					in 2000				
Clinton Scandals					Gore	43	86	8	5
Yes	49	24	64	10	Kemp	39	11	82	6
No	49	73	20	6	Would Not Vote	11	40	31	26

Source: "Presidential Election Exit Poll Results," CNN/Time AllPolitics, 1996, <http://allpolitics.com/elections/natl.exit.poll/index1.html> (November 8, 1996). The Voter News Service interviewed 16,359 voters at 300 precincts across the United States to produce this exit poll, which has a margin of error of plus or minus about 1.3 percent.

As expected, the Democrat won sizable majorities of Americans making less than $30,000 a year, and he also captured more narrow pluralities among those making $30,000 to $75,000. Upper-middle income and upper-income Americans were in the Republican's corner, with Dole winning 54 percent of those making over $100,000 annually—a group that may have been especially attracted to Dole's 15 percent income tax cut proposal.

Income is partially, but not totally, correlated with education in explaining the '96 vote. Majorities of those with little formal education cast ballots for Clinton, but so did those with the most education (at least some postgraduate training). Dole narrowly won those who had secured a college degree yet had no advanced education.

Much had been made during the campaign of disaffected Republicans, supposedly defecting to Clinton. Yet the exit poll results show that Clinton won only 13 percent of Republicans—not far from the 10 percent of Democrats that Dole won. Independents, not partisans, decided the election. Clinton attracted 43 percent of independents to Dole's 35 percent. Third-party candidates won the rest of the independent electorate. Perot received 17 percent, the rest of the minor party nominees together got 5 percent.

Incidentally, since Perot's 1992 share of the national vote shrank dramatically in 1996, where did the ex-Perotistas go? By a margin of 2 to 1, Dole was the beneficiary. Does this mean that if Perot had not run in 1996, Dole would have inherited the lion's share of the remaining Perot bloc? According to the exit poll, most 1996 Perot voters claimed they would not have even bothered to cast a ballot—a credible claim in light of the low turnout overall. Dole would have gotten most of the rest of Perot's backers, but this would only have added a couple of percentage points to his total.

Just as he garnered most of the Independents, Clinton won the election by dominating by 57 to 33 percent among the nearly half of the voters who described themselves as moderates. (This was another repeat from 1992.) Clinton also swept the liberal fifth of the electorate, 78 to 11 percent. Dole's refuge was of course conservatives, comprising a third of the voters, where he captured 71 percent to Clinton's 20 percent. Given Clinton's liberal first two years as president, his attraction to a fifth of all conservatives is remarkable, and a measure of how much the president moderated his politics in 1995 and 1996.

With the advent of the Christian Coalition, religion has become an even more vital point of political analysis. And indeed, among white "religious right" voters (that is, conservative Protestant evangelicals), there is again clear evidence of a Republican tilt. Bob Dole won nearly two-thirds of these voters, far less than George Bush's almost 80 percent in 1988, but impressive nonetheless. Dole also led among all Protestants, 50 to 41 percent. By contrast, Clinton scored landslides with Jewish voters (78 percent) and those with no religion (59 percent). Even more importantly, the president secured a solid 53 percent majority of the Catholic vote, despite the opposition of Church leaders angered by his pro-choice position on abortion and veto of a congressional bill than banned so-called "partial birth" abortions at the last stage of pregnancy. Despite the urgings of many campaign advisers, Dole never made partial birth abortions much of an issue—a decision that may have been a mistake, given these results. Catholics are a critical swing group, about 29 percent of the electorate compared to 38 percent for Protestants, 16 percent for other Christian groups, 3 percent for Jews, and 7 percent for the areligious. White "religious right" voters comprised 17 percent of the 1996 electorate.

Other definable groups in the electorate provided fascinating fodder for analysts, including:

- *Gun owners:* The pro-gun control Clinton won 54 percent of voters who did *not* own a gun, but just 38 percent of the votes of gun owners.
- *Singles vs. Married:* Voters who were married chose Dole narrowly, 46 to 44 percent, while Clinton was the overwhelming choice of the non-marrieds (57 to 31 percent).
- *Union Members:* Clinton and Dole almost evenly split the votes of non-union members, but union members and their households went for Clinton almost 2 to 1.
- *First-Time Voters:* Only 9 percent of the voters were first-timers, luckily for the Republicans since Clinton won them 54 to 34 percent.
- *Talk-Radio Listeners:* Dole had a tiny edge among those who described themselves as "frequent" talk-radio listeners—the expected "Rush Limbaugh effect," perhaps.
- *Gay Voters:* Among the 5 percent of voters who identified themselves as gay, lesbian, or bisexual, Clinton won two-thirds.
- *Cigarette Smokers:* Oddly, given Dole's general support of tobacco and Clinton's strong opposition to it, Clinton won the current smokers by 53 to 36 percent, and Dole nearly tied Clinton among those who have never smoked. This may be related to income, since non-smokers are more likely to be upper-income and more Republican, and smokers tend to be just the reverse.

Issues in the Exit Polls

The Democrat won the presidential election, but in some ways the Republicans seemed to have won the war of ideas. For example, by a margin 52 to 41 percent, voters wanted the federal government to do less rather than more. ("Less" voters favored Dole 2 to 1; "more" voters backed Clinton 3-to-1.) And Americans wanted an even *tougher* welfare law than the draconian one that passed in 1996; 18 percent said it "cuts welfare too much" but 39 percent said it "didn't cut welfare enough."

The philosophical tide had not moved in a Republican direction on two issues, though: Medicare and abortion. The Democrats' "Mediscare" campaign claiming the GOP was out to gut the popular program clearly convinced a plurality; by 42 to 17 percent, voters said the Republicans were more likely to cut Medicare, and those suspicious of the GOP's intentions gave Clinton 68 percent of their votes. On abortion, 60 percent of the voters wanted the procedure legal in *all* or *most* cases, with Clinton winning 63 percent of the vote among this group. Dole garnered the same percentage (63) with those favoring abortion in only a *few* cases or *never*, but only 37 percent of the voters expressed an anti-abortion rights position.

Without a doubt, however, the alpha and omega issue of the 1996 presidential election was the economy. Among the 55 percent of voters who called the national economy "excellent" or "good," Clinton captured 64 percent of the ballots. By contrast, Dole won just 52 percent among the smaller 43 percent who believed the economy to be "not good" or "poor." A solid 53 percent majority saw the country as "generally going in the right direction," and Clinton was the beneficiary of 69 percent of these votes. For the 43 percent who said the nation was "seriously off on the wrong track," Dole was the choice (by 61 to 23 percent).

Interestingly, while the voters appeared to be relatively optimistic about America, they were not necessarily so upbeat on the scandal-plagued incumbent they chose to re-elect. Fully 54 percent said Clinton was *not* "honest and trustworthy." An even larger 60 percent did not believe the president had told "the truth about Whitewater." Half expressed a more general concern about the scandal factor in a second Clinton administration, although by a margin of 58 to 38 percent voters pronounced issues more important than "character and values" in choosing a president. And what were the voters' "feelings" about the "feel-your-pain" president's prospective second term? Forty-seven percent were "excited" or "optimistic," but 52 percent were "concerned" or "scared."

Odds and Ends

Every exit poll has its share of revealing sidelights. From the 1996 version came these tidbits:

- Almost two-thirds of the voters did not think that Dole's age (73) "would interfere with his ability to serve effectively as president." But of the third who *did* have doubts about Dole's advanced years, 79 percent voted for Clinton.
- Late-deciders helped Dole to close the gap with Clinton. Among the 16 percent of the electorate that made up their minds in the last seven days of the campaign, Dole beat Clinton 41 to 35 percent. Perhaps the last-minute controversy about Democratic fund-raising from foreign sources and Dole's 96-hour

continuous campaign marathon in early November swayed some waverers, or maybe undecideds just naturally gravitate to the nonincumbent—a phenomenon many pollsters have reported over the years. In any event, voters who decided a month or more before election day picked Clinton 53 to 44 percent.
- The Republicans won one national contest, although it wasn't on the ballot. By a margin of 50 to 43 percent, voters preferred Elizabeth Dole to Hillary Clinton as First Lady.
- Suppose Colin Powell had been the GOP presidential nominee instead of Bob Dole. The exit poll found that Powell would have defeated Clinton 48 to 36 percent. (Of course, a tough campaign *might* have revealed less popular aspects of Powell's views and persona, so this poll result should be skeptically interpreted.)
- In the age of the permanent campaign, the end of one presidential contest signals the beginning of the next. And what would be the result of a match-up between Al Gore (D) and Jack Kemp (R) in 2000? If you believe 1996's voters, it would be a toss-up: Gore—43 percent, Kemp—39 percent, 11 percent for "other" or undecided.

THE CENTURY'S END ELECTION: A WHIMPER, NOT A BANG

Excitement was not much in evidence during the campaign of 1996—the polar opposite of the 1896 contest that featured fiery populist William Jennings Bryan and President-to-be William McKinley. While about 80 percent of the eligible electorate cast a ballot in that tumultuous McKinley-Bryan election, a paltry 48.8 percent of American adults turned out to the polls for the Clinton-Dole face-off. Turnout declined in every state, and all-time record lows were set in fifteen states. The meager participation rate yielded a particularly sad spin on the election: Bill Clinton won with the votes of just 24 percent of American adults, with Bob Dole attracting only 20 percent. This lack of voter interest in the 1996 race came as no surprise to campaign chroniclers. Television viewing of the party conventions was down almost 21 percent. The TV audiences for the presidential and vice presidential debates were down dramatically from 1992; the final presidential debate received the lowest rating of any such televised debate in history. Network news coverage of the presidential campaign on the nightly broadcasts dropped by 50 percent from four years earlier.[1] And even the network audience for election night itself was down 40 percent from 1992, with only 39 percent of the potential viewership tuning in—the lowest ever.

Reasonable people can debate whether this apathy signified mainly satisfaction with the status quo or frustration with the choice of candidates or anger about the tenor of the campaign. But few observers can remember an election that so utterly failed to engage the citizenry or contained less drama (at least at the presidential level).

Partly, it was simply that the election seemed so predictable, so exceptionally cut and dry. The glut of public opinion polls certainly contributed, as usual, to the front-runner's inevitability, including a few embarrassingly wrong surveys.[2] For example, the final CBS News/*New York Times* poll declared Clinton destined to win by a near-historic 18 percentage point margin, instead of his actual 8 points; perhaps the time-pressed surveyors accidentally substituted a poll of their constituent newsrooms.

The endless stream of nearly identical predictions from the polls and pundits, and the fact that no truly major event occurred in the campaign season to alter the forecasts, made the 1996 election an impossible climb for the challenger. As Democratic National Committee Chairman Don Fowler put it, "From March or April [1996] on, the election was a stable line, and there was never a time when there was anything in the mix that gave us any real cause for doubt or concern."[3] Republican National Committee Chairman Haley Barbour, while insisting that, "I do not accept the idea that Clinton's election was inevitable," admitted that "we started [presidential] polling in April, and we never measured Dole above 41 percent in a single survey, even during the [GOP] convention."[4] The turning points were obvious. The economic recovery peaked in the election year, and a solid, expanding economy helped to generate (directly and indirectly) encouraging news on virtually a daily basis: lower unemployment, higher worker wages and corporate earnings, a lower deficit as tax revenues climbed, most crime rates on the decline, a drop in infant mortality, and so on. Presidents are not singularly responsible for these glad tidings, but they get the credit (or blame) for events happening during their watch, and Bill Clinton was the clear beneficiary. Political scientists have long understood the economy's centrality in presidential elections, and their economic-based prospective models—released months before the election day—were for the most part highly accurate in projecting the dimensions of President Clinton's re-election.[5] Combined with relatively placid conditions abroad and the decision by independent counsel Kenneth Starr not to take any action during the campaign, the solid economy sealed the deal for President Clinton.

The Republicans played their part in Clinton's revival, too. After the president's repudiation at the polls in the 1994 midterm elections, the hubris-filled GOP Congress shut down the federal government in an attempt to force Clinton to bow to their budgetary priorities. The American public judged the Congress extreme and sided with the president, newly seen as a useful check on the legislative branch's excesses. The president's made-to-order foil was the Congress's most visible leader, House Speaker Newt Gingrich, whom the public perceived as egotistical and radical.

With a useful devil figure (Gingrich and the Republican Congress) at hand, Clinton skillfully underwent one of his periodic political makeovers, transforming himself from the liberal of 1993–4 into the "New Democrat" moderate that he had claimed to be in his 1992 campaign. Clinton signed a harsh "welfare reform" bill and another GOP-passed piece of legislation banning gay marriages, with surprisingly little protest from liberals. The 1994 election had so traumatized Democrats of all persuasions that Clinton was given wide latitude to do almost anything necessary for his political survival. Similarly, Clinton was handed renomination without a fight, a tremendous advantage (as we have already reviewed in Chapter Three). Targeting women and moderates in particular, Clinton also focused on education, the environment, Medicare, and middle-class concerns. Part of the Clinton campaign agenda was undeniably demagogic: in his "Mediscare" effort, the president claimed the GOP was bound to gut Medicare, conveniently ignoring that the program was heading toward bankruptcy and that his own proposed cuts were not much smaller than the Republicans. But other aspects of Clinton's agenda were shrewd, reasonable stratagems well suited to his strengths and purposes: targeted tax breaks for some college tuitions, V-chips to permit parental control of children's television viewing, support of school uniforms, a ban on "drive-thru" deliveries (short hospitalizations) for pregnant women, and so on.

While Newt Gingrich and his freshmen co-revolutionaries were an essential ingredient in the GOP's suicide stew, Bob Dole's lackluster campaign flavored the mix. The Dole general election effort has frequently been called the most disorganized and most unimpressive in modern times, and that may be an understatement. Frequently cited is the Dole organization's clumsy effort to get Ross Perot to withdraw in late October and endorse Dole, despite the Republican's successful effort to keep Perot out of the two presidential debates.[6] Horror stories galore have emerged from inside the campaign itself, including this evaluation from Dole's former media adviser Mike Murphy:

> The campaign was all about turf and personal relationships. None of the top people had ever done anything significant other than be RNC bureaucrats. They've produced a campaign that's, at best, strategically incompetent. The campaign ha[d] no real strategy, and never did. It's a group-think operation, with an overabundant use of polling and focus groups; they need a focus group to figure out what day it is . . . Dole was a great war horse, and he deserved a real campaign. It was heartbreaking to be a part of this thing and be powerless to change it.[7]

After the election, many prominent Republicans attributed Dole's loss mainly to his inadequate campaign—a faulty analysis that ignores the other factors discussed here. But a poor organization can expand the margin of the losing candidate's defeat, and such was probably Bob Dole's fate. The Dole team seemed incapable of creativity, even of implementing ideas that had substantial support within the team itself. Take, for example, Mike Murphy's clever suggestion to have Dole dominate the news between the two major-party conventions by riding a train through some swing states. [See the accompanying internal campaign memorandum.[8]] If the stratagem sounds familiar, it is because President Clinton's advisers eventually decided to do the same thing, and the trip was brilliantly successful. Given that the train ploy made eminent good sense, as recognized by the president's planners, why did the Dole campaign not act first (which it had had the opportunity to do)? According to Mike Murphy, "I sold Dole on the train trip. He'd bring it up in meetings, and they'd all say, 'We're working on that, senator.' And then they'd get back to him, shake their heads, and say, 'Impractical. Can't work. Don't want to do it.' "[9]

The contrast between the candidates' campaign abilities has rarely been as stark. Bill Clinton's political gifts and energies are already the stuff of legend. It is not simply his "I feel-your-pain" approach in public gatherings, but an insatiable appetite for people and their approval that distinguishes his style. As a Democratic official who had observed Clinton many dozens of times put it, "You put Clinton in a crowd, and he lights up. He has to talk to every

---

Confidential Internal Memo/Dole Campaign:

POST CONVENTION "WHISTLE-STOP" TRAIN TRIP CONCEPT

by Mike Murphy, 7/8/96

Strategic Idea: The Bob Dole "Tax Cut Express"

We grab momentum after our convention and steal news of the Democrat convention with a surprise whistle stop tour from San Diego to Chicago, where we announce our tax cut during the Democratic convention.

Tactics:

After the San Diego Convention, Senator Dole and the VP nominee embark on a whistle-stop train tour. We travel up through the critical swing "Inland Empire" corridor of California to Los Angeles. Then east across Arizona and New Mexico, and up to Denver. Then across

(Continued)

(Continued)

Kansas to Russell. Big Hometown Rally. Main street Values speech (Hollywood, workfare, etc.) Conclude speech in Russell with big SURPRISE announcement: *We are taking the fight for America to Clinton and the Democrats. We are continuing the train trip to Chicago.*

We roll east through Missouri and then north through Illinois. Arrive in Chicago during day two of the Democratic Convention. Big outdoor rally (we will run heavy ad campaign to promote big attendance.) Dole announces his Tax Cut plan. Train then rolls on through Northern Indiana (Elkhart) and up to Grand Rapids, Michigan and west to Detroit suburbs. Then south to a big finish in Cleveland.

Why We Should Do This:

- Media has nothing to write about at the Democratic convention. We create a huge story. Steal thunder. Put Clinton on defensive on his tax-increase record. Get Clinton way, way, off message.
- Put Dole tax cut versus Clinton tax hike at very top of campaign agenda. Get tax agenda set pre-Labor Day.
- Train idea is a good message bubble for Sen. Dole to travel in. Comfortable. One stump speech, given over and over again. Tele-prompter stage on rear of train. Lots of local news, color.
- The "rolling train" toward Illinois creates a wonderful day by day "countdown" story. Clinton campaign has to deal with daily countdown reaction as Dole, unstoppable, rolls toward big showdown in Chicago. (This is really a big bracketing operation. Gov. Edgar can plan "welcome party.")
- Good pictures for us to use in fall TV ads.
- Lots of surprises (first the Chicago destination, then tax cut announcement in Chicago at big rally), aggressive, momentum feel after San Diego. Makes news.
- A POSSIBLE ADVERTISING IDEA: We do a daily "greatest hits" 60 second TV ad on CNN (and maybe network) from the train each day from Russell to Illinois.

BOTTOM LINE: This is a great way for us to fill the vacuum between our convention and theirs, deny them a free message ride, and set the fall agenda for the campaign. We also hit six of our most important swing states (CA, CO, MO, IL, MI, OH) volunteer, shake hands with every cook and dishwasher at an event, touch the shoulder of every cop in the motorcade. It's a real passion; nobody could fake that." By comparison, Bob Dole's public speaking skills were barely passable, and he rarely connected with a crowd. The Republican flitted from issue to issue, theme to theme, desperately searching for a silver bullet. If he had one, according to leading Democrats, it was taxes. The president's advisers were worried about Dole's 15 percent income-tax cut since the Clinton team's research had shown "the one thing we were really weak on was taxes," remembered DNC chairman Don Fowler. "But Bob Dole's proposal was so inartfully crafted and delivered and sold that it had no effect."[10]

Finally, the RNC's Haley Barbour—who watched in frustration as Dole floundered—added several other ingredients to 1996's electoral stew, most of them a critical commentary on the inadequacies of Bob Dole and his campaign:

> My wife told me, "If you ask Dole voters to name three reasons why they're for Dole, almost all of them would say (1) 'I'm a Republican' and (2) 'He's not Clinton'. But none of them could give you a third reason . . . Some of it was [Dole's] age, but another thing that jumps out of the data is public concern about education. Dole said some things that left people with the impression that abolishing the Department of Education was about all he had to say on the subject . . . You can't ignore money, either. Clinton got $37 million for an unopposed nomination and spent it on the general election, which was grossly unfair but had a big effect. Plus he benefitted from tens of millions spent by labor unions, while most of big business sat on their hands and just decided not to take the same aggressive course as labor.[11]

From 1896 to 1996

On several occasions throughout this volume, we have drawn comparisons between the *fin de siecle* presidential contests of the nineteenth and twentieth centuries. One final comparison remains to be made: the remarkable similarity in the winning coalitions of the two President "Bills," McKinley and Clinton. As the accompanying map illustrates, McKinley—like Clinton—built his Electoral College majority upon a sweep of the Northeast, the Midwest, and the West Coast. While Bob Dole did not fare as well as William Jennings Bryan, both losing candidates secured substantial support in the South, the Plains states, and the Rocky Mountain region.

Democrats can only hope, and Republicans fear, that Clinton's twice-tested base becomes as enduring as McKinley's, which lasted until the Great Depression ushered in the New Deal majority in 1932. Of course, political parties mattered more to average voters a century ago, and an individual's partisan affiliation was usually deeply felt and thus not easily abandoned. At the twentieth century's end, a third or so of the citizens are essentially

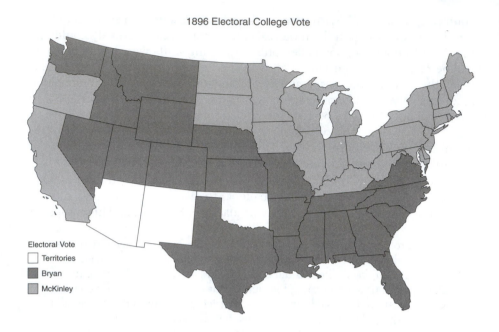

Figure 4   1896 Electoral College Vote

independent of party labels, and most of the other two-thirds are not strongly attached to the labels they embrace. Therefore, it is extraordinarily difficult to engineer a partisan realignment of any permanence. The Republicans, who had become cocky and overconfident after three straight landslides in the 1980's, learned this to their chagrin in 1992, and the odds are that the Democrats will be disappointed anew early in the new century. (How early? It is anybody's guess!)

Still, the 1996 contest for the White House was filled with warning signs for the Republicans. Their weaknesses with women, moderates, young people, and independents will not be easily remedied, unless a recession, an unpopular foreign war, or a major league presidential scandal conveniently unfolds in the next election year. Yet again, it is reminiscent of 1896, though in reverse.[12] William Jennings Bryan's brand of Democracy represented an economic populism and social conservatism that proved wildly attractive in rural America but deadly in the more moderate, populous precincts of urban America. Similarly, the Christian Coalition's Republicanism—now utterly dominant in the party's platform—is an article of faith in the GOP's new base (the rural South and heartland America) but increasingly troublesome in northern and western urban and suburban precincts of both coasts and the urban Midwest. Will today's GOP be able to build a bridge to the next century, transcending this cultural divide better than the Democrats in the 1890's who failed in the task? In large measure, their success in presidential elections may depend on it.

NOTES

1. See the *Hotline* 10 (Nov. 8, 1996): 1, 6–7.

2. See the *Hotline* 10 (Nov. 12, 1996): 9–10. Data are taken from the Markle Presidential Election Watch study conducted by the Center for Media and Public Affairs; ABC, CBS, and NBC evening news shows from Labor Day to November 5, 1996 were analzyed.

3. See the *Hotline* 10 (Nov. 6, 1996): 33–4. The CBS/*Times* survey was by far the least predictive.

4. Interview with Donald Fowler, November 11, 1996.

5. Interview with Haley Barbour, November 27, 1996. During the Republican convention, however, Clinton dropped to 46 percent—just a 5 point lead over Dole. The president recovered his larger lead after his own convention.

6. See James C. Campbell and Thomas E. Mann, "Forecasting the Presidential Election: What Can We Learn from the Models?", *The Brookings Review* 14 (Fall 1996): 24–31.

7. Russell Verney, the Reform Party's political director, claimed that Dole's campaign manager Scott Reed only got in Perot's door because the appointment was made by longtime Perot financial associate Ken Langone, a Perot supporter in 1992 who had decided to back Dole in 1996. Verney asserted, "Until the meeting began, Ross was unaware that there was going to be any discusion of him dropping out . . . It took him by surprise . . . If they wanted Ross to [endorse Dole], they should have sent somebody with a whole lot more stature [than Reed]." Interview, Novermber 12, 1996.

8. Interview with Mike Murphy, September 30, 1996.

9. Memo shared with the author by Mike Murphy. See also the ideas proposed by editorial writer John Fund in "Bob Dole's Best Shot," *The Wall Street Journal*, September 26, 1996, A12.

10. Interview, September 30, 1996.

11. Interview, November 11, 1996.

12. Interview, November 27, 1996. Barbour was particularly critical of the Business Roundtable, the flagship organization of some of America's largest corporations, which "took a powder and decided to do nothing" in case Democrats regained control of Congress.

13. See William Schneider, "Clinton is Building a New Majority," *National Journal* vol. 28, no. 44 (November 2, 1996): 2382.

CHAPTER 7

Campaigning for Congress

The Echo of '94

Richard E. Cohen

Congressional Correspondent, National Journal

For a Congress that had experienced a roller-coast four years for both parties, the 1996 election results surprisingly reinforced the status quo. In historical terms, the exception proved the rule. During most of the 20th century, power in Washington had moved steadily from the divided and often dysfunctional Congress to the White House's bully pulpit. Individual lawmakers, meanwhile, had learned to survive by keeping distance from their national parties' travails and by bringing home the bacon to their local constituents. But, after the Democrats' crash-and-burn failure to deliver on President Clinton's agenda caused their decisive ouster from control of both the House and Senate in 1994, the resurgent Republicans had an idea for how they would exercise their new-found majority: they thought that they could run Washington from Capitol Hill. On the biggest issue—their attempt to balance the federal budget and reduce the growth rate for Medicare and other fast-growing entitlement programs while they cut spending throughout most of the remainder of the budget—the Republicans' initiative to draw the line between the two parties was a spectacular failure in legislative terms. And their proposal gave Democrats and their allies a tailor-made campaign issue.

But, after all the campaign hullabaloo, surprisingly few incumbents were defeated and there was little net change in the balance of power anywhere in Congress. Nor, despite their post-election rhetoric about the need for bipartisanship, was there much evidence that neither party emerged from the campaign with significantly revised strategies. Meanwhile, several other trends that had developed during the past decade or two continued their slow but inexorable pace: Republicans reinforced their new-found majority in the South, in both the House and Senate; While both parties talked moderation, the center of gravity moved farther left among the Democrats and to the right for Republicans. And women gained numbers in both parties but they still were not in position to challenge the male control or mindset on Capitol Hill.

For both parties, the 1996 election had more than its share of disappointments. Democrats suffered the most obvious failures. In the House, where they held the majority for 40 years until 1994, their single-minded bid to regain control fell painfully short after a bitter and hard-fought campaign. In the Senate, Democrats actually lost two additional seats as they found that the presidential results provided virtually no coattails. The results appeared to make it unlikely that President Clinton's party will regain the majority in either chamber of Congress during his second term. But Republicans, although they obviously had reason for satisfaction, knew that they too faced problems. Their diminished House majority was the smallest for either party since the mid-1950s, and their tenuous control left embattled Republican leaders potentially captive to innumerable self-styled House GOP factions making all sorts of impossible and irreconcilable demands. In the Senate, the vigorous new Majority Leader Trent Lott already had learned difficult lessons about the limits of his influence before the November election, when the Republican Congress approved several major bills that Clinton enthusiastically signed. The rules of the Senate, the Republicans were reminded, assure that little happens without satisfying the minority—sometimes, even a minority of one. And the President showed that he wins the bulk of the political credit, no matter how much (or how little) sweat he drips to move legislation.

When the 104th Congress began in January 1995, House Speaker Newt Gingrich and his "Contract With America" were the dominant political forces in Washington. With most congressional Democrats reeling from the 1994 election blow to their solar plexus, and with Clinton playing defense while he sought to regain his political strength and seek a new direction for his presidency, Republicans seemed unstoppable. But it didn't turn out that way. First, they suffered some setbacks, chiefly in the Senate, where their constitutional amendment to balance the federal budget suffered a one-vote defeat. Then, the great debate in late 1995 on specific steps to achieve that balance by 2002 foundered in a shutdown of the federal government. Fittingly, the closing extended through the Christmas and New Year holidays while Clinton and Republican leaders continued their marathon talks; it ended the day before a once-in-a-century blizzard that shut down most of Washington for another week in early January. After the apparent failure by both sides to resolve anything, the political gods had decreed—from all the evidence—that the appropriate response was to cover the Capitol with a couple feet of snow.

As the Democrats pushed their relentless assault on Gingrich's legislative handiwork plus his personal foibles, the 1996 campaign for Congress took on a tone that was both unusually nationalized and targeted at the same time. With tens of millions of dollars of advertising assistance financed by organized labor, the Democrats' message was virtually the same from Maine to Arizona: the local congressman had "supported Gingrich's agenda to slash Medicare in order to provide a tax cut for the wealthy." Democratic strategists doggedly sought out the most vulnerable House Republicans, chiefly those from the 73 freshmen elected in November 1994. For the first several months of 1996, as national political attention focused on the battle for the Republican presidential nomination, Congress moved to the back seat, and members finally had the opportunity to make their case back home. Some were more successful than others. Those who were able to overcome the national stereotype by focusing on their own activities generally prevailed in November. But some Republicans from the start faced an uphill battle for survival, either because they lacked the political skills or because their 1994 victory in a Democratic-leaning district was a fluke.

If the 1996 campaign had been fought simply on the Democrats' challenge to the Gingrich agenda, the results make clear that they would have fared better. But a second major factor came into play for Democrats, which was a direct result of their 1994 election setback and the pessimism that settled into their ranks as they settled into the minority in both the House and Senate. Rather than adjust to their loss of control, many Democrats decided not to seek re-election. True enough, many of these lawmakers had served on Capitol Hill for a decade or two, or more, and it was time for them to move on. But there was another side to the story, which the retirees were less willing to discuss publicly: if they thought that there was a likelihood that Democrats would regain the majority and the gold-plated chairmanships that come with it, they would have been more likely to seek another term. But the angry tenor of the budget debate and the Republicans' seeming political dominance in the fall of 1995, when most incumbents were deciding whether to seek another term, provided an inhospitable climate for Democrats. Compounding the blow for their party was that a disproportionate share of the Democrats' many retirees were from the South, where their party had clearly moved to the defensive and was losing many of its seats as political control shifted from rural courthouses to fast-growing suburban subdivisions.

When the results trickled in on Election Night, the outcome in the House fell short of what the Republicans had hoped. About a dozen GOP freshmen lost their seats, and the massacre of the southern Democrats lost some of its intensity. Still, to the surprise of many Democrats, Republicans did well enough to retain their control. After a few December runoffs in Texas, the count showed 227 Republicans, 207 Democrats, and one independent. The Republicans had 230 seats immediately after the 1994 election, although five party switchers and one special election moved them to 236 in early 1996.

However, the problem at the end of 1996 was not as much the small net loss of nine seats as the changed political climate. With the combination of the Democrats' battering of Gingrich, the presidential campaign defeat of Robert Dole, plus their own somewhat inevitable fraying of unity as the glow of their 1994 triumph faded, House Republicans faced some loss of camaraderie and their strong sense of mission from two years earlier.

In the post-Dole Senate, the changes—both in the election results and in the party's leadership—pushed Republicans in the same direction the House had moved in the previous two years. The Senate GOP had become more southern, more conservative, and more aggressive. But, as in the House, their new enthusiasm and the growing ideological zeal of Trent Lott's Republicans were no guarantee of party unity or of legislative success. Despite their loss of two seats, Democrats had won enough Senate contests to gain some bragging rights in the new Congress. And after the 1994 election, in which not a single new Democrat had joined the Senate, the victory of six first-term Democrats in 1996 gave some needed revitalization to their side of the aisle. On the other hand, whether the Senate Democrats in the new Congress would find common ground with Republicans, with President Clinton or—for that matter—with each other remain open questions.

THE WASHINGTON SETTING

Because so much of the 1996 campaign rhetoric was based on the legislative developments of the previous two years, a brief review of the 104th Congress is essential to an understanding of the electoral dynamics. That two year period was marked by an unusually intense partisanship and by a striking supremacy of Congress over the White House in setting the national agenda. And more than any other single player in recent decades, House Speaker Newt Gingrich of Georgia was the dominant figure on Capitol Hill. Gingrich's highly publicized ascent to the national political stage was remarkable for several reasons. During his previous 16 years in Congress, he had played only a modest legislative role and he was little-known outside Capitol Hill, even by Washington's self-styled insiders. Instead, he had postured himself chiefly as a political strategist, working initially with a handful of comrades in the House and with activist allies in the Reagan Administration to press their conservative agenda. Even when House Republicans unexpectedly chose him by a one-vote margin in 1989 to become their number-two leader, Gingrich did not take the conventional role as a party "whip" to rally support for Republican policies. That was apparent in September 1990, when he became an outspoken opponent of the budget deal that President Bush reached with most House and Senate leaders from both parties. The split among Republicans over a modest tax increase ultimately caused serious political damage to Bush's re-election bid.

With Bush's defeat in 1992, Gingrich soon emerged as the ideological and political leader of congressional Republicans. With his hands-on direction, the GOP unanimously opposed Clinton's 1993 budget package, which the House and Senate each approved by one-vote margins. On Clinton's sweeping health-care reform proposal, Gingrich was instrumental in coalescing Republican opposition and in developing a modest alternative, which soon gained support from conservative Democrats. The GOP stance helped to sink the White House plan, which the Democratic-controlled House and Senate both failed to bring to a final vote. These events and others made it apparent that House Republicans wanted more aggressive leadership than they were receiving from Robert Michel of Illinois, who had been their party leader since 1981. So, when Michel announced in October 1993 that he would not seek re-election to the House, there was little doubt that the frequently pugnacious and blunt-spoken Gingrich was the heir apparent.

What came next was the defining event during Gingrich's command of House Republicans. With little publicity in the first half of 1994, he worked with a coterie of allies among House Republicans—most of them junior, but with a mixture of moderate and conservative views—to assemble a campaign strategy that would demonstrate to voters both that Democrats were no longer fit to run the House and that Republicans had the ideas and the determination to take command. Their focal point would be the "Contract with America"—a unique political document that promised legislative action on 10 basic proposals within 100 days, assuming the Republicans won control of the House. After 40 years in which Republicans had served, often with a sense of subservience and inevitability, as the downtrodden House minority, Gingrich led a new corps of Republicans who said that they had had enough and that they were prepared to show the American public that they were fit to become the majority. "Newt has great ideas, and I have wanted to make sure that they come out," said Representative Christopher Shays of Connecticut, one of the House's most liberal Republicans and a Gingrich ally. The ideas were basic and, according to public-opinion polls, popular: they featured a balanced-budget constitutional amendment, tax cuts, welfare reform, and overhaul of federal regulatory and crime laws. But what made Gingrich such a skillful advocate during the 1994 campaign was that he worked relentlessly to convince Republican candidates and, ultimately, the voters that the goals were attainable. By campaigning for scores of House candidates across the nation, by raising abundant funds for them and for the national party, by giving them a sense of confidence and of unity, and by developing a sense of teamwork, Gingrich became a new-style congressional leader. With the unifying themes of the Contract With America, which most of them signed in a ceremony on the Capitol steps in late September, House GOP candidates across the nation in 1994 sought to convince voters that their local election would have a national impact. Even if most voters did not actually read or comprehend the details of that campaign document, it helped to increase the party's credibility that Republicans offered what appeared to be constructive alternatives.

When the 1994 election results came in, Gingrich became the undisputed champion of a political revolution. The numbers were awe-inspiring. Republicans had gained 52 House seats, the largest shift since 1948. They had defeated 34 House Democratic incumbents, while losing none of their own members. And they had won control of the House for the first time in 40 years, ending the longest period of single-party control in Congress in the nation's history. Senate Republicans, too, had a successful campaign, with an eight seat gain that allowed them to capture Senate control. But their gain was less impressive, not only because the GOP had held the Senate majority for six years during the 1980s but also because Republican challengers defeated only two Democratic incumbents; the remaining party changes in the Senate were in seats that had been held by Democratic retirees. Besides, under the leadership of Robert Dole of Kansas, Senate Republicans had kept their distance from the young upstarts who prepared and campaigned on the Contract with America.

All Republicans now had their agenda in place for the start of the new 104th Congress. Even before they were sworn into office, Gingrich assembled the members of the new House majority to make early plans to overhaul their tradition-encrusted institution. They swept out many of the old offices and bureaucratic traditions that had slowed the House's advance into a new technological world. Although they failed to go as far as some reformers advocated, they eventually eliminated three House committees and 34 subcommittees and they made other jurisdictional changes in an attempt to rationalize an antiquated committee system. Perhaps most importantly, Gingrich worked with a cross-section of House Republicans to select committee chairmen on a basis other than strict seniority. At the powerful Appropriations Committee, for example, the top four Republicans were bypassed until Gingrich selected the conservative and temperamentally aggressive Bob Livingston of Louisiana as the new chairman.

With those changes in place, the Gingrich-led House moved quickly in 1995 to deliver on its campaign promises. With an initial majority of only 230-to-204, the slimmest margin in the House since 1954, Republicans would require internal discipline to achieve their goals. In an unprecedented display, the House debated and voted by early April on the 10 major items of the Republicans' Contract, some of which required passage of several bills. The lawmakers approved all but one of the proposals—the proposed constitutional amendment to impose term-limits on members of Congress, which required two-thirds approval. When Congress left Washington for the spring recess, Republicans basked in their success, and polls showed a positive public response. A poll conducted by the Gallup Organization with CNN and *USA Today* in early April 1995 showed that 53 percent felt that the Republican leaders of Congress were moving the country in the right direction, compared with only 37 percent who responded that it was moving in the wrong direction. But that poll and others also included disturbing results for Gingrich: a substantially negative rating in his own popularity. Only 37 percent approved of his own job performance, compared with 47 percent disapproval; by a 52–35 percent margin, the respondents said that they did not share his values.

The remainder of 1995 was marked by increasingly contentious debate in Congress over the Republicans' plan to balance the federal budget by 2002, as they had promised in a constitutional amendment that fell one vote short of the required two-thirds approval in the Senate. Although there were significant policy differences between the initial House and Senate versions, both made major cuts in the federal government's domestic spending, and they approved tax cuts for American families and for businesses. But, it quickly became clear, the partisan flashpoint of the GOP plan was an attempt to reduce the rate of growth in the federal Medicare program, which was established in 1965 to provide medical assistance for the elderly. Citing an official report of the Clinton Administration that the hospital-insurance portion of the program was falling short of funds and that it would go bankrupt by 2002, Republicans mounted what they considered a credible and well-publicized campaign to cut back projected Medicare expenditures by $270 billion over the next 7 years. In the process, Republicans repeated as a chorus, they were moving to "preserve, strengthen and protect" Medicare. But Democrats had a different perspective. Noting that the $270 billion reduction in Medicare spending matched the amount of the Republicans' proposed tax cut, Democrats said repeatedly that the GOP was "cutting Medicare to pay for tax cuts for the rich." That attack, which gained an especially favorable response from worried senior citizens, would become the Democrats' dominant partisan theme for much of the next year.

The budget clash, especially over Medicare, led to an unprecedented stalemate between the President and congressional Republicans over the money needed to operate the federal government in fiscal 1996. But they were unable to resolve their final differences. What gave the negotiations added drama is that they were conducted amid two separate shutdowns of most federal agencies because they had run out of operating funds or authority; the closings lasted a total of four weeks during a period between mid-November and early January. With the news media reporting that federal beneficiaries and government workers were not receiving payments that were essential for routine sustenance, the holiday season took on an unusually grim tenor. But the Democrats' use of more skillful public-relations tactics shifted the blame for the shutdown mostly to the Republicans, according to public-opinion polls. It was, Gingrich later confessed, a period in which he was outmaneuvered by a more politically adept Clinton. "I've got a problem. I get in those meetings and as a person I like the President," Gingrich told two top Clinton aides at the time, according to an account in *The Washington Post.* "I melt when I'm around him. After I get out I need two hours to detoxify. My people are nervous about me going in there because of the way I deal with this."[1] The Speaker also found himself torn by conflicting views within his own party. Many House Republicans—chiefly a large group of the ever-feisty freshmen— were unwilling to accept anything other than virtual surrender by Clinton. Senate Republicans, led by Dole, were far more willing to negotiate a deal. Democrats responded that, in contrast to the more popular Contract with America, the Gingrich agenda had become "extreme." But, agreeing to make only a modest budget compromise with Clinton, Republicans held firm and decided to take their differences to the public during what they hoped would be the pivotal 1996 election.

THE CAMPAIGN SETTING

American elections, of course, are not simply a matter of choosing between two parties. The results are influenced by such other factors as incumbency, candidate recruiting, and fundraising. In the House, two broad factors set the framework for the election, posing major risk for each party. The Democrats had to contend with their many retirees, especially from the South; the Republicans were concerned for their vulnerable freshmen. First, a brief look at some numbers. Of the 74 first-term Republicans (including Tom Campbell of California, who was elected to fill a vacant seat in December 1995), all but three sought re-election. Wes Cooley of Oregon and Enid Greene Waldholtz of Utah each retired because of ethical problems stemming, in part, from their 1994 election campaign; Sam Brownback of Kansas ran for Bob Dole's Senate seat. Approximately two dozen of the remaining GOP freshmen were marked from an early point as especially vulnerable by both parties. Some such as Phil English of Pennsylvania, Michael Patrick Flanagan of Illinois, and Fred Heineman of North Carolina held seats in traditionally Democratic areas. For others, their non-legislative actions had marked them for ridicule by Democrats or the press. In that category, for example, were Helen Chenoweth of Idaho, who had questionable financial transactions; David Funderburk of North Carolina, who was accused of fabricating the conditions of a traffic accident in which he may have been the driver; and Steve Stockman of Texas, who seemed to voice sympathy for militia groups after the April 1995 bombing of the federal building in Oklahoma City. Although many freshmen Republicans, notably those from the South, had no re-election worries, Democratic campaign strategists saw an opportunity from the start of the campaign to tie virtually all of them to their anti-Gingrich strategy. "No Speaker has been as polarizing a force as Newt," said Democratic Congressional Campaign Committee chairman Martin Frost of Texas. Polls showed that he was viewed as "hard-edged" and "mean-spirited," Frost added.

But Democrats faced at least as great a jeopardy to their own seats because 30 of their House members decided not to seek another term. Of that group, 19 were from the South and perhaps a dozen of them held seats that Republicans viewed as prime targets. The many retirements were a problem for Democrats on two levels. On a case-by-case basis, the southern departures were worrisome because of the Republicans' growing strength in that region and because the GOP won 22 of the 31 Democratic-held open seats nationwide in 1994. More generally, congressional retirements also serve as a leading indicator of election prospects: typically, many members decide to leave because they fear that they will have trouble winning another term. With the House Democrats' difficulty in adjusting to their unaccustomed life in the minority, the large number of retirees also signaled pessimism in party ranks that they would regain control and their accompanying chairmanships any time soon. Although House Republicans also suffered 23 retirements in their ranks, a large majority of those lawmakers held relatively safe Republican seats. For example, 12 of the departing GOP members were from districts where Bush won at least 60 percent of the vote in 1988, when he won 53 percent nationwide. The Democratic retirees, by contrast, were disproportionately in areas where their national party had fared poorly; of the 29 Democratic open seats, Bush won 20 of those districts in 1988.

In the Senate, retirements also became a big problem for Democrats, because of both the numbers and the geography. Of the 15 Democrats whose term expired in 1996, 8 decided not to seek re-election—a record number for a single party since popular election of senators began in 1914. Although some retirees were aging, like 78-year old Claiborne Pell of Rhode Island and 75-year-old Jim Exon of Nebraska, others like Bill Bradley of New Jersey, 53, and Sam Nunn of Georgia, 58, were in their peak political years. Even more troubling for Democrats was that all four of their southern senators at the end of their six-year term decided not to seek re-election; in addition to Nunn, they were Howell Heflin of Alabama, Bennett Johnston of Louisiana and David Pryor of Arkansas. This pattern of southern Democrats voting with their feet was similar to what took place in the House. Instead of running veteran senators who probably would have had little difficulty winning re-election, Democrats in the four southern states scrambled to find candidates to run against the reinvigorated Republicans. Senate Republicans, too, had retirement problems. Except for Mark Hatfield of Oregon, however, each of their five other retirees came from Republican-leaning states. They included the special case of Dole, who quit in June 1996, only to be replaced by appointee Sheila Frahm from historically Republican Kansas. She, in turn, lost the GOP primary to Representative Brownback less than two months later.

The record number of retiring senators triggered hand-wringing in the political community about the shrinking political center. The departures were "stripping the Senate of experienced lawmakers comfortable with compromise when it requires reaching across party lines," lamented an article in the *New York Times*.[2] The departure of many conservative Democrats and moderate Republicans depleted much of the Senate's already-diminishing corps for bipartisanship. Republicans Nancy Kassebaum of Kansas and Alan Simpson of Wyoming, like Democrats Johnston and Nunn, were examples of old-style senators uncomfortable with the growing partisanship on both sides of the aisle in an institution where such behavior until recently was far less prevalent than in the House. Although some of the newly-elected Senators probably would help shape a new center—a constantly evolving feature of almost any legislative body—the retirement parade seemed likely to have a major impact within the Senate.

Democrats also faced the problem that several of their senators seeking re-election faced highly competitive challengers. Paul Wellstone of Minnesota, who ranked as the most liberal senator in many ratings, had a rematch of his close 1990 victory over then-Senator Republican Rudy Boschwitz of Minnesota. Max Baucus of Montana and Tom Harkin of Iowa were early Republican targets in states where the GOP had shown growing strength and where Republicans relentlessly sought to pin the "liberal" tag on their opponents. And perhaps the most interesting Senate contest came in the liberal bastion of Massachusetts, where popular Republican Governor Bill Weld challenged the re-election of Senator John Kerry; the socially liberal Weld postured himself to the left of his opponent on some issues, but Weld's profile was considerably more conservative on federal spending and taxes.

On the other side of the aisle, Republicans had few seriously vulnerable incumbents. At the top of the Democrats' target list was Senator Larry Pressler of South Dakota—the chairman of the Commerce, Science and Transportation Committee—whom Democrats accused for years of having lost touch with his constituency. The GOP's other big problem came with otherwise secure incumbents whose age and long seniority made them inviting targets. The prime example was 93-year-old Strom Thurmond of South Carolina, who already held the record as the oldest-ever senator; first elected in 1954, he also was close to the record of the senator with the most years of service. Another worry for GOP officials was arch-conservative Jesse Helms of North

Carolina, 75, whose political career had been marked by close and controversial victories.

As they prepared for the 1996 campaign, both parties faced the challenge of adjusting to major changes in the political environment. The 1994 election was significant not only because of the Democrats' stunning defeats and their loss of congressional control. Also apparent was that incumbency was no longer the advantage that it had been for more than a decade. As recently as the previous mid-term election in 1990, for example, only 15 House members and one senator were defeated for re-election. Contrast that to the 36 lawmakers in the two chambers who were defeated four years later. True, every one of the losers in 1994 was a Democrat. But the results left a clear message that voters were restless and more willing to make change, for whatever reason. Even in 1992, the anti-incumbency message had started to resonate more loudly. Fed by such factors as the House-bank scandal, in which 325 members were listed as having written overdrafts without penalty or had received other special banking privileges from House employees, voters were making clear that they were increasingly disaffected by both parties. The 1992 election not only featured the independent presidential candidacy of Washington-bashing Ross Perot, but it also was notable because Democrat Bill Clinton, then governor of Arkansas, deliberately distanced himself in the presidential campaign from the congressional Democrats.

The weakening of the incumbency advantage was closely tied to another political change: the increasingly national strategy for congressional campaigns. For many years, most candidates in both parties had perfected former House Speaker Tip O'Neill's mantra that "all politics is local." In many cases, they had made a conscious practice of distancing themselves from their national party leaders and rhetoric. That was especially true for southern Democrats who sought to posture themselves as more conservative than their national party and for northern Republicans who sought to move to the left of their national party's rhetoric. But the Republicans' 1994 campaign and the subsequent legislative actions changed much of that conventional approach.

As Speaker, Gingrich undertook a grueling travel schedule on behalf of Republican candidates that was far more energetic than had been the case for recent leaders of either party. Gingrich is "unique and irreplaceable" as a GOP asset, said Representative Bill Paxon of New York, chairman of the National Republican Congressional Committee (NRSC). In what may have been a bit of overstatement he added, "Lloyds of London couldn't come up with a big enough insurance policy to cover what he gives us." Those visits provided both major financial assistance and forums to rally the party faithful behind the local candidate. "People later told me that they appreciate the opportunity to hear the Speaker," said freshman Representative Randy Tate, R-Wash., following Gingrich's visit to his politically centrist district in June, which drew more than 1,000 people.

Although the Republicans' nationalizing of campaigns was more of a factor for House candidates, their typically better-known Senate contenders also found that the financial heft of the NRSC gave its Washington operatives more opportunity to shape campaigns in the states. Those activities received a judicial boost from a landmark Supreme Court decision in June 1996, which removed many of the statutory constraints on party spending on behalf of candidates. National Republican committees responded with a barrage of advertising on behalf of many of their congressional candidates or against their Democratic opponents. GOP lawyers contended that because these ads were "legislative advocacy" and did not expressly advocate the election or defeat of a candidate, they were not covered by federal limits, which imposed a population-based formula on party expenditures in a Senate campaign. This new form of political expenditure allowed the parties—chiefly, the better-financed Republicans—to dump additional millions of dollars into Senate contests.

THE NEW GEOGRAPHY

As shown by the Republicans' takeover in 1994 and by the 1996 campaign, the most significant long-term change in congressional elections has come in the South. Although the region's switch to the GOP in presidential politics began with the 1968 election, Democrats managed to retain a solid majority of House and Senate seats in the South throughout the next two decades. But that ended in the first half of the 1990s as the result of three related factors: 1) the increasing difficulty facing southern Democrats—even conservatives—because their national party was viewed as too liberal; 2) the growth of the Republican Party in the South, chiefly as the result of suburban population growth and the gradual increase of local GOP elected officials and organizational strength across the region; and 3) the influence of redistricting, which created additional black-majority districts and, as a result, reduced the base of black voters for Democratic candidates in white-majority districts. Through the combination of retirements, election defeats, and party switches, the number of House Republicans in the 13 states that fall south of the line from the Virginia border to Oklahoma nearly doubled from 44 to 78 (of a total of 137 districts) from 1991 until the start of the 1996 campaign. In the Senate, the number of southern Republicans grew from 9 to 16 in the same period. With the many retirements in the region, Democrats knew that they faced an uphill struggle to prevent further losses in both the House and Senate in November 1996.

Starting with President Franklin Roosevelt's New Deal, the "Solid South" had been an essential cornerstone of Democratic Party politics. The "Boston-Austin" axis, symbolized by the quest for regional balance among the party's congressional leaders, acknowledged that the party's two wings needed each other to survive. Even though southerners after World War II gradually became more conservative than their northern colleagues in the Democratic Party, they remained powerful in Congress, chiefly because of the ironclad grip of the seniority system. Because the Republican Party barely existed on a local level in most of the South and because local Democratic leaders were able to discourage intraparty challenges to most of their officeholders, Democratic lawmakers from that region had little to fear once they first won their seats. The result: during most of the 1950 and 1960s, while northern liberals became the dominant force in the national Democratic Party, southern conservatives retained a majority of the chairmanships in the House and Senate. But that, too, began to change in the 1970s when revisions of the House Democrats' seniority rules resulted in the ouster of several southern committee chairmen who were deemed out of touch with the party's mainstream. Then, with the 1980 presidential election of Ronald Reagan, Republicans started to gain even more House and Senate seats and they increased the pressure on many southern Democrats to join with them on key legislative votes, especially on the economy. With the 1994 change in party control, conservative southerners saw even less reason to remain Democrats. That helps to explain why a record total of five southern House members and two Senators (one from Alabama, the other from Colorado) switched from the Democrats to the Republican Party during little more than a year after the election, thus increasing the momentum toward the wide-scale partisan shift within the region.

Compounding the problems for many Democrats in the House was the growing political and judicial pressure for the creation of black-majority districts to comply with the 1982 renewal of the Voting Rights Act. During the 1991–92 redistricting, a powerful coalition of local black politicians and President Bush's Justice Department demanded that legislatures across the South create as many black-majority districts as possible, even though some of the seats were created with bizarrely contorted boundaries. What had been five black-majority seats (in Atlanta, Houston, Memphis, New Orleans and rural Mississippi) before that round of redistricting became 17 after the 1992 election, with 11 of them in predominantly urban areas; each of those districts elected a black Democrat. (In 1994, J. C. Watts Jr. of rural Oklahoma became the first black southern Republican to win a House seat during the 20th century, but his district was only 7 percent black.) The creation of the additional black-majority seats had the effect, not surprisingly, of reducing the share of black population in the surrounding House districts. That helps to explain why, despite the net increase of nine House seats in 1992 throughout the South due to the separate shifts in overall population, Democrats suffered a major net loss of seats in the region as most of the neighboring districts elected Republicans.

For two reasons, the 1996 election grimly shaped up as possibly the House Democrats' last stand in the South. First, as noted earlier, the many retirements (19 southern Democrats, including two blacks, decided not to seek re-election, compared to only four Republican departures in the region) threatened an additional major loss of House seats. But Democrats had some hope that they could avoid the type of major losses that they suffered in 1992 and 1994. Some of the retiring white Democrats held largely rural and low-income districts where Republicans had not yet become a major local political force. In addition, Democratic strategists hoped that they could turn their anti-Gingrich message to their favor in several of these Democratic-leaning seats.

Second, an extended round of Supreme Court decisions overturned the 1992 redistricting in several southern states as unconstitutional. The five-member Court majority objected to what it called "racial gerrymanders" in the odd-shaped districts. As a result, the lines for the 1996 election were re-drawn in parts of Florida, Georgia, Louisiana and Texas, with the prospects of redistricting changes for 1998 in North Carolina and perhaps elsewhere. The changes threatened both black and white Democrats in the region. In Louisiana, black Democrat Cleo Fields decided not to run again when his district went from 67 percent black to 28 percent black. In Georgia, black Representative Cynthia McKinney lost more than half of her former district but she ran anyway in a revised district in suburban Atlanta. The last-minute changes of the Texas lines created problems for Democrats in three districts outside Dallas and Houston, which had been held by white Democrats, one of whom had already decided not to seek another term. Local Republicans, not surprisingly, welcomed those changes and contended that they would continue their gains of the previous two election cycles.

Redistricting had no impact, of course, in the Senate, where each state has two seats. But the shift to the Republicans seemed at least as dramatic. Republicans in both Arkansas and Louisiana had a strong opportunity to elect their first senator this century. The situation was especially difficult for Democrats in Arkansas, where Governor Jim Guy Tucker was forced to resign in July 1996, following his conviction in federal court on Whitewater-related charges not directly related to President Clinton. Although the resulting decision by Republican Lieutenant Governor Mike Huckabee to replace Tucker and give up his bid for the Senate initially caused some confusion for the GOP, Huckabee's decision ultimately worked in their favor as party leaders selected Representative Tim Hutchinson to replace Huckabee; running against Democratic Attorney General Winston Bryant, Hutchinson offered himself as a voice for change to voters tired of politics as usual in the Razorback State. Ironically, of the four states where their southern Senators had retired, Democrats had the best opportunity to retain the seats in Georgia and Louisiana because the increased Republican strength in each of those states resulted in a nasty GOP primary. In Georgia, Guy Millner won the nomination over Johnny Isakson in a contest in which Isakson contrasted his pro-choice position on abortion; each had previously waged a competitive contest for governor. Secretary of State Max Cleland, a former Carter Administration official, won the Democratic nomination without opposition. In Louisiana, there were six well-known or well-financed Republicans competing for the nomination in the state's unusual nonpartisan primary, in contrast to only two Democrats. Following the 1995 election of recent party-switcher Mike Foster as the state's Republican governor, party leaders saw a good opportunity for a pickup. Some Republicans had feared that Louisiana's unique rules might result in the two Democrats moving to the November runoff. But conservative state legislator Woody Jenkins—who had twice run for the Senate as a Democrat more than a decade earlier—actually finished first in the primary after Republican leaders rallied around his candidacy in the closing days of the primary campaign. Finally, in Alabama, Attorney General Jeff Sessions, a Republican, was the early favorite to defeat Democratic State Senator Roger Bedford. In each of the four open Senate seats in the South, the Republican nominee was an experienced candidate; that was a significant change from elections a decade or two earlier.

MESSAGE DEVELOPMENT

The combination of Gingrich's activist 1995 agenda plus the opportunities and the vulnerabilities posed to each party by the 1996 election contributed to a renewed emphasis on message development by congressional leaders. But that did not necessarily mean that all candidates in each party took on equivalent views. Instead, many of them excerpted parts of their national-party message or they took it as a starting point for their own local appeal; in a few isolated cases, candidates even pointed out the national approach to contrast their own independence. For Republicans, the temptation to repeat the strategy of their highly successful 1994 campaign was balanced by a growing recognition of its political unpopularity in many parts of the nation, which was fueled by the Democrats' often harsh criticism of their high-profile legislative efforts. Democrats, for their part, acknowledged that they had learned lessons from Republicans about the usefulness of party-wide campaign themes, but their candidates retained important elements of the local autonomy, which had contributed to their decades-old electoral success as the majority party in Congress. Two special elections for open seats halfway through the 104th Congress gave useful lessons on the limits of each approach. In California, the contest for a House seat made clear that Democrats could not regain the majority simply by running against Gingrich. The Senate campaign in Oregon demonstrated that Republicans could not prevail simply by repeating 1994.

The Democrats' false start came when Representative Norman Mineta gave up the San Jose-based House seat that he held for more than 20 years; the former chairman of the House Public Works and Transportation Committee, he became an executive with the Lockheed Martin company. Although Mineta had become invincible in local elections, the economically comfortable district was a "swing" seat politically, where Republicans—especially moderates—fared well. Republicans acknowledged that tradition when they nominated without opposition Tom Campbell, a Stanford University economics and law professor who served six years in the House before he narrowly lost in 1992 the Republican primary for an open Senate seat. In that contest, as the centrist alternative to the state's conservative party hierarchy, he lost by 38-to-36 percent to conservative Bruce Herschensohn, who lost the election that November to Democrat Barbara Boxer. Democrats, after several embarrassing setbacks in attempting to recruit well-known local officials to succeed Mineta, nominated Jerry Estruth, a little-known former member of San Jose's city council. In a campaign that was organized and financed heavily by the Washington-based Democratic Congressional Campaign Committee (DCCC), Estruth's advertising sought to portray Campbell as a Gingrich clone and he called the campaign a referendum on Gingrich. "The bottom line is, Tom Campbell will vote for Newt Gingrich for Speaker of the House, and I won't," Estruth said. Campaign committee chairman Frost of Texas repeatedly said that he had "one piece of advice" for Democratic candidates: "Their opponents' middle name is Gingrich." But Campbell responded that they chose the wrong contest to test-run their strategy. His previous service in the House had shown his independence from national Republican dogma, he said, especially on controversial topics such as abortion and the environment, where he had usually taken a liberal view. In what national Democratic leaders acknowledged was an embarrassing setback that caused them to reassess their national strategy, Campbell on Dec. 12 won an overwhelming 59-to-36 percent victory. In the midst of the budget crisis, Republicans asserted that the outcome showed that their own efforts were continuing to play well beyond the Washington Beltway.

But the special-election dynamics changed considerably a month later farther north on the Pacific Coast. That contest was forced after veteran Republican Senator Bob Packwood, the chairman of the powerful Senate Finance Committee, resigned to avoid Senate expulsion following a much-publicized, three-year ethics investigation of his alleged sexual harassment of female Senate and campaign aides. In the special election, Representative Ron Wyden won the hard-fought Democratic primary against Peter DeFazio, another House Democrat; Wyden operated more as a party insider but he sought to posture himself as a political centrist. On the Republican side, state senate president Gordon Smith easily won his party's primary. Although he had become a major player in Oregon politics and he won the backing of prominent conservatives, Smith sought to portray himself as an outsider who had been a successful local businessman. When the campaign started in October, Smith voiced comfort with the national Republican program and leaders; his campaign would be "a referendum on the national agenda," he said in October. As the campaign heated up and the budget crisis intensified in Washington, however, Smith began to distance himself from the Gingrich agenda. "I rather expect that each of us will stand on our own," he said in December, referring to himself and Wyden. The Oregon contest also became a testing ground for the national coalition of liberal organizations—including organized labor, environmental groups, and abortion-rights groups—that spent many hundreds of thousands of dollars for advertising and sophisticated voter-turnout operations. Wyden publicly kept his distance from these groups and their frequently harsh attacks, but there was a close coordination among the political operatives. Following a costly and intensive exchange of advertising, Wyden narrowly won the contest with 51 percent of the vote. Exuberant national Democrats, many of whom had been pessimistic in the final hours before the vote, responded that the Oregon election would be the turning point in the 1996 campaign because of the lessons that they had learned.

As the presidential campaign started to take shape, each party refined its national themes during the early months of 1996. For congressional Democrats, mindful that President Clinton was seeking to distance himself from both parties on Capitol Hill, the goal was to find as much common ground as possible on general terms and to identify specific issues on which they agreed with the President. On legislation, they set an increase in the minimum-wage as a top priority. On the other hand, many Democrats made clear their disagreement with Clinton's continuing interest in reaching a deal with Republicans on welfare reform legislation. When it came to campaign rhetoric, Democrats were less specific in their own views and more focused on criticizing their opponents. In June 1996, Senate Minority Leader Tom Daschle of South Dakota and House Minority Leader Richard Gephardt of Missouri, on behalf of their party, released their "Families First" campaign agenda. Daschle termed it "neither radical nor revolutionary."

Compared with the Republicans' 1994 Contract, the Democrats' 25-page document was a laundry list of incremental policy changes. More of a direct factor in their campaign strategy was the constant drumbeat of criticism by Daschle and Gephardt and their congressional team against what they termed Gingrich's "extreme" Congress. "Mr. Gingrich and his ilk have dug in their heels with an ideology that is mean-spirited," said Max Sandlin, the Democratic nominee for an open House seat in east Texas, which was a prime Republican campaign target. "People see cuts in Medicare and student loans as the government breaking its word." With Democrats across the nation echoing that theme, its impact was enhanced by additional tens of millions of dollars of broadcast advertising, much of it financed by organized labor. But Republicans weakened the impact of the opposition attack when they passed three major pieces of legislation in July 1996 with bipartisan legislative support and Clinton's signature: the minimum-wage increase, welfare reform, and a modest health care reform bill designed chiefly to assure that workers would not lose their medical insurance simply because they changed jobs.

For Republicans, the emergence in March of Robert Dole as the party's apparent presidential nominee gave Gingrich and their other legislative leaders a welcome opportunity to fade into the political background outside Capitol Hill. Although Gingrich continued to concede his stylistic differences with Dole, their close dealings during 1995 on the budget and other issues had raised their comfort level with each other and increased Gingrich's willingness to defer to Dole. Even when Dole announced in May 1996 his resignation as Senate majority leader—a decision that reflected, in part, Dole's frustration with the contentiousness on Capitol Hill—congressional Republicans maintained regular contact and sought to coordinate strategy with him. Those ties were further sealed by two vital steps that Dole took prior to the Republicans' San Diego convention in August. First, Dole's proposal for a 15 percent cut in income tax rates was enthusiastically received by Gingrich and other GOP leaders, who welcomed the proposal as consistent with their earlier agenda and as a big boost for party prospects in the fall campaign. Then, Dole's selection of Jack Kemp as his running mate was another 10-strike for congressional Republicans, who viewed Kemp as their ideological godfather. As a House member for 18 years, Kemp had worked closely with both Gingrich and Trent Lott, who had been House minority whip until his election to the Senate in 1988. The result was a striking camaraderie between two groups of Republicans that had spent much of the past two decades battling with each other on Capitol Hill: Dole's old-style Republicans, who placed the highest priority on deficit reduction and tended to seek bipartisan deals, and Gingrich's activist flock, who were more hostile to the federal government and modeled themselves as political outsiders.

CANDIDATE RECRUITMENT

Next to the local electorate's partisan and ideological leanings, the quality of the respective candidates often is the most important factor in determining election outcomes. Without a well-spoken and credible standard-bearer, even the most effective political message often becomes lost in the voters' focus on individual personalities and foibles. In the 1996 campaign cycle, many contests were shaped by the two national parties' growing role in crafting a broad message and financing the congressional campaign. With the financial size and political clout of the party-financed Democratic and Republican campaign committees, Washington politicians and their top aides have become important players in what until recent years were locally run campaigns. There are limits, of course, to the national parties' role. Rarely can outsiders successfully enter and take over a campaign where the candidate lacks the credibility and personal desire to mount a serious effort. But the national parties can and do play a role in determining which local races receive the most outside resources and attention from the political community. Take the New Jersey Senate race, for example. Even before Senator Bill Bradley announced his retirement in August 1995, third-term Representative Dick Zimmer was seeking the Republican nomination for the Senate seat. After Bradley surprised many local and national politicians with his retirement, several prominent New Jersey Republicans voiced an interest in the contest—including former governor Tom Kean. In the end, however, only two little-known state and county legislators, both of them conservative, decided to challenge the relatively moderate Zimmer. Why? First, Zimmer was aided by the early endorsements that he received from several House colleagues plus the encouragement of Republicans close to popular Governor Christine Todd Whitman. In addition, he received from the start the tacit support of Senator Alfonse D'Amato of New York, who chaired the National Republican Senatorial Committee. That was evident in such factors as the influential role that was played in Zimmer's campaign by Arthur Finklestein, an aggressive Republican consultant from New York who is a close ally of D'Amato. The senatorial committee also gave Zimmer an early commitment that it would provide the maximum $710,000 that the committee can provide under the federal-campaign law to pay his campaign's bills. In addition, the committee spent millions more to help Zimmer by financing television ads that criticized his opponent, Democratic Representative Robert Torricelli, as a big-spending liberal but did not engage in explicit campaign advocacy. In its June 1996 ruling, the Supreme Court sanctioned the practice, which the well-financed national Republicans had developed in recent years.

Even with all of that assistance, however, Zimmer fell unexpectedly short, losing by 10 percentage points. The Republican was a victim of several factors, including, 1) the high cost of introducing himself to voters—and retaining their attention—in one of the nation's most expensive states for campaigning, where candidates must spend millions of dollars to advertise on out-of-state television stations in New York City and Philadelphia; 2) Torricelli's effective attack on Zimmer's voting record on issues such as the budget, Medicare and the environment to show that the Republican cast votes that appeared at odds with New Jersey's moderate tradition; and 3) Clinton's unexpectedly strong showing in New Jersey—a 53 to 36 percent win over Dole in what both parties initially viewed as a battleground state for the presidential campaign. Perhaps the most significant factor in Zimmer's defeat, however, was the failure of Finklestein's campaign strategy that featured an endless stream of television advertising that sought to depict Torricelli as "foolishly liberal" for New Jersey.

The Republicans' recruiting of Senate candidates ran into a different kind of problem in Illinois, where state and national Republican leaders initially rallied behind Lt. Governor Bob Kustra as their nominee for the Senate seat of Democrat Paul Simon, who announced his retirement nearly two years before the 1996 election. But Kustra, who had been a little-known former school teacher before he was hand-picked to his position by Governor Jim Edgar, ran a low-key primary campaign against State Representative Al Salvi. Even with the support of party bigwigs, Kustra failed to respond effectively to Salvi's criticism that he had supported spending and tax increases. Salvi's grass-roots bid succeeded in the March Republican primary. As it turned out, however, Kustra probably would have been a stronger candidate in the general election. Salvi was trounced in November by Democrat Richard Durbin, who attacked Salvi's conservative views on issues such as abortion and gun control as out of the mainstream. In Kansas, one of the most heavily Republican states in the nation, Republicans also demonstrated their independence of party leaders when they nominated Representative Sam Brownback to run for the Senate seat to which Sheila Frahm had been appointed two months earlier by Governor Bill Graves. Despite early Democratic claims that Brownback was too conservative to win in November, however, he had no trouble defeating first-time candidate Jill Docking.

National Democratic leaders had their own trouble in seeking to recruit candidates for Senate races. Bob Kerrey of Nebraska, the chairman of the Democratic Senatorial Campaign Committee, developed the strategy of encouraging businessmen to enter several races against seemingly entrenched Republican incumbents. In each case, the Democratic challenger had little or political experience but each dug into his deep pockets to finance much of his campaign. Kerrey's cadre included Walter Minnick of Idaho, who had been an aide at the Nixon White House in the early 1970s and then moved to Idaho where he made millions of dollars as a wood-products manufacturer; Elliot

Close of South Carolina, whose family ran one of the state's large textile companies; and Mark Warner of Virginia, who made huge sums in the cellular telephone industry. As it turned out, however, these and other entrepreneurial Democratic candidates all failed.

In House races, the support of party leaders can often have a decisive impact, especially when a well-known local official is running against a political upstart. Because of the high cost of congressional campaigns and the brief attention span that most voters have for such contests, the low voter turnout in a primary gives an extra advantage to political insiders. That was evident, for example, when state lawmaker Rod Blagojevich and Alderman Danny Davis each won the Democratic nomination for House seats in the Chicago area; each had the support of that city's influential Democratic organization. But that rule does not always apply. In Iowa, Jack Hatch, a former state legislator and top aide to Senator Tom Harkin was the early favorite for the Democratic nomination for the House seat held by freshman Representative Greg Ganske. But he was defeated by Connie McBurney, who was well-known as a weather reporter for a local station even though she was a political neophyte.

McBurney was one of several women who were Democratic candidates in House and Senate contests that gained the national spotlight. But the total number of women candidates was smaller than in 1992, when the controversial Supreme Court nomination of Clarence Thomas made that election the "year of the woman." In the Senate races, four Democratic nominees were women but each ran as a moderate in their relatively conservative states: Louisiana, Wyoming and the two contests in Kansas. Although national women's organizations—led by EMILY's List—spent millions of dollars to recruit and finance women running for Congress, several of the leading female contenders were unexpectedly defeated in party primaries for House seats. As for the Republicans, who were successful in electing a corps of conservative women to House seats in 1994, their best women prospects in 1996 tended to be more moderate in their philosophy. As with male Republicans, however, they had to contend with the Democrats' attacks that they were supporting Gingrich's agenda.

The success rates for women candidates in 1996, however, were less dramatic than in the two previous elections. McBurney disappointed many Democrats with her showing in Iowa. Only Mary Landrieu of Louisiana prevailed among the four Democratic women who were nominees for Senate seats. Other women from both parties proved successful, chiefly by emphasizing their moderate credentials. Republican Susan Collins of Maine, a former Senate aide, won a vacant Senate seat in that state. With Olympia Snowe of her home state, who was elected in 1994, they are the first pair of Republican women to serve concurrently in the Senate from the same state. Among the 10 other new women tentatively elected to the House, seven Democrats and three Republicans, the one who generated the most attention was Democrat Carolyn McCarthy of New York, a former registered Republican who ran as a political neophyte with a gun-control campaign to avenge her husband's death in a firearm-triggered massacre on the Long Island Railroad. In addition, former Fort Worth, Texas mayor Kay Granger was actively recruited by both parties before she decided to run as a Republican in the district that had been held by House Speaker Jim Wright before he resigned in 1989. The November results produced records for the total number of women in each chamber: nine in the Senate and 50 in the House, small increases from the previous Congress.

CAMPAIGN END-GAME

As became clear in the mixed Election Day results for both parties, the congressional campaign increased the premium on the candidates' dexterity to respond to changing and local circumstances than was the case in the two previous campaigns. In 1994, of course, Republicans ran on the unifying themes of their Contract With America. In 1992, both parties promised to change "business as usual" in Washington. But the 1996 stretch run placed a premium on candidates' ability to fight for themselves amid the hazardous combination of rampant political clamor and an apathetic electorate.

For vulnerable Republicans, the first challenge was to respond to the Democrats' national campaign themes. Those incumbents who were more aggressive generally found themselves in a better position on Election Day. Freshman Representative Phil English of Pennsylvania, for example, responded to the national AFL-CIO attacks on him by running local television ads in his Erie-based district that cited his own efforts to address Medicare problems. He also held dozens of informal meetings with small local groups to lend a personal touch. His early damage control helps to explain why Democrats could find only a flawed, third-tier opponent to challenge English, and why the Republican narrowly prevailed in his "swing" district. Freshman Representative James Longley of Maine, by contrast, was slower to respond to similar attacks on him from national Democrats and their allies. Despite repeated pleas from Republican campaign strategists, Longley delayed in gearing up for the election. "He went to Washington to do a good job, and he wasn't thinking about the AFL," said Ron Bonjean, Longley's campaign press secretary. That gave a running start to Democrat Tim Allen, the well-known former mayor of Portland. Longley more lackadaisical approach made him a victim on Election Day.

As in 1994, congressional leaders from both parties frantically sought to bolster their candidates in weak districts across the nation. But they did not generate as enthusiastic a local response, nor was there as much of a national context in the 1996 campaign. Gingrich again proved to be a strong fundraising draw across the nation. But the controversy surrounding his performance in Washington led many Republicans to downplay publicity for his local visits on their behalf. Gephardt, too, found that candidates wanted to go their own way. The Democrats' "Family First" agenda, to which he and other party insiders had devoted months of work, was rarely mentioned by candidates during their local contests. Even when the popular Clinton made appearances with other Democratic contenders in the closing weeks of the campaign, he typically made few comments about them to the local audience. Engaging in excessive partisanship would be counterproductive, the candidates' polls had repeatedly shown.

But that caution did not discourage congressional candidates from making ample use of broadcast advertisements attacking their opponents. Democrats repeatedly attacked their opponents for backing the Republicans' "extreme" budget proposals, which President Clinton vetoed. "Who's behind Newt Gingrich's radical anti-Colorado agenda?" asked an ad for Tom Strickland, that state's Democratic nominee for a Senate seat. "Three-term Congressman Wayne Allard, that's who." In Kansas, Jill Docking criticized Sam Brownback, her Republican opponent for a Senate seat, for voting "with the extremists to cut funding for community policing and [for] safe and drug-free schools." Strickland and Docking both lost contests where Democrats contended that they had a good chance to win the seats. Many Republican candidates responded with repeated attacks on their opponents as too liberal. Citing his opponent's "embarrassingly liberal" record, Republican Rudy Boschwitz nominated Democratic Senator Paul Wellstone of Minnesota for the "1967 Liberal Hall of Fame." But GOP consultant Arthur Finklestein's cookie-cutter strategy for running against Democrats proved unsuccessful for Boschwitz as it did for Zimmer in New Jersey plus Nancy Mayer of Rhode Island and Senator Larry Pressler of South Dakota.

In the end, the Senate election was a split decision for the two parties. Southern Republicans reveled in their first Senate victory in Arkansas in the 20th century, and their veteran incumbents successfully struggled to retain seats in North Carolina and Virginia, but the GOP hopes in Dixie were dashed by narrow losses for open seats in Georgia and Louisiana, where the Republican candidates may have been too conservative for their states' "swing" voters. In the Midwest, South Dakotan Pressler was the only senator of either party to lose re-election, but Democrats were stunned when popular Governor Ben Nelson of Nebraska lost a Senate contest to Republican Chuck Hagel, who won his first contest for elected office. And in the Northeast, Republicans Bill Weld and Zimmer lost what had seemed to be good opportunities in Massachusetts and New Jersey, while the GOP held on in Maine and New Hampshire with the victory of Susan Collins, a moderate, and the narrow re-election of conservative Senator Bob Smith.

Some common threads emerged in the Senate elections. Each of the newly-elected Democratic Senators had extensive political experience; four served most recently in the House and the other two had been statewide elected officials—Cleland, the Georgia Secretary of State, and Landrieu, Louisiana's former state Treasurer. Most of the Republicans, too, had extensive political experience; all but Collins of Maine and Hagel of Nebraska had previously won public office. Advocates of term limits could cite the fact that Pressler was the sole Senate incumbent to lose re-election in 1996; that meant that only eight Senators—four Democrats and four Republicans—have lost re-election bids since 1990. On the other hand, the many Senate retirees in recent years account for the fact that 64 of the 100 Senators in the new 105th Congress will be in either their first or second six-year term. In 1991, by contrast, only 50 Senators had served fewer than 12 years.

The House results also painted a diverse picture. Republicans claimed satisfaction that their 227 seats were virtually the same as the 230 members that they held when the 104th Congress convened two years earlier. And they achieved their chief goal of winning House control in two successive elections; Republicans had not secured the majority in consecutive Congresses since the 1928 election. Still, Republicans were disappointed to lose far more of their House incumbents than did the Democrats—17 to 3, based on results as of late November. Of the Republicans' freshman class, a dozen lost their re-election bids. Most of the losses by GOP incumbents came in states where Clinton did especially well, including six in the Northeast and five on the West Coast. Although House Republicans were disappointed about losing two first-term incumbents in North Carolina, they performed well elsewhere in the South. For example, they gained the seats of two Democratic retirees in Alabama and two others in Texas, among others. In the South, Democrats could claim some satisfaction that two of their Black Caucus members—Sanford Bishop and Cynthia McKinney, both from Georgia—survived even though the redistricting changes forced both to run in redrawn districts with a dramatically smaller black population. In addition to retiring Democrat Cleo Fields of Louisiana, Republican Gary Franks of Connecticut was the only other black member to lose a House seat. Democrat Julia Carson of Indiana gained a House seat for the Black Caucus, and Harold Ford Jr. was elected to succeed his father, Harold E. Ford.

The House results reinforced the dramatic changes that have taken place in the nation's electoral map. With their continuing gains of seats in the

South, the House GOP's center of power has moved to the region where Democrats were the dominant force only three decades ago. Without their major gains in the South solely in the past two elections, Republicans would have fallen considerably short of gaining the House majority. In addition, most of the House Republicans' party leaders and committee chairmen are from the South, as was the case with the Democrats through the 1960s. The data also reveal that, despite some recent electoral problems in the Midwest and West, Republicans also hold a majority of seats in each of those regions, which had generally leaned Democratic until recently. Only in the East are Republicans clearly the minority party in the House. (See Tables 1 and 2.)

Predicting where these trends will head in the millennium is anyone's guess in a legislative body, which works on a two-year clock. When the election results were in, Republican strategists contended that their House and Senate majorities were secure for the next four years and that they are virtually certain to gain seats in each chamber in the 1998 election; Republicans also predict that Democrats will suffer from the continuation of a large flow of retirements in 1998, both in the House and Senate. (The party controlling the White House historically does poorly in midterm elections, especially during a president's second term). Democrats responded that the public made clear in the 1996 elections its opposition to the type of over-reaching that Republicans displayed when they won the congressional majorities. With the lessons that they learned following the 1994 election, Democrats claim that they will continue to overhaul their own party and will regain their long-held status as the nation's dominant party.

Regardless, from the shorter-term congressional perspective, several results are clear from the 1996 election. 1) President Clinton would have no prospect of winning support if he offered anything close to the health-care plan that dominated debate during his first two years at the White House.

Table 1 **Regional Breakdown of the U.S. House**

	East		Midwest		South		West		Total	
	D	R	D	R	D	R	D	R	D	R
1964	77	40	66	59	105	19	47	22	295	140
1968	68	49	46	79	93	31	36	33	243	192
1976	78	35	68	53	95	30	51	25	292	143
1980	66	47	58	63	80	45	39	37	243	192
1992	54	42	61	44	88	52	55	38	258	176
1996	57	39	49	56	58	82	43	50	207	227

Source: *National Journal*, November 9, 1996, p. 2421

Table 2   **Regional Breakdown of the U.S. Senate**

	East		Midwest		South		West		Total	
	D	**R**	**D**	**R**	**D**	**R**	**D**	**R**	**D**	**R**
1964	12	10	15	9	24	4	17	9	68	32
1968	9	13	13	11	21	7	15	11	58	42
1976	12	10	16	8	21	7	13	13	62	38
1980	11	11	10	14	17	11	9	17	47	53
1992	14	8	15	9	17	11	11	15	57	43
1996	12	10	13	11	10	18	10	16	45	55

Source: *National Journal*, November 9, 1996, p. 2440

2) Although congressional Republicans contend that the recent results have vindicated their 1995 budget strategy, they emerged from the 1996 election without the bravado that accompanied their advocacy of the Contract with America two years earlier. 3) Election results, especially in the House, likely will remain far more volatile than was the case during the 40-year era ending in 1994, when Democrats dominated. 4) Smaller majorities, in turn, increase congressional partisanship and the difficulty of enacting major legislation. 5) Perhaps most significantly, Congress almost always will respond to what its members collectively believe is the will of the American public.

NOTES

1. Michael Weisskopf and David Maraniss, "Personalities Shaped Events as Much as Ideology," *The Washington Post,* Jan. 20, 1996, A-1.

2. Adam Clymer, "Simpson Joins Ranks of Pragmatists Leaving Senate," *The New York Times,* Dec. 4, 1995, B-4.

CHAPTER 8

The State Elections of '96

Thad Beyle

University of North Carolina–Chapel Hill

THE KEY POLITICAL ROLE OF THE STATES

Despite what you may read elsewhere about our country's elections, there is a decidedly state and local cast to the selection of leaders at all levels of our governmental system. As former Speaker of the U.S. House Tip O'Neill constantly reminded us, "All politics is local."

In fact, aside from some specifics on eligibility for national office, timing for national elections, terms of service, and the unique role of the Electoral College, it is the states which are at the center of our electoral system. The states determine the format for the selection of candidates, the types of ballots, the process for registering voters and administering elections, the establishment of legislative districts, and the certification of results. The states also establish the "rules of the game" for local government and politics, their types of government, and election formats.

There are separate elections for offices at the national, state, and local levels at varying times. Each November, and often more times a year in some states and localities, voters have the opportunity to select leaders for some unit of government. Some critics argue that our system necessitates too much voter participation, which actually leads to voter fatigue and non-voting.

This decentralization of our politics also means there are no real national parties in our system. Each state has its own set of politics, political actors, and political configurations which are very different from other states'. In most states, very loose confederations of state and local party organizations and individual political leaders are grouped together under the heading of Democrats or Republicans. And every four years there is a presidential election focusing attention on these groupings of Democrats and Republicans as if they were more unified than they actually are. But there are often as great differences between some members and groups within these parties across the states as exist between the two parties themselves.

This bias toward letting states drive politics and the electoral system has several interesting consequences. Among them are: the unique rhythm of our politics; the often frustrating politics undergirding the constitutionally based separation of powers concept; the built-in political ambition ladder for individuals seeking leadership positions; the ability of residents and voters in some states to set and adopt issue agendas; the perverse nature of voter turnout for elections; and the occasional need for national government intrusion into these state based political processes in an attempt to redress inequities or discrimination on the part of the states. We will be addressing these consequences in this chapter as we examine the 1996 elections below the national level.

THE UNIQUE RHYTHM OF AMERICAN POLITICS

Our politics has a four beat rhythm or 4/4 march tempo to it with a strong first beat accent and a weak third beat accent. The first beat accent is tied to our quadrennial presidential elections such as in 1996. For example, the 1996 ballot not only included the presidential election, but election of the entire 435 member House of Representatives and 34 of the 100 member U.S. Senate. In addition, many state leaders were elected including 11 governors and nearly 6,000 of the over 7,300 legislators in states. To top that off, there were referenda held in states on separate constitutional amendments, bond issues, and other issues of concern to the voters.

The weak third beat of U.S. politics are those elections held in the off-presidential years on the even year as in 1994. Again, the entire U.S. House of Representatives was elected as was over one-third of the U.S. Senate. However, the big difference was the election of 36 of the 50 state governors plus many state legislators. While this third beat may be weak by national standards, it is a very solid and strong beat in many of the states.

There are also two off-beat years—the odd numbered years by the calendar—when many local elections are held so they will not be swamped by the noise of the national and statewide elections. In addition, there were two gubernatorial elections on the second beat (1993 in New Jersey and Virginia) and three gubernatorial election on the fourth beat (1995 in Kentucky, Louisiana and Mississippi plus some state legislative elections). The results of these off-beat years are usually examined very carefully for signs of what may be coming in the next presidential election. So, watch carefully the results of the 1997, 1998 and 1999 elections as possible harbingers of what the next first beat of the 2000 presidential election might be like.

POLITICS IN THE 1990s—PROBLEMS IN THE STATES

In the 1990s, politics across the states has been quite volatile. Coming into the 1990s, the country's economy was experiencing a recession which was having a considerable effect on the states. When the national economy faltered, some regions and states were hit harder than others economically. State revenues fell while the need for governmental programs and assistance increased. Governors and legislators were faced with no-win budgetary decisions—the need to raise taxes and/or cut programs just to keep the state's budget in balance while responding to the needs in the state. Unlike the national government, there is no printing press in the states' basements which can print up money as needed. While considerable borrowing does go on in the states, in effect the leaders of these governments must seek to balance their budgets each year. They do not have the luxury of just trying to reduce the deficit a bit each year—there can be no deficit.

There were also some serious issues which states were facing that had some high and growing price tags. The federal-state Medicaid program established to help those in need of health care was growing rapidly as Congress added more responsibilities to the program which the states had to pick up (unfunded mandates). The impact of this was termed the "PAC-Man" of state budgets. The costs of coping with rising crime also became a major budget item in the states as more prisons were needed to handle the rising number of people being incarcerated. Money which might have been normally aimed at education in the states often had to be shifted to corrections and prisons. The philosophical shift here was also important as the states were essentially moving from preventive to corrective efforts.

These factors, and other problems facing the states led to some adverse political situations for elected state leaders. Some faced an angry electorate over some of the decisions they had made while serving. They also faced a growing term limits movement in the states in which voters were adding restrictions to individual terms of office. Proponents of these changes were frustrated over incumbents' ease in staying in office. Incumbency had become such an electoral advantage that it was nearly impossible to beat those holding office. So, these proponents of political change turned to a new vehicle to achieve their goals by restricting how many times an individual can run for and hold a specific office, limiting their terms, and getting rid of them constitutionally.

THE RECENT IMPACT OF DIRECT DEMOCRACY IN THE STATES

The term limits movement highlights another fact of life in some of the states. While most of us are aware of and participate in representative democracy through our votes cast for candidates each year, some states have provisions in their constitutions for more direct participation. These provisions include the recall—the right of a number of citizens to petition to have a public official face an election which might recall them from office; the initiative—the right of citizens to have an issue placed before the legislature to act on or to come directly before the voters for consideration; and the referendum—the right of citizens to decide on a public issue in the voting booth.

While we may be used to having constitutional amendments and statewide bond issues on our ballots, there has been a rise of other issues placed on the ballot for the voters to consider. These include restrictions on taxes being imposed, term limits, the legality of alternative life styles and other very controversial issues. There are also some referenda items which are not of much interest to the majority of citizens but of great concern to some state interests, enough to get the item on the ballot. These referenda are being used by all types of participants in our political system—there is no one ideological cast involved. In a study of these vehicles being voted on between 1977 and 1984, 79 of the initiatives were backed by those on the liberal side of the political spectrum, 74 by those on the conservative side, and 46 were not classifiable in ideological terms. They also had about the same success rate—45 percent.

In the first 80 years of this century, there were about 500 separate initiatives placed on the ballots of the states—about six per year. Between 1981 and 1990, there were about 270 initiatives—about 25 per year.[1] The 1990s have been a banner decade for initiatives: 64 in 1990, 65 in 1992, 72 in 1994, and over 90 in 1996. California and some of the other western states with newer constitutions seem to have a cottage industry in such politics.

THE IMPACT OF RECENT ELECTIONS IN THE STATES

There are other things afoot in the states politically. One is the growth of "power splits" in the states like what we now see at the national level. In the 1990s, many states are ending up with split political leadership after an election. After the 1990 elections, 29 states found they had a governor belonging to one party and one or both of the houses of the state legislature controlled by the opposing party. After the 1992 elections, this number grew to 31 states but dropped to 26 states following the 1994 elections. No matter what the exact number is, in the 1990s split partisan control of state government has been the rule in more than half the states.

To political analysts and voters the reasons for this are a rise in the number of independent voters and split ticket voting where voters move their votes across party lines based on how they view the candidates. Many citizens no longer vote a straight party ticket. To political candidates and party lead-

ers, these voters are not becoming more independent, they are just more un-
reliable. There are several explanations for this, not the least being the decline
of "genetic party identification" where sons and daughters are growing less
likely to assume their parent's political identity just as they have assumed
their parents' religion.

Looking at some specific election results illustrates this situation. In
1992, the voters in Vermont elected Democratic Governor Howard Dean with
70 percent of the vote, Republican U.S. Senator Jim Jeffords with 50 percent
of the vote and Independent Congressman Bernard Sanders with 50 percent of
the vote. That same year Indiana voters reelected Democratic Governor Evan
Bayh (63 percent) and Republican U.S. Senator Dan Coats (58 percent) while
giving President George Bush only a plurality win with 43 percent of the vote.

The 1992 presidential election seemed to have a rather minimal impact
on the results further down the ballot. With Arkansas Governor Bill Clinton
(D) winning with only a plurality of the vote (43 percent) over President
George Bush (38 percent), it was no surprise that the partisan composition of
the Congress changed very little. Democratic strength in the U.S. Senate
dropped by one seat and by nine seats in the U.S. House. At the state level,
the Democrats picked up three governors' chairs formerly held by Republicans (Delaware, Missouri, North Carolina) while only losing one to the Republicans (North Dakota).

However, in the 1994 off year elections, the Newt Gingrich–inspired Republican Revolution had a significant impact on elections in the states. The
changes at the national level are well known as the Democrats lost their control over both houses of Congress. At the state level, the impact of this revolution was also very dramatic. Going into the election, Democrats held 29
governors' chairs to the Republican 19—there were two independent governors in Alaska and Connecticut. After the 1994 votes were counted, Republicans held 30 chairs to the Democrats 19 with one independent governor
elected in Maine. Further, the Republicans also won many of the state legislative seats up in 1994. Before the election they only controlled eight state legislatures, split control in 17 other states, with the Democrats controlling 24.
After the 1994 elections, the Republicans held control over both houses in 19
states to the Democratic control in 18 states, and there was split control in
13 other states.[2] Now, the burden of the problems created by a power split in the
control of state government fell more on Republican governors' shoulders.

In a few words, 1992 belied the fears of presidential coattails drastically
changing the outcome of other contests down the ballot, while the off-year
1994 election indicated that other factors than a national presidential election
can have a major impact on lower level contests. The stage was set for what
1996 would bring as most predictions based on past outcomes were now in
question.

THE 1996 POLITICAL SCENE IN THE STATES

Beneath the glare of presidential politics, the politics in many states was also gearing up. There would be gubernatorial contests in 11 states, and elections for control of all or part of 86 of the 99 separate state legislative chambers. Partisan control of 41 of these 86 chambers was up for grabs as the majority party had a five seat or less margin.[3] Elections would also take place for a few other state level offices coupled with a myriad of referenda.

While voters were often distracted by charges and counter-charges about the national candidates and some other highly visible races, and appalled by the panoply and number of negative television ads, there were some important issues and directions being discussed in the many state campaigns. One veteran observer suggested that on balance, the various campaigns in the states—governors and state legislators in particular—were not likely to lead to any significant changes in the major issues of taxes, spending and state regulation.

Specifically, during the 1996 campaigns it appeared that state level candidates were "speaking with a common voice" on these issues:

- Opposing higher taxes and suggesting specific taxes to reduce,
- Lowering local property taxes but not by raising state taxes or cutting educational spending,
- Promising to control or trim state level spending but offering no specific programmatic or spending cuts,
- Ending "welfare as we know it" by adopting a strategy emphasizing work and personal responsibility,
- Protecting the environment and consumers without restricting development unnecessarily or arbitrarily.[4]

THE 1996 GUBERNATORIAL RACES

The 11 gubernatorial contests were spread across the country, from New Hampshire and Vermont in New England to Washington State in the Northwest, and from North Carolina to North Dakota. Seven incumbent governors sought reelection, while two other incumbent governors in New Hampshire and Washington decided not to seek another term despite being eligible to serve again. Two other incumbent governors in Indiana and West Virginia were term limited so there were four open seats being contested in 1996. Going into the 1996 elections, Democrats held seven of these 11 chairs; when all the campaigning and voting was over, Democrats still held seven of these chairs.

The seven incumbent governors seeking reelection entered their campaigns with rather high popular approval ratings on their performance in office. In a September 1996 sweep of the 50 states, polls conducted by Mason-Dixon/Political Media Research asked likely voters in each state how they rated the performance of their incumbent governors—excellent, pretty good, only fair, or poor? As can be seen in Table 1, each the incumbent governors except Democrat Mike Lowry of Washington had positive approval ratings among likely voters above 50 percent in their states. Lowry had been dealing with a charge of sexual harassment within his office which obviously dimmed his luster among the citizens and voters of Washington.

The average approval rating for the seven incumbent governors seeking reelection was 65 percent positive, ranging from a high of 80 percent for Republican Marc Racicot in Montana to 54 percent for Democrat Mel Carnahan in Missouri. These positive approval ratings seemed to translate into votes in November as all but Democrat Howard Dean of Vermont saw their vote total percent to be within 5 points of their approval ratings. Dean's vote percentage was 11 points above his approval rating. Their average total was 68 percent ranging from Racicot's 80 percent in Montana to Hunt's 56 percent in North Carolina. The message seems clear: do a good job and get reelected.

The real politics at the gubernatorial level thus focused on the four states with an open seat: Indiana, New Hampshire, Washington, West Virginia. Democrats held three of these seats going into the election and came out holding three. However, there was some partisan turnover as New Hampshire

Table 1

State	Governor	Approval rating (%)[‡]	1996 Vote (%)
Delaware	Tom Carper (D)	64	69
Indiana*	Evan Bayh (D)	62	–
Missouri	Mel Carnahan (D)	54	57
Montana	Marc Racicot (R)	80	80
New Hampshire[†]	Steve Merrill (R)	64	–
North Carolina	Jim Hunt (D)	61	56
North Dakota	Edward Schafer (R)	64	66
Utah	Mike Leavitt (R)	73	75
Vermont	Howard Dean (D)	59	71
Washington[†]	Mike Lowry (D)	32	–
West Virginia*	Gaston Caperton (D)	55	–

*Term limited, could not seek reelection

[†]Retired; did not seek reelection

[‡]Approval Rating: percentage of voters indicating they felt the governor was doing an excellent or good job in a Mason-Dixon/Political Media Research September 1996 poll.

switched from a Republican governor to having a Democrat while West Virginia reversed this gain by moving from Democrat to Republican, and the politics in each of these states was different.

First, those two states where the early leaders in the race eventually faltered and lost:

Indiana

With popular Democratic Governor Evan Bayh term limited, the two major political figures in the state easily won their party's nomination. Democratic Lieutenant Governor Ed O'Bannon had no challenger for the Democratic nomination, while Indianapolis Mayor Steve Goldsmith had to beat a former state representative to gain the GOP nomination (55 percent to 37 percent).

Goldsmith, a well-known and nationally respected mayor, entered the race as the favorite, and the early polls backed this as he was running with a 7-to-11-point lead through August. Then, the race turned into a toss-up as Goldsmith began to have some problems at home in the Indianapolis police department and O'Bannon was stressing the conservative fiscal record of the "Bayh–O'Bannon" Administration years. By September, the race was a toss-up and O'Bannon finally won by a narrow 4-point margin.

West Virginia

With term limited Democratic Governor Gaspar Caperton leaving office, both parties had highly contested primaries to select their nominees for governor. On the Democratic side, the "coal miner's daughter" Charlotte Pritt narrowly defeated a state senator for the nomination (39.5 percent to 33 percent). Pritt came into the contest with some negative "political baggage" as she had challenged Caperton for the 1992 Democratic nomination, and then had run in the 1992 general election as an independent. On the Republican side, former Republican Governor Cecil Underwood (1957–1961) was able to best two other challengers for the party's nomination (41 percent to 33 percent/ 26 percent).

With neither party's candidate having received a majority of the primary vote, the contest initially seemed hard to read. An April poll had Pritt with a substantial 22-point lead but by late spring this lead was down to only 5 points. By summer her lead in the polls had evaporated and the race was a tossup as Underwood campaigned on economic development and no new taxes in the economically distressed state. Pritt's earlier efforts to unseat Caperton turned some Democrats toward Underwood, and he won narrowly by 4 points in November—the only Republican to win statewide. Once known as the youngest governor in West Virginia's history at the age of 35, now the moderate Republican becomes the state's oldest governor at 74!

The other two open seat races saw the eventual winners gain a lead in the polls and then build on it en route to victory in November.

New Hampshire

Politics in the Granite State suffered from over exposure during the presidential primary period. Incumbent governor Steve Merrill served as the leader of the Dole campaign perhaps with an eye toward serving in a high position in the potential Dole Administration. This was not a pipe dream as Governor Sherman Adams, who played the same role for Dwight Eisenhower in 1952, ended up as his chief of staff in the Eisenhower Administration, and Governor John Sununu, who also played that role for George Bush in 1988, earned the same job in the Bush Administration. So there were precedents for such dreams.

The Democrats chose three-term State Senator Jeanne Shaheen to carry their banner for the governorship in a lopsided primary contest over her nearest competitor (88 percent to 7 percent). She, too, had been active in presidential politics in the state as she ran the campaigns of Jimmy Carter and Gary Hart in the state. In a closely contested primary race, Republicans chose lawyer and former State Board of Education chairman Ovide Lamontagne over Congressman Bill Zelliff (48 percent to 43 percent).

Shaheen edged to a tentative lead in the early summer while half of the voters were still undecided. She ran on what she called "kitchen table issues" (expanding kindergartens, reducing utility rates, and working on college tuition plans) and took the pledge not to seek income or sales taxes, a pledge that every successful candidate must take. By September her lead had opened up into the high teens, and she won handily by an 18-point margin. The Shaheen Machine had a decided female cast to it as she won the women's vote by a 2 to 1 margin. She was only the third Democratic governor elected in the state since 1924 and will be the first woman governor to serve in the state.

Washington

With the negatives flowing from the retiring governor Mike Lowry's administration and the strong 1994 run by Republicans in the state, the governor's chair seemed ready to fall to a Republican. Yet, Washington's "jungle primary" seemed to change that set of calculations.

The September primary, held rather late in the political season, is unique among the states. All the candidates for an office are listed on the same ballot and the candidates who receive the highest votes in each party then vie in the general election. The Democrats selected King County executive Gary Locke over Seattle Mayor Norman Rice (24 percent to 18 percent) while the Republicans voted in former state senator and Christian conservative Ellen Craswell over several other candidates including a state representative (14 percent to 8 percent). These percentages are of the total vote in the primary for the gubernatorial nomination so it would appear that Locke started out with a 10-point lead coming out of the primary.

As a state legislator, Locke had voted for a tax increase during the Lowry administration and was tagged as a liberal in the campaign. But Craswell's views and statements stirred this campaign. She advocated putting "Bible-believing Christians in leadership of our state," attacked homosexuals as "sodomites" seeking to obtain "special rights," and as individuals who had a "life-style choice" which could be reversed if they worked hard enough at it. She also indicated that God would be placed high on her governor's office organization chart. Some moderate and well-known Republicans bolted and publicly supported Locke much to the chagrin of the state party's leadership.[5]

Locke's lead grew larger during October, and he won by 18 points in November. He is the epitome of the American dream. The son of Chinese immigrants, he grew up in public housing, received a law degree, became a prosecutor, then an elected county executive, and now governor. He is the first Chinese-American elected governor in the 50 states.

In sum, these results indicate two important political facts of life in the states. First is the importance of having already won a statewide race when seeking the governorship. In these 11 races, seven were won by incumbents, an eighth by a former governor, and a ninth by a lieutenant governor. Only two of the winners advanced from a substate political base—State Representative Jeanne Shaheen in New Hampshire and King County executive Gary Locke in Washington. A previous statewide candidacy overcomes the problems of creating name recognition and a statewide political organization.

Second is the considerable difficulties that mayors and former mayors of large cities have in winning the governorship. Over the past 10 election years, 1987–1996, only two of the 26 mayors and former mayors of a state's larger cities have run and won—Tony Knowles of Anchorage in Alaska in his second try in 1994 and George Voinovich of Ohio in 1990. In 1996, none of the three mayors running won—Steve Goldsmith (R) of Indianapolis in Indiana, Richard Vinroot (R) of Charlotte in North Carolina, and Norman Rice (D) of Seattle in Washington. The larger cities do not provide a large enough base or broad enough name recognition for these mayors and there are always hints of an anti-urban or anti-big city bias among those voters living outside that large city. This may also indicate that running and winning a governor's race is qualitatively different than running and winning a mayor's race. A mayor who perceives the state as just a larger city and the state's constituents as just a larger number of people obviously commits a strategic political error.

THE 1996 STATE LEGISLATIVE RACES

As at the national level, the two majority parties entered the 1996 state legislative races with conflicting goals—the Republicans wanted to build on their wins of 1994, and the Democrats wanted to recapture what they had lost. The Democrats had lost 501 seats to the Republicans in 1994 and the control of several legislative chambers in the states. Coming into the 1996 elections, Democrats controlled both houses in 16 states, the Republicans in 18 states, with 15 states having split control—Nebraska has a unicameral, non-partisan legislature.[6]

The 1996 results were mixed as they were for the governors' races, but there did seem to be a slight tilt toward the Democrats in these legislative races. The Democrats captured eight chambers which the Republicans previously held, but the Republicans gained control of four that the Democrats had held— a net gain of four for the Democrats. In sum, the Democrats came out of this election with control over both houses in 20 states, the Republicans in 17, with 12 state legislatures under split control.

Democrats became the majority party in the California, Illinois, Michigan and Nevada houses, and in the Connecticut, Maine, Tennessee and Vermont senates. The 1994 election results had turned the California Assembly into a partisan battleground where the victories and majority the Republicans had gained was thwarted by the political machinations of the out-going and long-time Democratic Speaker Willie Brown. Nevada had been "enjoying" the experience of an evenly split house so just having a party—any party—gain control would reduce the chaos of the no control situation.

Republicans took over the Florida House and the senates in Iowa and Washington. Politics in Florida were obviously volatile as the Republicans gained control of the State House for the first time since Reconstruction and maintained their control of the State Senate which they had won for the first time 1994. All of this occurred in the face of statewide Democratic wins for Governor Lawton Chiles in 1994 and for President Bill Clinton in 1996. Voters in Florida obviously enjoy splitting their tickets.

The results highlight the changes that are going on in the southern states. Not only is the South becoming a building block for GOP presidential races, but Republicans are now consistently winning further down the ballot. Between 1976 and 1992, Democrats controlled both houses in the 16 states of the South. In 1994, they gained control of the North Carolina State House.

Now, after the 1996 elections, Democrats control both chambers in only 11 of those states, the Republicans control both chambers in Florida, while four other states have split partisan control of their two houses.[7]

In North Carolina, the Republicans' surge in 1994 gave them control of the state house (68R-52D) and near control in the state senate (26D-24R). After the 1996 elections, the Democrats had been able to increase their margin in the State Senate (30D-20R), but the Republicans held on to a narrow margin in the State House (61R-59D). But there were some razor thin wins in some of the House districts, a 95-vote margin in one district, so recounts and challenged ballots could leave the state house in the same situation that the Nevada House has been facing.

With the considerable changes going on within our federal system right now and into the foreseeable future, split partisan control in many of the states may be a blessing in disguise. As Bill Pound of the National Conference of State Legislatures observed after the election results were counted, divided political control "also means that you govern in the center much more, because you have to compromise."[8]

DIRECT DEMOCRACY IN 1996—THE REFERENDA VOTING

There were a wide range of propositions put before the voters in 20 states to consider. California had a laundry list of eight issues for consideration ranging from banning affirmative action, to adding campaign finance restrictions, to regulating HMO's, to limiting lawsuit awards, to allowing the medical use of marijuana, to increasing the minimum wage, to trying to restrict tax increases. These November referenda were in addition to the 12 propositions that had appeared on the March primary ballots.[9] Oregon also had eight issues before the voters in November, and Nevada voters had to consider five separate issues.

Several of these statewide issues were of considerable note. The California Civil Rights Initiative (CCRI) which would end preferences in public hiring, contracting and educational institutions' admissions based on race or sex was the object of much concern from proponents and opponents. Strongly supported by Republican Governor Pete Wilson, who took it on the road with him during his short and ill-fated campaign for the Republican presidential nomination, it was later endorsed up by GOP Republican presidential candidate Bob Dole in his last minute attempts to pump some life into his faltering California campaign. President Clinton and a coalition of minorities, women, and labor unions opposed it.

The measure passed more narrowly (54 percent to 46 percent) than earlier polls had suggested it would. Wilson immediately took steps to implement the measure but opponents sought to stymie this by filing suit in federal district court alleging this initiative violated the equal protection clause of the U.S. Constitution.[10] This case may be another example of where a proposition voted into effect by state voters is negated by the decisions of the federal courts.

In the most recent example of such a set of judicial decisions, several states were reacting to a recent U.S. Supreme Court decision overturning the right of the states to impose term limits on federal officials elected within their states. In these earlier situations, voters in a number of states had adopted propositions limiting their U.S. congressmen and U.S. senators to the number of terms or years they could serve.[11] However, the Arkansas State Supreme Court ruled that action by its states' voters to be unconstitutional, a decision concurred with by the U.S. Supreme Court in *U.S. Term Limits v. Thornton* (1995). The rationale was that only restrictions in the U.S. Constitution counted and states could not make a series of separate decisions as to who was or was not eligible to run for office. In a few words, if the states and their voters wanted term limits on federal offices, the U.S. Constitution would have to be amended.

So, in 1996 elections some states took a new direction on the question of term limits. Voters in fourteen states were asked to pass a measure that would ask any candidates running for federal offices to seek to have Congress pass an amendment to the U.S. Constitution on term limits. Those who declined to do so would be duly noted on the ballot the next time they ran. These measures were successful in nine states but failed in five others.

There was another set of successful propositions causing observers to take notice this year. Arizona and California voters approved measures which would permit the use of marijuana for medical purposes if prescribed by a physician. California's proposition was drawn rather broadly while Arizona's was restricted to critically ill patients. This again set up a federal–state confrontation, as there are clear federal restrictions against growing, selling, or using marijuana.[12]

While there were obviously other propositions of note including some on taxes, one other proposition must be mentioned. For the first time in over 200 years, the voters of North Carolina were given the right to vote on whether their governor should have the veto power. The fear of the old colonial governors had been used for decades to hold this "modern reform" at bay. Championed by the Republicans in recent years as they saw their first elected governors in this century struggle with a state legislature controlled by the Democrats, they had to "bite the bullet" and send the proposed amendment out to the voters just when they had gained control of one house and had near control of the other. In the end, this whole issue turned out to be more about the power struggle between the governor and the legislature than any high minded call for reform. The voters approved the amendment overwhelmingly.

ON TO THE NEXT ROUND OF STATE POLITICS

The politics of 1996 is past and next will come the "off beat" 1997 elections. There will be interesting governors' races in New Jersey and Virginia, some legislative races, and probably a few more referenda to consider. All will be watched closely to see if these particular contests provide any signals as to what may happen in the many "third beat" year state and federal elections of 1998. Will they, along with the other "off-beat" elections of 1999, serve as harbingers of the next "first beat" election year of the twenty-first century in the year 2000? To twist a phrase, "The political beat goes on."

NOTES

1. "Liberals, Conservatives Share Initiative Success," *Public Administration Times* 8:4 (February 15), 12.

2. Joan M. Ponessa and Dave Kehler, "Statewide Initiatives, 1981–90," *Initiative and Referendum Analysis*, No. 2 (June), 1–2.

3. Stuart Rothenberg, "The Untold Story of November," *The Rothenberg Political Report* 18:1 (January 9).

4. *State Policy Reports*, v. 14, n. 21 (November 1996), 4.

5. *State Policy Reports*, v. 14, n. 21 (November 1996), 2.

6. Timothy Egan, "Battle in Washington Brings Soul Searching," *New York Times* (October 22).

7. Richard Wolf, "Legislatures Gain Clout As States' Authority Grows," *USA Today* (October 17).

8. "Party Control: Southern Legislatures," *State Government News* (December, 1996), 35.

9. Stephen Barr, "Control of 31 states now split," *The Washington Post* (November 6, 1996).

10. "California: Results of Ballot Propositions," *The Hotline* 9:127 (March 27, 1996), 21.

11. Jeffrey L. Katz, "Propositions: Pot to Parental Rights," *Congressional Quarterly Weekly Report*, 54:45 (November 9, 1996), 3243.

12. Thad Beyle and Rich Jones, "Term Limits in the States," *The Book of the States, 1994–95* (Lexington, KY: The Council of State Governments, 1994), 28–33.

13. Jeffrey L. Katz, "Propositions: Pot to Parental Rights," *Congressional Quarterly Weekly Report*, 54:45 (November 9, 1996), 3243.

CHAPTER 9

The Press' Performance

Diana Owen

Georgetown University

One of the big stories of the 1996 presidential campaign was that it failed from the start to capture the hearts and minds of the American public. As analysts and pundits delivered their post-mortems, the mass media were quickly accused of exacerbating, if not causing outright, the low level of voter engagement. Even members of the media community feared that they may have failed in meeting their public service obligations. CBS News President Andrew Heyward lamented in October, "If there's a lack of interest on the part of the public, is that to some degree because we're not doing a very good job?"[1]

The 1996 campaign was especially disappointing from a mass communication perspective, as it followed in the wake of the 1992 election. The previous presidential contest was a watershed for the mass media campaign. Candidates played the usual media management games and courted the traditional press. To an unprecedented degree, however, the candidates circumvented the journalistic mainstream by turning to alternative media to get their messages across. Talk radio and television programs, electronic town meetings, and other "new media" forums provided candidates with the opportunity to work outside of established journalistic norms and gatekeeping practices. At the same time, the public became a more direct part of the media spectacle. These media strategies fostered a campaign environment which generated a level of citizen enthusiasm about politics that was unprecedented in recent years, and which produced the highest voter turnout in decades.

The "new media" trends established in the 1992 presidential campaign did not carry over prominently into the 1996 contest. In part, this was due to the candidates' conservative campaign strategies. In addition, "new media" tactics work best when candidates are political outsiders, unlike ultimate Washington insiders Bill Clinton and Bob Dole, and can forge a more "sincere" bond with average citizens. Further, the "new media" aren't so new anymore; their novelty may have worn off. The populist component of the 1992 contest that seemed to hold some promise for future campaigns was less evident in 1996.

The 1996 election was not an anomaly, however. It marked perhaps the extreme case of American campaign politics as usual—a politics of prolonged tedium. But, are the mass media to blame? Did media coverage of the 1996 campaign contribute to the public's disaffection from the electoral process? In this chapter, we will examine the degree to which the media may be innocent or guilty of these charges. Because the mass media are the primary means by which most citizens experience campaigns, they are likely suspects. Critics contend that the media, because of their pervasive negativity, tabloid style of reporting, "feeding frenzy" mentality, and self-serving motives, trivialize campaigns to the point where voters tune out. Others disagree, citing the fact that today's communications environment offers diverse political programming that can satisfy the tastes of any voter. Further, it may be difficult in this campaign to place the blame entirely on the news media. The strong state of the nation, the candidates themselves, their campaign strategies, and the nature of the American election process had a lot to do with the kind of news that was produced.

We begin with a discussion of major trends in media coverage of politics and elections as they relate to the 1996 contest. These trends include the journalistic credo that "bad news equals news," the "star system" for reporters and pundits, poll driven reporting, and the "tabloidization" of news. Negative advertising also works to set the tone for political coverage. In addition, we examine some contextual issues surrounding the 1996 campaign which influenced press coverage. The state of the nation, the paucity of fresh and exciting campaign information, and the public's attitudes toward and professed familiarity with the candidates may have contributed to a slow news campaign. Finally, we analyze the role of the "new media" in the election, and speculate about why, after being so visible in 1992, they faded into the background in 1996.

TRENDS IN ELECTION MEDIA COVERAGE

Thomas E. Patterson argues that in the tug-of-war that exists between candidates and journalists for control over the campaign agenda, the mass media hold the balance of power. The media have become the chief intermediary in the relationship between candidates and voters. Media values and reporting practices have transformed American elections from a process once revered by citizens to one that is despised.[2]

Bad News Equals News

In the current era, political news is generally bad news. Journalists appear to be following the rule that if something is working in government and politics, it isn't worth reporting. Collectively, news stories leave the impression that politicians are corrupt, governmental institutions are dysfunctional, and political processes are being compromised. Yet, the barrage of negativity does not end with news reports. Pundits thrive on casting aspersions at political leaders and policies. Talk radio hosts and callers engage in frequently hostile rantings about lying politicians and unresponsive government. The net result, some fear, is to undermine public faith in government. Further, citizens may become so numbed by the continual bombardment of bad news that they withdraw from the political realm.[3]

Negative news abounds in campaigns as journalistic norms carry over into this arena. The press tends to report a different, far more conflictual campaign than the candidates generally wage, although candidates have been far from positive in their campaign rhetoric in recent years. One of the reasons candidates employed "new media" strategies in 1992 was to deflect some of the negative coverage they were receiving in the mainstream press. The tactic worked, as talk shows provided a comparatively friendly forum for candidates.[4]

Press coverage of recent elections has been especially negative. By comparison, coverage of the 1996 presidential contest was more civil. A Center for Media and Public Affairs (CMPA) content analysis reveals, however, that the candidates on balance received more negative than positive network television news coverage, although Bill Clinton had some periods where good news reports outweighed the bad. Overall, 47 percent of television news stories about Bill Clinton were positive, compared to 41 percent for Bob Dole. Interestingly, Bob Dole received his only break from the television media (47 percent positive coverage) during the Republican National Convention. Bill Clinton had his hardest time with the press during the convention period, garnering only 38 percent positive coverage. Press criticism was heavy largely because of the scandals surrounding his administration and criticism about his signing of the welfare reform bill.[5]

Voters did not find the 1996 campaign to be any more negative than previous elections, although they did not consider coverage to be especially positive. A *Washington Post*/Harvard University/Kaiser Foundation study conducted immediately following the election indicated that 55 percent of voters felt that this year's campaign was about as negative as those in the recent past, while 25 percent thought it was more negative and 19 percent considered it to be less negative. However, voters perceived that Dole received substantially less favorable press than did Clinton. While 56 percent of voters believed that the press treated Dole about right, 36 percent said that media reports were too negative, while only 6 percent felt they were too favorable. In contrast, 54 percent of voters considered Clinton's coverage to be fair, while 12 percent believed it was too negative, and 31 percent felt it was too favorable.

Voters who believed that coverage of Bob Dole was too negative were asked what factors contributed to this perception. Many people objected to the "horse race" aspect of coverage surrounding the Dole campaign. A full seventy-seven percent of these respondents felt that too much attention was paid to Bob Dole's standings in the polls, and 69 percent believed that news reports about the way his campaign was run were too negative. Only 39 percent of this group felt that coverage of Dole's record in Congress was problematic.

The *Washington Post* poll revealed that 66 percent of those who objected to Dole's media coverage felt that the pictures or the situations Dole was portrayed in were unfavorable. The prize for the worst campaign image should be awarded to Bob Dole. On September 18, Dole fell from a stage in Chico, California, when the railing collapsed as he was shaking a young boy's hand. A photo of Dole lying on the ground with an anguished look on his face graced the front pages of newspapers across the nation, was featured in full color in news magazines, and was shown repeatedly on television news programs. Dole's fall from the stage preoccupied the media for at least a week. Without the accompanying text, the picture of Dole prostrate and pained left the impression that he was suffering from a heart attack or some other physical malady and conjured up the issue of his age and health. Dole proved to be a good sport about the incident and developed a series of jokes which he used throughout the campaign. During the final presidential debate, Dole used one of these jokes to illustrate a point he was making about the need for litigation reform. "You know, I fell off a platform out in California, in Chico, a while back. Before I hit the ground, my cell phone rang, and this trial lawyer says, 'I think we've got a case here.'"[6] Dole used the same joke on a post election appearance on "Late Night with David Letterman."[7]

Voters surveyed by the *Washington Post* also believed that Bill Clinton was portrayed unfairly in pictures. However, no negative image of Clinton rivaled that of Dole's pratfall. The press did manage to capture pictures of Clinton with strange expressions on his face which they used to accompany stories about scandals plaguing his campaign and administration. Voters had the most problems with the media paying too much attention to the negative aspects of his character. Ninety-five percent of respondents who complained about Clinton's press coverage believed that the media overplayed the character issue, compared to 55 percent who felt that Dole's character was unfairly maligned. There were far fewer complaints about "horse race" coverage of the Clinton campaign. Only 44 percent felt that too much attention was being paid to Clinton's standing in the polls, and 49 percent disliked negative reports about how his campaign was being run.

Negative Advertising

Press reports of the presidential campaign exacerbated the attacks levied by the candidates. When the Dole campaign ratcheted up its assaults during the final three weeks of the campaign, press reports magnified their intensity. However, candidates themselves can contribute to negative campaign coverage through their advertising strategies, even when the policy content of their stump speeches outweighs anti-opposition rhetoric. The press spends significant time covering ads and advertising tactics, including the use of "ad watches," which critique candidate spots. The sheer number of ads makes them fair game for news coverage. From April 1 through October 31, 1996, 167,714 spots aired in the nation's top 75 media markets.[8]

Even as candidates condemn negative campaigning, they readily employ attack ads because they can work. Voters tend to remember negative ads, and they can undermine an opponents support, especially when the electorate is cynical.[9] In 1996, the presidential candidates spent over $90 million on advertising. Their ads were substantially more nasty than their campaign speeches, which was a strategic step taken to depersonalize the attacks. The Dole campaign's attack ads challenged Clinton's character and trustworthiness. The ads showcased Clinton's problems with Whitewater, ethical issues surrounding his administration, sexual harassment, and his attempt to smoke marijuana as a college student. The Clinton campaign's negative ads stressed that Dole was old and out of touch, even using his long record of government service against him. Reform Party candidate Ross Perot also ran negative ads, especially when he was not allowed to participate in the presidential debates, even though in his infomercials he urged voters not to support candidates who used attack spots.

Negative advertising strategies in the 1996 presidential contest were more sophisticated than in the past. The two major presidential campaigns created a wide range of ads that were designed to reach specific target audiences. In addition to the traditional direct attack spots, the Clinton campaign aired "empathetic negative" ads. These 30-second spots sandwich negative slams at the opponent in between positive portrayals of the candidate. Artfully filmed and softer in tone than the usual attack ads, these spots are designed to compare the candidates' positions on issues while appealing to the voters' emotions. An example of the empathetic negative ad is one that the Clinton campaign used to criticize Bob Dole's position on the Family and Medical Leave Act. The ad features working class parents walking along a country road talking about the death of their daughter, whose picture appears on the screen.

The ad goes on to describe how President Clinton signed the Family Leave Bill into law so that parents can be with sick children and not lose their jobs. A black and white photo of Bob Dole appears, as the announcers discusses Dole's six-year fight against the Family and Medical Leave Act. The ad concludes with a shot of President Clinton sitting in the White House garden accompanied by a little girl in a wheelchair.[10]

The negative ads in the presidential campaign paled in comparison to the spots employed in a number of congressional races throughout the country. Political scientist Darrell West studied advertising in Senate races in Rhode Island, Minnesota, and New Jersey, where the air wars were especially vicious. West found evidence of a public backlash against the ultra negative campaigns. A coordinated Republican strategy to demonize candidates by evoking the evil "liberal" label against opponents nationwide largely backfired. Similarly, the Democratic tactic of linking Republican candidates to unpopular Speaker Newt Gingrich were not effective. A particularly odious strategy involved "morphing" candidates into criminals. In a California race, Congressman Vic Fazio was transformed into the killer of Polly Klaas.

West discovered that candidates who focused on positive issue information rather than negative character information did better in the election. In fact, ads which employ humor, such as a fast-talking Paul Wellstone and his drag-racing campaign bus in the Minnesota Senate race, are more likely to grab voters' attention and receive high ratings than negative spots.[11] There is some anecdotal evidence to suggest that in states where the campaign was especially negative voters became disillusioned, and some reported that they did not bother to go to the polls.

Tabloidization of News

A common complaint about the current state of American political news is that it is more "infotainment" than information. In an era of increased competition for audience shares, mainstream news has become heavily infused with entertainment content. In addition, tabloid newspapers and television programs have taken on political roles, at times setting the agenda for the traditional press. Further, when tabloids break stories involving sex, scandal, and crime, they can force candidates to react to the charges. This was the case in 1992 when the *Star* tabloid broke the story of Bill Clinton's longstanding affair with Gennifer Flowers. As *Washington Post* reporter Howard Kurtz states, "The established media is increasingly covering the same sorts of things as the tabloids and finding that the supermarket papers are often better at the game."[12]

In such an environment, "feeding frenzies," where the press relentlessly pursues scandalous stories, especially those involving politicians' personal lives, flourish.[13] "Inside Washington" commentator Evan Thomas described the process by which personal scandal stories reach the mainstream press. "There is a media food chain which goes from supermarket tabloid, to New York tabloid, to CNN, to the mainstream press—in about 15 minutes."[14]

The 1996 contest was so dull that it did not even include especially good "feeding frenzies" to complain about. Most of the "frenzies" surrounded President Clinton, his administration, and his campaign officials and operations. Many of them were old news. The well-worn Whitewater story was around, as speculation about Hillary Clinton's role in an Arkansas real estate deal refused to die. Travelgate, the firing of seven employees in the White House travel office, was being kept alive by Independent Counsel Kenneth Starr, who was investigating allegations that Mrs. Clinton pressured Chief of Staff Mack McLarty into making the dismissals. Filegate, the White House's improper requisitioning of over 900 FBI files, also cast a shadow on the administration.[15] These stories failed to sustain public interest. More personalized "frenzies," such as those involving charges against Bill Clinton of sexual misconduct relating to an alleged affair he had with Paula Jones and his failure to release his medical records in their entirety, encouraging speculation that he had a sexually transmitted disease, also did not register much with citizens.

One feeding frenzy that caught the Clinton campaign off guard was sparked by the extramarital affairs of top aide Dick Morris. In late August, the *Star* tabloid broke the story that Morris had revealed secrets about the White House to a $200 an hour call girl named Sherry Rowlands, who recorded them in her diary. Allegedly, Morris told Rowlands that Hillary Clinton was behind the FBI file scandal, a charge Mrs. Clinton denied. Rowlands also claimed that Morris let her listen in on his phone calls with the president in order to impress her. The *Star* and the *National Enquirer* also revealed that Morris was the father of a six-year-old child by a Texas woman with whom he had had a relationship for fifteen years. Morris was writing an inside story about the campaign and had extensive notes on his portable computer. Congressional investigators were considering subpoenaing both Morris and the portable computer to find out what he actually knew about Filegate.[16]

The Morris story followed the typical path from the tabloids to the mainstream press. The *Star* had attempted to sell the story to news organizations but found no takers. Ever since the *Miami Herald* faced heavy criticism for uncovering Gary Hart's affair with Donna Rice, the serious media prefer to follow-up, rather than initiate, sex scandals. Interestingly, the *Star* received accolades from journalists, including *Washington Post* editor Bob Woodward, and magazines such as *Time*, as well as the networks for breaking the story.[17] The *Star* touted these credentials to its own readers in a story running simultaneously with the revelations about Morris's long-term mistress.[18]

The Dick Morris affair sparked minor "frenzies" surrounding the "shadowing culture of political consultants." The most sordid of these "frenzies" surrounded noted Republican activist and unpaid advisor to the Dole campaign Roger Stone. The *Star* and *National Equirer* printed stories that Stone and his wife, Nydia, solicited sex partners on the Internet and in swingers' magazines. Dole immediately sought to shield himself from the damage by distancing himself from Stone. Another minor frenzy involved GOP strategist Arthur Finkelstein, who had orchestrated the campaigns of some of the country's most vehement anti-gay legislators. Finkelstein was "outed" by *Boston* magazine, and admitted to being a homosexual.[19]

The Morris feeding frenzy fizzled after a few weeks. Some news organizations treated it less like a campaign story and more like a commentary on the problems of modern society. The September 30 cover of *Newsweek* bore the word, "Adultery," and the feature story debated the meaning of infidelity in the '90s, complete with polling data.[20] A sidebar story covered the reaction of Morris's wife, Eileen McGann, to the allegations. Ms. McGann had come under fire for standing by her man, as people speculated that she was doing so in order to benefit from the $2.5 million book deal that Morris had landed as a result of his inside knowledge of the Clinton White House.[21]

The "feeding frenzies" surrounding the Clinton administration, which did nothing to change the outcome of the election, may be more of a factor as the President enters his second term in office. While the individual scandals did not seem to register strongly with the public during the election, their collective effect may undermine his ability to garner trust for governing. In addition, the fallout from old "frenzies," such as Whitewater, and the new ones, especially Indogate, is a long way from being contained, as investigations continue.

The "feeding frenzy that wasn't" in the 1996 campaign involved allegations that Bob Dole had had an extramarital affair which began in 1968 while he was married to his first wife. During the campaign, the *Washington Post* and *Time* magazine investigated the story, and conducted extensive interviews with the woman. The story broke in the *National Enquirer* during the last week of October but did not stimulate the expected feeding frenzy. The *Washington Post* buried the allegations inside a lengthy campaign story after the *Enquirer* made its revelations. The *New York Daily News* published the story, while other news organizations, including the *Boston Globe, Newsday,* the *New York Post, Newsweek,* and CNN, gave the allegations a quick mention. Most media outlets chose to ignore the report, including the three major networks, the *New York Times,* the *Los Angeles Times,* the *Wall Street Journal,* and *USA Today.*[22] The story received far more play in the days following the election.

The reasons for the media's restraint in covering the alleged Dole affair are varied. Some news organizations felt that a twenty-eight year old story was not news. Others disagreed, citing Dole's use of the character issue against Clinton as justification for releasing the story. The Dole campaign struggled to keep the lid on the rumor. Members of Dole's campaign staff met with media officials to urge that the story not be printed. After the report broke in the *Enquirer*, Dole became reluctant to schedule too many press interviews, fearing that he would be questioned about the affair. Finally, the woman involved, Meredith Roberts, was a reluctant source. She declined $50,000 offered by the *Enquirer* for her story and tried to prevent the tabloids from exploiting the situation. She told the *Boston Globe*, "I am appalled at how the lines of distinction between the tabloid and the mainstream press get blurred. And how they use innocent people as pawns."[23]

Poll-Driven Reporting

Polls are a long-standing fact of American political life. In recent years, however, the amount of poll-generated news has increased along with the sources of polling information. In addition to news organizations' own polling data, the press regularly incorporates the results of surveys conducted by independent research organizations, think tanks, interest groups, and candidates into its reports. The overabundance of polling information disseminated during the 1996 campaign may have heightened the boredom factor in an already lackluster campaign.

Poll stories constitute manufactured news.[24] Polling data represent a snapshot of public opinion. On their own, poll results are not conducive to producing action-oriented stories which might draw audience members into the campaign. In an attempt to add drama to the numbers, reporters often will imply that shifts in the polls can be attributed to particular campaign events, however misleading these connections may be in reality.

The media often employ poll results to create political profiles of various demographic groups within the electorate, such as "soccer moms" and "angry white males." A *Time* magazine cover proclaimed a suburban, conservative, Midwestern working mother, thirty-five year old, a high school graduate, and earning $35,000 a year to be "the most wanted woman in America." The article made liberal use of polling data to indicate that this "crucial voter" had shifted her preferences dramatically toward Bill Clinton since 1992.[25] When written well, stories involving polling stereotypes can provide voters with information to guide voting decisions. More often, however, poll driven stories are reported in a manner devoid of meaningful historical or policy context. Further, polling data work to distance citizens from the human side of politics by reducing their attitudes and emotions to numbers without personal referents.[26]

One major criticism of poll intensive reporting is that it privileges the "horse race" aspect of the election over more substantive policy concerns. In 1996, "horse race" coverage abounded. The media, as has become the norm, became preoccupied with campaign strategy and the candidates' relative standings in the polls. CNN and *USA Today* even provided daily tracking poll data. A new form of political discourse has developed around presidential preference polls based upon the spin tactics of candidates, campaign managers, journalists, and pundits.[27]

The "horse race" was a more prominent and meaningful component of television network news coverage during the primaries than during the general election. A Center for Media and Public Affairs (CMPA) analysis of the content of ABC, CBS, and NBC election news stories during the primary season revealed that the lion's share of coverage was devoted to the Republican candidates' standings in the polls, their electability, and their campaign tactics. One-hundred-seventy-five of 315 stories—47 percent—focused on the "horse race," compared to 88 stories—29 percent—which featured candidates' policy proposals. The networks aired over three times as many "horse race" stories in 1996 as they did in 1992. At the same time, the candidates were stressing substantive themes in their campaign speeches and ads, relegating comparatively little time to discussing their poll standings or campaign strategies.[28]

The networks' coverage of the "horse race" diminished markedly during the general election. According to a CMPA content analysis, only 18 percent of post-primary campaign news (through September) dealt with poll results in terms of a "horse race." Reporters made frequent references to Bill Clinton's and Bob Dole's placement in the polls, but any semblance of a race was mitigated by Clinton's consistently large lead. As a result, the proportion of television news stories featuring policy information rose significantly to 46 percent, as a wide range of policy issues, including abortion, welfare reform, crime, drugs, anti-smoking, children's issues, and education made it on the media's agenda. The economy was less evident in 1996 television news coverage of the campaign than it had been in 1992.[29]

There is evidence that the public is growing impatient with "horse race" coverage. The *Washington Post* post-election survey asked voters if they felt that the news media should report polls showing which presidential candidate is ahead. Six percent of the respondents replied that the media should report more poll results, while 34 percent felt that the current amount of polling information was satisfactory. However, 32 percent responded that the media should report fewer polls, and 26 percent wanted no polling data whatsoever.[30]

Post-election analyses in 1996 speculated that pre-election polling had produced a kind of "bandwagon effect" which contributed to the low turnout in the campaign. Voters, perceiving that Bill Clinton was the certain victor, abstained from voting. However appealing this theory may be, given Clinton's clear front-runner status throughout the campaign, the influence of pre-election polling on voters' candidate choice and turnout is difficult to establish empirically.[31]

Celebrity Journalism

As the lines between journalism and entertainment have become increasingly blurred, the news industry has become more like Hollywood. One manifestation of this trend is the emergence of an elite corps of "celebrity journalists," who have the potential to earn large fees showcasing their talents outside of their traditional media roles. Celebrity journalists follow similar routes to stardom, which includes landing a prestigious job in the mainstream media, working the political talk show circuit, and branching out to entertainment media forums. The most in-demand star journalists can command upwards of $40,000 in speaking fees,[32] although recent criticism has curbed this practice somewhat.

Covering a presidential campaign offers wanna-be celebrity journalists the opportunity to establish their credentials and proven stars the occasion to hone their skills. At times, the press presence can overwhelm the candidates and the voters. During the New Hampshire primary, for example, the press blitz was so intensive that it created a wall between voters and the candidates. As *Washington Post* reporter Howard Kurtz asked, "Was the presidential primary about New Hampshire, or was it about Dan Rather, Tom Brokaw, Peter Jennings, Larry King, Mary Matalin, Tim Russert, Cokie Roberts, Bernard Shaw, Don Imus, Fred Barnes, Chris Matthews, and a few hundred of their closest friends?"[33]

A significant implication of the star system is that journalists spend more time telling the campaign story, as candidates have less of a chance to speak for themselves. Political scientist Thomas E. Patterson discovered that as the candidate sound bite has shrunk to approximately eight seconds, interpretation of candidates' messages by journalists has increased markedly.[34] This finding holds true for television news, where commentators are often featured speaking while footage of presidential candidates serves as a backdrop, and in print, where direct quotes by candidates are largely overshadowed by reporters' explanations. Add to this equation the plethora of news discussion programs, such as "The Capital Gang," "Washington Week in Review," "Crossfire," and even programs on Comedy Central, and the ratio of candidates' to commentators' words becomes even more lopsided.

The trends that Patterson identified for earlier elections were evident in 1996. A CMPA content analysis revealed that only a small percentage of the total network television news air time was devoted to comments by the presidential candidates. Commentary by reporters and anchors constituted more than 72 percent of election news reports. The average sound bite from a presidential candidate remained at eight seconds in length, consistent with the 1992 campaign. However, for every eight-second sound bite, reporters provided 52 seconds of observations. Other sources, such as voters, experts, campaign personnel, and interest group representatives also contributed to telling the candidates' stories. As such, less than 28 percent of network news coverage featured candidates speaking for themselves.[35]

Voters, it appears, would prefer to allow the candidates to have their say, rather than relying so heavily on the comments of reporters and pundits. The *Washington Post* survey asked voters if they would rather see more of the news devoted to reporters explaining where a candidate stands on the issues, or the candidates themselves giving their positions. A striking 77 percent of the respondents wanted to let the candidates speak, while 16 percent preferred reporters' commentary.[36]

Some journalists defend the practice of the media providing extensive commentary on political events. With the rise of CNN and other real time news outlets, many events are reported as they are breaking or shortly thereafter. Newspapers, in particular, must provide in-depth information and analysis in order to serve as a source of new information to audience members.

The networks did respond to a campaign waged by the Free TV for Straight Talk Coalition, spearheaded by Walter Cronkite, Senator Bill Bradley, and Senator John McCain, to provide prime air time for the candidates to deliver two-and-a-half minute mini-speeches on alternate nights. While balking at the idea at first, ABC, CBS, NBC, and FOX allowed the candidates the opportunity to engage in a running debate on air after the coalition ran full-page ads in major newspapers. The spots themselves were substantive. The problem was that the networks did not accommodate them at a uniform time each evening. Sometimes they appeared at the end of the nightly newscast, at other times, they were incorporated into a newsmagazine program. Thus, voters could not easily develop a routine for viewing these segments.

CAMPAIGN CONTEXT

There are some factors that were beyond the media's control during Campaign '96. The economy was stable and the country was at peace. There was no major crisis to arouse popular concern. The issues raised by the candidates were too trivial or too complex to galvanize citizen support. The candidates were overly familiar and their campaigns were unexciting. The electoral process was protracted and depersonalized. In a word, the campaign was *boring*.[37] Besides these factors, election news had to compete with the "story of the century"—the wedding of John F. Kennedy, Jr.—as well as a very exciting World Series.

Asked if a story of a cat being rescued from a tree by firemen could beat out presidential campaign news, Paul Dughi, a Columbus, Ohio television news director, replied, "It depends on the cat."[38] This statement captures the sentiment of many journalists who were themselves disappointed and bored by the lack of interesting campaign stories. ABC News correspondent Jeff Greenfield complained, "This is the most uninteresting presidential election of my lifetime. You don't have a cutting-edge candidate putting anything on the table. Clinton is running out the clock. It's not about anything."[39] NBC News anchor Tom Brokaw echoed these sentiments: "We're turning over every rock that we can without just making it up."[40]

The candidates themselves bear some of the responsibility for the shortness of campaign news. While Bill Clinton is a masterful campaigner, his organization felt that the most effective strategy was for the President to ride out his comfortable lead by attending to the affairs of state. His central message of "crossing the bridge to the 21st century," was the perfect accompaniment to his risk averse strategy, but it did little to stimulate press coverage. Bob Dole's personal style of campaigning frequently left reporters guessing about his message and searching hard for story angles until the end of the campaign. His speeches rarely contained new information, and his presentation was often confusing. For example, when Dole was in New York paying a courtesy call on Cardinal John O'Connor, a reporter asked if Dole had any message for Catholic voters. Dole replied, "No, I'm just here to visit. I've visited the cardinal before. He's a friend of my wife Elizabeth." The result was that Dole was shut out of the network newscasts that evening and received only a few lines in elite newspapers, as was the case quite a few times during the campaign.[41] To compound the problem, the press corps following Dole was kept at a distance from the candidate and had to rely on answers to shouted questions or information from a small pool of reporters who were granted access.

A Center for Media and Public Affairs study provides some support for the contention that journalists did not report as much campaign news as in previous contests. Their analysis reveals that between January 1 and September 30, the three major television networks reported 20 percent fewer election stories than for the same period in 1992, although coverage of the primary period actually exceeded 1992 levels. As the campaign progressed, the amount of network news coverage declined precipitously. From April through September, campaign news dropped to 30 percent below the 1992 comparables. For September, the coverage was almost 40 percent lower than in 1992.[42]

The public did not seem to have a compelling need to find out more about the candidates or their stands on issues. Unlike recent campaigns in which there was a large proportion of undecided voters late in the election, citizens in 1996 made up their minds early. Voters claimed that they knew as much about the candidates when the campaign began in September than when it concluded in November, and that they had enough information to make a decision.[43] Sixty-two percent of respondents to the *Washington Post* survey felt that they could make an informed choice. In fact, voters seemed to be fairly knowledgeable about key campaign issues. Seventy-nine percent of voters knew that Dole, and not Clinton, favored making abortions more difficult to obtain. Seventy-two percent understood Clinton's position on affirmative action. Seventy-nine percent of voters knew that Clinton favored increased federal funding for job-training programs, and 81 percent understood that Clinton wanted to expand family leave. A majority of voters—63 percent—correctly believed that Dole favored an increase in defense spending.

Voters, who are more interested in the campaign than the general public, did not demand more coverage of the campaign. In response to the question, "If you were the editor of the newspaper you most often read during this year's presidential campaign, would you have increased, decreased, or devoted the same amount of space as that newspaper did to the coverage of the presidential campaigns," 50 percent of voters would have kept it the same, 30 percent would have liked more, and 12 percent favored less coverage. A similar question asked voters to step into the role of the news director of the national news program they watched most often during the campaign. While 48 percent said that they would devote the same amount of time to election news, 24 percent favored decreasing coverage, and 23 percent wanted more reports.

WHITHER THE "NEW MEDIA"?

One of the novelties of the 1992 election was the "new media" foray into campaign politics. The "new media's" presence in the electoral arena had several implications. Talk radio, entertainment television, tabloid papers, and other alternative media created a dilemma for the mainstream press, which had to make decisions about whether or not to cover events that were reported first in these forums. In addition, the new media had significant popular appeal, as they have the ability to at least leave citizens with the impression that they have a political voice. On the downside, the "new media" contributed to the heavy integration of entertainment with politics, including the greater tendency toward the "tabloidization" of mainstream news stories.

The "new media," however, are fickle. They unabashedly acknowledge that their primary objective is economic. Entertainment is paramount, not public service. Therefore, the "new media" are under no obligation to bestow any more attention on the electoral process than the entertainment value of the campaign warrants. Talk radio hosts, for example, found that they could not sustain interest in the election, and that audience members did not feel much like discussing the campaign on air. In one case, a popular talk radio host opened his program with a discussion of politics and the election and received no calls when he opened up the phone lines. Changing the topic to whether or not young girls should get tattoos, the switchboard lit up.[44] Entertainment talk shows, such as "Oprah," turned down the opportunity to host Bob Dole, fearing that they would bore their audiences. Entertainment magazines, like *People,* which had featured a heavier than usual dose of political stories—even cover stories—in 1992, scaled back their coverage in 1996.

There are a variety of reasons why the "new media" faded into the background in 1996. The "new media" are decidedly anti-establishment, and the two major candidates epitomized everything that talk radio, in particular, targets for abuse. Ross Perot, who offered an amusing foil in 1992, was a tired cliché by 1996. None of the candidates pursued a vigorous "new media" strategy. Bill Clinton, who had used talk radio and television to his advantage in the 1992 campaign, discovered that talk shows turned quickly against a sitting president.[45] He was especially turned off by acidic comments made against him by talk jock Don Imus at the Radio and TV Correspondents Association dinner. By staying away from talk radio, Clinton strove to delegitimize it as a political force. Bob Dole used talk radio somewhat more than Bill Clinton, but not enough to satisfy conservative talk radio hosts. A *National Journal* cover story asked, "Talk Radio: Is Bob Dole Afraid of It?," summing up the candidate's relationship to the medium.[46] In September, Michael Harrison, editor of the industry magazine, *Talkers,* confronted Dole about his ignoring the medium and suggested that Dole make two to three minutes available in his daily schedule to call-in. From September on, Dole made regular calls to talk radio programs.

In 1992, the "new media" were a story in and of themselves. The mainstream press charted its competitors' course, levying criticism when possible and snatching their stories when convenient. By 1996, "new media" strategies had become incorporated into the arsenal of tried and true campaign tactics. "New media" had not supplanted the mainstream media's political audience base, or even eroded it slightly, as some media analysts had speculated. They no longer commanded the mainstream media's attention.

Yet, there is evidence that something of a "stealth campaign" was being waged in the "new media." Bob Dole unofficially announced his candidacy for president during a 1995 stint on "Late Night with David Letterman." "Larry King Live!" played host to the candidates, their wives, and a wide range of campaign functionaries. Both Bill Clinton and Bob Dole made the now requisite appearances on MTV, and fielded questions from Generation X correspondent Tabitha Soren on the "Choose or Lose" bus. The candidates and their wives were interviewed on television news magazine shows, such as "20/20."

Even if the candidates' appearances on talk shows were few, the campaign did come up in discussion. Late night talk show hosts, such as Jay Leno and David Letterman, regularly used material from the campaign in their opening monologues. In fact, a Pew Research Center report found that approximately 25 percent of the public learned something about the campaign from late night comics. On daytime, Rosie O'Donnell repeatedly raised objections to Bob Dole's candidacy on her talk show, even when his ads were shown during her program. The "new media's" influence was even felt during the debates, as the popular town meeting format employed in 1992 was reprised.

One particular "new media" innovation that received some attention during the 1996 campaign was the use of the Internet for broadcasting political information. Mainstream news organizations established home pages on the World Wide Web where everything from late-breaking stories to the most recent poll results could be found. The candidates established their own Web pages, which contained some creative ideas amidst the partisan information. The Dole home page, for example, allowed users to create their own posters. Bob Dole advertised his home page frequently throughout the campaign, perhaps to demonstrate that a 72 year old man was technologically current. Dole learned that a campaign in cyberspace can be hazardous. America Online invited users to write to President Clinton, Bob Dole, and Newt Gingrich. People who accessed the Dole site were mistakenly linked to a parody Web page, which gave them a responses like the following: "Thank you for your suggestions regarding the federal budget. As an important senator, and a candidate for president, it is important that I appear to care about your opinion."[47] So many citizens went on-line to track the results of the election that it caused a major traffic jam on the Internet.

If the general public was not particularly engaged by the "new media" in 1996, there is evidence that voters were. Television network news (66 percent), local television news (54 percent), and newspapers (54 percent) remain the most popular sources of campaign information for voters, according to the *Washington Post* survey. Voters relied on diverse communications outlets, including cybermedia. A Pew Research Center study found only a small fraction of the mass public followed the campaign in cyberspace. Only three percent of the public went on-line to follow the campaign once a week or more; an additional two percent tracked the campaign via computer less often.[48] However, the national exit poll showed that 26 percent of voters claimed to use the Internet regularly. The *Washington Post* survey revealed that seven percent of voters considered the Internet or World Wide Web to be a major source of campaign information and 26 percent used it as a minor source. Similarly, while the Pew Research Center study indicated that 14 percent of the public listened to political talk radio regularly, the national exit poll found that 36 percent of voters were frequent talk radio listeners.[49]

CONCLUSION

It is impossible to hold the mass media entirely responsible for the lack of public enthusiasm about Campaign '96. The entire dynamic of the contest worked against voter involvement.

Still, the public is disenchanted with media coverage of elections. Perhaps this is because American campaigns have become depersonalized spectacles. While the mass media serve as the conduit between candidates and voters, they also construct a wall.[50] Candidates work the crowd largely through their televised presence, and not in person. Their messages are delivered via unappointed emissaries, as even sound bites fade away. Perhaps by bringing citizens back into the media/election game, we might better stimulate public interest in campaigns.

NOTES

1. Howard Kurtz, "As Vote Nears, Americans Tuning Out Campaign '96," *Washington Post* (October 10, 1996): A1, A6.

2. Thomas E. Patterson, *Out of Order*, New York, NY: Knopf (1994).

3. See W. Lance Bennett, *News: The Politics of Illusion*, 3rd ed., White Plains, NY: Longman (1996); Matthew Robert Kerbel, *Remote and Controlled*, Boulder, CO: Westview (1996).

4. Bruce Buchanan, *Renewing Presidential Politics*, Lanham, MD: Rowman and Littlefield (1996).

5. Robert S. Lichter and Linda S. Lichter, *Media Monitor* (September/October, 1996): pp. 1–6.

6. "Campaign '96: Transcript of the Second Presidential Debate," *Washington Post* (October 17, 1996): p. A14.

7. Bob Dole appeared on Letterman on November 8, 1996.

8. "It Wasn't Your Imagination," *Boston Herald* (November 17, 1996): p. 17.

9. Darrell West, *Air Wars*, Washington, D.C.: CQ Press (1993); Shanto Iyengar *Going Negative*, New York, NY: The Free Press (1995); Howard Kurtz, "Candidates Get a Charge from Negative Ads," *Washington Post* (September 19, 1996): C1, C4.

10. Joe Klein, "The Limits of Negativity," *Newsweek* (September 23, 1996): p. 42; John Harwood, "Political-Ad Makers Struggle to Preserve Their Slice of the Pie," *Wall Street Journal* (September 17, 1996): A1, A12.

11. Amy Keller, "A Funny Thing Happened on the Way to the Polls: Humor in Campaign Ads," *Roll Call* (June 17, 1996): p. 15.

12. J. Peder Zane, "Liz's Love Life! Oprah's Diet! Dole's Foreign Policy!" *New York Times* (September 29, 1996): p. D1.

13. Larry J. Sabato, *Feeding Frenzy*, New York, NY: Free Press (1992).

14. A quote by Evan Thomas on "Inside Washington," November 16, 1996, when discussing the issue of the press "feeding frenzies."

15. Michael Isikoff and Daniel Klaidman, "A Starr-Crossed Term?" *Newsweek* (October 28, 1996): p. 38.

16. Richard Gooding, "The White House Love Diaries," *Star* (September 17, 1996): p. 6–9, 37, 45; Richard Gooding, "Clinton Aide Kept Mistress 15 Years," *Star* (September 17, 1996): p. 5; David Wright, "Clinton Aide Has Secret Love Child," *National Enquirer* (September 17, 1996): p. 29; Matthew Cooper, "Sifting Through the Rubble," *Newsweek* (September 16, 1996): p. 50.

17. Howard Kurtz, "Tabloid Journalism's Scoops for Scandal," *Washington Post* (September 16, 1996): p. D1, D4.

18. Richard Gooding, "How STAR Scooped America's Press," *Star* (November 16, 1996): pp. 5, 37.

19. Matthew Cooper and Mark Hosenball, "Private Lives, Political Ends," *Newsweek* (September 23, 1996): pp. 40–41.

20. Jerry Adler, "Adultery: A New Furor Over an Old Sin," *Newsweek* (September 30, 1996): pp. 54–60.

21. Eleanor Clift, " 'A Terrible, Terrible Trauma'," *Newsweek* (September 30, 1996): p. 57.

22. Howard Kurtz, "A Big Story—but Only Behind the Scenes," *Washington Post* (November 13, 1996): pp. D1, D6.

23. Howard Kurtz, (November 13, 1996): D6.

24. Albert H. Cantril, "Introduction," in *Polling on the Issues*, Albert H. Cantril, ed., Cabin John, MD: Seven Locks Press (1980): pp. 3–12.

25. Nancy Gibbs and Michael Duffy, "Desperately Seeking Lori," *Time* (October 14, 1996): pp. 45–52.

26. Sandra Bauman and Susan Herbst, "Managing Perceptions of Public Opinion: Candidates' and Journalists' Reactions to the 1992 Polls," *Political Communication*, vol. 11, no. 2 (April/June, 1994): pp. 133–144.

27. Bauman and Herbst, 1994, pp. 133–144.

28. S. Robert Lichter and Linda S. Lichter, "Whose Campaign Did You See?" *Media Monitor*, vol. 10, no. 3 (May/June, 1996): pp. 1–6.

29. Robert S. Lichter and Linda S. Lichter, "Take This Campaign—Please," *Media Monitor*, vol. 10, no. 5 (September/October, 1996): pp. 1–6.

30. *Washington Post*/Harvard University/Kaiser Foundation, *Politics 96 Poll Results*, (November 15, 1996).

31. Diana Owen, *Media Messages in American Presidential Elections*, Westport, CT: Greenwood Press (1991).

32. James Fallows, *Breaking the News*, New York, NY: Pantheon Press (1996).

33. Howard Kurtz, "Where the Media Mob Was in the Voters' Way," *Washington Post* (February 22, 1996): p. A14.

34. Thomas E. Patterson, *Out of Order,* New York, NY: Knopf (1994).

35. Robert S. Lichter and Linda S. Lichter, *Media Monitor* (September/October, 1996): p. 2.

36. Four percent of *Washington Post* survey respondents replied that they wanted information from both candidates and reporters; three percent said neither.

37. Multiple authors, "Bored to the Bone," *Newsweek* (November 11, 1996): pp. 38–42.

38. Quoted in "Perspectives," *Newsweek* (October 7, 1996): p. 27.

39. Kurtz, October 19, 1996, A6.

40. Kurtz, October 19, 1996, A6.

41. Howard Kurtz, "Dole Making Lots of Stops But Little News," *Washington Post* (June 28, 1996): A1, A12.

42. Robert S. Lichter and Linda S. Lichter, *Media Monitor* (September/October, 1996): p. 1.

43. Richard Morin and Mario A. Brossard, "Poll: Voters Knew Early, Knew Enough," *Washington Post* (November 15, 1996): p. A1, A14, A15.

44. Richard Davis and Diana Owen, *New Media in American Politics* (manuscript in progress).

45. Diana Owen, "Talk Radio and Evaluations of President Clinton," manuscript (1996).

46. "Talk Radio: Is Dole Afraid of It?" *National Journal* (April 27, 1996).

47. "Droll 'Dole'," *Washington Post* (November 6, 1995): p. A23.

48. Pew Research Center for the People & the Press, "Dole Can't Cash in on Mixed View of Clinton," Washington, D.C. (October 4, 1996).

49. Thirty-three percent of Clinton supporters, 40 percent of Dole voters, and 37 percent of Perot backers were regular talk radio listeners.

50. Roderick P. Hart, *Seducing America,* New York, NY: Oxford (1994).

CHAPTER 10

Financing the 1996 Campaign

The Law of the Jungle

Brooks Jackson

Political Correspondent, CNN

"All contributions by corporations to any political committee for any political purpose should be forbidden by law."

. . . *President Theodore Roosevelt, 1905*[1]

"This has shown us once again that our campaigns cost too much, they take too much time, they raise too many questions, and now is the time for bipartisan campaign finance reform legislation."[2]

. . . *President William Clinton, 1996*

Watching the hundreds of millions of dollars spent in the 1996 elections, citizens might be surprised to find that there were any laws limiting campaign finance at all. One business corporation gave nearly $2.2 million to the Republican Party, despite the fact that it had been illegal since 1907 for corporations to make any contribution in connection with a federal election. And even though it had been illegal since 1943 for labor unions to support federal candidates, the AFL-CIO spent up to $22 million in selected congressional districts on television ads accusing Republican House members of attempting to gut Medicare, slash student loans, and allow corporations to raid workers' pensions. An Indonesian couple, living most of the time in Jakarta, contributed $450,000 to the Democratic National Committee despite a law forbidding contributions by non-U.S. citizens who are not legal residents. Both parties spent tens of millions on television ads promoting their presidential

225

nominees, draining all meaning from the strict spending limits that both candidates had agreed to abide by in return for nearly $62 million in public subsidies granted to each campaign.

A few days before the election, a former president of Common Cause, Fred Wertheimer, called the 1996 campaign "the dirtiest ever," worse even than the illegal contributions to the 1972 Nixon campaign:

> (I)n 1996 the campaign finance system put in place following the Watergate scandals has been washed away. Though still on the books, campaign finance laws have been replaced by the law of the jungle.[3]

Indeed, laws were still on the books and they did have effect, but often not the effect that was intended. In the Republican primaries the limits gave a special advantage to a wealthy magazine publisher who had never held public office. And in the general election they gave a multi-million dollar head start to President Clinton, while financially handcuffing Republican Bob Dole for months. The system of using taxpayer money to publicly finance presidential campaigns was intended to purchase fairness, but instead has created inequities.

The rules that worked so poorly in 1996 originated as the most ambitious attempt in U.S. history to rid federal elections of special-interest money and to establish financial equity among candidates. They were inspired by abuses and crimes uncovered after a botched wiretapping and burglary of the Democratic Party's offices in the Watergate building the night of June 17, 1972.

THE POST-WATERGATE RULEBOOK

The Watergate money trail began with $100 bills found in the burglars' pockets, money that came from the Committee to Re-elect the President, which financed the political espionage attempt using political campaign contributions. Subsequent investigations uncovered widespread criminality in the financing of Nixon's re-election. The President's personal attorney Herbert Kalmbach served six months in federal prison after admitting he had promised to sell an ambassadorship for a $100,000 contribution to the Nixon campaign.[4] A list of corporations credited with giving $100,000 each was found in the possession of Nixon's personal secretary, Rosemary Woods, leading to convictions of 21 executives for illegally contributing business funds.[5]

Both parties were found culpable. Democrat Hubert Humphrey's 1972 campaign manager was jailed for accepting contributions from a corporation, Associated Milk Producers Inc. There was embarrassment enough all around. In response, Congress in 1974 enacted sweeping changes: public financing for presidential campaigns; spending limits for congressional and presidential candidates; a limit of $1,000 on the amount an individual could contribute to any federal candidate; an independent Federal Election Commission (FEC) to oversee enforcement; and to prevent end-runs around the new contribution limits, a ban on "independent" campaign spending to help favored candidates. It was a tight system, but it would not survive even a single election. (See Table 1.)

The new rules began to unravel almost immediately. In the 1976 *Buckley v. Valeo*[6] case the U.S. Supreme Court struck down, as violations of free speech, both the new limits on campaign spending by candidates for Congress, and the new ban on independent spending. And in 1978 the FEC allowed political parties to spend substantial amounts of "non-federal" money— regulated only by a patchwork of state laws, many of them quite permissive—for activities that benefited both federal and state candidates.[7] By 1980 the Republican Party was raising and spending substantial amounts of this so-called "soft money" to advance Ronald Reagan's re-election.[8]

An arms-race mentality soon took over, with Democrats and Republicans vying intently to raise ever-larger amounts in fear of being outspent by the other side. In 1988 Democratic fundraiser Robert Farmer announced he would seek a total of $50 million to create what he called a level playing field. In response, George Bush quickly put together his own "Team 100," so called because membership was limited to those who gave $100,000 each. According to a later estimate, Democrats actually raised $23 million in soft money during the 1988 presidential campaign, in which Republicans raised $22 million.[9] The escalation continued in later years.

The soft money loophole effectively eliminated all limits on where political parties could raise money. A single contribution of $1 million was accepted by the Democratic National Committee in 1987.[10] And just after the 1994 congressional elections, the Republican Party announced it had received $2.5 million from Amway Corporation to finance a new broadcasting center

Table 1   Federal Contribution Limits

	By a person	By a Political Action Committee
To a candidate	$1,000 per election	$5,000 per election
To a political party (national committee)	$20,000 per year	$15,000 per year
To a Political Action Committee	$5,000 per year	$5,000 per year
Overall limit	$25,000 per year	NO LIMIT

These limits apply only in federal elections: President, Senate, House. Differing laws apply to campaigns for state or local office.

at RNC headquarters. "We're extremely proud to receive this very generous gift," RNC Chairman Haley Barbour said.[11]

Still, until the 1996 campaign parties were somewhat limited in where they could *spend* the increasing flood of soft money. Some could be used to pay the parties' overhead expenses, particularly for buildings. But soft money could be used in campaigns only if spent for joint activities, benefiting both state and federal candidates. "Generic" television or radio ads saying "Vote Republican" or "Vote Democratic" were one such avenue, but were of limited use in campaigns. For the most part, soft money was used to finance voter registration drives and voter turnout efforts ostensibly benefiting a party's entire ticket, from president down to dog-catcher. Even so, a large fraction of the expense had to be "allocated" to the federal candidates on the ticket and paid for with "hard" dollars, raised and spent under the strict federal rules. Any use of soft money for traditional campaign commercials was ruled out—until the 1996 campaign when political parties and special-interest groups began spending massively on campaign commercials that posed as "issue ads."

As we shall see, the combination of soft money and "issue ads" effectively ended the post-Watergate restrictions on money in the general election. And even in the presidential primaries, where the rules were tattered but still in place, the role of money and the influence of an elite class of affluent contributors was stronger than ever.

THE INVISIBLE PRIMARY: "THE MOST RELIABLE FRIEND"

For Republicans the battle for the White House began February 23, 1995, nearly a year before the first real primary votes were cast in the snows of New Hampshire. The event was a Texas-sized political fundraising event in Dallas which raised $4 million for Republican Senator Phil Gramm. Gramm's quest for money and his attitudes about it tell much about the cash-driven nature of presidential politics in 1996.

California political legend Jesse Unruh once called money "the mother's milk of politics," but as Gramm looked out over the thousands of affluent supporters who had written him $1,000 checks that night, he outdid Unruh in characterizing the central role of money in American politics:

> Benjamin Franklin once said, in a sexist way that no one would say in 1995, that a man can have but three reliable friends in the world: an old wife, an old dog and ready money. Now, as you can all see, I have a young wife. I do have an old dog. But thanks to you and your support tonight, I have the most reliable friend that you can have in American politics, and that is ready money.[12]

During all of 1995 the presidential race was first and foremost a contest to raise money. Fundraising was a political campaign in itself, a long and strenuous struggle for the support of a few, affluent donors. Under federal law, no candidate may take more than $1,000 from any single donor ($5,000 in the case of a political action committee). But to be financially competitive, a candidate needs to raise between $20 million and $30 million over the course of the campaign, in addition to the federal matching funds those contributions would enable the candidate to claim. The arithmetic is brutal: just to raise one million dollars required 1,000 donors *if* each gave the maximum. And Gramm aimed to raise $25 million by the end of 1995. "If you can't raise it this year, you're out of business," predicted Gramm's finance chairman, Florida real estate developer Alec Courtelis.[13] There would be little time for raising money once the election year itself began, with so many caucuses and primaries loaded into the early months. Meeting that goal meant Gramm would have to find more than 2,000 donors *every month* of 1995, even if each gave the maximum.

This was true despite public financing. Eventually the U.S. Treasury would supply millions of dollars to the major candidates, matching their private contributions dollar-for-dollar, up to $250 per donor. But not a dime of that money would be paid until after Jan. 1, 1996. The candidates would have to depend entirely on private contributions during all of 1995, when the major contenders would be spending millions setting up large headquarters operations, establishing offices in key states, and in some cases starting TV advertising campaigns. There had been no such need for early money when the public financing law was written in 1974. But by 1995 the front-loading of the primaries had moved up the spending schedule. Candidates needed money long before any federal funds were available to help.

The need to campaign for money had also been magnified by two decades of inflation. Spending had gone up, but the amount that a single donor could give had remained the same, so more and more donors had to be found. Under the 1974 post-Watergate amendments to the Federal Election Campaign Act, the maximum amount that could be spent campaigning for a presidential nomination was $10 million. The law allowed for periodic inflation adjustments on the spending side, so that those contending for the 1996 nominations would be allowed to spend $30.91 million for campaigning.[14] But while the basic spending limit had more than *tripled,* the contribution limits stood still. The maximum that any one individual could give to a presidential candidate remained $1,000, exactly as it had been in 1974. As a practical matter, candidates needed three times more donors.

Furthermore, the "basic" limit of $30.91 million was just a starting point. The law also allowed an extra 20 percent for fundraising expenses, raising the overall limit to $37.09 million (the figure most often cited by the news media during the course of the campaign). And as a practical matter, the real limit was probably in excess of $40 million because the law also allowed *unlimited* additional spending for legal and accounting expenses.

The basic problem for all presidential candidates is that relatively few Americans are willing and able to give $1,000 to any candidate, or even $500. According to a remarkable set of unpublished calculations by Republican fundraising expert Rodney Smith, the average number of $1,000 donors to each presidential campaign since 1972 was only 4,308. The highest number was 18,768 who gave the maximum to George Bush's renomination campaign in 1992.[15] In a nation of more than 260 million, that is an extremely small elite, and nearly all of them are from the richest 1 percent of the population. Corralling large numbers of them and their money takes organization, effort, and intense courtship. "You're talking about being locked in a hotel room for four to six hours a day making phone calls to a bunch who would rather spend money on things other than yourself," said Republican political consultant Stuart Stevens. "That's not fun."[16] It forced candidates, Gramm included, to concentrate their efforts steadily for month after month on wooing a tiny and financially unrepresentative segment of the citizenry.

Typical of the courtship was a reception Courtelis arranged for Gramm at the $800,000 home of a Fort Lauderdale chiropractor, Dr. Rick Bruns, who was supporting Gramm in hopes of getting a tax cut. "I feel like I am mainstream public and here's somebody who's going to fight for my rights," said Bruns. But the affluent doctor was hardly mainstream in financial terms. As he spoke a sleek tuna boat bobbed in the canal just outside his back door. Courtelis, though he had raised millions of dollars for Presidents Ronald Reagan and George Bush, had never sought a Cabinet post or other position of power. Asked why, he said only half-jokingly, "Then *I'd* be working for *them* . . . "[17] Courtelis and fundraisers like him took long hours away from lucrative businesses and professions to raise money for candidates. "On the average, I spend between three and four hours a day calling different people and organizing," said Dr. Zach Zachariah, a Florida cardiologist who headed Bob Dole's fundraising team in the state. And these fundraisers expected and got access and influence as a matter of course. "I get a great satisfaction to feel that I am, in my way, shaping the future government of this country to have the principles that I have," Courtelis said.[18]

As for Gramm, he saw nothing amiss. If access was being bought, it was by people who deserved it. "You can't have too many people out in the country who are actually leading and working and creating jobs and making things happen, have too much access to a president," he said.[19]

Republican consultant Stevens called the presidential money derby "an invisible primary." The $1,000 donors collectively had the power to decide who would run, and who would not. Former Vice President Dan Quayle announced early that he would not be running for the Republican nomination. One reason is that Quayle had been turned down by several prominent party fundraisers who said—very privately—they did not think Quayle was up to the job. Other losers in the invisible primary included former Secretary of Defense Richard Cheney and former HUD Secretary Jack Kemp. "Dick Cheney said it probably better than I did," Kemp said. "What you have to do and what you have to be in order to raise money to compete in this climate is, if not obscene, pretty close to it."[20]

Gramm took a strong early lead in the "invisible primary." He had actually started his campaign in late 1994 by transferring into his newly formed presidential committee nearly $4.8 million left over from his Senate re-election committee. One of the quirks of the federal campaign finance laws is that they allow candidates to raise money for one federal office, say House or Senate, then transfer any or all of that money to a campaign for a different federal office. And the beauty of it is that all the donors to the first fund can be re-solicited for new contributions to the new campaign, even if they gave the legal maximum before. Gramm took full advantage of this. By the end of March 1995 he had brought in $8.4 million in new contributions from individuals.[21]

In second place, as of the end of March, was former Tennessee Governor Lamar Alexander, a favorite of the state's business establishment. Alexander had raised $5.1 million in contributions. Senate Majority Leader Bob Dole, starting later than Gramm and Alexander, was in third place with $4.2 million. Following far behind were Senator Arlen Specter of Pennsylvania at $1 million and conservative ex-broadcaster Pat Buchanan at $946,000. California Governor Pete Wilson was talking of jumping into the race and, to bolster his credibility in the "invisible primary," publicly claimed in early April to have secured promises of $8 million in contributions during a week of telephone calling. But as it turned out, it was easier to get those promises than the actual money.

Despite his early lead, Gramm eventually lost the invisible primary. By Dec. 31, 1995 Gramm had indeed managed to raise $20.8 million, counting the millions transferred from his leftover Senate campaign account. But Gramm had been left in the dust by an even better fundraiser—Bob Dole. After years of writing tax bills on the Senate Finance Committee, and brokering deals on business legislation as Senate Republican leader, Dole had an unparalleled list of contacts willing to give to him and solicit contributions from colleagues. Dole raised $24.6 million in 1995, including nearly $1 million from PACs. So what Gramm had been predicting at the outset would turn out to be true—the candidate who raised the most money before the election year began would indeed eventually become the party's nominee. But that man was not going to be Phil Gramm. Despite his early fundraising success and his massive early spending, he dropped out without winning a single convention delegate, thus replacing fellow Texan John Connally in the annals of politics as the presidential candidate who spent the most to gain the least.

Still, it was far from clear as 1996 began that Dole would be the nominee. The reason was Steve Forbes, a man who played by a different set of rules.

A "FAT CAT" BECOMES A CANDIDATE

Forbes had a personal fortune estimated at $440 million. He was just the sort of super-rich "fat cat" whose influence Congress in 1974 had hoped to diminish by enacting contribution and spending limits. Instead, in 1996 Forbes became a serious contender for the Republican presidential nomination. And he did so despite having no political following save for readers of his magazine column, no political organization beyond a small headquarters staff and a few hired consultants, and all the charisma of a tin robot. But Forbes did have money, and nobody knew how much he was willing to spend.

In an earlier era men like Forbes stayed behind the scenes, writing checks to finance their favored candidates, pushing their pet ideas by proxy. Forbes would have preferred that role. As one of the true believers in supply-side economics, Forbes had urged Jack Kemp to run. None of the other Republican candidates were crusading for tax cuts in the damn-the-deficits way that Forbes favored. But Kemp refused to face the grueling, year-long beg-a-thon dictated by rising campaign costs and the $1,000 limit on individual contributions. "We broke the news that he was going to have to do 250 fundraising events in 1995, and he just took the book and about stuck it down my throat," recalled a Kemp aide who later worked for Forbes.[22] So Forbes decided to run himself. If the law would not allow him to be Jack Kemp's financial angel, he could be his own.

Forbes could spend as much as he wanted from his own very deep pockets, because the Supreme Court had ruled nearly 20 years earlier that in politics, money is speech. It follows, the Court ruled, that under the First Amendment guarantee of free speech Congress cannot limit what a candidate may spend, or what a candidate may contribute to his or her own campaign. Billionaire Ross Perot had taken advantage of that ruling in 1992, spending $63.5 million of his own money running as an independent candidate for president, and getting 19 percent of the vote. Forbes could afford to spend on a similar scale in the Republican primaries.

Money gave Forbes special advantages. He had no need to spend months striving to raise contributions from thousands of donors. And there was no limit on his spending, while the other candidates had agreed to limit their own spending in return for getting public financing.[23] And they had accepted not

Table 2   **The Forbes Advantage**[24]

State	Spending Limit	Forbes Spending
Iowa	$1,047,984	$4 million
New Hampshire	$618,200	$3–$3.5 million
Delaware	$618,200	$2 million
Arizona	$1,496,044	$4 million

only the $37.09 million *overall* limit, but limits on what they could spend in *each state* as well.

It was freedom from those state-by-state limits, more so than the lack of an overall spending limit, that made Forbes a potent factor in the closing months of 1995. The Forbes strategy called for knocking Bob Dole out of the race by outspending him significantly in the early primaries. "We had always known our only shot was to take him out early. If we could take him out, we could outlast everybody else," one campaign official said. In Iowa, where Dole and other candidates labored under a spending limit of just over $1 million, Forbes spent $4 million. And in New Hampshire, between September and December 1995, Forbes spent $371,150 advertising on a single television station in Manchester. It was an amount larger than all his rivals combined to that point.[25] (See Table 2.)

At first the strategy worked: in a matter of months Forbes rose in the polls from asterisk to contender, as high as second place in some polls. Talk of his flat-tax plan was everywhere. His message was all positive: "Hope, growth and opportunity," repeated over and over again, so often than the slogan became abbreviated to "HGO" in conversations among Forbes aides. But results of the early, positive advertising did not satisfy Forbes' handlers. "HGO wasn't getting us anyplace against Bob Dole," said a campaign official. So Forbes, the sunny optimist, spent much of his money on ads attacking Dole as "a Washington politician" with "Washington values" who was "deceiving voters" and who voted for hundreds of billions in tax increases and supported a $16 million subway that ran three blocks from the Capitol to senators' offices.[26]

Forbes' ads backfired. Voters turned off by the nasty attacks and counter-attacks sought out other candidates to support. "We pounded the hell out of Dole, and he pounded the hell out of us, and together we created Lamar Alexander," a Forbes official recalled.[27] Forbes finished fourth in the Iowa caucuses, behind Lamar Alexander in third.

Forbes later went on to win in Delaware, where he had invested $2 million as part of the plan to knock Dole out early. But Dole and the other candidates side-stepped that contest, emptying Forbes' win of meaning. Forbes also won in Arizona, where he had spent $4 million, nearly triple the spending limit. The Arizona money went mostly for TV and radio ads that ran at saturation levels for month after month, starting in October 1995. Forbes' victory there showed what a really massive media campaign can do, particularly when opponents cannot come close to matching it. But by then Dole, with his support from the party establishment, was on the way to winning a crushing string of primary victories in other states. In the end, Forbes spent nearly $42 million—almost 90 percent of it from his own pocket—to lose.

Money failed to give either Gramm or Forbes a decisive advantage, but *lack* of money may have been decisive for Lamar Alexander. The former Tennessee governor enjoyed golden contacts in the business community, but his fundraising stalled, and he never came close to his original goal of raising $20 million in 1995. Instead, on the eve of the New Hampshire primary, Alexander's campaign was practically broke. He had spent more than $12 million but had only $425,606 in the bank as of January 31, 1996. At that point, Dole had $4.8 million in cash.

Tracking polls showed Alexander gaining, and Dole headed for a possible third-place finish that could well have been fatal to his candidacy. Dole, however, unleashed an expensive barrage of ads and telephone-banking attacking Alexander as a liberal who increased sales taxes in Tennessee. They worked: Alexander's surge in the polls stopped and it was he, not Dole, who eventually finished third and soon after dropped out. One reason, according to Alexander's media consultant, Mike Murphy, was that the Alexander cam-

Table 3   **The Final Tally: Sources of Funds for Major Party Candidates for Presidential Nomination**

	Individuals	**PACs**	**Candidate**	**Federal**	**Other**
Democrat					
Bill Clinton	$28,310,247	$0	$0	$13,412,197	$805,872
Republicans					
Bob Dole	$29,699,398	$1,212,305	$0	$13,545,770	$299,528
Steve Forbes	$4,203,792	$2,000	$37,407,000		$31,265
Phil Gramm	$15,879,881	$400,879	$0	$7,356,218	$5,155,666
Pat Buchanan	$14,834,832	$18,280	$0	$10,067,785	$11,496
Lamar Alexander	$12,635,365	$286,766	$9,583	$4,573,442	$114,084
Sen. Richard Lugar	$4,803,952	$129,015	$0	$2,657,242	$193,283
Gov. Pete Wilson	$5,286,889	$242,349	$0	$1,724,254	$110,723
Morry Taylor	$37,854	$0	$6,475,096	$0	$3,900
Alan Keyes	$3,444,981	$1,000	$7,500	$971,491	$5,274
Sen. Arlen Specter	$2,280,106	$158,791	$0	$1,010,455	$36,148
Rep. Bob Dornan	$298,206	$1,000	$44,000	$0	$4,374

paign could afford far fewer ads on the expensive Boston television stations, which reached a substantial number of New Hampshire voters in the heavily populated southern part of the state. "We were running on fumes," Murphy said later. "I think if we had another million dollars in New Hampshire, we would have won the nomination."[28]

FINANCING THE GENERAL ELECTION: A "BLACK HOLE" FOR DOLE

The post-Watergate rules were supposed to create a level playing field between major party candidates, who would compete on the basis of their ideas, not their money. It didn't work out that way in 1996. For all practical purposes the general election contest between President Clinton and Bob Dole began March 19, 1996, as Dole swept the Midwestern primaries and clinched the Republican nomination. But for nearly five months Dole would be at a severe financial disadvantage—hobbled by the very campaign finance rules that were intended to create an equal contest.

The rules seemed fair at first glance. The same $37.09 million spending limit applied to all candidates for nomination (except self-financed candidates like Forbes). And identical spending limits would apply in the general election to the two parties' nominees: each would have just under $74 million to spend under the limits ($61.82 million in public funds to be spent by the candidates' campaign committees directly and $11.99 million in private funds to be spent by their political parties in coordination with the candidates.) But while the rules were equal for both men, Dole and Clinton faced far different circumstances.

Those who drafted the rules never imagined that the nomination process would ever begin so early, go on so long, or be decided so many months before the nominating conventions. But because Dole had been forced to spend heavily to defeat a field of challengers that included Forbes and his unlimited millions, he was coming dangerously close to exceeding the $37.09 million spending limit months before receiving the nomination officially. Dole had spent nearly $28 million by the end of January.[29] Clinton on the other hand had faced no opposition. While Dole had spent his money attacking Forbes, Alexander, and Buchanan, Clinton could spend his "primary" money inoculating himself against Dole's future attacks, and even attacking Dole.

Republican political consultant Ron Kaufman described the problem for Dole in an interview at the end of February:

> Assuming that Dole gets the nomination in March, April, May, there then comes what I call a 'black hole' period of time. From then to the convention

he'll be out of money. President Clinton is sitting back on $20-$25 million, and our biggest problem will be that Bill Clinton will be able to define Bob Dole and the Republican Party in that time at his own will.[30]

Kaufman's words proved to be prophetic. The "black hole" would prove to be nearly $20 million deep.

By the end of April, despite a series of staff reductions and other economic maneuvers, the Dole campaign's reports to the FEC showed it had spent all but $177,000 of the allowed limit and began a series of bookkeeping gymnastics in an attempt to avoid going over. The Dole primary campaign ran a sort of "campaign yard sale," selling $1.2 million worth of items to the Dole general election campaign. Physical items such as TV sets, two-way radios, computers, telephones, video recorders, and a system for feeding tape-recorded "actualities" to local radio stations would be sold for 60 percent of their original purchase price. Reels of video shot for Dole primary ads, which might be recycled in Dole general election ads, would go for 50 cents on the dollar. Treating those sales as a reduction of previous spending, it would leave Dole $1.4 million under the limit. With that Dole would have to finance his campaign travel and a skeleton staff operation until the nomination became official. Meanwhile, Clinton had roughly $20 million left to spend.[31]

Clinton forces pressed the advantage relentlessly. On June 12 the Democratic National Committee filed a complaint with the FEC claiming the Dole campaign had actually exceeded its pre-nomination spending limit by $343,751 as of the end of May. The Dole campaign called the complaint "groundless." The matter remained unresolved as of election day. But it was clear enough that Dole could afford no advertising at all between March and his nomination in late August. (See Table 3, page 234.)

THE BIGGEST LOOPHOLE: SOFT MONEY AND "ISSUE ADS"

Clinton compounded his advantage over Dole through aggressive use of a new gimmick: campaign commercials posing as "issue ads," financed by tens of millions of dollars raised from sources that were supposed to be illegal in presidential campaigns. It was the biggest loophole of all, and in the general election of 1996 it all but obliterated the effect of the post-Watergate limits.

In theory, the ads merely discussed the issues of the day, and were not technically contributions to a federal campaign. But the distinction was almost entirely academic. Democratic Party "issue" ads attacked Bob Dole relentlessly by name while praising President Clinton as the protector of "America's values." Republican Party "issue" ads accused Clinton of promoting a big tax increase while waffling on welfare reform and a balanced federal budget.

As a practical matter, the "issue" ads were indistinguishable from commercials the Dole and Clinton campaigns produced for themselves. In fact, they were produced by the same media consultants. Democratic consultant Bob Squier's firm produced ads for the Clinton campaign and the pro-Clinton "issue" ads run by the DNC. And the RNC's pro-Dole ads were produced by consultants Don Sipple and Mike Murphy, the same men who were producing the Dole campaign's ads in the months before and immediately after the Republican convention. Some Republican Party "issue" ads even used the very same video clips Sipple and Murphy had used earlier in Dole campaign commercials. (See Table 4.)

After his March 19 victories, Dole's own TV ads went off the air. For weeks after that a massive advertising campaign for President Clinton dominated the air in key states, financed by the DNC. Between March 19 and April 29, pro-Clinton ads appeared 7,765 times in 40 cities in 24 states. The RNC during the same six-week period managed to run ads only 2,000 times in 18 cities in 15 states.[32] And many of the GOP ads were aimed mainly at boosting Republican members of Congress, not Dole.

Table 4　**When Is a Campaign Ad NOT a Campaign Ad? When It's an "Issue Ad."**

Democratic National Committee "Finish" Released May 6, 1996	Republican National Committee "More" Released June 20, 1996
Announcer:	Announcer:
Head Start. Student Loans. Toxic Cleanup. Extra Police. Anti-drug programs.	Did you know there are over five million illegal immigrants in the U.S.?
Dole–Gingrich wanted them cut. Now they're safe.	And that you spend five and a half billion dollars a year to support them with welfare, food stamps and other services?
Protected in the '96 budget, because the President stood firm.	
Dole–Gingrich? Deadlock. Gridlock. Shutdowns.	Under President Clinton, spending on illegals has gone up. While wages for the typical worker have gone down.
The President's plan? Finish the job. Balance the budget. Reform Welfare. Cut taxes. Protect Medicare.	And when efforts were made to stop giving benefits to illegal immigrants, Bill Clinton opposed them.
President Clinton says, get it done.	Tell President Clinton to stop giving benefits to illegals, and end wasteful Washington spending.
Meet our challenges. Protect our values.	

Neither of these "issue ads" specifically urged a vote for or against either candidate, so the parties claimed the right to spend as much as they liked on them and also financed them largely with "soft money".

Then the RNC ads disappeared entirely, while the Democratic ads kept hammering away with different variations of the same message: Dole and Newt Gingrich (always pictured together in grainy, sinister black-and-white) opposed everything good, from Medicare to cleanup of toxic waste. A typical line: "A hundred thousand new police, because President Clinton delivered. Dole and Gingrich voted no, want to repeal it."[33]

The unequal contest went on for weeks. RNC officials claimed that they could not afford to respond. But party leaders also believed that the early advertising would have little lasting effect, and that money might be spent more effectively closer to election day. RNC Communications Director Ed Gillespie said on May 1, "I had one pollster tell me the other day that if the election were held today—most people would be surprised. It's a little early in the season to worry about who's who in polling data."[34]

When Dole announced his resignation from the Senate, the RNC claimed it would begin a $20 million advertising campaign, but no such campaign materialized. Instead, the RNC released a series of TV ads to the news media while spending minimal amounts buying a token number of commercial runs, only in Washington D.C. and on CNN, where reporters would be most likely to see them. Most news organizations fell for the ruse, repeatedly running snippets of the anti-Clinton ads in news and public affairs programs. An ad showing Clinton waffling on a timetable for balancing the budget ran only 54 times. Another RNC ad falsely accusing Clinton of favoring welfare benefits for illegal aliens aired only five times. The most notorious example was an RNC ad called "Stripes" that said Clinton was "trying to avoid a sexual harassment lawsuit claiming he's on active military duty." But that ad was nothing more than a video press release—it never ran at all. Except, of course, for free on numerous news and political talk-programs.[35]

The real effort did not begin until May 31, when the RNC began running ads in more than a dozen states. But by that time Dole had been hammered by literally tens of thousands of Democratic Party ads. These Democratic "issue" ads praised Clinton as a welfare-reforming, budget-balancing, crime-fighting, savior of women, children and the elderly, while painting Dole as a Gingrich clone keen to slash Medicare, aid to education, pollution cleanup, and even police hiring. By this time the DNC had spent an estimated $15 million on such ads without any effective response from Republican side. "The President's run 10,000 commercials and it's not even June yet," complained Republican media consultant Alex Casetellanos. "And it's clearly helped him."[36]

In all, the DNC spent $42.41 million on issue ads before Clinton was nominated, some as early as October 1995.[37] The DNC's spending had attracted little notice in the news, because the ads were running only in states Clinton strategists believed were "in play," and not at all in Washington, D.C.

where most national political reporters lived. "I think that it's been missed by many people," said Democratic political consultant Carter Eskew. "It's sort of been under the radar."[38]

At this point, both parties were massively exploiting a legal gray area, eviscerating the post-Watergate limits. For one thing, none of the "issue" ads were being counted against any spending limits. And they were also being financed largely with soft money from corporations and other sources that were supposed to be legally contraband for use in presidential campaigns. How could they do it? Dole explained, in a remarkably candid exchange while speaking via TV hookup to a gathering of ABC's television affiliates:

> *Dole:* We can, through the Republican National Committee, do what we call the Victory '96 Program, run television ads and other advertising, it's called generic. It's not Bob Dole for president . . .

> *Interviewer:* You said generic spending and then it says Bob Dole for president. Is that considered generic spending?

> *Dole:* It doesn't say Bob Dole for president. It has my—it talks about the Bob Dole story. It also talks about issues. It never mentions the word that I'm—it never says that I'm running for president. I hope that it's fairly obvious since I'm the only one in the picture.

> (LAUGHTER)

> *Ted Koppel* (moderating): I love those technicalities.[39]

As Dole spoke, however, the U.S. Supreme Court was considering a case in which the FEC had ruled that just such an "issue ad" was in fact a campaign commercial. A federal appeals court had upheld the FEC's interpretation, but the Colorado Republican Party appealed and asked the Supreme Court to declare all spending limits on parties an unconstitutional restriction of free speech. The Court heard arguments on the case in April, and the ruling did not come down until 20 days after Dole's remarks to the ABC executives. But only two justices voted to uphold the Court of Appeals decision finding such ads illegal. Four others voted to overturn all limits on party spending. In a compromise decision, the three justices in the middle wrote a murky ruling allowing parties to spend unlimited amounts of money on ads if they were somehow "independent" of the candidates.[40] So the spending on both sides continued in a legal fog.

There were complaints all around that laws were being broken. On July 2 the Dole campaign filed a complaint accusing the DNC of making what it estimated to be $25 million in illegal expenditures for its pro-Clinton "issue ads." How could those ads be illegal and the RNC's pro-Dole ads legal? The

Dole campaign's "Exhibit A" was a book by reporter Bob Woodward, *The Choice,* which described President Clinton as "personally controlling tens of millions of dollars worth of DNC advertising" from within the White House, even dictating to his consultants Bob Squier and Dick Morris when pictures of Dole and Gingrich could appear in the ads.[41]

But how were the DNC's ads any different from the RNC's ads? If Clinton had conversations with Squier and Morris about the DNC's ads, Dole seems to have done the same with his consultants Sipple and Murphy, who were also producing the RNC ads. One sunny afternoon, in the midst of the RNC's pro-Dole media campaign, the candidate himself sat in a lawn chair on the rooftop of his campaign headquarters building talking to Sipple and Murphy. The scene was videotaped by a CNN camera from the network's Washington bureau next door.[42]

Meanwhile Dole's spending-limit squeeze had become so severe that by the time he reached the San Diego convention in August, he was reduced to setting up a "Kemp for Vice President" committee, which paid for $328,000 in convention expenses, including "Dole-Kemp" signs that delegates carried onto the floor and waved in front of television cameras. As a legal matter Kemp could set up a separate committee with a separate spending limit to "campaign" for the vice presidential nomination for which Dole had hand-picked him, and for which he was unopposed.[43] (See Table 5.)

FINANCING THE CONVENTIONS

The post-Watergate limits broke down in spectacular fashion at both the Democratic and Republican national conventions. Both consumed record

Table 5   **The Tilt: Bill Clinton's Financial Advantage**

	Clinton	Dole
"Primary" May-August	$20.0	$1.4
Kemp Vice-Presidential		$0.3
Conventions (Federal)	$12.4	$12.4
Conventions (Private)	$20.7	$23.0
Federal Matching Funds	$61.8	$61.8
Party "Coordinated"	$12.0	$12.0
Party "Issue Ads"	$42.4	$18.0
TOTAL	$169.3	$128.9

President Clinton was able to outspend Bob Dole by more than $40 million, because spending limits hampered Dole in the months before his nomination was official, and because the Democratic Party spent more aggressively on "issue ads" that party lawyers claimed did not count against any spending limits.

amounts of money, even though the conventions had long since lost their original function: choosing a candidate. The August conventions were simply another episode in a general election campaign that had been going on since March. And they were financed largely by corporations, despite a law that was supposed to prevent such special-interest funding. Both parties received $12.36 million in public funds to finance their conventions. But they also took in millions in business contributions through local "host committees." (See Table 6.)

To allow for local boosterism, FEC rules allowed companies with a local business connection to give to local host committees. But not a single Fortune 500 company is headquartered in San Diego. So Republicans took the position that almost any company selling its products in San Diego was "local" enough—contributions rolled in from Microsoft, Philip Morris, Time Warner, and Lockheed Martin. AT&T gave nearly $2.7 million.

One contribution solicited directly by the RNC was $1.3 million from Amway Corp., the same Michigan-based company that had given $2.5 million two years earlier. The Amway money was intended to finance the Republican Party's live television "coverage" of its own convention, "anchored" at times by RNC Chairman Haley Barbour and featuring floor reporters including Republican Rep. J. C. Watts of Oklahoma. The party bought 13-½ hours of time on two cable channels—the Family Channel and USA Network—and claimed to reach more than 500,000 viewers on each of the convention's four nights.[44] It amounted to an epic infomerical for Bob Dole and the Republicans, made possible by corporate money.

The Democratic convention in Chicago left news coverage to others, but solicited even more business money than the Republicans. According to

Table 6 **A Tale of Two Cities: Top Corporate Donors to the Democratic and Republican Conventions**

San Diego Host Committee		Chicago's Committee for '96	
AT&T	$2,653,226	Ameritech	$2,425,625
Amway Corp.	$1,320,000	Motorola	$1,108,830
Pacific Bell	$512,060	AT&T	$558.741
Philip Morris Co., Inc.	$502,500	United Airlines	$432,917
Microsoft	$257,319	Kemper Securities Inc.	$339,775
Del Mar Country Club	$250,000	Microsoft	$300,000
Chevron	$250,000	Sara Lee Corp.	$281,204
San Diego Padres	$250,000	Mayer, Brown & Platt	$266,449
San Diego Port District	$250,000	RR Donnelley & Sons	$224,267
Time Warner Inc.	$250,000	Chicago Mercantile Exchange	$178,670
United Airlines	$250,000	Philip Morris Co., Inc	$175,000

reports filed with the FEC long after the conventions were over, the San Diego Host Committee had raised $11.2 million from private donors, while Chicago's Committee for '96 had raised nearly $21 million.[45] Many corporations gave to both conventions, including AT&T, Microsoft Corp., and Philip Morris.

FINANCING THE PARTIES—THE ARMS RACE

On January 24, 1996 the Republican National Committee held the most successful fundraising event in its history—more than $16 million raised in a single evening. "It's the biggest fundraiser anywhere, any time," the RNC's Finance Chairman Howard Leach proudly announced. No hotel in Washington was large enough to accommodate the throng of donors. The party instead held the event in Washington's old National Guard Armory, a venue better known for hosting the Ringling Brothers Circus than for black-tie dinners. One reason: corporate lobbyists and wealthy businessmen eager to help the Republicans hang onto control of Congress. "The revolution has only begun," Senator Trent Lott promised the group. An investment banker who sold $2 million worth of tickets for the event explained that donors gave because they thought they would do better financially under Republicans. "These people buy into the agenda because it's going to create the kind of atmosphere in the country that's going to allow them to prosper."[46]

Then, a few months later on May 8, the DNC held the most successful fundraiser in *its* history, bringing in $12 million in one night at what they called the "National Presidential Gala." The DNC's communications director David Eichenbaum said that was triple the party's previous one-night record. With Bill Clinton leading Bob Dole by 20 points in public opinion polls, the President was becoming a magnet for money. "People want to be with a winner and they see where this election is going," Eichenbaum said.[47] Platoons of lobbyists were pressed into service as money-collectors. Dozens of corporations, from ARCO to Zeneca, Inc., were listed in the dinner program as contributors, along with many lobbyists, labor unions and wealthy individuals.[48] It was a situation ripe for scandal. Indeed, the scramble for contributions had already caused considerable embarrassment to the President.

In 1995 a one-page memo, uncovered by *Chicago Sun-Times* Washington bureau chief Lynn Sweet, stated boldly that for $100,000 a donor could become a "managing trustee" of the Democratic Party and be entitled to two annual events with the President, two more with the Vice President, "honored guest" status at the 1996 convention, and annual retreats with party leaders. The *Sun-Times* called it "The President's Price List."[49] The memo also offered annual economic trade missions: "Managing Trustees are invited to participate in foreign trade missions, which afford opportunities to join Party leaders in meetings with business leaders abroad."

That was especially troubling, since it seemed to offer official government favors in return for political contributions. The administration's trade missions were being led by Ron Brown himself, whom Clinton had promoted from party chairman to Secretary of Commerce. And the missions were being organized in part by Melissa Moss, a Commerce Department official who previously had been finance director of the DNC under Brown. The DNC quickly backed down when its memo to potential donors was made public, saying its trade mission offer had been "inaccurate and erroneous."

A red-faced Clinton ordered a review of the DNC's fundraising practices. During the 1992 campaign Clinton had denounced such access-selling in his campaign book *Putting People First,* complaining that American politics "is being held hostage to big money interests . . . while political action committees, industry lobbies and cliques of $100,000 donors buy access to Congress and the White House." Now his own party was issuing a formal price list for access to him.[50] Clinton said he had ordered an end to the party's tactics. "I think that the President and any other person in public office ought to meet with his or her supporters, including financial supporters," he said. "But it is wrong to raise money on the promise of guaranteed specific kinds of access. That is wrong and we stopped that." But in fact, as events would prove, little really changed in the DNC's fundraising shop.

RNC chairman Haley Barbour called the Democrats' price list "crass," but as *Time* magazine reporter Jeffrey Birnbaum later revealed, Barbour himself personally offered a similar list. In a letter signed simply "Haley," he promised that those who raised $250,000 for the RNC's January fundraiser would get lunch with Bob Dole and House Speaker Newt Gingrich. For $45,000 a donor could have breakfast with Gingrich. "That's just sort of the way it's done," said RNC spokeswoman Mary Crawford.[51]

The access-selling took on the aspects of an arms race, each side stockpiling more millions in fear that the other side would gain an advantage. The Republican and Democratic national committees were taking in more than double what they had raised in the 1992 presidential election. Far more than double, in fact (see Figure 1). Furthermore, the fastest increases were in unregulated soft money, the very kind of huge contributions, often from corporations, that had caused Congress to revise the campaign finance laws after the Watergate scandal 24 years earlier.

Not all the money went for advertising, of course. Barbour said the RNC spent $61 million during 1996 alone on fundraising expenses, chiefly the cost of running expensive direct-mail programs aimed at smaller donors. Also during 1996, the party spent $18.7 million on its "Victory '96" program, sending 84.8 million pieces of targeted mail and making 14.5 million telephone calls

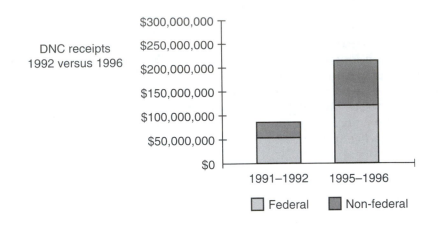

	1991–1992	1995–1996		1991–1992	1995–1996
Federal	$72,260,446	$169,977,294	Federal	$54,475,878	$121,651,204
Non-federal	$31,843,421	$94,499,921	Non-federal	$26,257,183	$89,026,804
Total RNC	$104,103,867	$264,477,215	Total DNC	$80,733,061	$210,678,008

Republican National Committee and Democratic National Committee, total receipts, 1/1/91–10/16/92, vs. 1/1/95–10/16/95. Figures are for the last report filed prior to each election.

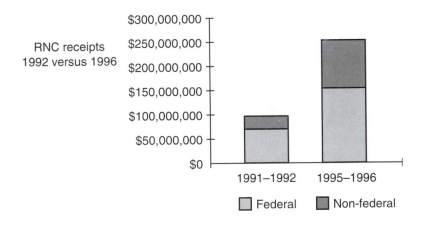

Figure 1   Double Their Money—The Race for Party Funds

Table 7   **Top Soft-Money Donors: All National Party Committees (1/1/95–10/16/96—incomplete tabulation)**

Republican Party Committees		Democratic Party Committees	
Philip Morris	$2,185,118	Jos. E. Seagram & Sons	$1,155,000
RJR Nabisco	$995,175	Walt Disney Co.	$866,800
Atlantic Richfield	$702,921	Communications Workers of	
Jos. E. Seagram & Sons	$646,600	American	$770,750
American Financial Corp	$562,000	Food & Commercial Workers Union	$573,050
AT&T	$549,590	MCI Telecommunications Corp.	$536,136
Brown & Williamson		Dream Works SKG	$525,000
Tobacco	$515,000	Integrated Health Services Inc.	$524,000
US Tobacco	$502,403	Assn of Trial Lawyers of America	$515,000
Mariam Cannon Hayes	$500,000	Goldman, Sachs & Co.	$510,000
Enron Corp.	$469,100	Arnold Hiatt	$500,000
Chevron Corp.	$461,056	Loral Corp.	$495,500
Eli Lilly & Co.	$441,985	Revlon Group, Inc.	$491,250
General Motors	$410,125	Philip Morris	$480,250
Coca-Cola Co.	$408,680	AFSME (union)	$471,212
News Corp.	$404,700	Laborers Union	$456,400
Amway Corp.	$396,000	Lazard Freres & Co.	$420,000
Bristol-Meyers Squibb	$392,900	Connell Co.	$407,000
Tobacco Institute	$384,795	Atlantic Richfield	$388,500
Pfizer Inc.	$379,395	AT&T	$382,184
Blue Cross/Blue Shield	$377,053	Ziff Communications	$380,000

Source: Center for Responsive Politics. Includes contributions from affiliates or subsidiaries.

to Republican-voting households by election day in an attempt to raise GOP turnout.[52] These were the kinds of efforts aimed at helping the entire party ticket, from "Dole to dog-catcher."

But much of the money was poured into "issue ads." The RNC spent about $30.5 million on such ads, $18 million of it for Dole and the remainder in selected Senate and House races.[53] And the ads were being paid for largely with soft money. As the RNC interpreted the rules, up to 35 percent of each ad could be paid for with soft money if the RNC itself purchased the station time. But if *state* party organizations paid, between 50 percent and 78 percent could be paid for with soft money, depending on the state.[54] So typically the RNC would ship the money to state parties and allow them to buy the time, so as to get the maximum campaign use out of the soft money. The DNC followed the same practice.

To many outsiders, what the parties were doing was an open scandal. Common Cause, the group that had lobbied for enactment of the original post-

Watergate campaign finance rules, denounced what the parties were doing as blatantly illegal. "These are not technical violations of the law," said the group's president Ann McBride. "These are not pushing the envelope to take advantage of loopholes in the law. What is at issue here are massive illegal schemes to violate the presidential primary spending limits and to violate the prohibitions on corporate and union contributions and the restrictions on large individual contributions." Common Cause filed an official request for Attorney General Janet Reno to begin steps needed to appoint an independent counsel to conduct a criminal investigation.[55] But Reno denied the request shortly after the election.

Another chain of events, however, guaranteed that the financing of the 1996 campaign would be under investigation long after the election was over. It was the Indonesian Affair, a scandal that hit Democrats at the climax of the long campaign. The first stirrings came when the *Los Angeles Times* reported that one of the Democratic Party's largest soft money donations was illegal. The $250,000 contribution had been given by a Los Angeles company named Cheong Am America, Inc., which turned out to be little more than a U.S. bank account for a South Korean corporation. Federal law makes it illegal for non-U.S. corporations to give unless the money comes from a U.S. subsidiary and from the subsidiary's own revenues. The DNC returned the money.

The Cheong Am incident attracted little attention at first: even the *Los Angeles Times* played the story on page 16. Such episodes had become more or less routine in national campaigns. Earlier, one of the financial vice-chairmen of the Dole campaign, Massachusetts businessman Simon Fireman, had been fined a record $6 million for making $120,000 in illegal corporate donations to the Dole primary campaign and others by getting employees to make donations and then reimbursing them from company funds.[56] Prosecutors said there was no evidence Dole knew the donations were illegal, and Dole simply returned the money, with little political fallout.

But the Democratic fundraising story soon developed into a sensation. Another news organization discovered that an Indonesian couple who had contributed $425,000 to the DNC were living in Jakarta, not at the address in the Washington D.C. suburbs shown on the DNC's campaign-finance reports. (The couple, Arief and Soroya Wiriadninata, had actually contributed another $25,000, which showed up later, making their total $450,000.) The *Wall Street Journal* ran a front-page story implicating DNC fundraiser John Huang and detailing his connections to the Lippo Group, an Indonesian conglomerate. Huang had not only raised the illegal $250,000 that the DNC had to return, but had also solicited the $450,000 from the Indonesian couple, heirs to a deceased founder of the Lippo conglomerate. Huang's involvement put the affair at the President's own door; Clinton had publicly called Huang "my long-time friend" and had also met personally with Huang in the White House, as well as with James Riady, son of Lippo's founder and chairman, Mochtar Riady.

Republicans seized the issue. Senator John McCain, a Dole campaign adviser, called for an independent counsel to conduct a criminal investigation. Speaker Gingrich—never prone to understatement—claimed grandly that the Indonesian affair would make Watergate "tiny by comparison." Dole, on the campaign trail, accused the DNC of running a "money laundry." Ross Perot predicted Clinton would face investigations and worse during a second term. "Would you allow a person with pending criminal charges to baby-sit your children? It's a joke," Perot said. "We are headed for a second Watergate, a constitutional crisis."[57]

Soon the DNC was returning more contributions, some illegal and some merely suspect. By election day the total reached more than $700,000, including $325,000 that Huang had solicited from Yogesh Gandhi, a California resident who later turned out to have sworn in a lawsuit that he had little money of his own. Huang disappeared for a time, and stories were appearing almost daily as the election approached. The DNC inflamed matters by attempting to avoid filing a pre-election disclosure report for the first time in its history, giving the impression it had even more embarrassing revelations to hide. The RNC announced it would file a lawsuit to compel disclosure, but embarrassed Democrats already had announced they would file the report after all. It contained little of note, but by that time the damage had been done.

Between September 20 and election day the DNC returned contributions totaling $762,000, of which $590,000 had been solicited by the President's "long-time friend" John Huang. And even afterward the DNC was still turning up problems, returning more large contributions including the $450,000 given by the couple in Jakarta. They failed to file U.S. income tax returns, the DNC said. In its eagerness to increase its intake of money, and despite the review of fundraising practices that the White House said it had ordered more than a year earlier after the presidential "price list" leaked out, DNC officials conceded that they had not bothered to ask even their largest donors about the source of their gifts. The party also had ceased its practice of making routine checks of computerized news libraries for potentially disqualifying information about would-be donors. (See Table 8.)

Democrats passed the matter off as a series of honest mistakes, but the scandal may have caused serious political damage. President Clinton's margin of victory over Dole was narrower than most polls had been showing, and he was elected with less than 50 percent of the total vote, hardly the mandate for which he had hoped. Republicans held onto control of the House, which had been rated a tossup by several independent analysts before the Indonesian

Table 8   **The Smoking Funds—Contributions Returned by the DNC**[58]

Donor	Amount	Date Refunded	Reason
Cheong Am America*	$250,000	9/20/96	Foreign Corporation
John H.K. Lee*	$10.000	10/16/96	Foreign National
Man Ya Shih*	$5,000	10/21/96	Fronting for real donor
Jorge Cabrera	$20.000	10/16/96	Drug dealer
Gulf Canada Resources Ltd.	$10,000	10/28/96	Foreign Corporation
Onex Corp.	$2,000	10/28/96	Foreign Corporation
Richard Tienken	$25,000	10/29/96	Alleged Mafia ties
Interactive Wireless	$50,000	10/31/96	Alleged Mafia ties
Carolina PCS	$15,000	10/29/96	Defaulted on government loan
Yogesh Gandhi*	$325,000	11/7/96	Unable to substantiate source of funds
Psaltis Corp.	$50,000	11/5/96	Foreign Corporation
Praitun Kanchanalak	$253,500	11/20/96	Given in name of another
Jao Yi Lu	$1,000	11/20/96	Cannot locate address
Arief & Soroya Wiriadinata*	$450,000	11/22/96	Unpaid U.S. Taxes

*solicited by John Huang

affair began to unfold. DNC Chairman Don Fowler, asked by a reporter whether the scandal had cost Democrats the House, said, "It didn't help."[59]

NOW HERE'S THE DEAL—FINANCING PEROT

The third man in the presidential race, Ross Perot, was an insignificant factor politically but may have scored an important victory in terms of political finance. In 1994 he had spent $63.5 million of his own money to finance his independent candidacy, making himself a national (if controversial) political force overnight. But in 1996, for a mere $10 million or so in additional personal funds, Perot bought a new party and secured for it a claim on the U.S. Treasury for future subsidies that could total in the tens of millions. He did it by exploiting the intricacies of the campaign finance laws, again. Perot did not win a single electoral vote in 1992, but he did win a valuable chit that he cashed in at the U.S. Treasury four years later—the right to public financing.

   Under the law the Democratic and Republican Party nominees were effectively guaranteed full public financing for their general election campaigns. The nominee of any party whose 1992 candidate had received at least 25 percent of the vote would get the full amount—$61.82 million—in 1996. Nominees of other parties also could qualify—in theory. But only if their candidate had received more than 5 percent of the vote in 1992. Perot himself could qualify for $29.06 million in public funding in 1996, a pro-rata amount based on getting 19 percent of the vote in 1992. Perot, however, had run before essentially as an independent, not as the nominee of any single national party.

To get that money Perot would have to agree to spending limits, including a limit of $50,000 on the use of his personal funds to advance his candidacy. But there was no limit on what could be spent to qualify a new party for access to state ballots. On March 1, 1996 Perot established the "Perot Reform Committee," and later reported contributing nearly $8.7 million to the committee for such things as paid petition drives needed to get the new Reform Party on the ballot. It is also estimated that Perot spent roughly $2 million on such activities before triggering any federal disclosure requirement, bringing the total to between $10 million and $11 million.

As the Reform Party took shape, the FEC made it clear that the only way its nominee could get public funding in the 1996 general election was for that nominee to be Perot himself. Perot forces asked the commission for an advisory opinion saying that any nominee of the new party would qualify for funding based on Perot's showing, but the commission pointedly refused, unanimously, to give such an opinion unless Perot made a better case. Chairman Lee Ann Elliott put the matter bluntly: "I cannot conceive of any information they could furnish us that would let another candidate under the Reform Party as it existed anywhere get federal funds under our current system."[60]

In the end, of course, Perot was the nominee and did get $29 million in public funds for "Perot '96," his campaign committee. He could have spent the full $62.82 million, the same spending limit that applied to the fully-funded Dole and Clinton campaigns. But Perot would have had to make up the difference by raising private contributions, which of course were limited to $1,000 per donor. He raised only $624,818 in private contributions.[61]

Since Perot's vote easily exceeded the 5 percent threshold for future public funding, the Reform Party qualified for a range of future benefits. Any future candidates for the party's nomination can qualify for federal matching funds to finance their pre-nomination efforts. These would be paid on the same basis as those campaigning for the Republican or Democratic Party nominations, matching every privately donated dollar up to $250 per donor. The party itself can claim $2.5-$3 million to finance its convention, if it has one, in the year 2000. It would only be a fraction of what the major parties will get, but perhaps enough to rent a hall, buy balloons and gain some media attention. And most important, *anyone* nominated by the Reform Party for president—even if that person is not Ross Perot—can claim an estimated $15 million to $16 million in public funds to finance a general election campaign in the year 2000.

Whether the Reform Party will become "institutionalized" in future elections, as Perot aides claim, remains to be seen. But Perot's 1996 candidacy secured a financial lifeline for the fledgling party independent of Perot's personal wealth.

FINANCING CONGRESS—"INTERESTS COULD BE AFFECTED"

Within days of Newt Gingrich taking the gavel to become Speaker of the House, a remarkable memorandum was sent to business lobbyists in Washington. Sent by Charles S. Mack, president of the Business-Industry Political Action Committee; it said:

> In meetings with the new leadership, I am being told that they are scrutinizing to whom companies and business associations are currently giving—that they take a very dim view indeed of access contributions to lawmakers who have tended to vote against business . . .

> What I am told is this:

> Legislative interests of those who help the congressional enemies of business, and don't support our friends, could be affected negatively. Some committee chairmen are reportedly denying access to lobbyists who support the other side . . . Lobbyists who are hedging their bets with an eye to reversal of last November's outcome in 1996, will find the next two years rather lean ones, I'm informed . . . If ever there was a time for the business community to help its friends, it is now.[62]

When the memo leaked out, Mack refused to identify *which* Republican leaders had told him all this. "I really can't say, specifically. But they are important, influential people in Congress and I respect their point of view," he said.[63]

Nevertheless, what followed was a marked shift in giving patterns. When Democrats controlled Congress, political action committees run by corporations and trade associations gave roughly half their money to Democrats. Republicans may have been more sympathetic to business, but Democrats had the power to award tax breaks or impose painful regulations, and pragmatic business lobbyists gave accordingly. That pragmatism had come to infuriate many Republicans. Now that Republicans had the power, they intended to dry up the business money that had been flowing to the enemy and direct it instead into their own re-election efforts.

Within days of taking control the new masters of the House invited lobbyists to pay tribute to them at a fundraising event they called the "New Majority Dinner." They might as well have called it the "new contributor" dinner. Veteran Republican lobbyists said they were seeing a lot of PAC managers at the event who, in the past, had gone only to Democratic events. Representative Bill Paxon, head of the National Republican Congressional Committee, proudly announced: "This is the most successful event in the 129-year history of the NRCC. Two million dollars and counting." Speaker Gingrich was touched. "Your response makes me teary-eyed," he told the dinner guests, who had paid $1,000 each to attend (more if paying with corporate money).[64]

The changed giving habits of the lobbyists soon began to show up in totals reported to the FEC. Former NRCC chairman Guy Vander Jagt, who had retired from Congress and was working in Washington as a lobbyist, explained: "They're changing now for the same reason that they gave to Democrats before," he said.[65] In the House, Republican incumbents more than doubled their overall intake of PAC money during the year. Their total rose to $26 million in 1995, up from just over $11 million two years earlier. At the same time the total realized by Democratic House members fell to $18.5 million from $25.5 million in 1993. (See Figure 2.)

But despite those dramatic figures, Republicans had been only partially successful. Much of the change resulted from the fact that there were simply many more Republican House members, and fewer Democrats, to whom PACs could contribute. For the most part, PACs continued to give almost as much as ever to the individual Democrats who had survived the 1994 election, if only because they had defended the PAC system in the past when Republicans attacked it, and because the next election could well return those Democrats to their old committee and subcommittee chairmanships once again. The *average* House Democrat took in almost exactly the same amount of PAC money in 1995 than in the previous off-year, 1993. Where Republicans

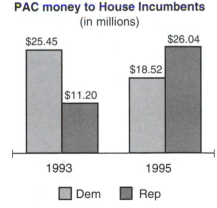

PAC money to House Incumbents
(in millions)

$25.45 $26.04

$18.52

$11.20

1993   1995

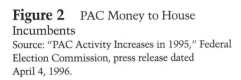

Dem   Rep

Figure 2   PAC Money to House Incumbents
Source: "PAC Activity Increases in 1995," Federal Election Commission, press release dated April 4, 1996.

succeeded was in boosting the amounts PACs gave to them. The *average* House Republican took in 67 percent *more* PAC money in 1995 than in 1993. For the whole year, House Republicans averaged $117,850, Democrats $107,035.[66]

The change was profound. In past elections PACs had given far more to Democratic congressional candidates overall—counting House and Senate, incumbents, challengers and candidates running in open seats. But in the 1995–1996 election cycle PACs were giving more to Republicans. Figures released by the FEC on September 27, 1996 documented the historic shift. After tabulating all the contributions reported by all 4,430 registered political action committees between Jan. 1, 1995 and June 30, 1996, the FEC reported that the PACs had given just under $72 million to Republican candidates and less than $55 million to Democratic candidates.

At another level, very little had changed. PACs were still giving overwhelmingly to incumbents. As of 20 days before the 1996 election, all 50 House candidates who reported receiving the most money from PACs were incumbents. Not a single challenger or open-seat candidate of either party was on the list.[67] And this time, most incumbents in both the House and Senate were Republicans. The pro-incumbent bias was most pronounced among business PACs, which gave far more than labor PACs in total. In the House, for example, corporate PACs gave nearly 93 percent of their money to incumbents in the first 18 months of the 1996 election cycle.[68] The pro-incumbent bias was less evident in Senate races, but still the dominant tendency. Overall, PACs gave 79.1 percent of their Senate and House contributions to incumbents in the first 18 months of the '96 campaign.[69] (See Table 9.)

LABOR'S COUNTERREVOLUTION: BATTLING "NEWTIE"

As business PACs shifted their giving to Republicans, there was a change underway within organized labor as well. Under the new and more militant leadership of President John Sweeney, the AFL-CIO undertook an unprecedented program of political action. If Newt Gingrich's leadership of the House marked a Republican "revolution," as Republicans liked to claim, then labor was plotting the counterrevolution.

Labor was limited in what it could do through its political action committees, however. Union PACs tended to be large, but few in number and were vastly outspent overall by business PACs. In 1994, labor PACs had given $40.6 million to House and Senate candidates, and 96 percent of it had gone to Democrats. This time the AFL-CIO would add to its PAC total another $35 million, taken directly from union treasury funds. And the money would be

Table 9   **PACs Favor Incumbents**[70]
(Senate & House Candidates—1/1/95–6/30/96)

PAC Type	Contributions	Percent to Incumbents
Corporations	$47,847,867	86.7%
Trade & Professional Associations	$34,244,631	82.1%
Labor Unions	$25,817,626	62.9%
Ideological	$11,649,999	73.4%
Other	$4,656,511	83.5%

targeted for a relative handful of races where Republican incumbents were thought to be most vulnerable to defeat. It amounted to real money. By itself, labor would be spending more in some districts than the average winning candidate spent altogether.

The $35 million plan was approved at an AFL-CIO convention March 25. The legal justification for spending union treasury money for such political activities was dicey—it was illegal to use union dues money to make a direct contribution to a federal candidate, or run a TV ad explicitly advocating a candidate's election or defeat. The AFL-CIO would claim to be spending to educate the public about "issues affecting working people." But the real political agenda was apparent at the convention. President John Sweeney attacked Speaker Gingrich and House Republicans as "Newtie and the blowhards," to the applause of delegates. Executive Vice President Linda Chavez-Thompson said the federation had spent $7 million on such "education" in 1995, "and we stopped the Contract with America dead in its tracks. Now we need to spend about six times as much to bury it six feet under." In practice, it would become difficult to see a distinction between burying the Republican agenda and burying the political careers of the Republicans themselves.

Much of the $35 million went into organizational efforts, such as training for political workers. But AFL-CIO officials said about $22 million of the total went for TV and radio advertising. In addition, an allied public-interest group, Citizen Action, said it spent an additional $7 million on similar ads during 1996.

Republicans attacked the ads as illegal and dishonest and fired off letters to station managers demanding that they refuse to broadcast the AFL-CIO commercials. "They are factually challenged at best," said Republican Representative Dick Chrysler of Michigan, one of the prime targets for labor's campaign.[71] As an example, he cited an ad blasting Chrysler and other Republican freshmen for opposing an increase in the federal minimum wage. The ad said, "In 1991 the federal minimum wage was $4.25 an hour. Since then, corporate profits and executive salaries have skyrocketed. And Congress gave itself a 30 percent increase." It was all true enough, except that the unpopular congressional pay raise had been enacted in 1989, long before Rep. Chrysler and other freshman had been elected to the House. Criticizing them for supporting a pay increase they never had a chance to vote against was obviously misleading. Even so, only five stations refused to run the ad, an AFL-CIO spokeswoman said, while 107 stations kept it on the air.

Business lobbyists tried riding to the rescue. The U.S. Chamber of Commerce and several business lobbying groups banded together in an ad hoc group they called "The Coalition" and raised money for a similar issue-ad campaign supporting Republicans. The business effort was less successful, however, and in the end it only spent about $5.1 million. The Chamber of Commerce itself also spent $1.8 million for a series of ads praising Republicans on the Medicare issue, a major point of attack by the AFL-CIO.[72] In one of the Chamber's ads, a 72-year-old man named Clinton Smith said "I was scared to find out that Medicare was going broke. The Republicans have a reform plan that saves Medicare."[73]

The Republican Party itself did little to counter the ads at first, except for a flurry of press releases denouncing "labor bosses." But in the final weeks of the campaign the Republican National Committee and the National Republican Congressional Committee together ran an advertising campaign they said cost $15 million, far outspending labor in the final weeks. Some Republican strategists called it a deliberate strategy of waiting to fire until "the whites of their eyes" could be seen. One of the ads showed heavy-set men chewing cigars sitting around a table piled with money in a smoke-filled room. "The big labor bosses in Washington D.C. have a scheme to buy the Congress," it said. "Tell the big labor bosses, Idaho is not for sale."[74] The GOP ads were "issue ads" too, so the party could use its own soft money from business to counter labor's money.

After the election both sides claimed victory. For all the millions spent, "Newtie and the blowhards" were still in charge of the House. Some of the AFL-CIO's targets had been defeated, but others, including such stars of the GOP freshman class, such as J. D. Hayworth of Arizona and John Ensign of Nevada, survived.

AFL-CIO vice president Richard Trumka said the ads had been a factor in pushing the Republican Congress to enact a minimum-wage increase, and also had forced many Republicans to moderate their positions on issues raised in the ads. "To get elected they had to say that they wouldn't slash Medicare and Medicaid, that they wouldn't slash education, that they would stand with us on workplace health and safety," Trumka said. "You are going to see a radically different 105th Congress this time around because of our efforts."[76]

But the $35-million effort also produced resentment and promises of retaliation. Republican Bill Paxon said the GOP House "withstood the largest special-interest power grab in American history."[77] And RNC Chairman Bar-

Table 10   Labor's Top Targets[75]

Jim Bunn	(R., Oregon)	$1,050,000	**Defeated**
J.D. Hayworth	(R., Arizona)	$750,000	Re-elected
Randy Tate	(R., Washington)	$630,000	**Defeated**
Rick White	(R., Washington)	$630,000	Re-elected
John Ensign	(R., Nevada)	$575,000	Re-elected
Martin Hoke	(R., Ohio)	$475,000	**Defeated**
Fred Heineman	(R., North Carolina)	$460,000	**Defeated**

(Amounts spent by the AFL-CIO for "issue ads" in selected House districts.)

bour said, "The very first thing that must be done in campaign finance reform is, we must stop the practice of Washington union bosses taking the compulsory union dues of working men and women in this country—without their permission, involuntarily, dues that in most states are paid as a condition of employment—and spending that money for political purposes."[78] (See Table 10.)

"INDEPENDENT" PARTY MONEY—THE "WALL OF STEEL"

The June 26 Supreme Court decision allowing unlimited amounts of "independent" spending for candidates by political parties presented an opportunity for Republicans, who had more money to spend, and a problem: *how* could a political party's spending possibly be independent of its own candidates? Candidates, and the poll-takers and media consultants they hired, were in constant touch with political party organizations as a matter of course. New York Senator Al D'Amato, head of the NRSC, thought he had found a way around the problem.

The NRSC exiled five staff members from its headquarters on Capitol Hill, and sent them to a small suite of offices rented month-to-month on the eighth floor of the Barr Building downtown. "We sent these guys over there to work on independent expenditures, and told them they couldn't have any contact with any of our candidates," said NRSC attorney Craig Engle.[79] Engle said a "wall of steel" had been erected between the NRSC and the independent-spending unit it had spun off, insisting that the two groups would not even have so much as a cup of coffee together until after election day.

The "independent" unit raised no money of its own, however. All funds were supplied by D'Amato's NRSC. And James Perry of the *Wall Street Journal* reported that the "wall of steel" failed to stop contact between the "independent" unit and one of the candidates it was supporting. Republican Senate candidate Mike Enzi called the unit to complain about an ad it was running on his behalf, and which he wanted pulled off the air. The ad criticized his opponent for supporting a sales-tax increase which he had also supported. Enzi said when he finally got through to someone at the unit she hung up, but the ad came off the air nonetheless.[80]

The "independent" ploy allowed the Republican Party to supply $10.8 million in support to candidates in Rhode Island, New Jersey, Wyoming, Kansas, and Colorado, among others. NRCC executive director John Heubusch said, "We just overwhelmed them."[81]

CONCLUSION: THE COLLAPSE OF REFORM

As a practical matter, 1996 saw the final collapse of campaign finance regulations enacted 22 years earlier in the wake of the Watergate scandal. And as if on schedule, another scandal began to unfold, causing another embarrassed president to call for yet another round of reform. It was the completion of a cycle that has replayed itself more than once in American history: financial excesses by office-seekers causing public disgust, followed by red-faced but reluctant lawmakers enacting ineffective reforms that fail to prevent more excesses, leading to even deeper public distrust of the nation's government.

While the total amounts of money raised and spent vaulted to new records, voter turnout drooped to one of the *lowest* on record in a presidential year. Public revulsion over the spiraling political money race showed up at the ballot box in California, where voters approved by 61 percent to 39 percent a ballot proposition sponsored by Common Cause, the League of Women Voters, and Ross Perot's lobbying arm, United We Stand America. Called Proposition 208, it provides for contribution limits in state races of between $100 and $500. In Bill Clinton's Arkansas, voters approved the "Clean Government Initiative" by 66 percent to 34 percent, imposing donation limits ranging from $100 to $300, and calling for a 100 percent tax credit for donations up to $50, to encourage small givers. Colorado voters approved Amendment 15 by 66 percent to 34 percent, banning corporate donations, and setting donation limits of $100 for state legislative races and $500 for statewide races. Maine, Montana, and Nevada voters also approved campaign finance limits.

But despite the demonstrated public appetite for change, prospects at the national level remained uncertain. President Clinton promised to make reform a top priority of his administration, but Congress remained firmly in the hands of Republicans who had deep differences with Clinton over how to proceed. Dwight Morris, a veteran journalist and political money-watcher, rated prospects for reform at "below zero" in a column published just before election day.[82]

NOTES

1. Center for Responsive Politics, *A Brief History of Money in Politics* (Washington, 1995).

2. "Excerpts from President Clinton's News Conference," *Washington Post*, Nov. 9, 1996, p. A16

3. Fred Wertheimer, "The Dirtiest Election Ever," *Washington Post*, Nov. 3, 1996, p. C1.

4. *Facts on File*, January 11, 1975, p. 6.

5. Among those convicted was George Steinbrenner, an Ohio shipbuilding executive who, in 1996, was owner of the World Series-winning New York Yankees.

6. 424 U.S. 1 (1976)

7. Federal Election Commission, *Advisory Opinion 1978–10* In this case the FEC granted permission to the Kansas Republican Party to use corporate and union funds, legal under Kansas state law, in a voter drive that benefitted both federal and state candidates. The case represented a reversal of an earlier FEC advisory opinion in which the commission told the Illinois Republican State Central Committee that corporate and union money could NOT be used to to fund "any part" of a joint federal-state voter drive even though such funds were legal under Illinois state law. Had the earlier opinion held, "soft money" would be illegal.

8. Elizabeth Drew, *Politics and Money: The New Road to Corruption*, p. 105. (Republican fundraiser Robert Perkins told Drew he had raised $9 million in soft money for Reagan's 1980 election. But others later said this figure was inflated and Perkins himself admitted that he had no records to back up his claim and that "the truth is that nobody really knows" how much was raised. (Brooks Jackson, *Honest Graft: Big Money and the American Political Process* (Alfred A. Knopf, New York, 1988, p. 163).

9. Brooks Jackson, *Broken Promise: Why the Federal Election Commission Failed* (Priority Press Publications, New York, 1990), pp 52–4 The amount of soft money raised before 1990 can only be estimated because the Federal Election Commission did not even require parties to make disclosure until a federal judge ordered the commission to revise its regulations in this area.

10. Maralee Schwartz, "Common Cause Slaps DNC," *Washington Post*, August 16, 1987, p. A4.

11. "Amway Underwrites Cost . . . ," Republican National Committee, press release dated Nov. 23. 1994.

12. Quote supplied by Larry Neal, Gramm's press secretary. Neal says Gramm was quoting from Benjamin Franklin's *Poor Richard's Almanac,* 1773.

13. Interview with author, May 1995

14. "FEC Announces 1996 Presidential Spending Limits," Federal Election Commission, press release dated March 15, 1996. (In 1976, the first presidential election held under the new FECA amendments, the basic prenomination campaign limit had already been increased to $10.9 million, due to inflation.)

15. Rodney Smith, "Major Presidential Campaigns: 1972–1992," unpublished study in author's possession.

16. Brooks Jackson, "Quayle-Money Race," CNN segment aired Feb. 9, 1995.

17. Conversation with author, May 1995. Courtelis, who had survived a bout with cancer of the pancreas, suffered a relapse a few months later and died.

18. "Presidential Money," op. cit.

19. Ibid.

20. Brooks Jackson, "Quayle-Money Race," CNN segment aired Feb. 9, 1995.

21. All figures regarding presidential primary contributions and disbursements are from unpublished tabulations prepared by Robert Biersack, chief statistician of the Federal Election Commission. Mr. Biersack's calculations adjust the sometimes misleading gross receipts and disbursements reported by candidates, removing the effects of such things as loan repayments, contribution refunds and transfer payments. These "adjusted" receipts and disbursement figures allow "apples-to-apples" comparisons among candidates.

22. Interview with author, June 8, 1996.

23. The exception was tire manufacturer Morry Taylor, who did not accept any limits and eventually spent $6 million of his own money before dropping out of the race. The limits were voluntary, but as a practical matter none of the major candidates could afford to go without public financing given the difficulty of raising private contributions.

24. Forbes spending from interview with Forbes campaign official, June 8, 1996. Spending limits from "FEC Announces 1996 Presidential Spending Limits," Federal Election Commission, press release dated March 15, 1996.

25. Brooks Jackson, "Factcheck Forbes," CNN segment aired Dec. 7, 1995.

26. Forbes TV ads: "Tax Cut," Oct. 30, 1995, "Subway," Dec. 7, 1995.

27. Interview with Forbes campaign official, June 8. 1996.

28. Interview with author, 1995.

29. Brooks Jackson, "Dole Limits," CNN segment aired Feb. 26, 1996.

30. Interview with author, Feb. 26, 1966.

31. Brooks Jackson, "Dole Money," CNN segment aired May 20, 1966.

32. Brooks Jackson, "Presidential Ads Spin Patrol," CNN segment aired May 1, 1996. Data from Competitive Media Reporting.

33. DNC "Photo" ad, released April 19, 1996.

34. Interview with author, May 1, 1996.

35. Brooks Jackson, "Duelling Ads Spin Patrol," CNN segment aired May 31, 1996. Data from Competitive Media Reporting.

36. Interview with author, May 31, 1996. The $15 million estimate is from Castellanos, based on a count of the number of times the ads had run in the 75 largest media markets as measured by Competitive Media Reporting, multiplied by the going rates for commercial time in those markets.

37. $42.41 milllion figure supplied by DNC press office, November 25, 1996. Of the total, only $837,886 was spent by the DNC directly.

The remaining $41,576,507 was transferred to state party organizations, which could make more liberal use of soft money to buy the ads.

38. Interview with author, May 31, 1996.

39. Federal Document Clearing House, transcript of Dole remarks to ABC Affiliates meeting, Orlando, Florida, June 6, 1996. Legally, the term "generic" actually described a different kind of ad, which urged citizens to "vote Republican" or "vote Democratic" without specific reference to candiates or office. Under long-standing FEC rules such ads could be paid for with a mix of federal and non-federal soft dollars, on the theory that they benefitted both federal and state candidates. The legal stratagem Dole described exploited a distinction the courts had drawn in some cases between campaign commercials that expressly advocated the election or defeat of a clearly identified candidate, and so-called "issue ads" that avoided such terms as "vote for" or "vote against."

40. *Colorado Republican Federal Campaign Committee v. Federal Election Commission*, U.S. Supreme Court No. 95-489, decided June 26. 1996.

41. Douglas Wurth, general counsel, Bob Dole for President Committee, letter to the Federal Election Commission, July 2, 1996.

42. Brooks Jackson, "Playground Politics," CNN segment aired July 5, 1996.

43. Kemp for Vice President reports on file at the Federal Election Commission.

44. Ruth Marcus, "Party Switches Method of Funding TV Coverage," *Washington Post*, Aug. 13., 1996, p.A17. At first the Amway money was routed through the San Diego Convention and Visitors Bureau, a private entity where it might have escaped disclosure. But when word of the huge grant leaked out, the Democratic National Committee filed a complaint with the Federal Election Commission. The money was returned to Amway, which immediately contributed it to the San Diego Host Committee, the entity that raises private contributions to help finance the convention.

45. San Diego Host Committee chairman Gerald Parsky insisted in an inverview Nov. 20, 1996 that even more money had come from private sources. The Host Committee's reports listed a $5.2 million contribution from the "San Diego Convention Fund," which Parsky said had come originally from private donors. Who those donors were, however, could not immediately be determined.

46. Brooks Jackson, "Republican Money," CNN segment aired Jan. 25, 1996.

47. Interview with author, May 7, 1996.

48. Brooks Jackson, "Democratic Money," CNN segment aired May 8, 1996.

49. Lynn Sweet, "The President's Price List," *Chicago Sun-Times*, June 30, 1995, p. 1.

50. Lynn Sweet, "Clinton Orders Donor Perk Review," *Chicago Sun-Times*, July 13, 1995, p. 3.

51. Jeffrey Birnbaum, "The Appetizers Better Be Good . . . ," *Time*, Dec. 11, 1995, p. 47.

52. Haley Barbour, "Memorandum to Republican Leaders," Nov. 4, 1996.

53. Interview with Mary Crawford, Republican National Committee, Nov. 18, 1996.

54. "State Pary Allocation Formulas," RNC document, undated (supplied by RNC press office).

55. Common Cause news conference, October 9, 1996.

56. Ralph Z. Hallow, "Ex-fundraiser for Dole Faces Jail Term," *Washington Times,* July 11, 1996, p. A4.

57. Renee Haines, "Perot says Clinton to face criminal charges," Reuter, San Antonio, Texas, Nov. 4, 1996.

58. Adapted from "Democratic National Committee contributions Returned Since September, 1996," DNC press relase, Nov. 12, 1996.

59. News conference, Nov. 12, 1996.

60. June 13, 1996, in open session of the Federal Election Commission.

61. Through Oct. 16, 1996.

62. Memorandum dated January 12, 1995. Copy in author's possession.

63. Interview with author, Feb. 7, 1995.

64. Brooks Jackson, "Money," CNN segment aired Jan. 27, 1995.

65. Brooks Jackson, "Business PACS," CNN segment aired April 14, 1995.

66. Averages calculated by author from FEC releases.

67. "Congressional Spending for '96 Elections . . . ," Federal Election Commission, press release dated Nov. 1, 1996, p. 48

68. "1995–96 PAC Contributions Increase . . . ," Federal Election Commission, press release dated September 27, 1996, p. 6

69. "1995–96 PAC Contributions Increase . . . ," Federal Election Commission, press release dated September 27, 1996, p. 2 (Percentages calculated by author).

70. "1995–96 PAC Contributions Increase . . . ," Federal Election Commission, press release dated September 27, 1996, p. 2 (Percentages calculated by author).

71. News conference, May 22, 1996.

72. Figures supplied by Frank Coleman, spokesman for the U.S. Chamber of Commerce, Nov. 18, 1996.

73. U.S. Chamber of Commerce Ad, "True Stories/Clinton Smith," released June 7, 1996.

74. RNC "Chapter" ad, released Oct. 10, 1996.

75. Spending figures supplied by AFL-CIO. They are unverified, as there is no requirement for disclosure of "issue ad" spending. District-by-district estimates by Republican Party officials ran considerably higher, but were vehemently denied by AFL-CIO officials.

76. Interview with author, Nov. 6, 1996.

77. News conference, Nov. 6, 1996.

78. News conference, Nov. 6, 1996.

79. James Perry, "Senate Republicans Prepare to Spend Millions . . . ," *Wall Street Journal,* Sept. 23, 1996, p. A22.

80. James Perry, op. cit.

81. Interview with author, December 1996.

82. Dwight Morris, "Below Zero: The Prospects for Reform," *Politics Now* World Wide Web site, Oct. 28, 1996.

CHAPTER 11

Final Thoughts

Ken Bode

DePauw University
Moderator, PBS "Washington Week in Review"

THE MATTER OF A MANDATE

For three successive elections, beginning with 1990, network analysts reported an angry electorate and the prevailing mood as anti-Washington and anti-Congress, with incumbents as an endangered species. There was no doubting the sour, hostile mood, but initially the results were inconsequential. In 1990, for example, polls showed that respect for Congress had reached a historic low point, fueled by public anger over the savings and loan bailout. However, by the end of the evening broadcast analysts were at pains to explain why 98 percent of incumbents were re-elected, the highest rate ever. Voters had a distaste for Congress, but apparently they refused to exercise that disgust by tossing out their own incumbent congressperson, the only member they could affect.

In 1992, results began more clearly to reflect the anti-incumbent mood of the electorate. In the three-way presidential contest between incumbent Republican George Bush, Democrat Bill Clinton, and Independent Ross Perot, the voters ended 12 years of Republican rule. Again, over 90 percent of congressional incumbents were re-elected, but there were signs that the voters were "getting a bead" on them in hunter's parlance. Many were re-elected with vastly diminished margins. All this, of course, presaged the Republican revolution of 1994, when voters broke the 40 year hold of the Democrats on the House of Representatives and turned over control of both houses of Congress to the GOP, with Georgia's Newt Gingrich, a self-proclaimed revolutionary and historical figure, as Speaker of the House.

In 1996, there was no similar anger apparent in the electorate. After two successive china-rattling elections, voters seemed ready to take a breather, ready to step back, look things over, and, perhaps, let them settle for awhile. We often look for large adjectives to describe election results. They are "re-aligning," "redefining," "confirming." How do you describe an election that brought back to office the most conservative member of the Senate (North Carolina's Jesse Helms) along with its most liberal (Minnesota's Paul Well-stone)? An election in which California voters threw out affirmative action and voted in medical marijuana? Where an incumbent president, whose party lost in a landslide referendum on him and his policies two years before, was re-elected, but his power to act was stalemated by opposition control of both houses of Congress? Perhaps you call it just that, a stand-pat "stalemated out-come," a reasoned endorsement of the status quo.

From Little Rock on election night, feeling truly like "the comeback kid," President Clinton grandly thanked the American people for the great honor they had bestowed upon him. There were three measures, all of them put in play by the President's "spin doctors" in the weeks and days before November 5, by which to judge the magnitude of Clinton's victory and mandate: the Electoral College margin, the President's fervent desire to be elected by a majority of the popular vote, and the control of Congress.

First, the Electoral College, in which Clinton's goal was to break 400. That was not achieved; however, by most measures 379 to 159 indeed looks like a landslide. But remember that the winner-take-all feature of the College was intended to inflate margins and provide at least the image of a decisive result. Also, who remembers the Electoral College totals? This is a classic "one-day story," today's front page, tomorrow's fish-wrap.

Second, the popular vote mandate. Two weeks before the election, the Clinton campaign was ebullient with a solid 16 to 20 point lead in national polls supported by similar margins in large, battleground states. These data raised hopes that the popular vote landslide would make Clinton the first Democrat since Franklin Roosevelt to be re-elected, and that the sheer margin of this victory inevitably would sweep to power a Democratic House and possibly Senate. In the final days of the campaign, the Clinton–Gore team watched its lead wither under a constant barrage of attacks about tainted campaign money from foreign sources, in one instance, cash laundered through a Buddhist temple in Los Angeles. Republican Bob Dole promised there would be indictments after election day, and Reform Party candidate Ross Perot raised the specter of another Watergate. In the closing days, tainted money was the most prominent and important issue on the media agenda. If money matters more than sex in the contemporary coverage of campaigns and concerns of voters, Clinton's opponents had found the character issue that seemed to stick. The popular vote division—49 percent for President Clinton, 51 percent against—approaches nothing like consensus. In fact, it resembles almost perfect "dissensus."

Obviously, the Democrats failed in the third measure of victory, control of Congress, meaning that the President must continue to govern within the parameters set by Republican control of the legislative branch. Because the Electoral College result has no enduring effect and the popular vote outcome carried no substantial weight, this is the most important measure of the 1996 election, a result that strongly suggests a stand-pattism in the electorate and rocky shoals ahead for William Jefferson Clinton. If we are entering an era in which the Republicans have captured the South as a base for control of Congress, it is also true that the South has captured the Republican Party in the process, reflected not only in the leadership of Senate Majority Leader Trent Lott, a Mississippian, and Speaker Newt Gingrich of Georgia, but in their lieutenants and major committee chairmen in both bodies, along with their legislative agenda. GOP control also means continued investigations of Whitewater, FBI files, Travelgate, and foreign campaign contributions, not good news for either Bill or Hillary Clinton.

It is no surprise that the President's election night exuberance of the great honor accorded him had, by the time of his first press conference, receded into a more realistic assessment: "I think what the American people were telling us is that they want us to get along and get things done." The next week, Newt Gingrich was unanimously nominated to continue as Speaker in the Republican-controlled House. Gingrich had survived, by his own estimate, despite $35 million of independent expenditure money in which he was demonized in an effort to defeat Republican freshmen. Though most of the freshmen were re-elected, Gingrich's personal ratings were as low as Richard Nixon's in his worst days, and the subdued Speaker found a message in the election results similar to the one discerned by the President. "If the 104th was the confrontation Congress," he said, "this will be the implementation Congress."

In those assertions by Clinton and Gingrich may lie the common ground needed for progress. Though there were no large mandates asked for and none delivered in the 1996 election, the stand-pat result may offer a window of opportunity. America now has a speaker chastened by public disapproval over budgetary deadlocks that twice closed down the government, and a president whose second term plurality mandate rests on a promise to balance the budget along with an aggregation of small proposals—V-chips, 48-hour maternity care, school uniforms, teenage curfews, and cleaning up a welfare bill he did not want to sign. The President admitted even before the election that he was studying the pitfalls of recent second term presidencies. If Mr. Clinton and Mr. Gingrich each want a larger legacy than they had built prior to 1996, both may be spurred to an effort to solve the larger problems that were not seriously addressed in last year's campaign, namely campaign spending and entitlement reform.

VALUES VERSUS VISION

If ever there was a candidate of the party establishment, it was Majority Leader Bob Dole. Dole's 35 years on Capitol Hill, his tenure as national party chairman, the hundreds of campaign trips on behalf of Republican colleagues, and his relentless pursuit of campaign funds for himself and others built up chits that were negotiable in a presidential nominating contest. As we saw in Chapter Three, when the primaries began Dole had sealed the endorsements of a majority of GOP senators and governors along with a substantial bloc of House members and state chairmen. After some difficulty fending off challenges from Steve Forbes and Pat Buchanan, he wrapped up the nomination by mid-March. Then set in a massive case of Republican buyers' remorse.

If there was a moment when the doubts began to congeal, it might have been when Dole selected himself to respond to Bill Clinton's 1996 State of the Union address, in which the President announced to a roar of bipartisan approval, "the era of big government is over." Dole sat in a room by himself looking at a single camera with a speech prepared before the President's text was available. He had none of the supporting atmospherics of a joint session of Congress with all of official Washington to add luster, and his speech seemed weak, flat, and forced. The disappointment was almost universal. "What are we going to do? How can we nominate Dole? The guy is inarticulate, he has no vision, and he is old."

Republican pundits were especially merciless. Led by the *Weekly Standard*'s Bill Kristol and syndicated columnist Arianna Huffington, they fueled the embers of doubt, suggesting that Dole would lose and probably end the Republican revolution by costing the party its control of the House and Senate, even suggesting that as an act of loyalty he should stand aside and allow the convention to pick a different candidate.

Throughout the summer and fall, Dole was vexed by what George Bush used to call, "the vision thing." Arthur Schlesinger has deemed vision to be the first requirement of presidential leadership, and Robert Dallek in *Hail to the Chief* says, "No candidate has been able to attain high office without some expression of faith in a greater America."[1] Dole's media strategists pointed to Depression-era Russell, Kansas, along with Dole's wartime injury and rehabilitation as the embodiment of the candidate's essential character. To avoid making him seem a Washington insider, his three-and-a-half decades as a creature of the nation's capital were less aggressively marketed. But even if you could accept that Dole's vision was, " . . . the sum of his roots and his experiences," as a CNN documentary put it, the candidate himself seemed rooted in the flat, understated language of western Kansas combined with the legislative parlance of the U.S. Senate.[2] Try as he might, Bob Dole could never project a larger sense of himself to audiences.

On the other hand, Clinton had to shed his image of a politician whose vision was too large, too ambitious, and unshared by the people he hoped to lead. He came to office promising a health care plan within 100 days, to reform welfare as we know it, and he assured the nation in his inaugural address that "the era of gridlock is over." After the disastrous health care defeat and his landslide rejection in the 1994 mid-term election, an unusual referendum on a president who was not even on the ballot, Clinton commissioned his famous make-over. His "repositioning," according to its architects, consultant Dick Morris and pollsters Mark Penn and Doug Schoen, was based on "values."

It is not the first time values issues were used in presidential politics. In 1988, with Vice President Bush lagging in the polls behind unabashedly liberal Michael Dukakis, Bush's campaign manager James Baker outlined his strategy to a home-state Texas audience. He explained that the key to overtaking the Democrat would be value issues, which he said were those questions on which most Americans knew on a visceral basis where they stood. Baker presented his list: abortion (they're for it, we're against), gun control (they favor it, we don't), a mandatory pledge to the flag in school (Governor Dukakis vetoed it in Massachusetts, Mr. Bush would have signed it), and weekend prison furloughs for convicted murderers.

Baker's litany was drowned out in a foot-stomping ovation. The ensuing campaign featured the famous Willie Horton commercials, visits by both candidates to flag factories, attacks on Governor Dukakis' American Civil Liberties Union membership, and promises never to raise taxes—all in the name of "values."

For Clinton, the issues were as different as the target audiences. Until 1996, social and religious conservatives held the franchise on family values. As it fit the rest of their ideology, their model was to get government out of people's lives, including their schools and workplaces. Clinton's handlers developed the first full scale competing model of family values in politics. Needing 10 to 15 points from social conservatives, Dick Morris and his colleagues targeted people in their 20s, 30s, and 40s, people trying to raise a family in difficult times. Morris explained this strategy in an interview with the author:

> They are fairly straight. They may have rock-and-rolled and used drugs, but not anymore, and they particularly do not want a culture that encourages their children to use them. They have friends who are gay but do not want a culture that encourages or glorifies gays. They want someone who understands this. They don't care what Clinton did in the past. That was debated and decided in 1992. This election will be about his stewardship of the White House.[3]

Much has been written about how Clinton moved to the center to preempt Republican issues, particularly a balanced budget, welfare, and crime.

The specifics of his repositioning—family leave, handguns and assault weapons, 100,000 cops, school uniforms, tobacco advertising, targeted tax cuts for education—were all considered small bore issues, but they all added up. Clinton developed a family based agenda that did not reject government, but also did not include any large, ambitious initiatives like his original health care plan. Clinton redefined himself into a kind of compassionate national father. What can government do to help with teenage social disorder? What can government do to help with the lifetime educational needs of the American worker? What can be done to get excessive violence and sex off TV?

Clinton constantly talked of community (preserving and promoting families), responsibility (the duty we owe to one another), and equality (providing opportunity for all Americans).[4] It worked. A year before the election, if a voter was married with children, he or she was unlikely to be a Clinton supporter. Through the spring and summer of 1996, while Dole was otherwise occupied, Clinton appealed to these voters by relentlessly aggregating his issues and carefully inoculating himself against future Republican attacks. In presidential politics, Republicans do best when crime, welfare, and taxes make up their issue constellation. When Dole finished the nomination contest and resigned from the Senate, he found the traditional GOP ground had been preempted by Clinton.

Age, also, was a factor in "the vision thing." In his convention speech, Dole purposely reached back to his formative years in small town Kansas, arguing that America was a better place when it was simpler, safer, friendlier, and more down to earth. For those old enough to remember and willing to be carried back in time, it was a compelling metaphor. But most Americans seem to understand that in very fundamental ways, our world is very different, far more complicated, and far less sage than the times Dole described. We face two inevitable and very large challenges. Along with the rest of the world, we are moving from a national to a global economy, and from the industrial age to the information age. Our children will bear the brunt of these challenges, but we must see that they are adequately prepared.

When President Clinton used the overworked metaphor of his "bridge to the 21st century," it, along with all the small bore education and family oriented programs he proposed, conveyed the impression that he understood these challenges and was better prepared to help us meet them than was the 73-year old Bob Dole. Every visual image of the Clintons and Gores, with teenage children still in school, reinforced that image. (They care about the things we care about, because they must.) Dick Morris felt that age was an important point of contrast between Clinton and Dole: "It is less a physiological thing than a matter of perspective," he said. On hearing Dole argue that tobacco is not necessarily addictive, a young voter put it more succinctly: "His clock is in the 1950s."

DO WE NEED A COMMISSION?

The famous New Hampshire photo-op handshake between President Clinton and Speaker Gingrich during the summer of 1995 is all but forgotten. At a joint appearance, the two men were challenged by the audience to pledge, on-the-spot, to do something about campaign finance reform, and on-the-spot they agreed to do so. Nothing has happened as of this writing.

Commissions are a tried and true American way of dealing with complicated problems. They have bailed out Social Security; examined urban violence, race in America, and the assassination of a president; reformed the presidential nominating process; closed superfluous military bases; and examined sexual harassment and the spread of gambling. Not all are popular, nor is every one successful. But they bring together experts with a mandate to focus on a perceived problem. And after the 1996 election, there was no shortage of perceived problems.

The Primaries

The GOP is the party of primogeniture; the front-runner almost always wins. This year, Bob Dole, anointed candidate of the establishment, ended it quickly, which ordinarily is what party leaders want— no drawn-out, divisive, expensive primary battles. But by the end of March, Dole was battered and broke. Millionaire Steve Forbes had taken a poll to discover just how vulnerable the front-runner might be among true-believer primary voters. Depict Dole as a creature of the establishment, Forbes' pollsters advised, and show him entangled in the special interest politics and compromises that go into the making of tax policy. Depict him as a flip-flopper, a pork barreler, weak, dull, harsh, bad of temper. Tell primary voters that Dole voted for 13 tax increases, for a big salary for himself, that he took trips paid for by special interests, criticized President Reagan for spending too much money for defense, and supported President Bush when Bush broke his promise not to raise taxes. Forbes used Dole as a punching bag as he tried to become the candidate of anti-establishment, anti-Washington, anti-politician Republicans.

It was over by mid-March, as Chapter Three explained. Dole lost Arizona to Forbes, New Hampshire to Pat Buchanan, but when he hit the South he won every primary thereafter. The rush to be first, or as near to the starting line as possible, had turned March into a month of madness, 27 primaries in 25 days, accounting for 65 percent of the delegates to be selected and beginning just eleven days after the first-in-the-nation New Hampshire primary. In 1996, Republicans had a special reason to complain. Their putative nominee had spent virtually every penny of the legal expenditures limit and was without funds for months before federal stipends kicked in after the August convention.

In a reasonable effort to afford the voters a sense of genuine involvement in the nomination of a president, states had created a lopsided system that favored front-runners, early money, and a surprise quick start. As Ohio Secretary of State Bob Taft asserted, "It has been 20 years since our voters had any real impact on the outcome of presidential nominating contests."[5] For that reason, Ohio moved its traditional May primary back to the third Tuesday in March, joining Michigan, Illinois, and Wisconsin to create a de facto midwestern industrial state regional primary. However, as it happened, Dole had already locked up the nomination by that point, so there was virtually no campaigning in Ohio, and voter participation fell to an all-time low. Front-loading had frustrated the reformers, creating unintended consequences.

In each nominating cycle, there has been an effort to displace Iowa and New Hampshire as the first two opening acts. In 1996 Arizona, Louisiana, and Delaware all flirted with stealing a jump, and Louisiana actually held unauthorized caucuses attended by a tiny minority of the Republicans in the state. After the primary season Republican National Committee Chairman Haley Barbour, recognizing the dangers in a continued unregulated race to be first, established a presidential primary task force to examine the situation. Without action, it was feared, the nominating process would eventually become a de facto national primary the first week of March. The National Association of Secretaries of State, composed of the chief elections officer in each state, also began a review of the nominating process and called for a commission to prescribe action.

These efforts have intensified the debate about whether Iowa and New Hampshire should go first. Critics argue they were too small, generally unrepresentative of the rest of the country, and attracted far too much attention from the candidates and the media. Yet there is also an appreciation of the "retail campaigning" that takes place in these states, the face-to-face candidate–voter interaction in cafes, courthouses, sale barns, union halls, living rooms, and church basements. Additionally, the equal footing theme these early, relatively level playing fields afford longshots and front-runners alike has merit. From the testimony taken by the secretaries of state and the GOP task force, there seems to be an emerging consensus that the presidential selection process needs to begin in small states, whether they be Iowa and New Hampshire or other similar venues on a rotating basis.

Before the rush to front-load, the campaign season lasted from late February to early June with primaries and caucuses across the country gradually winnowing out the weaker candidates. In calling for a bipartisan commission to deal with this problem, the secretaries of state recommended that a system be designed that once again would spread the voting over three or four months, and that a firm date be established after which no state may change the scheduling of its primary or caucus.

Do we need a full-fledged national commission to deal with front-loading? Yes, to reverse the current trend and raise public consciousness about the necessity of more considered judgment about presidential nominees.

The Polls

Everett Carll Ladd minced no words when he termed 1996 "a Waterloo . . . a terrible year for election polling."[6] Ladd's first and most obvious reason was that the polls missed the mark by greater margins than usual. As noted in Chapter Six, the final CBS/*New York Times* poll, for example, predicted a Clinton landslide of 18 points over Bob Dole. In fact, Clinton won by a far more modest eight points. Though that poll was the least accurate, polls throughout the campaign suggested that Dole's fate was hopeless. In early August, before either nominating convention, The Pew Research Center issued a poll headlined, "A Dull Campaign, Clinton Will Win Say More Than 70% of Voters."[7] Dole's campaign efforts were graded at D+, and interest was down compared to 1992, but nearly seven-in-ten voters polled by Pew said they were "absolutely certain" to vote. Actual turnout was 20 points below that.

In a presidential year, the process is infused with polls of one kind or another. There are focus groups to test themes and messages, candidate polls, media polls, tracking polls, and exit polls. Ladd estimates that from September 1 to election day, there were about 300 national polls checking presidential preference, with the results widely disseminated, bombarding voters with the idea that the election was over. This compares with about half as many in 1992, and only ten such polls as recently as 1968.

Pollsters have traditionally insisted that there is no evidence that voters are influenced by poll results. As quoted in the *New York Times*, October, 30, 1972, George Gallup said, "I have never in my life seen any hard evidence that people are influenced by polling results. If there is any effect, it is so negligible that it is impossible to measure." But the logic and force of that argument are gradually slipping away. Major newspapers and television networks poll cooperatively (NBC and the *Wall Street Journal*, ABC and the *Washington Post*, CNN and *USA Today*), and the poll results frequently lead the evening news broadcasts and are reported as front-page news. Some critics, such as Elizabeth Drew, claim, "So many news organizations themselves got into the polling business, and then they want to advertise their own results. So that a higher percentage of the reporting becomes about the polls which then affects the reporting."

Others are even harsher on the media polling, arguing that it amounts to reporting news that has been bought and paid for, featuring on the front page something that has not really happened. In any case, there is little doubt that if the press should be criticized for excessive coverage of the horse race in presidential elections, polls contribute mightily to that tendency.

Exit polls, of course, are a constant problem. Networks believe in them, and in combination with analysis of key precincts, they have an enormously high level of accuracy, which enables election night calls to be made in many races just as the polls close. However, they are vexing to many voters who do not understand their basis and who fix upon the inevitable errors. In 1996, for example, all the networks called the New Hampshire Senate race for the Democratic challenger immediately upon the 7:00 P.M. poll closing. Over the course of the evening, all had to take it back, since the Republican incumbent Bob Smith won. Of course, the practice that evokes the most strenuous reaction is the tendency to call landslide presidential elections over before the polls close on the West Coast. Election officials in California, Oregon, and Washington brush aside the arguments of network executives that such calls do not depress turnout in their states.

Again I ask, do we need a commission? Everett Carll Ladd says that the performance of election polls in 1996 was so flawed that the entire enterprise ought to be examined by a blue ribbon panel of high professional standing to review what went wrong and why, and to suggest corrective measures. He argues that impartial observers also ought to look at the extent to which the coverage of campaigns is driven by the infusion of polls into reporting. Ladd is right, and we need that commission.

Presidential Debates

In 1992, 97 million viewers watched President George Bush, Governor Bill Clinton, and Independent Ross Perot square off in the final debate broadcast from East Lansing, Michigan. Though some, such as journalist Tom Wicker, consider them to be "gushing fountains of misinformation, disinformation, posturing, prevarication, puerility," in the era of television, these high-stakes showdowns are here to stay.

Ever since modern presidential debates began in 1976, we have learned certain things about them. They are relatively civil, a break from negativity in the campaign process. They afford candidates time to detail unreported matters of policy from their stump speeches and to justify those policy positions. Ninety minutes of discussion about taxes, the size of government, Medicare reform, drug policy, health care, school choice, crime, defense and foreign affairs is a must-see tonic for those voters who believe that issues and policy are underreported in daily press coverage.

For voters who are inclined to make up their minds based on the personal qualities of contenders, debates provide a venue where candidates are more judicious and sober than in their campaign appearances, also less patronizing, more thoughtful, and personally involved.[8] We also know that viewers do not tend to remember the lengthy points of public policy. What sticks are those magic television moments such as Ronald Reagan's vowing not to make age an issue; Lloyd Bentsen's chastising Dan Quayle for comparing himself to Jack Kennedy; George Bush's checking his watch; Gerald Ford's liberating Poland from communist domination; and Michael Dukakis' failing to respond with anger about a hypothetical attack on his wife.

Finally, we know that however widely anticipated, watched, and reported debates may be, they are not events that massively sway voters. Voters, like network commentators, may be willing to pick a winner, but it doesn't necessarily change their minds about whom they support.

So, if debates are here to stay, the questions are: Who should be included? And who should decide? At the present time, the Commission on Presidential Debates, a creation of the two major parties, co-chaired by former national party chairmen from each, holds that franchise. Since the candidate of the Democratic or Republican Party has been elected to the presidency for more than a century, the invitation to those two nominees is automatic.[9] However, we are now in an era where independent candidates and nominees of third and fourth parties are more likely than not to be on fifty state ballots.

For inclusion in the debates, these "non-major party candidates" are required to meet a series of thresholds involving their electoral viability ("more than theoretical"), their newsworthiness, and signs of national enthusiasm, all relatively subjective criteria. In 1996, the commission formed a five member team of academic experts led by Harvard's Richard Neustadt to examine the field and make recommendations. It was relatively easy to deal with candidates like Harry Browne of the Libertarian Party, Ralph Nader of the Green Party, and Dr. Joseph Hagelin, a follower of the Maharishi Mahesh Yogi, and candidate of the Natural Law Party. The difficult question was whether to include Reform Party candidate Ross Perot, and if not, why not?

In 1992 Perot, who had just returned to the race after dropping out in July, was included by the commission when neither of the two major-party candidates objected. During this hiatus, he had allowed his state organization to continue gathering petitions to put his name on the ballot, and when he reentered, polls showed him at 7 percent. Perot used the debates effectively to reestablish his viability. In polling one day after the first debate, 37 percent thought Perot won, compared to 24 percent for Clinton, and only 11 percent for President Bush.[10] After this debate, Perot rose a dramatic 16 points in the polls. On the debate stage and through his paid television infomercials, he forced both Bush and Clinton to discuss the federal budget deficit. Perot ended the election season winning 19 percent of the popular vote, more than any third-party or independent candidate in modern times, but he won no states, no electoral votes.

Against that backdrop, the commission also needed to consider that since 1992, Perot had built upon his independent candidacy, incorporating it into the Reform Party, which had achieved ballot status in all 50 states. As that party's nominee, he was entitled to receive over $29 million in federal funds, based on his 1992 vote totals. Perot accepted those funds, agreeing to forgo spending many millions more of his own money, on the assumption that doing so would better establish the Reform Party on the electoral rolls and guarantee him a place on the debate stage.

The editorial press was divided. Based on his 1992 performance, the *New York Times* argued that allowing Perot to debate "seems minimally fair." The *Los Angeles Times* agreed, arguing that the country would benefit by live interrogation of Perot by someone other than "television's Larry King and other deferential questioners."[11] The *Wall Street Journal* argued that Perot was a pretender with no possibility of winning, that if he were serious about the federal deficit he would give back to the Treasury his $29 million of taxpayers' money.[12] And the Republican-leaning *Weekly Standard* advised the commission to "Just Say No" and help rid American public discourse of this meddlesome twerp.[13]

The commission did say no to Perot. He was at only 5 percent to 8 percent in the polls and deemed to have no realistic chance of winning. The decision was unanimous, and there was plenty of evidence that it reflected uncompromising demands from the Dole campaign that Perot be excluded. Analysis from the 1992 debates indicated that Perot had been harder on George Bush than on Bill Clinton, attacking Bush for his involvement in the Iran-Contra cover-up and the savings and loan crisis. Republicans were wary that Dole would be a more tempting target for Perot than would Clinton. There was also a common assumption that Perot siphoned more votes from Bush than from Clinton in 1992. The Dole campaign effectively exercised a veto over Perot's participation.

The ensuing two presidential debates were among the least watched in history. Who knows what would have happened if Perot had been included, but his endgame campaign themes focused almost exclusively on Clinton's foreign money sources. Campaign finance reform was one of Perot's major campaign themes both in 1992 and 1996, and without the Texan on the debate stage it was all but ignored. One more point: Perot had nearly $30 million of taxpayers' money; we were entitled to see how he spent it. Do we need a commission? No, we already have a commission, and *it* is the problem. What we need is a law.

Campaign Finance Reform

As we write, the true story of campaign money can be told no better than Brooks Jackson did in Chapter Ten. But that, inevitably, will not be the last word. There may well be a Justice Department investigation to determine whether criminal violations of federal campaign finance laws occurred. Republican Senator John McCain of Arizona has asked for a congressional investigation of the Democratic National Committee's sources of foreign campaign contributions. The DNC has returned over $1.5 million in funds that it suspects may have been contributed illegally. The FBI has decided an investigation into potential criminal conduct is warranted, particularly involving the possibility that donors made contributions using other people's money. And while President Clinton makes his first post-election trip to Asia, there was speculation in the press that the Bangkok stayover may be related to a $253,000 contribution to the DNC from a lobbyist for a Thai property development company and a supporter of the outgoing Thai prime minister. The money was given back by the DNC, because the committee said some of the funds came from sources other than the listed contributor.[14]

In the final days of the 1996 campaign, as Bill Clinton seemed to be coasting to a landslide re-election, the most important story in the media was the rapidly untangling story of his campaign money. Two major news weekly magazines did cover stories: *Time*, "The Money Trail,"[15] and *Newsweek*, "Candidates for Sale, Clinton's Asia Connection."[16] Both Clinton and Dole took time away from their standard stump speeches to propose campaign spending reform, a subject not otherwise much mentioned throughout the fall. Even as Bob Dole appealed, "Wake up, America. The liberal media is about to re-elect Bill Clinton," he was citing facts about the Clinton foreign money scandal gathered by the *Los Angeles Times*, the *New York Times*, and the *Wall Street Journal*.

Ross Perot made an infomercial and an appearance at the National Press Club. He said that Clinton faced " . . . huge moral, ethical, and criminal problems that could force him from office in a second term. We are headed for a second Watergate!" Perot accused the president of abusing his office by changing U.S. trade policy in return for giant, possibly illegal, campaign contributions from foreign interests, and by accepting a $20,000 contribution from a convicted drug dealer who was later invited to a White House social event. Dole and the Republicans, said Perot, had also abused the campaign finance system and traded favors for contributions.

All overblown campaign rhetoric? Probably not this time. For years there has been common agreement that America's post-Watergate campaign finance laws are outdated and porous beyond tolerating. The need for huge campaign budgets, incessantly swelled by the costs of television advertising—not only for president, but for House and Senate races as well—has caused both parties to begin to recruit millionaires, political amateurs willing to foot their own bills.

There is the further common assumption that nothing will happen as long as the matter is in the control of incumbents of both parties who know the game and benefit from the present rules. No matter how onerous the job of raising money, no matter how obvious the connection between contributors with an interest in government and the ensuing access to policy makers, both parties will find a way to niggle and delay, leaving the present system in place until it, too, explodes in a scandal like Watergate.

Two things happened this year that may change this pessimistic assessment. First, the amateur millionaire Steve Forbes dipped into his deep pockets and ran one of the most negative presidential primary campaigns ever witnessed, doing serious damage to the Republican front-runner and eventual nominee. In the end, Forbes spent $30 million, nearly every penny of it his own, to win 900,545 votes, or $33,313.16 per vote.[17] He probably could have done better by just handing out checks at polling places. Second, the victory of the first Democratic president to be re-elected since Franklin Roosevelt was badly tarnished by the foreign money scandal in the final days of the campaign. Although President Clinton insisted the Democrats had done nothing wrong, he admitted that changes in the system must be made. Criminal investigations and Republican-run congressional hearings will certainly follow. As surely as Ross Perot put the deficit on the national agenda in 1992, the campaign of 1996 did the same for the campaign spending reform.

Do we need a commission? Yes, but not in the normal sense. What we need is a commission with the same authority as the one that examined the need to close military bases around the country, a commission with authority to send a set of recommendations to Congress, which Congress can vote up or down, but not amend. Of all the commissions we need, we need this one most of all.

Final, Final Thoughts

The problem with campaigns run on "values" is that truly important issues are usually buried. In 1988, the savings and loan crisis was all but ignored. George Bush had nothing to say. His son Neil's ties to the failed Silverado Savings and Loan Association in Colorado Springs were potentially embarrassing. Michael Dukakis gave one speech about the crisis, but he was warned off by fellow Democrats. Democrats were responsible for the legislation liberalizing the banking laws that made the irregularities possible, he was told. Distracted by Willie Horton and the flag factories, voters heard nothing about the savings and loan crisis until a year later, when the $50 billion tab arrived.[18]

Throughout the 1980s public concern about the federal deficit crawled along at the bottom of the charts at about 5 percent in most polls. That was exactly the period of a threefold increase in the national public debt.[19] But the deficit did not register clearly on the national agenda until Ross Perot took $68 million of his own money and put it there during the campaign of 1992.

What was missed in the values-based campaign of 1996? Obviously, entitlement reform and campaign spending reform would lead that list. Medicare was a campaign issue, the subject of millions of dollars in emotional campaign advertising, but never intelligently discussed during the debates. And with Ross Perot banished from the debate stage, campaign spending reform was a non-issue until the foreign money stories began to break late in October.

Do we need a commission? Yes, we need several. But the good news is that the campaign of 1996 may have pointed to the problems clearly enough, and the divided-government outcome of the election— guaranteeing both parties a voice—may have provided the window of opportunity necessary to address these problems. At least we the public can hope so.

NOTES

1. Robert Dalleck, *Hail to the Chief: The Making and Unmaking of American Presidents* (Hyperion: New York, 1996), 1.

2. Ken Bode, "Bob Dole's Odyssey," CNN, October 20, 1996.

3. Interview with author, May 30, 1996.

4. Mark J. Penn and Douglass Schoen, "Why Our Gameplan Worked," *Time Extra: The Election of 1996* (Fall, 1996), 82.

5. Ohio Secretary of State Bob Taft in testimony before the GOP Task Force on Presidential Primaries, May 30, 1996.

6. *The Chronicle of Higher Education*, November 22, 1996, A52.

7. Pew Research Center press release,"A Dull Campaign, Clinton Will Win Say More Than 70% of Voters," August 2, 1996.

8. Annenberg School for Communication, "Tracking the Quality of Campaign Discourse: No. 10 What we know from 1960–92 about debates," October 3, 1996.

9. Commission on Presidential Debates, "Candidate Selection Criteria," 1996.

10. Annenberg School for Communication, "Tracking the Quality of Campaign Discourse: No. 10 What we know from 1960–92 about debates," October 3, 1996.

11. "Perot Should Have a Part in the Presidential Debates," *Los Angeles Times,* September 12, 1996.

12. "The Debates: Two or Five," *Wall Street Journal,* September 12, 1996, A14.

13. "Performance in the Debates: Just Say No," *Weekly Standard*, September 16, 1996, 9.

14. "Clinton: Visit to Thailand Raises New Questions," *Hotline,* November 26, 1996.

15. "The Money Trail," *Time*, November 28, 1996.

16. *Newsweek*, November 28, 1996.

17. "I'll Do It My Way," *Newsweek*, December 2, 1996, 65.

18. Ken Bode, "Welcome to the '88 Campaign," *New York Times*, May 28, 1996.

19. Robert Dalleck, *Hail to the Chief*, 24.